D1558032

# AMERICAN CRIMINAL COURTS

**Cliff Roberson, LLM, Ph.D.**

*Academic Chair, Graduate School of Criminal Justice,*
*Kaplan University*
*Emeritus Professor of Criminal Justice,*
*Washburn University*

**Frank DiMarino, LLM**

*Dean, School of Criminal Justice,*
*Kaplan University*
*Executive Editor, Professional Issues in Criminal*
*Justice Journal*

**Prentice Hall**

Boston   Columbus   Indianapolis   New York   San Francisco   Upper Saddle River
Amsterdam   Cape Town   Dubai   London   Madrid   Milan   Munich   Paris   Montréal   Toronto
Delhi   Mexico City   Sao Paulo   Sydney   Hong Kong   Seoul   Singapore   Taipei   Tokyo

**Vice President and Executive Publisher:** Vernon Anthony
**Senior Acquisitions Editor:** Eric Krassow
**Editorial Assistant:** Lynda Cramer
**Media Project Manager:** Karen Bretz
**Director of Marketing:** David Gesell
**Senior Marketing Manager:** Adam Kloza
**Senior Marketing Coordinator:** Alicia Wozniak
**Production Manager:** Holly Shufeldt
**Creative Director:** Jayne Conte
**Cover Design:** Suzanne Duda
**Cover Illustration/Photo:** Fotolia
**Full-Service Project Management/Composition:** Nitin Agarwal/Aptara®, Inc.
**Printer/Binder:** Edwards Brothers
**Cover Printer:** Lehigh-Phoenix Color

---

**Library of Congress Cataloging-in-Publication Data**

Roberson, Cliff
    American criminal courts / Cliff Roberson, Frank DiMarino.
        p.  cm.
    Includes index.
    ISBN-13: 978-0-13-511111-6
    ISBN-10: 0-13-511111-0
    1.  Criminal courts—United States. 2.  Criminal justice, Administration of—United States.  I. Title.
    KF9223.R59 2012
    345.73'01--dc22                                                           2010034540

10 9 8 7 6 5 4 3 2 1

**Prentice Hall**
is an imprint of

www.pearsonhighered.com

ISBN 10:       0-13-511111-0
ISBN 13: 978-0-13-511111-6

## Dedication

*First, we would like to dedicate this book to the men and women serving and those that have served in America's criminal courts as judges, counsel, and court professionals. We are truly fortunate to have such fine devoted professionals working in our criminal courts. Thank you.*

*On a personal note, we also dedicate the book to Susan DiMarino and Elena Azaola for their support and encouragement during the long hours involved in preparing this manuscript. Thank you for everything.*

# PREFACE

American Criminal Courts is designed as a one-semester textbook for students in courts-related criminal justice courses. The primary goal is to present a clear and balanced overview of the American criminal court systems. The courts are examined from both its historical foundation and in their contemporary form. The material is presented in an easy-to-comprehend manner, thus freeing the instructor from text review during class time. This will allow the instructor to pursue more meaningful discussions and group exercises involving criminal court concepts.

While we are listed as the sole authors of this text, it would not have been possible without the help of many dedicated friends and associates, including Greg Matoesian, University of Illinois-Chicago; William (Nelson) Barnes, a Texas prosecutor; Kristin Winkour, a Florida criminal justice researcher; and appellate attorney Cloud Miller. Thanks to the following reviewers: Albert D. Bettilyon, ITT Technical Institute, Tucson; Robert Boyer, Luzerne County Community College; Joseph R. Budd, Brown Mackie College; James L. Guffey, Bryant & Stratton College; John Hill, Salt Lake Community College; David LaRose, Westwood College; Cassandra L. Renzi, Keiser University; Elizabeth Salazar, Centura College; and Christine L. Stymus, Bryant & Stratton College.

The material in the text is designed for a one semester course involving the American criminal courts. The approach used is to examine each aspect of the court system with the goal of encouraging critical examinations of the various court decisions, rules , and procedures. American criminal courts have gained prominence in the past few decades with the increasing concerns about the accountability of the courts from a wide variety of viewpoints including court decisions and court expenditures. The courts are and have always been a vital policymaker. The ever present challenges that confront the courts are explored in the text as the courts continue to adapt to the needs of a complex and rapidly changing society.

## SUPPLEMENTS

Several online supplements available to instructors using this text include:

- Online Instructor's Manual with Test Bank (0-13-511112-9)
- Online PowerPoints (0-13-511113-7)
- MyCrimeKit (0-13-511196-X)

## Download Instructor Resources from the Instructor Resource Center

To access supplementary materials online, instructors need to request an instructor access code. Go to **www.pearsonhighered.com/irc**, to register for an instructor access code. Within 48 hours after registering you will receive a confirming e-mail including an instructor access code. Once you have received your code, locate your text in the online catalog and click on the Instructor Resources button on the left side of the catalog product page. Select a supplement, and a login page will appear. Once you have logged in, you can access instructor material for all Prentice Hall textbooks. If you have any difficulties accessing the site or downloading a supplement, please contact Customer Service at *http://247.prenhall.com.*

# CONTENTS

# 1

# Our Criminal Courts

**What You Need to Know About Criminal Courts**

After you have completed this chapter, you should know:

- The study of the criminal courts in the United States includes the ideas, principles, and values about which reasonable persons can and do disagree.
- Criminal courts are guided by procedural rules and statutes.
- The two questions regarding the burdens of proof in criminal proceeding are: (1) Who has the burden of proving an issue? And (2) what is the magnitude of the burden? The magnitude may be (1) proof beyond a reasonable doubt, (2) clear and convincing evidence, or (3) preponderance of evidence.
- Criminal courts in the United States are generally based on English common law.
- The primary state agency involved in criminal law administration in most states is the state department of justice or office of attorney general (criminal division).
- The two competing models of criminal procedure are the crime control model and the due process model.
- Jurisdiction is the authority by which courts and judicial officers take cognizance of and decide cases. There are two types of jurisdiction: (1) over the subject matter and (2) over the person.
- Venue refers to the geographical location of the trial, that is, the judicial district or county in which the trial should be conducted.
- When an appellate court reverses a conviction of a lower court, the case is returned to the original court for a determination by the trial court as to whether or not the case will be retried or dismissed.

**Chapter Outline**

- Introduction
- Development of Common Law Courts
- Criminal Law Administration
- Competing Models
- Judicial Decisions
- Legal Research

## INTRODUCTION

The study of the criminal courts in the United States is more than the study of the various courts. It includes an examination of the ideas, principles, and values that are present in the courts and the individuals involved in the courts. An additional fact to remember is that our criminal court system is not fixed in stone; it is changing and flexible. Understanding our concept of justice requires a thoughtful comprehension of the historical background, social values, moral standards, and political realities that give direction to our system. The United States' systems of courts have one primary goal: to promote justice. In our court systems there are civil courts and criminal courts. This textbook examines only the criminal courts.

This text focuses on criminal courts at both the state and federal level. Chapter one provides the reader with an overview of our criminal courts. In subsequent chapters, the key issues introduced in this chapter are discussed and expanded in more depth. For purpose of this text, the phrase "criminal courts" is defined to include all courts that regularly handle criminal cases, either at the trial or appellate level. Frequently references will be made to criminal procedure and substantive criminal **law**. Criminal procedure refers to those laws and rules that govern the criminal justice process. Substantive criminal law defines those acts that are crimes. Criminal procedure describes those laws and rules by which crimes are investigated and prosecuted. Conduct that constitutes a crime is covered in substantive criminal law.

There are two basic criminal court systems in the United States—federal and state. The term dual federalism often is used to describe the concept of two complete court systems. Over 95 percent of the criminal cases, however, are tried in state courts. There are some counties in the United States whose state courts prosecute more criminal cases each year than are prosecuted annually in the entire federal system. Los Angeles County, California, Harris County, Texas, and Cook County, Illinois, are three of those counties.

## Court Guidelines

Criminal courts are guided by certain rules, regulations, and laws. The sources of the laws, rules, and regulations include:

1. **Constitutions**—both state and federal.
2. **Statutes**—Both the state and federal governments have enacted statutes to regulate the administration of the criminal justice system. The primary state regulatory statute is the state code of criminal procedure that regulates procedure in state criminal courts. The primary federal statute that governs the trial of criminal cases in federal

**LAW IN ACTION**

**What is Law?**

In *United States Fidelity & Guaranty Co. v. Guenther*, 281 U.S. 34 (U.S. 1930), a civil case, an insurance company issued to respondent an automobile insurance policy, which provided that it did not cover any liability that arose while the automobile was being operated by any person under the age limit fixed by law. While the automobile was being operated by a 17-year-old driver, it was involved in an accident in which a third person was injured. The city in which the accident occurred had enacted an ordinance that made it unlawful for an automobile owner to permit anyone under the age of 18 to operate a motor vehicle within the city. The state's statute made it unlawful for a minor under the age of 16 to drive an automobile. The injured person sued respondent and recovered judgment, which respondent paid. Respondent then sued the insurance company on the insurance policy, the suit was removed to federal court, and petitioner recovered a judgment, which was affirmed by the appellate court. The United States Supreme Court granted certiorari and reversed, holding that the city was acting within its authority in enacting the municipal ordinance in question and that petitioner's liability was thus excluded under the plain meaning of the phrase "age limit fixed by law."

The Supreme Court stated that the term "law" when used in a generic sense, means the rules of action or conduct duly prescribed by controlling authority, and having binding legal force, including valid municipal ordinances as well as statutes.

court is Title 18, U.S. Code. Except for constitutional issues, federal procedural rules apply only to federal criminal cases. State procedural rules apply only to state trials.

3. **Judicial opinions**—Judicial opinions construe the constitutionality, meaning, and effect of constitutional and statutory provisions.
4. **Court rules**—Court rules consist of the various standard procedures used by the courts, which were developed as the result of a court's inherent supervisory power over the administration of the criminal justice system. Court rules regulate the guilt-determining process in the courts in the areas not regulated by other rules. Most students of criminal procedure fail to consider the importance of court rules in the trial of criminal cases.

Examples of court rules that impact on the criminal justice system are as follows:

**LOS ANGELES COUNTY MUNICIPAL COURT RULE 532.6 PROVIDES:**

Each judge is required to list [report] all causes [cases] under submission for more than 30 days, with an indication of the length of time each has been pending (30 through 60 days, 61 through 90 days, or over 90 days).

**CALIFORNIA SUPREME COURT RULE 22 [REGARDING ORAL ARGUMENTS BEFORE THE COURT] STATES:**

Unless otherwise ordered: (1) Counsel for each party shall be allowed 30 minutes for oral argument, except in a case in which a sentence of death has been imposed where each party shall be allowed 45 minutes. . . .

**U.S. DISTRICT COURT (EDCA) RULE 5A STATES**

(1) The trial of a defendant held in custody solely for purposes of trial on a federal charge shall commence within 90 days following the beginning of continuous custody.

## Foundational Judicial Concepts

As an introduction to the study of criminal courts, certain foundational concepts should be considered. These concepts will be explained in the text and are listed below in order to create an awareness of their existence.

- The guarantees of the Bill of Rights in the U.S. Constitution apply directly only to the federal government.
- The Due Process Clause of the Fourteenth Amendment by selective incorporation applies most of the rights contained in the Bill of Rights to the states.
- State constitutions may provide additional rights to citizens than those provided for in the U.S. Constitution but may not restrict the rights granted by the federal constitution.
- The two questions regarding the burdens of proof in criminal proceeding are:
  1. Who has the burden of proving an issue? and
  2. What is the magnitude of the burden?
  The magnitude may be (1) proof beyond a reasonable doubt, (2) clear and convincing evidence, or (3) preponderance of evidence.
- Formal charges in a criminal trial must first be formalized by either an indictment returned by a grand jury or by information prepared by a prosecutor.
- Prior to trial both the prosecutor and the defense may submit pretrial motions, and both have discovery rights imposed on them.
- Our judicial system is based on the adversarial process.
- Two famous quotes from Oliver Wendell Holmes should be noted:
  - Whatever disagreement there may be as to the scope of the phrase "due process of law," there can be no doubt that it embraces the fundamental conception of a fair trial, with opportunity to be heard. [*Frank v. Mangum*, 237 N.S. 309, 347 (1914)]

- The life of the law has not been logic, it has been experience. [The Common Law (1881) 1.]

## Decisional Concepts

Should the courts adopt "bright-line rules" or use a case-by-case adjudication? A bright-line rule is a rule that is clear and definite. Advocates of bright-line rules contend that police officers must make instant decisions, and to do their jobs they need clear rules. Advocates of the case-by-case approach contend that we desire rules that lead to the right result as often as possible—that the world is not clear and definite; that the development of bright-line rules for all situations makes the law illogical in many situations. The issue of the utility of bright-line rules were discussed in both the majority and dissenting opinions in *Gant v. Arizona* (2009). As noted by Associate Justice Stevens:

> The State does not seriously disagree with the Arizona Supreme Court's conclusion that Gant could not have accessed his vehicle at the time of the search, but it nevertheless asks us to uphold the search of his vehicle under the broad reading of Belton. The State argues that Belton searches are reasonable regardless of the possibility of access in a given case because that expansive rule correctly balances law enforcement interests, including the interest in a bright-line rule, with an arrestee's limited privacy interest in his vehicle (p. 1720).

Associate Justice Alito; joined by Chief Justice Roberts, Kennedy, and Breyer; noted in his dissent in the Gant case:

> In Belton we set forth a bright-line rule for arrests of automobile occupants, holding that . . . a search of the whole passenger compartment is justified in every case. . . . Belton and Thornton held that arresting officers may always search an arrestee's vehicle in order to protect themselves from hidden weapons. This "bright-line rule" has now been interred (p. 1774).

### LAW IN ACTION

### Excerpts from the majority opinion in *Arizona v. Gant* Case

[Justice Stevens's opinion] We do not agree with the contention in Justice Alito's dissent that consideration of police reliance interests requires a different result. Although it appears that the State's reading of Belton has been widely taught in police academies and that law enforcement officers have relied on the rule in conducting vehicle searches during the past 28 years, many of these searches were not justified by the reasons underlying the Chimel exception. Countless individuals guilty of nothing more serious than a traffic violation have had their constitutional right to the security of their private effects violated as a result. The fact that the law enforcement community may view the State's version of the Belton rule as an entitlement does not establish the sort of reliance interest that could outweigh the countervailing interest that all individuals share in having their constitutional rights fully protected. If it is clear that a practice is unlawful, individuals' interest in its discontinuance clearly outweighs any law enforcement "entitlement" to its persistence. The mere fact that law enforcement may be made more efficient can never by itself justify disregard of the Fourth Amendment. In observing that Miranda has become embedded in routine police practice to the point where the warnings have become part of our national culture, the Court was referring not to police reliance on a rule requiring them to provide warnings but to the broader societal reliance on that individual right.

A similar concept involves whether the propriety of police officers' conduct should be judged from the subjective or objective states of mind of the officers. The subjective approach requires that the officer's conduct be motivated by constitutionally appropriate motives. The objective approach disregards the officer's motives and measures the officer's conduct based on objective standards. While the Supreme Court has adopted both subjective and objective rules, the present tendency is to use the objective approach (*Whren v. United States*, 1996).

## DEVELOPMENT OF COMMON LAW COURTS

Many aspects of our present-day criminal courts are based upon English common law. All states except Louisiana can trace their legal systems to the English common law system. In 1805, Louisiana, whose system was originally based on the French and Spanish codal law concept, officially adopted the common law of England as the basis for their system.

Prior to the invasion by William the Conqueror and the Normans, England first used blood feuds and later a system called compurgation to keep law and order. Under compurgation, when an individual was accused of crime or the wrongful withholding of property, he could take an oath that he was innocent of any wrongdoing. He then called other witnesses (oath-helpers) to swear, not to the facts of the case, but that they believed the accused told the truth. If the accused gained the support of a sufficient number of "oath-helpers," he was acquitted. The system was based on the widespread fear of divine retribution for false swearing. It was from this practice that the present-day requirement for the witnesses to present their testimony under oath originated.

If the accused was unable to obtain sufficient oath-helpers, the judges had the alternative of leaving the case undecided or referring the case to a trial by ordeal. There were several forms of trial by ordeal. One test required the accused to put his hand in a kettle of boiling water. When the hand was withdrawn, it was bound with cloth for three days. At the end of three days when the cloth was removed, if the hand was unscathed, the accused was acquitted. Another ordeal required the accused to carry in his bare hands a red-hot bar of iron. If the accused was unable to carry the iron for a given distance without dropping it, he was considered guilty. Another ordeal consisted of walking barefooted across a number of heated plowshares placed side by side.

Still another popular method of trial by ordeal was to lower the accused with his hands tied behind his back into a body of cold water. If he floated, it meant that he was possessed by the devil and thus was guilty. This was based on the concept that when Satan invaded a person's body, his specific gravity was less than that of the water. If he sank, he was considered innocent. One problem with this ordeal was that often the "innocent" person drowned before he could be rescued. In most cases, the ordeals by hot irons were used for the nobility and ordeals by water for the commoners.

As the Normans gained power, they reintroduced the old feudal concept of "Trial by Duel." Under this system, in the case of a dispute a duel would be fought, and the winner of the duel became the winner of the case. Later, "Champions" could be hired by those involved to fight a duel.

Trial by jury emerged in the twelfth century to replace trial by ordeal and trial by duel. The county sheriff selected members of the jury. It was a common practice to select members who were favorable to the Crown. The sheriff also had the power to withhold food from the jury until they reached a decision. If the jurors made a "wrong decision," they could also be punished. The power to punish jury members was considered necessary to prevent the jury from siding with the accused against the Crown. The determination that a jury had made a wrong decision was based upon a retrial of the case before a jury of Knights.

In 1166, King Henry II ordered that 12 family heads of each 100 be placed under oath and report to the king all individuals accused or known to be robbers, murderers, or thieves. This order was known as the Assize of Clarendon. Assize referred to an order of the king. He provided that certain questions regarding conduct of an accused were resolved by a jury of 12 men selected from those who lived nearby. The procedure used to comply with the assize was similar to the process now used by grand juries. (Note: A grand jury is presently used as an investigative body that investigates and indicts persons suspected of committing criminal behavior. This also appears to be the origination for the size of a trial jury being 12 in number.)

By 1240, the use of trial juries was common. Persons accused of crime by a grand jury were given the option of banishment or trial by a jury. To discourage some persons accused of serious crime from choosing the option of banishment, many were tortured until they accepted the trial by jury alternative. The most common form of torture used was "pressing to death." The accused was first placed in solitary confinement, then stripped naked, and starved. His body was subjected to increasing weights of iron until he pleaded to the indictment and accepted a jury trial or died. Pressing to death lasted until the 1800s and was finally replaced with the automatic entry of a "not guilty" plea when the accused refused to plea.

To understand the common law, we must understand the English customs and traditions that evolved into what is now known as common law. Medieval England was divided into tribal areas known as shires. The king's justice was administered by "shire-reeves," who presided over the shire courts. A sheriff is the modern counterpart of the shire-reeve. The law was based on ancient custom and varied with each tribal area.

Common law was the earliest source of criminal laws. It originated during the period of time in which William the Conqueror was the king of England. At the time of the Conquest in 1066, there was no uniform criminal law in England. Individual courts were dominated by sheriffs who enforced the village rules as they saw fit. In order to reduce the arbitrary aspects of the law, William decreed that all prosecutions would be conducted in the name of the king. A similar practice exists today where all cases are prosecuted in the name of the people, the state, or the commonwealth.

The first known English code was written in the seventh century by King Aethelbert. The proclamations of the code were called dooms. The dooms were social class orientated. For example, theft was punishable by fines that ranged widely in magnitude according to the status of the victim. Stealing from the king was punishable by a fine equal to nine times the value of the property stolen. Theft from a person of the holy order was punishable by a fine three times the value of the property stolen. Crimes committed in the presence of the king were considered a violation of the "king's peace" and increased the punishment for the crime. In the ninth and eleventh centuries, the code was rewritten, but little new was added.

Most historians trace the common law of England to William the Conqueror who invaded England in 1066. At the time of the invasion, each county was controlled by a sheriff (shire-reeve), who also controlled the courts in that county. Accordingly, there was no uniform English system. William took over the courts and made them royal courts, that is, under the control of the king. He sent representatives to the many courts in England to record the decisions of the judges. William distributed selected decisions of the judges to all the judges. The judges then utilized the selected decisions in making their own decisions. As the routine of these courts became firmly established, it was possible to forecast their decisions in terms of similar cases decided by them in past cases. From this the doctrine of stare decisis developed.

William also compiled the law for the crimes that were common in most areas of the kingdom. These crimes became the common law crimes of England. Later new statutory crimes were added by the king and parliament. The concept of common law crimes was so ingrained in England that the traditional crimes such as burglary, larceny, and murder were not defined by statute in England until the 1960s.

During William's time, very few people could read or write. The king, the judges, and the church authorities determined the elements and the scope of criminal offenses. In some cases they even created new crimes. As William unified England as a nation rather than isolated villages, the judges developed familiarity with the general customs, usages, and moral concepts of the people. Judicial decisions began to be based on these general customs, usages, and moral concepts.

By the 1600s, the primary criminal law of England was based on the mandatory rules of conduct laid down by the judges. These rules became the common law of England. Prior decisions were accepted as authoritative precepts and were applied to future cases. When the English settlers came to America in the 1600s, they brought with them the English common law. Except for a few modifications, English common law became the common law of the colonies. During the American Revolution, there was a great deal of hostility toward the English in America. This hostility extended to the common law system. Accordingly, most of the new states enacted new statutes defining criminal acts and establishing criminal procedures. The statutes, however, basically enacted into statutory law what was formerly English common law.

## LAW IN ACTION

### Lady Justice

In America's criminal courts, justice is symbolized by "Lady Justice." The exact origin of the Lady Justice is debated. Most researchers agree that Lady Justice is a depiction of the Roman goddess Justitia and the Greek Titan Themis. The Lady holds in one hand a sword that symbolizes the power of the state. In her other hand she holds the scales of justice, which signifies impartiality. She also wears a blindfold that demonstrates her lack of prejudice as she can't see the parties before her (Copland, 2009). The Lady of Justice was an allegorical personification of the moral force in judicial systems long before the colonies were founded.

The earliest Roman coins depicted Justitia with the sword in one hand and the scale in the other, but with no blindfold. Justitia has been commonly represented as "blind" since about the end of the fifteenth century. The first known representation of blind Justice is Hans Gieng's 1543 statue on the Gerechtigkeitsbrunnen (Fountain of Justice) in Berne. As noted by several researchers, the blindfold raises some interesting questions. For example, do you want to blindfold someone with a sword? And how is she supposed to read the scales if she is blind? Some Lady of Justice statutes give her two faces like Janus, with the side bearing the sword prudently left unblindfolded (Hamilton, 2005).

At the Old Bailey courthouse in London, a statue of Lady Justice stands without a blindfold. A courthouse brochure explains that because Lady Justice was originally not blindfolded, and because her "maidenly form" is supposed to guarantee her impartiality it renders the blindfold redundant (Hamilton, 2005).

A different Lady is depicted by a statute at the Shelby County Courthouse in Memphis, Tennessee. The Shelby County statute depicts a blindfolded Lady Justice seated and acting as a human scale, weighing competing claims in each hand.

### Case Law

"**Case law**" is the phrase used to indicate appellate court interpretations of the law. A substantial majority of "law" is case law, that is, court opinions which interpret the meaning of constitutions and statutes. Case law also helps clarify and narrow statutory law. For example, the U.S. Constitution (Fourteenth Amendment) provides that no state shall deprive any person of life, liberty, or property without due process of law. What constitutes "due process of law" is decided almost daily in the courts. There are hundreds of published opinions issued by federal and state appellate and supreme courts each year.

Court decisions interpret the relationship of one code provision to another, the meaning of words used in the code provision, the legislative intent in enacting the code provision, the scope and effect of the code provision, and whether or not the provision violates any constitutional restrictions.

The term precedent is used when a legal principle has been decided by a court. The court decision is then a precedent (guide) for similar situations. There are two basic types of precedent: mandatory and persuasive. Under mandatory precedent, when a higher appellate court renders a decision on an issue, the lower courts under the supervision of that court must follow the ruling or face reversal on appeal. For example, if the Arizona Supreme Court decides an issue, state appellate courts in Arizona must follow that precedent. Persuasive precedent indicates a court decision that is not binding on a second court but is persuasive to the second court. For example, a court in New Mexico is faced with an issue that has never been decided by a New Mexico court. There is, however, a court in Nevada that has considered the same issue. The Nevada court decision is not binding on the New Mexico court but is of some persuasive authority. Precedent is based on the principle of stare decisis, which is discussed below.

Stare decisis is a Latin word meaning "to abide by, or adhere to, decided cases." The doctrine provides that when a court has once laid down a principle of law as applicable to a certain state of facts, it will adhere to that principle and apply it to all future cases where the facts are substantially the same (*Moore v. City of Albany*, 1885). Stare decisis is a policy founded on the theory that security and certainty require that accepted and established legal principles, under which rights may accrue, be recognized and followed (*Otter Tail Power Co. v. Von Bank*, 1947).

## CRIMINAL LAW ADMINISTRATION

The primary state agency involved in criminal law administration in most states is the state department of justice or office of attorney general (criminal division). This department is usually composed of the state attorney general and the division of law enforcement. The typical goals of the department are to seek to control and eliminate organized crime in the state, to publish and distribute a compilation of the state laws relating to crimes and criminal law enforcement that are of general interest to peace officers, to operate the state's teletype and law enforcement telecommunications systems, and to promote training and professionalism of peace officers.

### State Attorney General

The chief law officer of most states is the attorney general. It is the Attorney General's duty to see that all laws of the state are uniformly and adequately enforced. The attorney general, however, does not have direct supervision of district attorneys, sheriffs, and other law enforcement officers as may be designated by law, in all matters pertaining to the duties of their respective offices. In most states, however, the attorney general may require any of the officers to make reports concerning the investigation, detection, prosecution, and punishment of crime within their jurisdiction.

The attorney general in most states may prosecute any violations of law of which a superior or district court has jurisdiction when he or she is of the opinion that the law is not being adequately enforced in any county. Also, when directed by the governor, the attorney general shall assist any district attorney in the discharge of the duties of the district attorney. If a district attorney is disqualified to conduct a criminal prosecution, the attorney general may appoint a special prosecutor (*Sloane v. Hammond*, 1927).

Regarding the broad authority given to the attorney general by the state constitution, one court opinion noted that the authority has been tempered by judicial construction. The court stated:

> These officials are public officers, as distinguished from mere employees, with public duties delegated and entrusted to them, as agents, the performance of which is an exercise of a part of the governmental functions of the particular political unit for which they, as agents, are active. . . . [I]t is at once evident that 'supervision' does not contemplate control, and that sheriffs and district attorneys cannot avoid or evade the duties and responsibilities of the respective offices by permitting a substitution of judgment (*People v. Brophy*, 1942, p. 28).

### District or State's Attorneys

District attorneys are elected county or judicial district officers in most states. In a few states, they are appointed. They also are officers of the state. The district attorney is, in most cases, the public prosecutor. Duties of a district attorney in criminal matters normally include

- institution of proceeding before magistrates for the arrest of persons charged with or reasonably suspected of public offenses,
- presents cases to the grand jury in those states that use grand juries for indictments, and
- conducts all prosecution for public offenses.

In a few states there are state attorneys who are appointed rather than elected that perform those duties normally performed by the district attorney. In a few states, they are called county attorneys. In other states there are both county attorneys and district attorneys, with the county attorneys involved mostly in misdemeanors cases.

## COMPETING MODELS

The two competing models of criminal procedure are the **crime control model** and the **due process model**. Advocates of the crime control model contend that crime control is the most important goal of the criminal justice system. Included within the crime control model are the sub-goals of efficiency, uniformity, and presumption of factual guilt. According to the advocates of crime control, increasing the efficiency of the system will foster crime prevention and to be efficient, the system must be routinized.

The competing due process model stresses the importance of individual rights and the presumption of innocence. The advocates of this model contend that the role of the criminal justice system is more than just preventing crime. Its primary purpose should be to protect human rights. These advocates lack trust in informal police procedures and have a preference for formality. They believe that the best way to reduce abuses of individual rights is by the early intervention of judges and lawyers in the process. The due process advocates also are concerned with the effects of economic inequality on the judicial system.

The role of the judiciary varies according to the competing models. The crime control model sees less of a need for an active judiciary. On the other hand, due process

## LAW IN ACTION

### Competing Models of Criminal Justice

Herbert Packer, a Stanford University law professor, constructed two models, the crime control model and the due process model, to represent the two competing systems of values operating within criminal justice. The tension between the two accounts for the conflict and disharmony that now is observable in the criminal justice system. [Herbert L. Packer (1968). The Limits of Criminal Sanctions. Palo Alto, CA: Stanford University]

| Issue | Crime Control *Prosecutor's* | Due Process *Defense-Attorney's* |
|---|---|---|
| Primary mission | Controlling crime | Protecting individual rights |
| Systematic view | Assembly line | Obstacle course |
| Important values | Efficiency, speed, and finality | reliability |
| Focus | Factual guilt | Legal guilt |
| Process | Informal screening by prosecutor | Adversarial and formal procedures |

advocates contend that the courts must take an active role to reduce the inequalities in the criminal justice system. A comparison of the decisions of the Supreme Court of 2000s with those of the Earl Warren Court of the 1960s is an excellent example of the two competing models, with the Supreme Court of 2000s more inclined to follow the crime control model while the Warren Court tended to follow the due process model.

## CHOOSING THE CORRECT COURT

### Jurisdiction

Jurisdiction is the authority by which courts and judicial officers take cognizance of and decide cases. There are two types of jurisdiction: (1) over the subject matter and (2) over the person. A court must have jurisdiction over both the subject matter and the person before the court may decide the case. For example, a family court in Utah normally would not have jurisdiction over a criminal matter (subject matter jurisdiction).

Jurisdiction over the person in criminal cases normally is obtained by forcing the defendant to appear before the court. For example, Larry robs a bank in Texas. The state district court or criminal district court would have subject matter jurisdiction. The district court obtains jurisdiction over Larry (over the person) when he is brought before the court. If after the robbery Larry moves to South America, the district court would still have jurisdiction over the subject matter. The court, however, would lack jurisdiction over Larry until he is caught and taken before the court to answer the charges against him.

Jurisdiction over the subject matter cannot be conferred by consent or the failure to object. For example, Robert commits murder in Texas in violation of Texas penal statutes. He cannot be tried for that crime in an Iowa court because the Iowa court has no subject matter jurisdiction over a Texas crime. If Robert pleads guilty in the Iowa court and is convicted, the conviction will be set aside. Despite his guilty plea, he cannot waive the court's lack of jurisdiction. Accordingly, the Iowa proceedings would be null and void.

## LAW IN ACTION

### Where can the trial be held?

Joe and his wife Sue are separated and considering a divorce. Since both are residents of the State of California, a divorce would mean that Joe would be required to share the community property with his soon to be ex-wife. The couple's residence is in San Diego. Joe travels to Las Vegas. While in Las Vegas he mails Sue a box of poisoned candy. The day Sue receives the box of candy, she is getting ready to travel to Tucson, Arizona to see her mother. So she takes the candy with her. While in Arizona, she eats the candy and dies.

### As District Attorney for San Diego County, California, do you have venue and jurisdiction to prosecute Joe for the murder?

In answering the question, consider California Code of Criminal Procedure, Section 781:

> When a public offense is committed in part in one jurisdictional territory and in part in another, or the acts or effects thereof constituting or requisite to the consummation of the offense occur in two or more jurisdictional territories, the jurisdiction of such offense is in any competent court within either jurisdictional territory.

### What if Joe's crime was one involving a terrorist attack?

California Code of Criminal Procedure, Section 787 (added in 2002) provides that when multiple offenses constituting terrorist attacks occur in more than one jurisdictional territory, and the offenses are part of a single scheme or terrorist attack, the jurisdiction of any of those offenses is in any jurisdiction where at least one of those offenses occurred.

## Venue

**Venue** refers to the geographical location of the trial; the judicial district or county in which the trial should be conducted. A change of venue from a court of one county to the same court in another county does not affect the latter court's jurisdiction over the subject matter of the case.

Unlike jurisdiction, the parties to a trial may consent to venue. For example, by pleading guilty to the sale of a controlled substance without objecting as to the proper venue, the accused admits or consents to the venue of the court. As a general rule, proper venue is in the county where the crime was committed. Since venue represents a question of fact, it must be alleged in the pleadings. This is normally accomplished by alleging that the offense occurred in X county or at X location.

## Federal or State Court

Federal courts have jurisdiction on federal issues and state courts have jurisdiction on state issues. The general rules on whether the offense will be tried in federal or state courts are as follows:

If the act is a violation of federal law, it will be tried in federal court. For example, the criminal violation of an individual's civil rights under federal law will normally be tried in federal court.

If the act is a violation of state law, it will be tried in a state court. For example, the murder of a person in New York would be a violation of the New York Criminal Code and thus the trial should be in a New York state court.

If the act violates both state and federal law, the case may be tried in both. For example, if a police officer uses excessive force in the arrest of a suspect, the officer may be charged with assault and battery in state court as a violation of that state's criminal code. The officer also may be tried in federal court if the officer's conduct also violates the federal civil rights of the suspect.

Federal courts may not decide issues originally tried in state courts unless there is a federal question involved, for example, the state criminal court conviction infringed a right protected by the U.S. Constitution or a federal statute. For example, the police officer discussed above is tried in state court for assault and battery. During the trial, a statement made by the officer is used in evidence against her. After conviction, the officer files a writ in federal court alleging that the statement was taken in violation of her federal constitutional rights under the Fourth and Fourteenth Amendments to the U.S. Constitution. Whether or not the statement was taken in violation of her federal constitutional rights is a federal question and may be decided by the federal courts.

State courts are required to protect an individual's federal rights and those rights guaranteed by the state constitution or state statutes. Accordingly, while state courts are responsible for protecting a person's federal civil rights, the court normally has no jurisdiction to try and punish a person for violations of U.S. criminal laws. If exclusive federal jurisdiction exists or the offense is only a federal crime, then a state court has no jurisdiction.

The state supreme court or court of criminal appeals is the highest court of appeal for state criminal cases that do not involve federal issues. The decision of a state supreme court that a particular practice violates the state constitution is not subject to review by the U.S. Supreme Court (*Payton v. New York*, 1980).

In most states, death penalty cases are reviewed automatically by the state supreme court. The state supreme court generally has original jurisdiction (along with court of appeals and superior courts) in habeas corpus proceedings. In other criminal cases, the state supreme court accepts only those cases decided by the court of appeals. Except in death penalty cases, an accused generally has no absolute right to have the state supreme court decide his or her appeal of a criminal conviction.

The state supreme court may in most states, before a decision is entered, order a case transferred from a court of appeal to the state supreme court. The state supreme court generally also may review any decision of a court of appeals.

State supreme courts generally do not have the jurisdiction to render advisory opinions (*Younger v. Superior Court*, 1978). Accordingly, there must be an actual case or controversy pending in the court before an opinion will be issued. For example, New

## LAW IN ACTION

The court of last resort for citizens in Arizona is the Arizona Supreme Court. Following is a description of the court. It is very typical to most state courts. One interesting fact regarding this court is that the justices must retire at the age of 70. Contrast that with the history of the U.S. Supreme Court where many of the justices serve well into their 80s and even 90s. Another interesting fact is the requirement that the justice have been a resident of Arizona for at least 10 years prior to appointment. While Arizona requires that the justices to the state supreme court be attorneys, there is no similar requirement for membership on the U.S. Supreme Court although there has never been a non-lawyer appointed to that court.

### The Arizona Supreme Court

The Arizona Supreme Court's primary judicial duties under Article VI, § 5 of the Arizona Constitution, are to review appeals and to provide rules of procedure for all the courts in Arizona. It is the highest court in the state of Arizona and is often called the court of last resort.

The Supreme Court has discretionary jurisdiction, meaning that the court may refuse to review the findings of the lower court. Cases in which a trial judge has sentenced a defendant to death, however, automatically go to the Supreme Court for review.

## Supreme Court Justices

Five justices serve on the Supreme Court for a regular term of six years. One justice is selected by fellow justices to serve as Chief Justice for a five year term. In addition to handling case work like the other justices, the Chief Justice oversees the administrative operations of all the courts in Arizona.

## The Supreme Court

- may choose to review a decision of the court of appeals when a party (the plaintiff or defendant in the original case) files a petition for review;
- always hears the appeal when the superior court imposes a death sentence;
- regulates activities of the State Bar of Arizona and oversees admission of new attorneys to the practice of law;
- reviews charges of misconduct against attorneys, and has the authority to suspend or disbar them; and,
- serves as the final decision making body when disciplinary recommendations are filed against Arizona judges by the Commission on Judicial Conduct .

## The Court's Role in the Impeachment Process

Impeachment is a political process designed to deal with public officials accused of committing high crimes, misdemeanors, or misconduct in office. The person is charged, tried and, if convicted, removed from office.

The Chief Justice of the Supreme Court presides over Senate impeachment trials, but renders no decision as to the guilt or innocence of the public official on trial. Formal charges for an impeachable offense are initiated by a majority vote of the Arizona House of Representatives. Conviction for the impeachable offense requires a two-thirds vote in the Senate. Upon conviction, a public officer is removed from office. The role of the Supreme Court in the impeachment process is set forth in Article VIII, Part 2, § 1 of the Arizona Constitution.

## Court Personnel

The Arizona Constitution authorizes the Supreme Court to appoint a clerk of the court and assistants. According to A.R.S. § 12-202, the clerk shall attend sessions of the court, issue legal paperwork, enter all court orders, judgments and decrees, keep other books of record and perform other duties as required by law or the court. The clerk's office maintains the court's official files and assists in scheduling matters for decisions and oral arguments. The clerk's office is also responsible for publishing and distributing the court's written opinions.

## Supreme Court Justice Qualifications

A Supreme Court Justice:

- Must be admitted to the practice of law in Arizona and be a resident of Arizona for the 10 years immediately before taking office;
- May not practice law while a member of the judiciary;
- May not hold any other political office or public employment;
- May not hold office in any political party;
- May not campaign, except for him/herself; and,
- Must retire at age 70.

[Source: Arizona Supreme Court web site: http://azcourts.gov/AZSupremeCourt.aspx Accessed on August 10, 2010]

Jersey enacts a new statute making it unconstitutional for a citizen to move from one county in the state to another county in the same state. In most instances, the New Jersey Supreme Court would not issue an opinion as to the validity of the statute until there is an actual case involving the statute before the court.

Courts of appeals decide appeals from superior or district courts and have original jurisdiction in habeas corpus proceedings. In most cases, an accused has a right to have his or her appeal of a criminal conviction in superior or district court decided by the court of appeals.

Superior or district courts are considered as courts of general jurisdiction and have original jurisdiction in all cases except those given by statutes to other trial courts. Superior or district courts have jurisdiction to try misdemeanors not otherwise provided for and felonies (criminal offenses punishable by death or by imprisonment in the state prison). Generally, a superior or district court has no jurisdiction over a case charging only a misdemeanor in a county with a county, municipal, or justice court. Superior or district courts in most cases have appellate jurisdiction in criminal cases that are tried in county, municipal, and justice courts.

Municipal, county, and justice courts usually have jurisdiction in criminal matters as follows:

1. to hear and decide cases involving misdemeanors and infractions;
2. to conduct the following procedures in felony cases:
   a. arraignment,
   b. bail setting and reduction,
   c. accept pleas, and
   d. preliminary hearings; and
3. to issue search and arrest warrants.

## JUDICIAL DECISIONS

Most state constitutions provide that no judgment shall be set aside, or new trial granted, in any cause, on the ground of misdirection of the jury, or of the improper admission or rejection of evidence, or for any error as to any matter of pleading, or for any error as to any matter of procedure, unless, after an examination of the entire cause, including the evidence, the court shall be of the opinion that the error complained of has resulted in a miscarriage of justice.

### COURTS IN ACTION
**Do you agree with Chief Justice John Jay, that juries are the best judges of facts? How do you distinguish between a question of fact and a question of law?**
**Chief Justice John Jay, U.S. Supreme Court on the province of the jury**
Georgia v. Brailsford, 3 U.S. 1, 4 (U.S. 1794)
It may not be amiss, here, Gentlemen, to remind you of the good old rule, that on questions of fact, it is the province of the jury, on questions of law, it is the province of the court to decide. But it must be observed that by the same law, which recognizes this reasonable distribution of jurisdiction, you have nevertheless a right to take upon yourselves to judge of both, and to determine the law as well as the fact in controversy. On this, and on every other occasion, however, we have no doubt, you will pay the respect, which is due to the opinion of the court: For, as on the one hand, it is presumed, that juries are the best judges of facts; it is, on the other hand, presumable, that the court are the best judges of law. But still both objects are lawfully, within your power of decision.

## LAW IN ACTION

### What should be the burden of proof to convict someone of a criminal act?

Do you agree that in cases of doubt, it is better to let the defendant go free? There is an old Chinese proverb that states: "it is better to hang the wrong fella than no fella." This proverb is based on the concept that punishment should be certain—if a crime is committed, someone will be punished. Which of these two concepts is more acceptable to you?

### Excerpts from Brown v. Greene, 577 F.3d 107, 108 (2d Cir. N.Y. 2009) on standards of proof required for conviction

Petitioner-Appellant Dwayne Brown was convicted of second-degree robbery after a jury trial in 2002 in the New York State Supreme Court. On appeal thereafter to the First Department of the Appellate Division of the New York Supreme Court, Brown argued that his trial counsel was constitutionally ineffective. The jury charge, Brown contended, may have led the jury to convict him under a preponderance of the evidence standard and not, as is constitutionally required, under the beyond a reasonable doubt standard.

### Background.

In January 2002, two men stopped Claudio Degli-Adalberti in a subway station on the Upper West Side of Manhattan and, after a brief scuffle, stole his wallet. A few minutes later, Degli-Adalberti contacted the police. He described the physical appearance of the two thieves, which the officers quickly broadcast over the police radio. A nearby squad car stopped two men thought to match the description: Brown and Eric Burwell. The police took Degli-Adalberti to view Brown and Burwell; he indicated that they were the men who had robbed him.

The key issue at trial was whether Brown and Burwell were the two individuals who had robbed Degli-Adalberti. The opening and closing statements of both the defense and the prosecution focused on this aspect of the case and also included numerous statements to the effect that the jury must employ the reasonable doubt standard to convict the accused. The jury convicted Brown and Burwell after two and one-half hours of deliberation, and Brown received a sentence of 11 years to life in prison.

### Excerpts from the dissenting opinion of Circuit Judge Straub, U.S. Court of Appeals, Second Circuit:

At the core of my disagreement with the majority lies my view that the jury charge is fairly read to have instructed the jury to use a mere preponderance of the evidence standard in deciding the identity of Degli-Adalberti's robbers rather than the constitutionally required standard of proof beyond a reasonable doubt. This reading is conveyed by the following portions of the jury charge:

We have different functions. You are the exclusive judges of the facts. Only you can make the accuracy and credibility assessments that are the starting point of your decision-making. . . .

Your chief function as finders of fact is to determine the accuracy and the credibility of the people who testify in front of you. The way you do that is really the way you do it in your own lives. Only you can say that a person who testified was truthful or not truthful and what weight or emphasis you should give to the testimony; was the person accurate or inaccurate.

I'm going to give you some suggestions, but you'll see that these are things that any functional, intelligent adult human being considers instinctively in his or her effort to decide accuracy and truthfulness. . . .

It is the quality [of the evidence] and not the quantity which must control.

That principle, quality not quantity, is the reason why New York has the one-witness identification rule about which you were alerted during the jury selection. The testimony of one person is sufficient for there to be a conviction, provided [that] testimony is of sufficient persuasiveness and credibility that [it] permits the jury to be satisfied beyond a reasonable doubt that the People have proven their case. . .

Crimes are defined by elements. The focus of a trial is to determine whether or not the prosecution can prove each of the elements of a crime beyond a reasonable doubt.

During the course of a trial, things happen. You hear testimony. You can spend your deliberation time trying to resolve each and everything that you heard. My suggestion is you try to resolve only the things that you need to resolve in order to make a determination whether the People have proven the elements of a charge beyond a reasonable doubt.

A jury makes factual findings. The elements must be established beyond a reasonable doubt if they're going to be established at all. . .

What your concern is: Did the People prove beyond a reasonable doubt the elements of a robbery; and, equally, if not more importantly, the accuracy of the identification of Mr. Burwell and Mr. Brown as the person or persons involved in the crime. . .

With regard to identification cases, as this is, it's the judge's responsibility to focus the jury on the considerations that a jury should go through in deciding whether or not the People have proven an accused's guilt beyond a reasonable doubt. I'll go through these things.

But, with respect to the credibility factors and the identification considerations, you'll see that an intelligent, functioning adult human being instinctively would think of or examine, assess virtually all these things, if not all these things, in trying to determine whether the People have met their burden.

First of all, you've got to decide the credibility of Mr. Degli-Adalberti, as well as any other witness. Because only by initially making factual decisions do you have a basis on which to draw your ultimate conclusions. You've got to decide what facts you're working with. That means you've got to decide as the witnesses are conveying testimony here, is their testimony accurate and credible.

So, with respect to whether the identification is truthful, that is not deliberately false, you must evaluate the believability of the witness who makes an identification. In doing so, you may consider the various factors for evaluating the believability of a witness' testimony that I listed for you a while ago with regard to whether the identification is accurate....

These factors are common sense things that any intelligent person would assess in making the determination whether the defendant or defendants are correctly identified.

You heard me say crimes are defined by elements. Essentially, there are three elements with regard to robbery. . .

So, there are three elements, each of which must be proven beyond a reasonable doubt.

Was there a theft? Ordinary meaning.

Was there force used? Force is any physical force beyond some incidental touching.

And, was there a person present who was present, ready, willing and able to aid in the commission of the robbery, the theft. . .

Those three elements have to be proven separately as to each person, Mr. Burwell and Mr. Brown.

If the People prove the three elements as I've just described them beyond a reasonable doubt, each one of them, then you have no choice, you must convict the person. If the People miss any one or more or all of the elements, miss proving that beyond a reasonable doubt, you have no choice, you have to acquit the person. . .

Does the jury unanimously agree as to the charge against Mr. Burwell, as to the charge against Mr. Brown? When you get into the jury room, conceivably, there would be disagreements among you. Not surprising.

The two most important civic functions that people do are to vote and to serve on juries. And for centuries elections have been closely decided. 50.1 beats 49.9 every time, and then you're stuck with somebody for two, four, six or in the case of some judicial elections fourteen long years. And, yet, for 230 years now, juries, the same pool of people who can't agree on a candidate, have been unanimously deciding cases. So, how does that happen? It happens, obviously, because within the jury deliberation context, people sometimes change their minds.

In our system of justice, an accused is not guaranteed a perfect trial, only one that is substantially correct. A miscarriage of justice occurs only if, based on the entire record, the appellate court concludes that it is probable that a result more favorable to the defendant would have been reached in the absence of the error (*People v. Foster*, 1985). Errors of trial, however, which deprive a defendant of the opportunity to present his or her version of the case, are ordinarily reversible, since there is no method to evaluate whether or not a missing defense resulted in a miscarriage of justice (*People v. Fisher*, 1984).

The accused may normally appeal a court's decision in the following situations:

- a final conviction,
- a sentence,
- an order that commits the defendant for insanity or for controlled substance addiction, and
- an order granting or denying probation.

The state (people) may not appeal an acquittal. Generally, the prosecution may appeal the rulings listed below:

- an order dismissing the case before the defendant has been placed in jeopardy,
- a judgment for the defendant upon the sustaining of a demurrer (objection to pleadings),
- an order granting a new trial,
- an order arresting judgment, and
- any order made after judgment affecting the substantial rights of the people.

When an appellate court reverses a conviction of a lower court, the case is returned to the original court for a determination by the trial court as to whether or not the case will be retried or dismissed. Exceptions to this general rule occur when the appellate court rules as a "matter of law" that there was insufficient evidence to sustain the conviction, or the appellate court rules that the original court lacked jurisdiction to try the case.

## LEGAL RESEARCH

This section is designed for those readers who do not have an extensive background in legal research and is provided to help the reader understand some of the uniqueness when researching court issues. Researching legal issues and cases is different from standard literature research. Once the student has mastered the concepts and methodology, the legal issues, case laws, and statutes can be located quickly and efficiently. Most research involving courts and other legal issues is accomplished online with either the Westlaw or Lexis-Nexis search engines. When using either of those search vehicles, the programs provide the researcher with online assistance in framing the search question or issue and in conducting the search.

In conducting legal research, the researcher should:

1. Research the subject systematically, going sequentially from one source (e.g., statutes, court decisions, or law reviews) to the next.
2. Check to insure that the latest available information has been consulted. For example, use only the latest copy of the penal code. Using only the latest references is essential because legal information and points of authority change frequently due to results of statutory modifications and new court decisions.
3. Be patient and thorough when researching legal questions. To many questions, the law frequently does not yield easy "yes" or "no" answers. At times, the answers will be considered as ambiguous and conflicting.

## Legal Citations

**Legal citations** are a form of shorthand used to assist in locating legal sources. Appellate court decisions are published in case law books, more popularly known as reporters. The basic rules of legal citation are as follows:

1. In most citation formats, the volume or title number is presented first.
2. Following is the standardized abbreviation for the legal reference source.
3. In the case of court cases, the page number of the first page of the decision is listed last. In the case of statutory references, it is the section number of the statute.

For example, the citation 107 U.S. 468 refers to the case starting on page 468 of volume 107 of United States Reports. A citation of 18 U.S.C. 347, refers to title 18 U.S. Code, section 347.

## National Reporter System

West Publishing Company's **National Reporter System** is the standard for researching court reports. The system includes, in bound volumes and advance sheets, decisions of all state and federal appellate courts and selected trial court opinions. Included in the bound volumes are the table of cases, table of cited statutes, criminal and appellate procedure tables, words and phrases, and a key number digest.

The Reporter system was started 1876 by two brothers doing business under the name of John B. West and Company. The brothers reported the decisions of courts in Minnesota in a series of pamphlets known as The Syllabi. In 1879, the name of the series was changed to North Western Reporter. By 1887, the venture had expanded to a total of seven regional reporters covering all the states. The seven regional reporters are still being published with only slight modifications in state coverage. The present day coverage is as follows:

Atlantic Reporter: Me., N.H., Conn., Vt., Pa., Del., Md., and N.J.

North Eastern Reporter: Mass., N.Y., Ohio, Ind., and Ill.

North Western Reporter: N.Dak., S.Dak., Nebr., Minn., Iowa, Wis., and Mich.

Pacific Reporter: Kan., Ok., N.M., Col., Wyo., Mont., Id., Utah, Ariz., Nev., Or., Wash., Ca., Alaska, and Ha.

South Eastern Reporter: Ga., S.Car., N.Car., Va., and W. Va.

South Western Reporter: Tex., Ark., Tenn., Ky., and Mo.

Southern Reporter: La., Miss., Ala., and Fla.

In addition to the regional reporters, West publishes the Supreme Court Reporter that reports only decisions of the U.S. Supreme Court; The Federal Reporter that reports decisions of the U.S. Courts of Appeal; and the Federal Supplement that reports selected U.S. District Court decisions, decisions of federal judicial panels, and other special federal courts. The New York Supplement, which also reports New York state appellate cases, was started in 1887, and the California Reporter that reports current decisions of the California Supreme Court, district courts of appeal and superior court (appellate department) decisions, was started in 1960.

## Official Reporters

As noted above, West's National Reporter System is the standard case reporter. In most cases they are not considered as the **official reporter**. Each high court designates a publisher as its official reporter. For example, the official reporter of the U.S. Supreme Court is the U.S. Reports (U.S.) whereas the reporter is the Supreme Court

Reporter (S. Ct.). Contained in each case reported in the West reporter is the official reporter citation.

## Legal Digests

**Legal digests** are not legal authorities but can be used as research tools. Legal digests identify and consolidate similar issues by topical arrangement. Most legal digests, using West's standard format, divide the body of law into seven main divisions that encompass thirty-two subheadings and approximately four hundred topics. West also publishes a digest for each series of case reporters. Each topic is assigned a digest "key" number. For example, Crim Law 625 is the key number for the legal issue of "exclusion from criminal trial."

The key number is the same for each digest published. Legal points from court decisions are published with a brief statement of the legal point involved and the case citation for the court decision being digested. If, for example, a point being researched is located in a digest under Crim Law 625, then reference to other digests using the same key number (Crim Law 625) will help locate other court decisions on the same or similar issues.

## Shepard's Citations

Shepard's Citations, started in 1873 by Frank Shepard, are widely used to ascertain the current status of a statute or court decision. Shepard's Citations, more popularly known as citators, analyze each appellate court decision as to the history of the case, other decisions where that decision has been cited, and whether or not the rule of the case has been modified, overruled, or approved by other cases. A similar analysis is used for statutes. For a detailed explanation of how to use Shepard's Citations, read the first pages of any citatory volume.

## Legal Dictionaries and Encyclopedias

Like Shepard's Citations and legal digests, legal dictionaries and encyclopedias are not legal authorities but research tools. The most popular legal dictionary is Black's Law Dictionary.

Legal encyclopedias provide discussions on various legal points in encyclopedic form based on court decisions and statutes. They are arranged by broad legal topics and subdivided by individual areas. Most state legal encyclopedias provide detailed discussions on state legal issues. For example, the citation "17 Tex Jur 3d (Rev) 125" refers to volume 17 of Texas Jurisprudence, third edition (revised), section 125. The cited section provides a detailed discussion on robbery.

## Law Reviews

The major law schools publish law reviews. In general, law reviews contain scholarly articles on various aspects of law. They are not legal authority but are often cited as persuasive authorities. Law reviews are cited similarly to court cases. For example, in volume 50 of the Texas Law Review an article that begins on page 192 would be cited as 50 Tex. L. Rev. 192.

## Standard Jury Instructions—Criminal

Standard Jury Instructions—Criminal are collections of standard jury instructions that a judge may use to instruct the jury regarding elements of crimes, defenses, and other matters relating to the trial. They also are used by nonjudges as references, since the instructions contain explanations of crimes and criminal procedural matters.

### Westlaw and LexisNexis

Westlaw and LexisNexis are electronic legal research services that provide access to tens of thousands of databases composed of cases, statutes, regulations, law review articles, practice materials, newspaper articles, and many other materials. The vast majority of these materials are available full text.

Both Westlaw and LexisNexis started in the 1970s as dial-up services with dedicated terminals. The earliest versions used acoustic couplers or key phones; then smaller terminals with internal modems. Around 1989, both started offering programs for personal computers that emulated the terminals, and when Internet access became available, both used an internet address as an alternative option.

As of May 2010 to serve its user population of about 5 million subscribers, LexisNexis hosted over 100 terabytes of content on its 11 mainframes (supported by over 300 midrange UNIX servers and nearly 1,000 Windows NT servers) at its main datacenter in Miamisburg, Ohio (LexisNexis Data Centers Fact Sheet, 2010) .

Judges and attorneys usually prefer one or the other for their legal research. For example, co-author of this book Frank DiMarino prefers to use Westlaw and co-author Cliff Roberson prefers to use LexisNexis. To some extent the choice of service depends on which service the attorney or judge is more familiar with. When Frank was with the U.S. attorney's office in Savannah, Georgia, the office used Westlaw, whereas Cliff previously worked as a case editor for LexisNexis.

## Questions in Review

1. Why is there a dual court system in the United States?
2. What are the primary duties of an appellate court?
3. Explain the importance of jurisdiction and venue.
4. What steps does an appellate court take when it reverses a case?
5. Explain the jurisdiction of federal courts?
6. Explain the role of a court that has original jurisdiction?
7. Do criminal defendants have a right to demand a change of venue? If so, when?
8. What are the three foundational rules regarding how to conduct legal research?
9. Explain what type of rulings of a trial court that the defendant is able to appeal?
10. Can the government appeal? If so, when?

## Practicum

Jay Arnold, while a resident of Ohio, opened an office in Missouri. From his office in Missouri, he mailed letters to possible investors in Texas, New York, and California in an attempt to sell them counterfeit gold. What state or states have jurisdiction over his criminal acts? Why? Does the federal government have criminal jurisdiction over his acts? If so, on what basis?

## Web Resources

Federal Judicial Center:
www.fjc.gov

United States Sentencing Commission:
www.ussc.gov

Administrative offices of the U.S. Courts:
www.uscourts.gov

Sourcebook of Criminal Justice Statistics online:
www.albany.edu/sourcebook

American Prosecutors' Research Institute:
http://www.ildaa.org/apri

Federal Defense Attorneys:
http://www.afda.org

Indigent Defense, Bureau of Justice Statistics:
http://www.ojp.usdoj.gov/hjs/id.htm

National Association of Criminal Defense Lawyers:
http://www.nacdl.org

National District Attorneys Association:
http://www.ndaa.org/index.html

Prosecution Statistics, Bureau of Justice Statistics:
http://www.ojp.usdoj.gov/bjs/pros.htm

Prosecutors in State Courts, Bureau of Justice Statistics:
http://www.ojp.usdoj.gov/bjs

United States Department of Justice, Office of the Attorney General:
http:Ilwww.usdoj.gov/agl U.S. prosecutors Web sites:
www.prosecutor.info

## Key Terms (study for exam 1)

**Case law:** The phrase used to indicate appellate court interpretations of the law.

**Crime control model of Justice:** The model that advocates that crime control is the most important goal of the criminal justice system.

**Due process model:** The model of criminal justice that stresses the importance of individual rights and the presumption of innocence.

**Law:** When used in a generic sense, means the rules of action or conduct duly prescribed by controlling authority, and having binding legal force, including valid municipal ordinances as well as statutes.

**Legal citations:** Forms of shorthand used to assist in locating legal sources

**Legal digests:** Legal reference books that identify and consolidate similar issues by topical arrangement.

**National Reporter System:** West Publishing Company's case reporting system that includes decisions of all state and federal appellate courts and selected trial court opinions.

**Official Reporter:** Each high court designates a publisher as its official reporter that will publish its decisions.

**Venue:** The geographical location of the trial; the judicial district or county in which the trial should be conducted.

## References

### CASES

*Frank v. Mangum*, 237 N.S. 309, 347 (1914).

*Gant v. Arizona*, 129 S. Ct. 1710 (2009).

*Moore v. City of Albany*, 98 N.Y. 398 (1885).

*Otter Tail Power Co. v. Von Bank*, 72 N.D. 497 (1942).

*Payton v. New York*, 445 U.S. 573 (1980).

*People v. Brophy*, 49 CA2d 15, 28; 120 P.2d 946 (1942).

*People v. Fisher*, 153 Cal. App. 3rd 826 (2nd Dist. Cal. 1984).

*People v. Foster*, 169 Cal. App. 3rd 519 (1st Dist. Cal. 1985).

*Sloane v. Hammond*, 81 CA 590, 254 P. 648 (1927).

*United States Fidelity & Guaranty Co. v. Guenther*, 281 U.S. 34 (U.S. 1930).

*Whren v. United States*, 135 L.Ed 2d. 89 (1996).

*Younger v. Superior Court*, 21 Cal. 3d. 102 (Cal. 1978).

### BOOKS, JOURNAL ARTICLES, AND OTHER REFERENCES

Copland, James R.. "What of Impartiality? *National Law Journal* 22 (June 1, 2009).

Hamilton, Marci. *God vs. the Gavel*. London: Cambridge University Press, 2005.

Holmes, Oliver Wendell. . *The Common Law*. Mineola, NY: Dover Publications, 1881.

LexisNexis Data Centers Fact Sheet (2010), www.lexisnexis.com/presscenter/mediakit/datacenter.asp (accessed May 1, 2010).

# 2

# Judicial Power

**What you need to know about Judicial Power**

After you have completed this chapter, you should know:

- Constitutions create the branches of government, including the executive, legislative, and judicial branches.
- A court is an institution authorized to resolve disputes between parties.
- Criminal courts decide the guilt or innocence of defendants charged with a crime.
- Most courts are created by constitutions and legislation.
- Federal courts are created by the U.S. Constitution and legislation passed by the U.S. Congress.
- State courts are created by individual state constitutions and legislation passed by state legislatures.
- Judicial power and authority is created by constitutional provisions and legislation.
- Jurisdiction means the power and authority of the court to hear a case and render a decision binding upon the parties.
- Court decisions set standards for conduct by applying the law to resolve disputes.
- As courts decide cases, the law is applied to practical disputes and plays a vital role in the fabric of our society.
- Courts are divided into three levels: trial courts, intermediate appellate courts, and courts of last resort.
- Access to courts and the protections of law are open to everybody, including citizens and noncitizens.
- Traffic courts, municipal courts, juvenile courts, small claims courts, probate courts, and family courts, are known as "inferior courts" because they have limited authority to only hear certain types of cases.
- Trial courts have witnesses testify, admit evidence, and are the triers of fact in any criminal prosecution.
- Appellate courts review the procedures and conclusions made by a trial court based upon the record made during the trial court's proceedings.
- Appellate courts do not admit testimony or other evidence during the consideration of an appeal.
- Appellate courts decide cases based upon briefs and arguments submitted by counsel and the record of the proceedings in the trial court.
- Courts of last resort decide what appeals will be heard by the court based upon the Supreme Court's discretion.
- A judge presides over court proceedings to assure that procedures and laws are followed, proceedings are orderly, and resolution is fairly and justly obtained.
- In the federal court system, judges are appointed for life.
- In the state court system, judges must run an electoral campaign to be elected to their position for each term.

**Chapter Outline**

## INTRODUCTION

In the United States, the state and federal governments are separated into three branches each with its own specific responsibilities. The branches are: (1) the executive branch, lead by the U.S. president or in a state by a governor; (2) the legislative branch, made up of the House of Representatives, the Senate, and the state legislatures; and (3) the judicial branch, composed of trial and appellate courts.

Among the three branches of government, the trial courts have the closest contact with criminal defendants, law enforcement personnel, and the lawyers involved in the prosecution and defense of criminal charges. This chapter describes how courts are created and organized, what the role of judges is, how judges are selected, and what powers do courts exercise in enforcing decisions.

## CREATION OF COURTS AND JURISDICTION

A court is an institution designed to resolve legal disputes between parties according to the established law, procedure, and court rules. As courts conduct their daily business of deciding cases through interpreting and applying the law in legal disputes, the law assumes a vital role in the societal fabric of our lives.

The "law" as embodied in court decisions sets standards or principles that are part of the reasonable expectations of how people and institutions will interact with each other in a diverse and complex society. Court decisions impact the freedom of individuals, the economic status of businesses, and the relationship among citizens in communities. The fair, just, and expeditious resolution of disputes promotes the general welfare of our society.

Often, courts are called on to uphold limitations on the government's exercise of power. Courts protect against abuses by each branch of government, including administrative agencies, the president, Congress, and even lower courts.

Courts protect the rights of minorities from unrestrained actions by the majority and protect the rights of people who can't protect themselves. As will be discussed later, this is considered as part of the "rule of law" concept. Courts also embody principles of equal treatment and fair play. Access to courts and the protections of the law are open to everybody, including citizens and noncitizens. Courts provide to criminal defendants, who are unable to afford representation or are indigent, during the trial and on appeal, appointed counsel to act zealously on their behalf.

Courts hear both civil cases and criminal cases. Civil cases involve disputes about business contracts, negligence, or property. Criminal cases are prosecutions brought by the government against defendants charged with criminal offenses. Courts decide what really happened and what should be done about it. In criminal cases, courts decide if a crime was committed and what the punishment should be administered.

Both state and federal courts are created through authority granted by a constitution. Although we study the U.S. Constitution to learn the structure of federal courts, each state has its own constitution, too, that gives the states the authority to establish courts within the state's boundaries. The founding fathers of the United States drew on several early state constitutions for guidance and the federal constitution inspired the later development of state constitutions.

Both the federal constitution and state constitutions deal with similar issues of government structure, the balance of power, and individual liberties. It is necessary that courts are independent. Courts should be free from outside influence, favoritism, and political pressure so that the parties will be treated fairly and objectively. A judge must decide the issues brought before the court based solely upon the law and the facts of each case rather than being swayed by improper interests.

The "**jurisdiction**" of a court is also defined by a statute. Jurisdiction is the power or authority of a court to legitimately hear and decide certain cases. Legislation may impose additions or limitations on the authority of courts to hear cases and further define the jurisdiction of courts. Before a court has jurisdiction or power to hear and decide a case, the court must have jurisdiction over the subject matter and over the parties to the case. Jurisdiction of the subject matter is generally established by statute and in criminal cases jurisdiction over the person is generally established by having the person present in court.

## Federal Courts

The federal judiciary is created by Article III of the U.S. Constitution that specifically establishes federal courts. Article III states, in part: "The judicial Power of the United States, shall be vested in one supreme Court, and in such inferior Courts as the Congress may from time to time ordain and establish." Legislation, as early as the Judiciary Act of 1789, created "inferior courts" such as the 96 district courts, which try criminal cases and the 12 geographically based circuit courts of appeals, which decide criminal appeals. Courts have been created as the population of the United States has grown and court caseloads have increased.

In all states, there are not one but two distinct court systems: state courts and federal courts. The vast majority of cases—over 95 percent—are handled by the state courts. The great bulk of legal business—traffic offenses, divorce, wills and estates, buying and selling property—is handled by the state courts, because all these areas are governed primarily by state laws.

Courts in the United States are divided into three levels:

- Trial courts, where cases start. Trial courts resolve the dispute by determining the facts and applying legal principles to decide who is right.
- Intermediate (appellate) courts, where most appeals are first heard. Appellate courts determine whether the law was applied correctly in the trial court.
- Courts of last resort (usually called supreme courts), which hear further appeals and have final authority in the cases they hear.

This division is generally true of both state courts and federal courts. The federal judiciary follows a similar organization of having three levels of courts.

## State Courts and Jurisdiction

Each court system in the 50 states of the United States is not exactly the same. For example, the names of trial courts are different and some states have separate "supreme courts" to hear civil cases and criminal cases. Yet there are some common similarities to provide a general description about the organization and authority of the courts of typical state court systems.

## State Trial Courts of Limited Jurisdiction

Most state court systems are made up of two types of trial courts. First, there are trial courts of limited jurisdiction or authority such as traffic court, family court, and probate court. Frequently, these courts are referred to as the lower trial courts. Second, there are trial courts of general jurisdiction, which are the primary trial-level courts in which felony matters are prosecuted.

Trial courts of limited jurisdiction are courts that deal with specific types of cases and subject matters. Such courts are usually presided over by a single judge who presides over cases without a **jury**. Examples of limited jurisdiction courts and the types of cases they handle include:

*Traffic court*—minor violations of traffic laws, such as speeding and negligent driving;

*Municipal court*—offenses against city ordinances, such as liquor laws, beach regulations, and building codes;

*Juvenile court*—cases involving delinquent children who are minors not having reached the age of 18 or 21;

*Small claims court*—disputes between private persons or businesses involving low dollar amounts, for example in Ohio, of less than $15,000;

*Probate court*—matters concerning administering the will or estate of a person who has died; and

*Family court*—matters concerning adoption, divorce, alimony, custody, and child support.

## State Trial Courts of General Jurisdiction

Trial courts of general jurisdiction are the primary trial courts that hear felony cases. A single judge presides over the trial. The judge decides legal issues about the interpretation of the law and legal procedure. A jury also sits during a trial to decide factual issues and render a verdict. A complete record of the trial and all other sessions, called a verbatim transcript, is made. This record is used on appeal to review the trial proceedings.

Courts of general jurisdiction are known by a variety of titles among the states, including "circuit courts," "superior courts," "courts of common pleas," and, in New York, "supreme courts."

In certain cases, these courts of general jurisdiction may hear appeals from courts of limited jurisdiction, such as an appeal from a municipal court or a traffic court. Table 2-1, which contains the estimated number of felony convictions in State courts during the calendar year 2004, provides us with an estimation of how busy our state courts are.

## State Intermediate Appellate Courts

Most states have intermediate appellate courts between the trial courts of general jurisdiction and the highest court in the state. Any party who is unsatisfied with the trial court's **judgment** may appeal to the intermediate court. In criminal cases, however, the state may not appeal a not-guilty verdict.

An appeal from a trial court must be heard by an intermediate appellate court. An appeal from a trial court is considered a matter of right. When appellate courts review a criminal case, they limit their review to alleged procedural flaws and errors of legal interpretation. On appeal, the procedures followed by the government during the investigation and prosecution phase of the case may be reviewed for violations of the

| TABLE 2-1 | Estimated number of felony convictions in State courts, 2004 | |
|---|---|---|
| | Felony convictions in State courts | |
| **Most serious conviction offense** | **Number** | **Percent** |
| **All offenses** | 1,078,920 | 100.0% |
| **Violent offenses** | 194,570 | 18.0% |
|   **Murder** | 8,400 | 0.80 |
|     **Murder** | 5,660 | 0.50 |
|     **Manslaughter**[a] | 2,740 | 0.30 |
|   **Sexual assault**[b] | 33,190 | 3.10 |
|     **Rape** | 12,310 | 1.10 |
|     **Other sexual assault** | 20,880 | 1.90 |
|   **Robbery** | 38,850 | 3.60 |
|     **Armed** | 8,990 | 0.80 |
|     **Unarmed** | 8,950 | 0.80 |
|     **Unspecified** | 20,910 | 1.90 |
|   **Aggravated assault** | 94,380 | 8.70 |
|   **Other violent**[c] | 19,750 | 1.80 |
| **Property offenses** | 310,680 | 28.8% |
|   **Burglary** | 93,870 | 8.70 |
|     **Residential** | 15,100 | 1.40 |
|     **Nonresidential** | 18,230 | 1.70 |
|     **Unspecified** | 60,540 | 5.60 |
|   **Larceny**[d] | 119,340 | 11.10 |
|     **Motor vehicle theft** | 16,910 | 1.60 |
|     **Other theft** | 102,430 | 9.50 |
|   **Fraud**[e] | 97,470 | 9.00 |
|     **Fraud** | 48,560 | 4.50 |
|     **Forgery** | 48,910 | 4.50 |
| **Drug offenses** | 362,850 | 33.6% |
|   **Possession** | 161,090 | 14.9 |
|   **Trafficking** | 201,760 | 18.7 |
|     **Marijuana** | 22,180 | 2.10 |
|     **Other** | 60,650 | 5.60 |
|     **Unspecified** | 118,930 | 11.0 |
| **Weapon offenses** | 33,010 | 3.10% |
| **Other offenses**[f] | 177,810 | 16.5% |

*Note:* Detail may not sum to total because of rounding.

[a]Defined as nonnegligent manslaughter only. A small number of cases were classified as nonnegligent manslaughter when it was unclear if the conviction offense was murder or nonnegligent manslaughter.

[b]Includes rape.

[c]Includes offenses such as negligent manslaughter and kidnapping.

[d]When vehicle theft could not be distinguished from other theft, the case was coded as "other theft." This results in a conservative estimate of vehicle thefts.

[e]Includes embezzlement.

[f]Composed of nonviolent offenses such as receiving stolen property and vandalism.

http://bjs.ojp.usdoj.gov/content/pub/html/scscf04/tables/scs04101tab.cfm (accessed March 28, 2010).

Constitution or established procedural rules. Also, the rulings of the trial judge may be reviewed for error.

In some states, when a defendant appeals from a conviction in lower court, he or she will receive a "trial de novo" in a primary trial court, which means that a new trial will be held in the reviewing court.

Appellate courts, except in trial de novo cases, decide the case based upon the written **briefs** submitted by the parties and the record of the trial proceedings. The appellate courts will not accept additional evidence through witness testimony. These courts usually sit in panels of two or three judges to decide an appeal and a majority vote will decide a case.

## Highest State Courts

Each state has a court of last resort. In most states, such courts are referred to as "supreme courts." Some states, however, such as Maryland, refer to their highest court as the "court of appeals." In New York, the supreme court is a trial court and the court of last resort a court of appeals. In two states, Texas and Oklahoma, the state supreme court does not handle criminal cases. In those states, the court of criminal appeals is the court of last resort for criminal matters.

Generally, the highest state court has authority to select the cases that the court will decide. This is considered as a discretionary appeal in that the defendant does not have a right to an appeal. There are some issues or cases that the state high court must accept— for example, the appeal in a capital case (case with the death penalty).

Like the intermediate appellate courts, an appeal to a state supreme court usually alleges a mistake of law rather than a factual issue. Most state high courts do not have "fact finding" authority, which means that they must accept the facts as found by the courts below and decide whether or not the court below committed an error involving a legal matter. The exception to this rule in most states is that a defendant may claim that the facts were insufficient as a matter of law to sustain the findings of the court. The claim alleges that the evidence was so deficient that a reasonable jury would not have found the defendant guilty.

Parties do not have an automatic right to an appeal to the highest court. A state high court has "discretionary review," which means that the court decides whether to accept a case and what issues they will hear. For example, the state supreme court may grant leave or permission to appeal criminal cases from the intermediate courts of appeal. Again, the state supreme court may not grant an appeal in a particular case because it may exercise its discretion or prerogative against reviewing a particular case.

It should be noted that some states require or "mandate" state supreme court review in all cases involving the death penalty, issues arising under the U.S. Constitution or the state constitution, and cases in which there have been conflicting opinions from two or more courts of appeals.

Depending upon the state constitution, some state supreme courts have original jurisdiction in certain matters. This means that the state supreme court is the first and only state court to hear and decide these cases. For example, the highest courts in several states have original jurisdiction over issues regarding elections and the reapportionment of legislative districts.

For most litigants, the state supreme court is the court of last resort. State supreme courts often review a case by sitting, depending upon the size of the court, in a panel of three, five, seven, or nine judges sometimes referred to as "justices." The chief justice serves as the leader of the state's judiciary and is responsible for assuring ethical conduct among the jurists in the entire state and the admission of lawyers into the state's bar.

### Practical Example of a State's Court Structure—Ohio

Many states have a similar court structure as the state of Ohio. The Ohio courts are created by the state Constitution that says: "[T]he judicial power of the state is vested in a Supreme Court, Courts of Appeals, Courts of Common Pleas and divisions thereof, and such other courts inferior to the Supreme Court as may from time to time be established by law" (Article IV, Section 1, of the Ohio Constitution).

In Ohio, the courts of common pleas are the trial courts that hear felony cases. All trial courts empanel juries, hear the testimony of witnesses, receive evidence, and, through the advocacy of the prosecutor and the defense counsel, decide cases by juries rendering a verdict.

Courts of appeals or intermediate courts are the primary courts of review from judgments made at the trial court level. Appeals must be heard by intermediate appellate courts so long as procedural rules and filing timelines are complied with. Appeals of felony convictions to the court of appeals in the 12 districts in Ohio are part of the court's mandatory jurisdiction as opposed to the type of discretionary appeals heard by Ohio's supreme court.

The Ohio Supreme Court is the court of last resort for most litigants unless the Supreme Court of the United States grants the rare opportunity of an appeal. For a case to be heard by the Ohio Supreme Court, the Court must grant leave to appeal a case. Thus, similar to most other state supreme courts, the Ohio Supreme Court has the prerogative or the discretion to decide which appeals it will hear.

The jurisdiction of Ohio courts is also specified by the Ohio Constitution and legislation. In Ohio, for example, the judges on the general division of the courts of common pleas have what is called "general jurisdiction" to conduct civil and criminal trials. Since they are the court of the first impression, they are said to have original jurisdiction in such cases.

Criminal jurisdiction for the courts of common pleas mostly includes all crimes defined by statute as felonies that carry a minimum punishment of a year or more. For minor offenses, such as **misdemeanors** and traffic violations in Ohio, lesser courts known as "**municipal courts**" have jurisdiction to hear and dispose of such cases.

Figure 2-1 reflects the organization and jurisdiction of the state courts in Ohio, The organization and jurisdiction of the Ohio State courts is similar to the other states in the United States. Generally, there are three levels of courts: (1) The trial courts that try felony cases (known in Ohio as the court of common pleas); (2) the courts of appeals that review the felony convictions for errors in law or procedure; and (3) the Supreme Court of Ohio that review decisions of the courts of appeals.

## ROLE OF THE JUDGE

The judge has been called "the pillar of the entire justice system." The judge as also been referred to by unhappy litigants as the "last American dictator." As the judge presides over courtroom proceedings, she has numerous responsibilities. The judge assures that all hearings are conducted in a fair and orderly fashion. Also, the judge interprets the law and applies the rules of evidence and procedure as well as acts impartially and without bias.

The trial calendar and docket schedule is also the judge's responsibility. She must assure that cases are litigated without undue delay. Criminal cases may have speedy trial provisions imposed by the state that require that the defendant be brought to trial within a specified time limits or the case could be dismissed. These rules are meant to provide the defendant a speedy trial.

In cases where the judge's knowledge of the parties or her interests would preclude a fair and disinterested control of the proceedings, the judge should withdraw from the

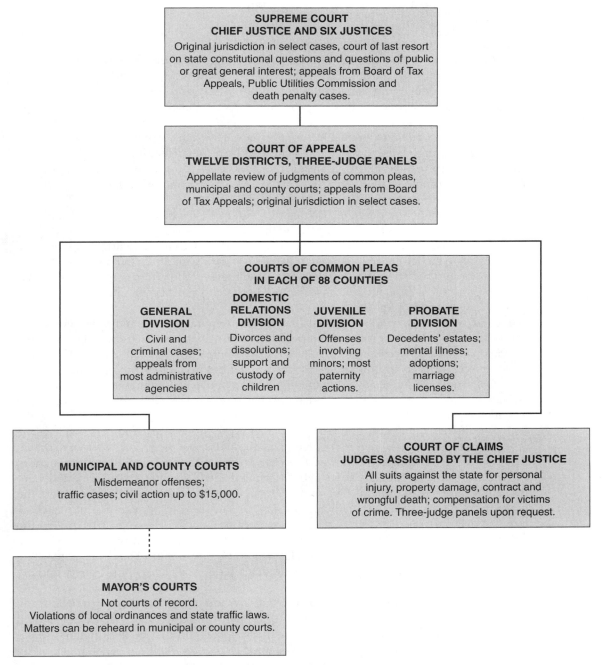

**FIGURE 2-1**  State Court structure for the State of Ohio.

case. A withdrawal from sitting in judgment of the case is known as a "**recusal**." A judge would withdraw from a case if the case involved friends, family, a former client, or a former law firm or business associate. The judge's recusal would operate to assure that another independent and unbiased judge would preside over the proceedings.

In criminal cases, the judge presides over the trial. A jury, composed of 12 citizens, sits to decide factual issues and assess the truthfulness of witness testimony. During the trial, the judge must determine whether any evidence offered is illegal or improper, give the jury legal definitions and instructions about the law that applies to the case, and, in cases that result in a conviction, **sentence** the defendant.

Criminal trials have two adversaries, the prosecutor and the defense counsel, present their cases through a legal contest between opposing sides. The **adversary system** assures that evidence and legal arguments will be fully and forcefully presented. The judge must remain above the fray by providing a dispassionate and objective application of the law to the facts.

Judges must be knowledgeable about the law. They must have the mental discipline to conduct thorough legal research to assure that the most current laws are being applied appropriately to resolve issues. Many of their decisions are given in written opinions. They need to communicate their judgments in a clear and concise manner that will withstand logical scrutiny by others.

Judges must be good listeners so that they can make the best informed decision fairly and with an open mind. They must possess the intellect to seek answers to pointed questions that are at the heart of the issues to be resolved. Judges must avoid the appearance that they have made their minds up in advance of hearing all of the evidence.

Although they should be respectful of the lawyers, the court personnel, the jury, and the parties to a case, judges must also not hesitate to sanction an unprepared lawyer, a disorderly litigant, or an unruly spectator.

The judge's personal life must also be above reproach. Judges must avoid conduct, events, and speeches that create an impression or an appearance that the judge is biased or personally interested in the outcome of a case. While off the bench, judges should not socialize with lawyers or other persons who appear before them in any hearing.

Consequently, judges avoid being involved in the local communities while they are actively hearing cases. Judges may undertake charitable work but they refrain from political activities, including fundraising and campaigning for candidates. Judges should have the highest standards of integrity and ethical conduct in the professional and personal lives.

As noted in *State v. Jacobson* (2008), it is important that the judicial system maintain an appearance of propriety. The Due Process Clause set forth in the Fifth Amendment to the U.S. Constitution entitles parties in both criminal and civil matters to an impartial, neutral, and disinterested tribunal. The public's respect and confidence in the integrity of the judicial system can only be maintained if justice satisfies the appearance of justice. A judge is presumed by law to be unbiased and not prejudiced. However, to maintain the judiciary's appearance of propriety, a judge is to recuse (remove) himself or herself from any matter in which the judge's impartiality would be questioned. The codes controlling judicial disqualification in all states mandate that a judge shall avoid impropriety and the appearance of impropriety.

In *State v. Jacobson* (2008), Jacobson was convicted of assault following a bench trial. Prior to the trial, the judge had disclosed to the parties that he was socially acquainted with a physician who was going to be a witness at trial and that he was inclined to believe the physician's testimony. The parties agreed to proceed with the bench trial [trial by judge alone] despite the judge's familiarity with the witness. Defendant argued that the judge committed reversible error by failing to recuse [remove] himself under the North Dakota judicial conduct code. The state supreme court approved the conviction, stating that the judge disclosed information that he believed the parties might have considered relevant to his disqualification and provided an opportunity for the parties to agree to waive his disqualification. Defendant agreed to proceed with the judge conducting the bench trial and only after he was convicted did he move for a new trial. While the judge was disqualified from the proceeding, his disqualification did not require him to immediately remove himself from the proceeding. He properly disclosed information relevant to the question of disqualification. The parties agreed to proceed, thus waiving the judge's disqualification.

## COURTS IN ACTION

## Why is it important that the judicial system maintain an appearance of propriety?

*State v. Jacobson, 2008 ND 73, P6 (N.D. 2008)*

**Excerpts from court opinion**: It is important that our judicial system maintain an appearance of propriety. The Due Process Clause of the United States Constitution entitles parties in both criminal and civil matters to an impartial, neutral, and disinterested tribunal. The public's respect and confidence in the integrity of the judicial system can only be maintained if justice satisfies the appearance of justice. A judge is presumed by law to be unbiased and not prejudiced. However, to maintain the judiciary's appearance of propriety, a judge is to recuse [withdraw from the case] himself from any matter in which the judge's impartiality would be questioned.

A judge's disqualification decision [in North Dakota] is directed by the North Dakota Code of Judicial Conduct. The Code mandates that a judge shall avoid impropriety and the appearance of impropriety. A judge shall disqualify himself or herself in a proceeding in which the judge's impartiality might reasonably be questioned. The Code provides a non-exhaustive list of instances when a judge must recuse himself from a matter:

**a.** the judge has a personal bias or prejudice concerning a party or a party's lawyer, or personal knowledge of disputed evidentiary facts concerning the proceedings;

**b.** the judge served as a lawyer in the matter in controversy, or a lawyer with whom the judge previously practiced law served during such association as a lawyer concerning the matter, or the judge has been a material witness concerning it;

**c.** the judge knows that he or she, individually or as a fiduciary, or the judge's spouse, parent or child wherever residing, or any other member of the judge's family residing in the judge's household, has an economic interest in the subject matter in controversy or in a party to the proceeding or has any other more than de minimis interest that could be substantially affected by the proceeding;

**d.** the judge or the judge's spouse, or a person within the third degree of relationship to either of them, or the spouse of such a person:

(i) is a party to the proceeding, or an officer, director or trustee of a party;

(ii) is acting as a lawyer in the proceeding;

(iii) is known by the judge to have a more than de minimis interest that could be substantially affected by the proceeding;

(iv) is to the judge's knowledge likely to be a material witness in the proceeding.

An objective standard is used to determine whether a judge must recuse himself. The judge must determine whether a reasonable person could, on the basis of all the facts, reasonably question the judge's impartiality. Even without intentional bias, disqualification can be essential to satisfy the appearance of justice.

## JUDICIAL SELECTION

Federal judges are nominated by the president of the United States and, once confirmed with the advice and consent of the U.S. Senate, are appointed for life.

Most state court judges are not appointed for life but are either elected or appointed (or a combination of both) for a certain number of years. Judges are elected or appointed to the bench after having served as a lawyer for a number of years and making a significant contribution to the legal profession and their communities. Judges who have served on a lower court are sometimes promoted to a higher court, such as a from a trial court to an appellate court.

## LAW IN ACTION

### What happens when the elected local judge is unable to serve?

Ohio General Code § 1579–85 provides for the appointment of an acting judge by the chief justice of the municipal court when the incumbent judge of that court shall be temporarily absent or incapacitated from acting. Ohio Constitution, article IV, § 10 limits the length of terms of elective judges other than those provided for in the Constitution. A municipal court is a creature of legislative action in which the qualifications of a municipal judge are set up. Ohio Constitution, article IV, § 13 authorizes the governor to fill by appointment vacancies occurring during the regular term in the office of any judge, but its language is restricted to vacancies in office which contemplate that the incumbent of the office has died, resigned or has been removed from the office as distinguished from temporary absence or incapacity. The same observation may be made as to Ohio Constitution, article XVII, § 2.

For example, in Texas, judges at the three levels of court are elected in partisan elections by the state's electorate. Judicial candidates run for office by organizing a political campaign, seeking donors, publishing political advertisements, making speeches, and offering different positions from their opponents. The ballot box decides whether a trial judge will serve a term of 4 years or an appellate judge will serve a term of 6 years. Besides winning the election, to be a trial judge, a judicial candidate must be at least 25-years old and have practiced law for 4 years. To be an appellate judge, the candidate must be 35-years old and have practiced law for 10 years.

## COURTS IN ACTION

### How does a judge differ from other public officials?

Edward Ryan, a delegate to the 1846 Wisconsin constitutional convention and later chief justice of the Wisconsin Supreme Court stated that unlike other elected officials the judiciary "represents no man, no majority, no people. It represents the written law of the land . . . it holds the balance, and weighs the right between man and man, between the rich and the poor, between the weak and the powerful." [Edward G. Ryan, Elective Judiciary, Address at the Wisconsin Constitutional Convention (Nov. 30, 1846), in 2 THE CONVENTION OF 1846, at 590, 594 (Milo M. Quaife ed., 1919) (contained in Collections, Vol. 27).]

David B. Rottman and Roy A. Schotland stated that to appreciate the uniqueness of judicial elections, we must first note the differences between judges and other elective officials.

Executive and legislative officials are elected in all democracies, but the United States is all but unique in having judges stand for election. Rottman and Schotland noted that the role of the judge:

> The ideal judge has integrity. He or she not only appears to be, but actually is scrupulously honest, impartial, free of prejudice, and able to decide cases on their merits without regard to the identity of the parties or their attorneys, his or her own interests, or the likely criticism. The ideal judge is committed to the rule of law—he or she will respect the authority of higher courts, follow existing precedent, and adhere to accepted procedures for interpreting statutes and deciding issues. Finally, the ideal judge is humane. [David B. Rottman and Roy A. Schotland (2001, June) What Makes Judicial Elections Unique? Loyola of Los Angeles Law Review, Vol. 34 pp. 1369–1370]

## LAW IN ACTION

## Judicial Campaigns

Judges who are elected to their offices must run an electoral campaign, which has many similarities to other political campaigns. Television and radio advertisements, speeches, and public relations play a significant part in getting a candidate elected for a state judicial office.

Fund raising consultants, campaign advisors, and media relations experts have built an industry to guide judicial candidates to get elected. Businesses such as Whitestar Communications and Judicial Campaign Consultants specialize in the strategic planning of getting judges elected.

An example of a successful campaign involved Michigan's Forty-Second District Court Judge Denis LeDuc, whose testimonial about his consultant addressed as a note of appreciation indicated that the consultant was "instrumental in the drafting of our many campaign messages and themes. The plan you developed to target likely voters worked almost flawlessly. I cannot thank you enough."

Media that provides a message appealing to voters is necessary to succeed in judicial campaigns. One such commercial that promoted successful electoral results for a judicial candidate was the one that aired for Kentucky's Jefferson County District Court Judge candidate, Katie King. To see one of her commercials, follow this link: www.youtube.com/watch?v=1D949HjW6X8&feature=player_embedded.

Other commercials, directly attack sitting judges for decisions they made while in office and are facing reelection. The commercials may be paid for by interest groups that seek to unseat judges who disagree with their priorities or by opposing candidates. A sampling of so-called negative-attack advertisements from such states as Michigan, Ohio, Illinois, and Alabama used in judicial campaigns can be viewed at: www.youtube.com/watch?v=XzFbpXCVgfY.

Some state judicial campaign conduct committees have concluded that judicial elections have become "noisier, costlier, and nastier" in the last three decades. Calls for reform of judicial elections have mounted because some campaigns advance a candidate's personal views of matters that are likely to come before the courts. Such campaigns may threaten a judge's impartiality and call into question the judge's ability to decide by applying the law to the facts presented in a case after hearing the evidence presented by opposing parties.

Also, reform movements recognize that the judiciary is different from the political branches of government and is composed of the legislative and executive branches. Judges should not represent any interest group, party, or constituent.

Up to the late 1970s, judicial elections in Texas were unremarkable events. The Democratic party dominated the state's judiciary. The party's primary election was the main battleground among the judicial candidates. Even those contests rarely inspired much voter turnout because most judges resigned before the end of their terms so that governors would be allowed to appoint their judicial successors. The political appointees often won easy reelection.

In Texas, the costs of judicial campaigns continue to increase. According to the American Judicature Society, in 1980, Texas became the first state where the cost of a judicial campaign was over $1 million. During the next decade, the seven winning candidates for the Texas Supreme Court raised nearly $9.2 million. The American Judicature Society claims that more than 40 percent of that $9.2 million "was contributed by parties or lawyers with cases before the court or by contributors linked to those parties." These elections have drawn more money, political influence, and debate about judicial selection.

## ENFORCEMENT OF JUDICIAL RULINGS

Courts rely upon the executive branch of the government for the enforcement of their decisions and rulings. Courts do not have their own enforcement units. In criminal cases, when a judge sentences a defendant to incarceration, the defendant is held in custody by the federal or state authorities.

In federal criminal cases, defendants are held in custody by the U.S. Marshals Service. The Marshals Service is responsible for housing and transporting all defendants who are arrested by law enforcement agencies and charged with a federal offense. The Marshals Service is also responsible for all prisoners who have been sentenced by a federal court until they are delivered to the designated Federal Bureau of Prisons facility to serve the period of confinement. According to the Marshals Service, it is responsible for about 58,500 detainees in its custody on any given day.

At the state and local level, the county **sheriff**'s office is primarily responsible for the enforcement of court rulings. In many counties, the sheriff is the chief law-enforcement officer, elected by residents in the county, and considered an officer of the court.

Deputy Sheriffs serve civil process and enforce court orders. The sheriff's office also operates the county jail that holds defendants pending trial when bond has been denied

### LAW IN ACTION

### Historical enforcement of U.S. Supreme Court orders

In the history of the U.S. Supreme Court, it has had to issue decisions that have provoked considerable controversy as to how its ruling would be enforced. In 1832, the Court considered the case of the Cherokee Indian tribe that lived in the state of Georgia on land that had been guaranteed to them by a treaty with the United States. Gold was discovered on the land. The state of Georgia tried to seize the land. The Cherokees sued. In *Worcester v. Georgia*, the Court held in favor of the Cherokees ordering Georgia to cease laying any claims to the land or the gold. Georgia refused to obey the Court. President Andrew Jackson reportedly said, "John Marshall [the chief justice of the Supreme Court] has made his decision; now let him enforce it. Jackson sent federal troops to evict the Cherokees, who traveled the Trail of Tears to Oklahoma, thousands dying along the way.

In 2001, the Court decided *Bush v. Gore*, a case about the validity of the presidential electoral results in the state of Florida. Essentially, the Court decided the winner of a close presidential election. Although much commentary followed, the defeated party, Vice-President Al Gore respected the Court's decision and conceded the election. The most remarkable characteristic of recent cases is the fact that the public as well as the losers and winners abide by the Court's decisions.

The Constitution promises the people the rule of law. Justice Stephen Breyer, an Associate Justice of Supreme Court, in remarks made to the Boston College Law School, said that the rule of law in the United States has been promoted by a legal profession that reaches out to others, teaches by example, and instills respect for the rule of law.

"Habits, customs, expectations, and settled modes of behavior" engaged in by judges, lawyers, and the general public all serve to protect the constitutional system in our nation. Chief Justice John Marshall recognized, however, "the people made the Constitution and the people can unmake it." Justice Breyer believed that the continued existence of the rule of law depends upon the next generation of Americans participating in our democratic governing process and understanding the constitutional importance of doing so.

and until they have been convicted. Once convicted, depending upon the local procedure, the defendant is transferred to the state correctional institution or held in county jail until their appeal is heard and then transferred to prison.

Courts have power to hold persons in contempt of court. Courts are deemed to have inherent power to punish all persons for violating their rules and orders, for disregarding procedural requirements, and for interrupting the proceedings.

For example, this contempt power extends to persons who have failed to appear as a witness in response to a subpoena or to attend a hearing as a defendant when issued a summons. If held in contempt, the person may be compelled to pay a fine or serve time in jail, or both, depending upon the nature of the violation.

## COURTS IN ACTION

## U.S. Supreme Court in 2010

**Chief Justice———— Year Appointed by President**
John G. Roberts Jr. 2005 George W. Bush
**Associate Justices——Year Appointed President**
John Paul Stevens 1975 Ford
Antonin Scalia 1986 Reagan
Anthony M. Kennedy 1988 Reagan
Clarence Thomas 1991 George H.W. Bush
Ruth Bader Ginsburg 1993 Clinton
Stephen G. Breyer 1994 Clinton
Samuel A. Alito Jr. 2006 G.W. Bush
Sonia Sotomayor 2009 Obama
Elena Kagan 2010 Obama

The 11 U.S. presidents from 1945 to 2010 have appointed 29 Supreme Court members. Republicans have appointed 17 and the Democrats 12.

| President | Party | Appointments |
| --- | --- | --- |
| Harry Truman | Democrat | 4 |
| Dwight Eisenhower | Republican | 5 |
| John Kennedy | Democrat | 2 |
| Lyndon Johnson | Democrat | 2 |
| Richard Nixon | Republican | 4 |
| Gerald Ford | Republican | 1 |
| Jimmy Carter | Democrat | 0 |
| Ronald Reagan | Republican | 3 |
| George Bush | Republican | 2 |
| Bill Clinton | Democrat | 2 |
| George W. Bush | Republican | 2 |
| Barack H. Obama | Democrat | 2 |

## Questions in Review

1. What role do state constitutions play in the creation of courts?
2. Do legislatures affect the power and authority of courts to hear cases? If so, how?
3. What is jurisdiction?
4. Describe the three levels of courts in the federal and state systems.
5. What is the role of the judge during a trial?
6. What do appellate court judges do?
7. On appeal, what does an appellate judge consider to make a decision?
8. How are judges selected in the federal system?
9. How are judges selected in the state system?
10. What is the best way to select judges? Why?
11. What reforms in the selection of judges would you like to see?
12. Consider the court of last resort (e.g. state supreme court or court of criminal appeals) in your home state, what types of jurisdiction does it have?

## Practicum

Ohio Revised Code Annotated § 2705.01 provides: A court, or judge at chambers, may summarily punish a person guilty of misbehavior in the presence of or so near the court or judge as to obstruct the administration of justice.

### CATHOLIC SOCIAL SERVICES V. TIMOTHY HOWARD, 666 N.E.2D 658 (1995)

Attorney Michael D. Slodov ("appellant") appeals the finding of the trial court that he was in contempt of court. Appellant had appeared before the Juvenile Court representing his client, Timothy Howard, in a matter. Apparently, he made the trial judge unhappy because the judge ordered him not to appear before it or to be present near the courtroom during the current proceedings. Later when he was seen in a hallway near the courtroom, he was held in contempt pursuant to Ohio Rev. Code Ann. § 2705.01, and sentenced to a fine and incarceration.

Appellant appealed.

In his first assignment of error, appellant contends the trial court erred in finding him in contempt. Appellant argues the trial court could not lawfully prohibit his presence in the area near the courtroom or in the courtroom itself.

### AS AN APPELLATE JUDGE, WOULD YOU VOTE TO AFFIRM (APPROVE) THE FINDING AND SENTENCE?

**Appellate Court decision:** Contempt of court is defined as disobedience of an order of a court. It is conduct which brings the administration of justice into disrespect, or which tends to embarrass, impede or obstruct a court in the performance of its functions. The purpose of contempt proceedings is to secure the dignity of the courts and the uninterrupted and unimpeded administration of justice.

Contempt is either civil or criminal in nature. Civil contempt seeks to coerce compliance while criminal contempt's purpose is to punish. Both the character and purpose of the finding of contempt must be examined in determining whether the contempt was civil or criminal. Criminal contempt is usually characterized by an unconditional prison sentence or fine. It is designed to vindicate the authority of the court.

In the instant case, the trial court found appellant to be in violation of its previous order that appellant not be in or near the courtroom. The purpose of the sanction was to punish appellant for his transgression. He was unconditionally sentenced to thirty days in jail and fined $ 250.00. Therefore, this was direct, criminal contempt.

The trial court found appellant's behavior to be in violation of its previous direction that he not be near or in the courtroom and that appellant's presence obstructed the administration of justice. The trial court did not indicate how appellant obstructed the administration of justice. Direct contempt usually requires conduct which poses an imminent threat to the administration of justice. The mere presence of a person does not constitute an apparent intention to disrupt the administration of justice. There is no evidence of conduct by appellant which impeded or interrupted any proceedings in the trial court's courtroom or anywhere in the vicinity of the courtroom.

The determination of contempt is within the trial court's discretion. However, evidence of guilt beyond a reasonable doubt must be shown on the record and the offending conduct must constitute an imminent threat to the administration of justice. There is no evidence appellant engaged in conduct which obstructed the administration of justice. The trial court abused its discretion in holding appellant in contempt.

Further, the trial court's order prevents appellant from appearing in its courtroom. Such an order effectively restricts appellant from practicing law before the trial judge. In State, ex rel. Jones, v. Stokes (1989), 49 Ohio App. 3d 136, 551 N.E.2d 220, this court granted a writ of prohibition when two trial judges sent a letter to the Legal Aid Society ordering the director to not assign a certain attorney to their courtrooms. When the attorney appeared, the trial court issued an order to show cause why the director should not be held in contempt. This court stated:

> Certainly, this broad sanction goes beyond disqualification or mere regulation of the conduct of counsel in a particular proceeding. Respondents have imposed a continuing restriction on Reisman's ability to practice law in their two courtrooms. This

restriction differs only by degree from the sanctions imposed through the grievance procedures which are supervised by the Supreme Court of Ohio. Yet, the Supreme Court's "jurisdiction over the discipline of attorneys is exclusive and absolute." Smith v. Kates (1976), 46 Ohio St. 2d 263, 266, 75 Ohio Op. 2d 318, 320, 348 N.E.2d 320, 322. As a consequence, the conduct of respondents which gave rise to this action in prohibition is the type of usurpation of jurisdiction by an inferior court which necessitates relief in prohibition.

The order in the instant case bars appellant from practicing law before the trial court. Appellant was not disqualified from a specific case but from all future proceedings. Such an order is beyond the trial court's jurisdiction as it conflicts with the exclusive power of the Supreme Court of Ohio to govern the practice of law. Appellant's first assignment of error is well taken. The finding of contempt was reversed.

## Key Terms

**Adversary System:** The process of litigation in trials and on appeals used in the United States, which depends upon each opposing side to present its case and argue its contentions before the court so the court can rely upon the parties' efforts to present the facts and the legal considerations.

**Brief:** A written pleading prepared by each side in a lawsuit or criminal prosecution, usually presented to an appellate court to explain and argue to the court its view of the facts, its interpretation of the applicable law, and the conclusions the court should reach.

**Judgment:** The final disposition of a civil lawsuit or criminal prosecution.

**Jurisdiction:** The jurisdiction of a court is its power and authority to hear a case and legitimately render a decision that is binding upon the parties. The jurisdiction of a court is established by the provisions in a constitution and by legislation.

**Jury:** In a criminal prosecution, 12 persons plus some alternates, selected from lists of registered voters or licensed drivers, who are sworn to listen to the evidence admitted into court, consider no matters outside of court, and determine the facts by rendering a verdict at the conclusion of deliberations.

**Juvenile Court:** Court specifically established by legislation to hear criminal cases concerning minors who are under the age of 18, depending upon the state's definition of who is considered to be a minor.

**Misdemeanor:** Less serious criminal offense, as compared to a felony, which is usually punishable by a sentence of one year or less. Such sentences are usually served in county jails.

**Municipal Courts:** According to the judicial organization of some states, these are courts whose territorial authority is confined to a city or community and whose jurisdiction includes hearing only petty offenses and civil violations of municipal codes and zoning ordinances.

**Recusal:** The withdrawal or disqualification of a judge from hearing a case because of the judge's personal interests, financial holdings, or other conflicts of interest, which may create an impression that the judge is unfair or biased.

**Sentence:** The punishment ordered by a court for a defendant convicted of a crime, which may include incarceration and a monetary fine.

**Separation of Witnesses:** A court order, requested by one of the parties during a hearing, which requires all witnesses who may testify at the hearing to remain outside the courtroom until each is called to testify and to not discuss their testimony. In federal criminal cases, the defendant and the investigating case agent may remain in the courtroom.

**Sheriff:**  An officer of a county, often chosen by popular election, whose principal duties are to aid the courts. In criminal cases, the sheriff serves processes (such as subpoenas), summons juries and executes judgments (by incarcerating defendants in county jails).

## References

### CASES

*Bush v. Gore*, 531 U.S. 98 (2000)
*State v. Jacobson*, 2008 ND 73 (N.D. 2008)
*Worcester v. Georgia*, 31 U.S. 515 (1832)

### BOOKS, JOURNALS AND ARTICLES

*Black's Law Dictionary* 4th ed. St. Paul, MN: West, 1957.

Bureau of Justice Statistics. *State Court Sentencing of Convicted Felons, 2004—Statistical Tables*. "Felony Sentences in State Court." http://bjs.ojp.usdoj.gov/content/pub/html/scscf04/tables/scs04101tab.cfm (accessed March 28, 2010).

Becker, Daniel, and Malia Reddick. "Judicial Selection Reform: Examples From Six States." *American Judicature Society* (2003). www.judicialselection.us/uploads/documents/jsreform_1185395742450.pdf (accessed April 24, 2010).

Breyer, Stephen. *Commencement Remarks to the Boston College Law School*. Newton, Massachusetts, May 22, 2003.

www.abanet.org/publiced/courts/court_role.html (accessed April 24, 2010).

www.judicialcampaignconsultants.com/Judicial_Campaign_About_Us.html (accessed April 24, 2010).

www.usmarshals.gov/duties/factsheets/pod-1209.html (accessed April 24, 2010).

Posner, Richard A. "The Role of the Judge in the Twenty-First Century." *Boston University Law Review* 86 (2006): 1049–1068.

# 3

# The Judicial Process

## What you need to know about the judicial process

After you have completed this chapter, you should know:

- Venue refers to the geographic location where the trial may be held.
- The Sixth Amendment to the U.S. Constitution establishes the right of the defendant to be tried by a speedy and public trial, by an impartial jury of the state and in the judicial district wherein the crime was committed.
- Although the defendant is entitled to have the trial in the district where the crime occurred, this right may be waived and a request made that the trial be held in some other district.
- Because the defendant has a constitutional right to be tried within the judicial district within which the crime was committed, the government has no right to move for a change of venue over the objections of the defense.
- In setting the trial date, many factors must be considered, such as what a reasonable length of time is, to permit each side to prepare its case and whether the accused is in jail or has posted bail.
- Although the right to a speedy trial is primarily for the benefit of the accused, this right, like others rights, may be waived by the defendant, and often is. Defendants make frequent requests for continuances in bringing the case to trial.
- Fourteenth Amendment guarantees a right of jury trial in state courts in all criminal cases which—were they to be tried in a federal court—would come within the Sixth Amendment's guarantee.
- The laws of every state guarantee a right to jury trial in serious criminal cases.
- Another guarantee under the Sixth Amendment is the right to a public trial. Although this right appears to be a clear and explicit right, what constitutes a public trial is not defined either by the Sixth Amendment or by any of the laws of the states.
- The nation's accepted practice of guaranteeing a public trial to an accused has its roots in the English common-law heritage.
- Rules of evidence are used by the courts in an attempt to secure fairness in administration, elimination of unjustifiable expense and delay.
- The rules of evidence are designed to regulate the process of proving facts
- Evidentiary rules should be construed in a manner to attempt to secure fairness in administration, elimination of unjustifiable expense and delay, and promotion of growth and development of the law of evidence to the end that the truth may be ascertained and proceedings justly determined.
- The right of pretrial discovery in criminal matters is of comparatively recent origin. It was unknown at common law and still is not recognized in criminal matters in some states.

- The right of discovery is the pretrial right of the adversary to inspect, review, and copy certain materials held by the opposition—the materials that are anticipated to be introduced as evidence during the trial.

- In a criminal trial, there are two separate issues regarding the mental state of the defendant, insanity and competency to stand trial. Note both are legal, not medical definitions.

- The defense of insanity refers to the defendant's mental state at the time when the alleged crime was committed.

- Competency to stand trial refers to the defendant's mental state at the time of the trial.

- Plea negotiating, or plea bargaining, as it is more commonly known, is nothing more than agreement between the prosecuting attorney and the defense to reduce a charge to a lesser crime, to drop certain charges, or to receive a lessened sentence in return for a guilty or nolo contendere plea.

- Plea negotiating usually takes place shortly after the initial appearance or the arraignment of a defendant.

## Chapter Outline

- **Time and Place of Trial**
- **Right to Speedy Trial**
- **Right to Jury Trial**
- **What Constitutes a Public Trial**
- **Outline of Trial Proceedings**
- **Rules of Evidence**
- **Right of Discovery**
- **Mental Status of Defendant**
- **Presentation of Evidence**
- **Plea Bargaining**

## TIME AND PLACE OF TRIAL

> In all criminal prosecutions, the accused shall enjoy the right to a speedy and public trial, by an impartial jury of the State and district wherein the crime shall have been committed. . . .
>
> —U.S. Constitution, Sixth Amendment, 1791

### Venue

Venue refers to the geographic location where the trial may be held. The Sixth Amendment to the U.S. Constitution establishes the right of the defendant to be tried by a speedy and public trial, by an impartial jury of the state and in the judicial district wherein the crime was committed.

This guarantee was placed in the Sixth Amendment as a result of the colonists' having been dragged from their homes to some secret place, often to England, and tried away from their peers (Roberson and Wallace 2009). This guarantee applies to the states through the Due Process Clause of the Fourteenth Amendment. Thus, the place of the trial, or venue, lies within the judicial district in which the crime occurred.

The term venue is derived from the French word *visne*, meaning neighborhood. If the charge is a felony, the judicial district is the county; if it is a misdemeanor, the judicial district is the specific area of the county so designated and established by law. The burden is on the prosecution to present evidence during the trial to prove that the crime was committed within the judicial district in which the trial is being held. Proving venue may be accomplished merely by an investigating officer's testifying on the specific location within the county where the crime was committed.

If venue is not established by the prosecution, a conviction may be reversed on appeal because it is the right of the defendant to have the jury chosen from the judicial district in which the crime was committed.

## Motion To Change Venue

Although the defendant is entitled to have the trial in the district where the crime occurred, this right may be waived and a request made that the trial be held in some other district. This outcome is particularly true in felony cases. The defendant often believes that a fair and impartial trial cannot be had in the county in which the crime was committed. This viewpoint is usually based on a belief that adverse publicity, the nature of the

## COURTS IN ACTION

### The Fourteenth Amendment and State Judicial Proceedings

The Fourteenth Amendment to the U.S. Constitution is the only place in the Constitution where the idea of human equality is recognized (Epps, 2010). The idea of human equality was never endorsed by the original framers of the Constitution. They constructed a government with classes of people beginning with "free persons" and descending through "Indians not taxed" and then the euphemism they used for slaves. The drafters of the Fourteenth Amendment, however, drafted the Amendment to cover not just citizens, but "any person" and barred the states from denying any person "the equal protection of the laws."

It should be emphasized that the amendment was directed to the states to prevent them from depriving any person of life, liberty, or property without due process of law. But it raised a question regarding the interpretation of the term due process of law as it related to the administration of justice.

The courts later concluded that if an accused had his day in court with the right to appeal a conviction, the due process of law clause of the Fourteenth Amendment had been satisfied. The U.S. Supreme Court has since placed a different interpretation on the meaning of the due process of law clause of the Fourteenth Amendment. The Supreme Court has ruled that the following particular Bill of Rights guarantees are applicable to the states: the Fourth Amendment right to be free from unreasonable searches and seizures and to have any illegally seized evidence excluded from criminal trials; the Fifth Amendment privilege against self-incrimination and the guarantee against double jeopardy, and the Sixth Amendment rights to counsel, to a speedy trial, to a public trial, to confront opposing witnesses, and to an impartial jury. For practical purposes, these amendments are as applicable to state and local officers as they are to federal officers.

[Garrett Epps, (2010, August) "Graham: It's an Election Year, Let's Dismantle the Constitution" The Atlantic. pp. 4–9.]

## Due Process and the 14th Amendment

Whatever disagreement there may be as to the scope of the phrase "due process of law" there can be no doubt that it embraces the fundamental conception of a fair trial, with opportunity to be heard.—Oliver Wendell Homes in Frank v. Mangum, 237 U.S. 309, 347 (1915).

There are two due process clauses in the U.S. Constitution; one in the Fifth Amendment and one in the Fourteenth Amendment. The courts have held that the due process clause in the Fifth Amendment protects individuals' rights from the federal government and the one in the Fourteenth Amendment protects us from state and local governments.

crime, or community hostility makes it impossible for the defendant to obtain an impartial jury. Under these circumstances, the defendant will file with the trial court a written request, known as a motion to change venue. The trial judge will hold a **hearing** on this request, at which time the defendant will present evidence in an effort to convince the judge that a change of venue should be granted.

Because the defendant has a constitutional right to be tried within the judicial district within which the crime was committed, the government has no right to move for a change of venue over the objections of the defense.

## RIGHT TO SPEEDY TRIAL

The Sixth Amendment provision that the "accused shall enjoy the right to a speedy trial" is included in the constitution of all the states. The constitutional right to a speedy trial is a fundamental right of an accused; otherwise, many injustices may be suffered. The people, or society, also have an interest in the guarantee that an accused will be brought to trial without unnecessary delay. This is the only way in which society can be properly protected from the offender.

These guarantees provide few guidelines on exactly when a trial must be held in order to comply with the speedy trial regulation, so the decision on when to hold a trial becomes a troublesome and difficult one to make. The right to a speedy trial does not permit the defendant to demand that a trial be held the same day as the arrest because the prosecution has the right to prepare its case against the defendant. But the prosecution may not take an indefinite time in its preparation.

In setting the trial date, many factors must be considered, such as what a reasonable length of time is, to permit each side to prepare its case and whether the accused is in jail or has posted bail. The rules of procedure of most states require that criminal trials be set for those in jail ahead of those who have posted bail when other factors are equal. Even if a trial date is set, the trial may not necessarily begin on that date, since continuances may be granted that will cause delays.

The constitutional right to a speedy trial is set forth in the Sixth Amendment to the U.S. Constitution. The federal government and most states also have statutory rights to a speedy trial. In the case of federal trials, it is the Speedy Trial Act of 1974 which provides the statutory right.

The people or the state also has a right to a speedy trial. In most cases, it is the prosecution that is trying to bring a case to trial because it has the burden of establishing guilt, and delay generally weakens the case.

Although the right to a speedy trial is primarily for the benefit of the accused, this right, like others rights, may be waived by the defendant, and often is. Defendants make frequent requests for continuances in bringing the case to trial. Often months pass between the time that an arrest is made and when the defendant is brought to trial, particularly in felony cases.

Regardless of the hardships that may be suffered in not having a speedy trial, the defendant often will delay the trial date as long as possible. Delay often works to the advantage of the accused because, with the passage of time, witnesses for the prosecution are more likely to become unavailable and their memories are more likely to dull. In addition, physical evidence becomes difficult to identify and is likely to become lost or contaminated.

## RIGHT TO A JURY TRIAL

After the colonists gained their independence from Great Britain, a new government was established. To prevent possible future interference with the right to a trial by jury in this newly formed government, the Sixth Amendment to the U.S. Constitution contained

**COURTS IN ACTION**

**Williams v. Fla., 399 U.S. 78 (U.S. 1970)**

## Holding

The 12-man panel is not a necessary ingredient of "trial by jury," and a state's refusal to impanel more than the six members provided for by state law does not violate any Sixth Amendment rights as applied to the states through the Fourteenth.

## Excerpts from opinion

In Duncan v. Louisiana, 391 U.S. 145 (1968), we held that the Fourteenth Amendment guarantees a right to trial by jury in all criminal cases that—were they to be tried in a federal court—would come within the Sixth Amendment's guarantee. Defendant's trial for robbery on July 3, 1968, clearly falls within the scope of that holding. The question in this case then is whether the constitutional guarantee of a trial by "jury" necessarily requires trial by exactly 12 persons, rather than some lesser number—in this case six. We hold that the 12-man panel is not a necessary ingredient of "trial by jury," and that judge's refusal to impanel more than the six members provided for by Florida law did not violate defendant's Sixth Amendment rights as applied to the States through the Fourteenth.

We had occasion in Duncan v. Louisiana, supra, to review briefly the oft-told history of the development of trial by jury in criminal cases. That history revealed a long tradition attaching great importance to the concept of relying on a body of one's peers to determine guilt or innocence as a safeguard against arbitrary law enforcement. That same history, however, affords little insight into the considerations that gradually led the size of that body to be generally fixed at 12. Some have suggested that the number 12 was fixed upon simply because that was the number of the presentment jury from the hundred, from which the petit jury developed. Other, less circular but more fanciful reasons for the number 12 have been given, but they were all brought forward after the number was fixed, and rest on little more than mystical or superstitious insights into the significance of "12." Lord Coke's explanation that the "number of twelve is much respected in holy writ, as 12 apostles, 12 stones, 12 tribes, etc.," is typical. In short, while sometime in the 14th century the size of the jury at common law came to be fixed generally at 12, that particular feature of the jury system appears to have been a historical accident, unrelated to the great purposes which gave rise to the jury in the first place. The question before us is whether this accidental feature of the jury has been immutably codified into our Constitution.

It might be suggested that the 12-man jury gives a defendant a greater advantage since he has more "chances" of finding a juror who will insist on acquittal and thus prevent conviction. But the advantage might just as easily belong to the State, which also needs only one juror out of twelve insisting on guilt to prevent acquittal. What few experiments have occurred—usually in the civil area—indicate that there is no discernible difference between the results reached by the two different-sized juries. In short, neither currently available evidence nor theory suggests that the 12-man jury is necessarily more advantageous to the defendant than a jury composed of fewer members.

Similarly, while in theory the number of viewpoints represented on a randomly selected jury ought to increase as the size of the jury increases, in practice the difference between the 12-man and the six-man jury in terms of the cross-section of the community represented seems likely to be negligible. Even the 12-man jury cannot insure representation of every distinct voice in the community, particularly given the use of the peremptory challenge. As long as arbitrary exclusions of a particular class from the jury rolls are forbidden the concern that the cross-section will be significantly diminished if the jury is decreased in size from 12 to six seems an unrealistic one.

We conclude, in short, as we began: the fact that the jury at common law was composed of precisely 12 is a historical accident, unnecessary to effect the purposes of the jury system and wholly without significance "except to mystics." To read the Sixth Amendment as forever codifying a feature so incidental to the real purpose of the Amendment is to ascribe a blind formalism to the Framers which would require considerably more evidence than we have been able to discover in the history and language of the Constitution or in the reasoning of our past decisions. We do not mean to intimate that legislatures can never have good reasons for concluding that the 12-man jury is preferable to the smaller jury, or that such conclusions—reflected in the provisions of most States and in our federal system—are in any sense unwise.

Legislatures may well have their own views about the relative value of the larger and smaller juries, and may conclude that, wholly apart from the jury's primary function; it is desirable to spread the collective responsibility for the determination of guilt among the larger group. In capital cases, for example, it appears that no State provides for less than 12 jurors—a fact that suggests implicit recognition of the value of the larger body as a means of legitimating society's decision to impose the death penalty. Our holding does no more than leave these considerations to Congress and the States, unrestrained by an interpretation of the Sixth Amendment that would forever dictate the precise number that can constitute a jury. Consistent with this holding, we conclude that petitioner's Sixth Amendment rights, as applied to the States through the Fourteenth Amendment, were not violated by Florida's decision to provide a six-man rather than a 12-man jury. The judgment of the Florida District Court of Appeal is affirmed.

## COURTS IN ACTION

### Excerpts from Apodaca v. Oregon, 406 U.S. 404 (U.S. 1972)

Robert Apodaca, Henry Morgan Cooper, Jr., and James Arnold Madden were convicted respectively of assault with a deadly weapon, burglary in a dwelling, and grand larceny before separate Oregon juries, all of which returned less-than-unanimous verdicts. The vote in the cases of Apodaca and Madden was 11-1, while the vote in the case of Cooper was 10-2, the minimum requisite vote under Oregon law for sustaining a conviction. After their convictions had been affirmed by the Oregon Court of Appeals and review had been denied by the Supreme Court of Oregon, all three sought review in this Court upon a claim that conviction of crime by a less-than-unanimous jury violates the right to trial by jury in criminal cases specified by the Sixth Amendment and made applicable to the States by the Fourteenth. We granted certiorari to consider this claim, which we now find to be without merit.

The purpose of trial by jury is to prevent oppression by the Government by providing a safeguard against the corrupt or overzealous prosecutor and against the compliant, biased, or eccentric judge. Duncan v. Louisiana, 391 U.S., at 156. "Given this purpose, the essential feature of a jury obviously lies in the interposition between the accused and his accuser of the commonsense judgment of a group of laymen. . . ." Williams v. Florida, supra, at 100. A requirement of unanimity, however, does not materially contribute to the exercise of this commonsense judgment. As we said in Williams, a jury will come to such a judgment as long as it consists of a group of laymen representative of a cross section of the community who have the duty and the opportunity to deliberate, free from outside attempts at intimidation, on the question of a defendant's guilt. In terms of this function we perceive no difference between juries required to act unanimously and those permitted to convict or acquit by votes of 10 to two or 11 to one. Requiring unanimity would obviously produce hung juries in some situations where non-unanimous juries will convict or acquit. But in either case, the interest of the defendant in having the judgment of his peers interposed between himself and the officers of the State who prosecute and judge him is equally well served.

[The Supreme Court held that the Sixth Amendment did not require that defendants be convicted by unanimous jury verdicts. Note: All states except Louisiana and Oregon permit a non-unanimous verdict in felony cases. If there jury size is less than 12, then a unanimous verdict is required.]

the provision that all persons accused of a crime had the right to be tried by an impartial jury. The Sixth Amendment right to trial by jury is made binding on the states through the Due Process Clause of the Fourteenth Amendment, as is the right to a speedy trial. These rights are also contained in all state constitutions or statutes. Although the Sixth Amendment did not mention the number of persons required to constitute a jury, it was generally accepted that the common-law rule of 12 persons would prevail. So strongly was it felt that a jury must consist of 12 persons in a criminal case that a trial by jury consisting of fewer than 12 would be a denial of due process of law.

The idea of an accused's being permitted to waive a jury trial and have the case heard by a judge alone was practically unthought-of. It was not until 1930 in the case of *Patton v. United States* that the U.S. Supreme Court held that a verdict rendered by a jury comprising fewer than 12 members was not a violation of an accused's constitutional right to a trial by jury.

In the Patton case, the trial started with a jury comprising 12 persons, but during the trial 1 of the jurors became incapacitated. The defendant agreed to continue the trial with only 11 jurors. He was convicted, and the case was taken to the U.S. Supreme Court to determine whether a defendant has the right to waive a jury trial. The defendant did not waive the entire jury in the Patton case, but even waiving 1 juror and continuing with only 11 was so foreign to the common-law procedure that the U.S. Supreme Court felt that the matter was worth their consideration.

The Court in the Patton case stated that, after an examination of Article III, section 2, and the Sixth Amendment of the U.S. Constitution, they had come to the conclusion that a jury trial was a right that the accused might "forego at his election" and that this right was a privilege and not an "imperative right." As such, the defendant could waive a jury comprising fewer than 12 persons. This decision gave an implied permission to waive the jury entirely and have the case heard by a judge sitting alone.

## LAW IN ACTION
### Excerpts from *Duncan v. Louisiana*, 391 U.S. 145 (U.S. 1968)

### Summary of the case

Duncan was charged with simple battery, a misdemeanor punishable by a maximum of two years imprisonment and a $ 300 fine in a Louisiana court. He sought trial by jury, but because the Louisiana Constitution grants jury trials only in cases in which capital punishment or imprisonment at hard labor may be imposed, the trial court denied the request. Defendant was convicted and sentenced to serve 60 days in the parish prison and pay a fine of $ 150. After the state supreme court denied appeal, he sought review in the federal court. The Supreme Court held that a crime punishable by two years in prison was a serious crime and not a petty offense. Consequently, the defendant was entitled to a jury trial and the trial court erred in denying it. In so ruling, the Court opined that the right to trial by jury guaranteed defendants in criminal cases in federal courts by the U.S. Constitution Article III and by the Sixth Amendment was also guaranteed by the Fourteenth Amendment to defendants tried in state courts.

### Excerpts from Justice Bryon White's majority opinion

The claim before the Court is that the right to trial by jury guaranteed by the Sixth Amendment. . . . The position of Louisiana, on the other hand, is that the Constitution imposes upon the States no duty to give a jury trial in any criminal case, regardless of the seriousness of the crime or the size of the punishment which may be imposed. Because we believe that trial by jury in criminal cases is fundamental to the American scheme of justice, we hold that the Fourteenth Amendment guarantees a right of jury trial in all criminal cases which—were they to be tried in a federal court—would come within the Sixth Amendment's guarantee. Since we consider the appeal before us to be such a case, we hold that the Constitution was violated when appellant's demand for jury trial was refused. . . .

The history of trial by jury in criminal cases has been frequently told. It is sufficient for present purposes to say that by the time our Constitution was written, jury trial in criminal cases had been in existence in England for several centuries and carried impressive credentials traced by many to Magna Carta. . . .

The laws of every State guarantee a right to jury trial in serious criminal cases; no State has dispensed with it; nor are there significant movements underway to do so. Indeed, the three most recent state constitutional revisions, in Maryland, Michigan, and New York, carefully preserved the right of the accused to have the judgment of a jury when tried for a serious crime. . . .

So-called petty offenses were tried without juries both in England and in the Colonies and have always been held to be exempt from the otherwise comprehensive language of the Sixth Amendment's jury trial provisions. There is no substantial evidence that the Framers intended to depart from this established common-law practice, and the possible consequences to defendants from convictions for petty offenses have been thought insufficient to outweigh the benefits to efficient law enforcement and simplified judicial administration resulting from the availability of speedy and inexpensive nonjury adjudications. These same considerations compel the same result under the Fourteenth Amendment. Of course the boundaries of the petty offense category have always been ill-defined, if not ambulatory. In the absence of an explicit constitutional provision, the definitional task necessarily falls on the courts, which must either pass upon the validity of legislative attempts to identify those petty offenses which are exempt from jury trial or, where the legislature has not addressed itself to the problem, themselves face the question in the first instance. In either case it is necessary to draw a line in the spectrum of crime, separating petty from serious infractions. This process, although essential, cannot be wholly satisfactory, for it requires attaching different consequences to events which, when they lie near the line, actually differ very little.

In determining whether the length of the authorized prison term or the seriousness of other punishment is enough in itself to require a jury trial. . . . In the federal system, petty offenses are defined as those punishable by no more than six months in prison and a $ 500 fine. . . . It is sufficient for our purposes to hold that a crime punishable by two years in prison is, based on past and contemporary standards in this country, a serious crime and not a petty offense. Consequently, appellant was entitled to a jury trial and it was error to deny it.

## WHAT CONSTITUTES A PUBLIC TRIAL

This nation's accepted practice of guaranteeing a public trial to an accused has its roots in our English common law heritage. The exact date of its origin is obscure, but it likely evolved long before the settlement of our land as an accompaniment of the ancient institution of jury trial. In this country the guarantee to an accused of the right to a public trial first appeared in a state constitution in 1776. Following the ratification in 1791 of the Federal Constitution's Sixth Amendment, which commands that "In all criminal prosecutions, the accused shall enjoy the right to a speedy and public trial . . ." most of the original states and those subsequently admitted to the Union adopted similar constitutional provisions. Today almost without exception every state by constitution, statute, or judicial decision, requires that all criminal trials be open to the public.  [Supreme Court Justice Hugo Black in In re Oliver, 333 U.S. 257, 266-267 (U.S. 1948)]

**COURTS IN ACTION**

**Juror decision making**

**Do jurors listen to the trial judge's decision and make their decisions based on the court instructions and the evidence admitted at the trial?**

Scholars have long debated juror decision making and what jurors use in making their decisions. Jurors are only allowed to consider admissible evidence and therefore a lot of information is withheld from them at the trial. As any courtroom veteran will quickly note, the decision makers (jurors) know less about the case than probably anyone else in the courtroom.

A 1998 public opinion poll indicated that most Americans eligible to serve on a jury asserted that they would act on their own beliefs as to right and wrong, regardless of a judge's instructions on the law of the case. Leonard Levy claims that if a similar poll had been taken in the 1650s, the results would have been the same. According to Levy, jury verdicts then and now reflected jury opinions. Levy describes the prosecution of John Lilburne, an irrepressibly cantankerous defendant, in 1649. Lilburne appealed to the jury over the heads of his judges and depicted the court as his oppressors and the jurors as his protectors. The jury acquitted him. He was tried again in 1653 and was once more acquitted. The foreman of the jury would say only that he had acted in accordance with his conscience. [Leonard W. Levy (1999) The Palladium of Justice: Origins of Trial by Jury. Chicago: Ivan R. Dee.]

Another guarantee under the Sixth Amendment is the right to a public trial. Although this right appears to be a clear and explicit right, what constitutes a public trial is not defined either by the Sixth Amendment or by any of the laws of the states. The problems that arise are the following:

- What is a public trial?
- Who constitutes the public?
- How many persons must be in attendance to make a trial a public one?
- And since the right to a public trial is basically a right of the accused, may the right be waived, resulting in a private trial?

Over time, partial answers to these questions have come from court decisions, but the answers to some questions have not been unanimous. It is clear that a public trial is one that is not secret. The commonsense interpretation of a public trial is one that the general public is free to attend. The doors of the courtroom are expected to be kept open. However, if no member of the public is in attendance, there is no requirement that a trial be stopped in order to satisfy the guarantee of a public trial. Under ordinary circumstances, the public includes persons of all classes, races, ages, and both sexes (Roberson and Wallace 2009).

In some cases, even though the trial is open to the public, certain items of evidence are not open for public view. For example, pictures of children involved in a sexual pornography case, if entered into evidence, would not be open for public view.

There are times when it may not be necessary to permit every person to attend trial proceedings in order for a trial to be a public trial. It has been held that to satisfy the constitutional guarantee to a public trial, it is not necessary to provide a stadium large enough to accommodate all who might want to attend a particular trial. Yet a courtroom

## LAW IN ACTION

### How would you rule?

Jose Rodriguez was tried in a New York state court for selling cocaine to an undercover officer. At a hearing held on the state's motion to close the courtroom during the undercover officer's testimony, the undercover officer testified that he was afraid that Rodriguez's relatives would recognize him and spread the word that he was a police officer. The state court ruled that defendant's relatives would be permitted to attend petitioner's trial only if they sat behind a screen obscuring the undercover officer's appearance.

### Has the defendant been denied the right to a public Trial?

The appellate court held that the state court's decision to exclude defendant's family from segments of his trial did not involve an unreasonable application of clearly established federal law because (1) the state had an overriding interest in protecting the identity of its undercover officers, (2) the undercover officer had been threatened before and he intended to return to the same area in the near future, (3) the closure was to last only for the duration of the undercover officer's testimony, (4) the state court made sufficient findings to support the closure, and (5) the state court considered the use of a screen as a reasonable alternative to closure. See: *Rodriguez v. Miller*, 537 F.3d 102 (2d Cir. N.Y. 2007)

should be large enough to permit a reasonable number of the public to observe the trial proceedings. It also has been held that a judge may limit the number of persons attending a trial to the seating capacity of the courtroom facilities without violating the right of a public trial. A judge may eject any spectator or member of the public who becomes unruly and disrupts the trial proceedings. The judge may even clear the courtroom of all spectators if they become disruptive. However, this action does not permit locking the courtroom doors and prohibiting other members of the public who conduct themselves properly from attending the trial.

## OUTLINE OF TRIAL PROCEEDINGS

To provide the reader with an overview of the general procedure in a criminal trial the generalized steps in the trial are listed in this section. Depending upon the jurisdiction, there may be some slight deviation from following procedures:

1. Accused is formally charged by indictment, information or other charging document.
2. Accused appears before a magistrate (judge) for a bail hearing and if necessary the appointment of counsel.
3. Arraignment is held at which time the defendant's plea is entered.
4. Pretrial hearing is held at which time evidence issues are decided and parties exchange discovery if not previously accomplished.
5. Selection of jury
6. Swearing in of jury (trial technically begins at this time)

**COURTS IN ACTION**

**Wi-Fi for Jurors**

According to the Charlotte Observer, Mecklenburg County, N.C., is trying to make jury duty less of a chore. The juror assembly room in the downtown Charlotte courthouse has free wireless Internet, a business center, a day care center and even a place where mothers can pump breast milk. There's a 90-minute lunch break and two movies are offered. The courthouse provides free popcorn. Court officials recognize most people don't look forward to jury duty, so the amenities and services aim to make performing the public obligation more pleasant, officials said.

Of course, there's another incentive to performing your civic duty: Those who don't show up may have to explain their absence to a judge. The efforts seem to make a difference. The benchmark-setting National Center for State Courts says fewer than five percent of jurors should be no-shows. In Mecklenburg County, four percent of those called from motor vehicle and voter registration records never show up. [Cleve R. Wootson, Jr. "Comfort in the courthouse" Charlotte Observer, Monday, Aug. 02, 2010, B-1; web site http://www.charlotteobserver.com/2010/08/02/1596124/comfort-in-the-courthouse.html#ixzz0vlyjcJAq.Accessed on August 7, 2010.]

7. Reading of charge and plea
8. Opening statement by prosecuting attorney
9. Opening statement by defense (this may be waived entirely or until prosecution rests)
10. Calling of first prosecution witness and administration of the oath
11. Direct examination
12. Cross-examination (may be waived)
13. Redirect examination (may be waived)
14. Recross-examination (may be waived)
15. Calling of additional prosecution witnesses, administration of oath, direct examination, and other procedure as in case of first witness
16. Prosecution rests
17. Motion for judgment of acquittal by defense (if denied, then the following procedure)
18. Opening statement by defense (if not previously given)
19. Calling of first defense witness and procedure followed as in case of first prosecution witness
20. Defense rests
21. Rebuttal presentation by prosecution
22. Closing arguments by prosecution and then by defense
23. Rebuttal closing argument by prosecution
24. Instructing the jury
25. Deliberation
26. Return of verdict (if guilty verdict returned, then the following procedure)
27. Request for new trial by defense (if denied, then the following procedure)
28. Sentencing the defendant if adjudged guilty.

**LAW IN ACTION**

**Grand Jury Indictment**

UNITED STATES DISTRICT COURT FOR THE
SOUTHERN DISTRICT OF GEORGIA
STATESBORO DIVISION

| | | |
|---|---|---|
| UNITED STATES OF AMERICA | ) | INDICTMENT NO. |
| | ) | |
| v. | ) | VIO: 18 U.S.C. § 656 |
| | ) | EMBEZZLEMENT BY |
| SUSAN W.. JOHNSON | ) | BANK EMPLOYEE |
| | ) | |

**COUNT ONE**

**(18 U.S.C. § 656
EMBEZZLEMENT BY BANK EMPLOYEE)**

From on or about September 1, 2003, and continuing through on or about December 22, 2004, the exact dates being unknown to the Grand Jury, in Toombs County, within the Southern District of Georgia, the defendant,

**SUSAN W. JOHNSON**,

being an employee, that is, a bank teller at the Vidalia Branch of the First State Bank located at 1005 East First Street, Vidalia, Georgia, a financial institution, the deposits of which were then insured by the Federal Deposit Insurance Corporation, with intent to injure and defraud said bank, did knowingly and willfully embezzle and purloin the sum of approximately $6,970 of the funds and credits of the Montgomery County Bank which had come into her custody and under her care by virtue of her position as a bank teller of the First State Bank.

All done in violation of Title 18, United States Code, Section 656.

A TRUE BILL

_____
FOREPERSON

_____
HARRY WILLIAMS
UNITED STATES ATTORNEY

_____
Joseph D. Young
Assistant United States Attorney
Chief, Criminal Section

_____
Frank J. DiMarino
Assistant United States Attorney

UNITED STATES DISTRICT COURT FOR THE
SOUTHERN DISTRICT OF GEORGIA
STATESBORO DIVISION

| UNITED STATES OF AMERICA | ) | INDICTMENT NO. |
| | ) | |
| v. | ) | VIO:    18 U.S.C. § 656 |
| | ) | EMBEZZLEMENT |
| SUSAN W. JOHNSON | ) | BY A BANK EMPLOYEE |
| | ) | |

**PENALTY INFORMATION**

COUNT ONE    18 U.S.C. § 656

EMBEZZLEMENT BY A BANK EMPLOYEE

NOT MORE THAN THIRTY (30) YEARS IMPRISONMENT, OR A
FINE OF $1,000,000, OR BOTH; SUPERVISED RELEASE OF NOT
MORE THAN FIVE (5) YEARS; AND A SPECIAL ASSESSMENT OF
$100.00.

_____
Frank J. DiMarino
Assistant United States Attorney

**DEFENDANT INFORMATION SHEET**

PLEASE ISSUE:_____ BENCH WARRANT__X__ SUMMONS
_____IN CUSTODY                    Recommended Bond
NAME:                                SUSAN W.. JOHNSON
ADDRESS:
PHONE:
EMPLOYMENT:
SEX:                                 F
RACE:                                Black
DOB:                                 1/10/69
SSAN
FOR FURTHER INFORMATION CONTACT:
AGENCY:                              FBI
AGENT:                               Sam Harris, GENCY CASE #:    30K AT
                                     86619PHONE:
COUNSEL FOR DEFENDANT:

# RULES OF EVIDENCE

Rules of evidence are used by the courts in an attempt to secure fairness in administration, elimination of unjustifiable expense and delay. The rules are designed to regulate the process of proving facts (Roberson and Wallace 2009). As noted earlier in Chapters 1 and 2, the judge determines the law that should apply to the case and the jury determines the facts of the case. If there is no jury, then the judge does both.

The finding of a fact is a finding as to what happened. For example, the determination that the accused was the one who took the money from the victim is a finding of fact. Whether this fact constitutes the crime of robbery is a question of law for the judge to decide.

Evidence law was originally almost entirely decisional law. Now it is codified in statutes and court rules. The federal and state rules of evidence do not depart significantly from the common-law decisions. Most state rules of evidence are based on the Federal Rules, with only slight differences among the states. Evidence is a very complex and difficult subject for attorneys in law school.

Evidentiary rules should be construed in a manner to attempt to secure fairness in administration, elimination of unjustifiable expense and delay, and promotion of growth and development of the law of evidence to the end that the truth may be ascertained and proceedings justly determined.

The two basic themes found in the federal rules and in most state rules are:

- The rules favor admissibility of evidence. As the third circuit court of appeals stated in *United States v. Pelullo* (1992), while the Federal Rules "are to be liberally construed in favor of admissibility, this does not mean that we may ignore requirements of specific provisions merely because we view the proffered evidence as trustworthy."
- The trial judge has considerable discretion as to the admissibility of evidence.

### Evidentiary Rulings

Rulings made by the trial judge regarding the admissibility or non-admissibility of evidence is not considered by the appellate courts as grounds to overturn a case unless (1) a substantial right is affected and (2) the nature of the error was called to the attention of the judge, to alert him or her to the proper course of action and enable opposing counsel to take proper corrective measures. The objection and the offer of proof are the techniques for accomplishing these objectives. An exception to this requirement is the **plain error rule.** Under the plain error rule, an appellate court may consider a judicial ruling on the evidence if the ruling was clearly wrong and prejudiced the defendant.

In jury cases, proceedings regarding evidentiary questions are generally conducted, to the extent practicable, outside of the presence of the jury to prevent inadmissible evidence from being suggested to the jury by any means, such as making statements or offers of proof or asking questions in the hearing of the jury.

In some states, each time that the evidence is offered or referred to, the opposing party must renew its objections to the evidence. Most courts take a more flexible approach, holding that the renewal of objections is not required if the issue decided is one that (1) was fairly presented to the trial court for an initial ruling, (2) may be decided as a final matter before the evidence is actually offered, and (3) was ruled on definitively by the trial judge. Other courts distinguished between objections to evidence, which must be renewed when evidence is offered, and offers of proof, which need not be renewed after a definitive determination is made that the evidence is inadmissible (Roberson and Wallace 2009).

### Judicial Notice

The concept of judicial notice is used when a relevant fact is so well known that to require that it be proved would be a waste of time. For example, a trial judge may take judicial notice that July 4th is a court holiday. A judicially noticed fact must be one not subject to reasonable dispute in that it is either (1) generally known within the territorial jurisdiction of the trial court or (2) capable of accurate and ready determination by resort to sources whose accuracy cannot reasonably be questioned.

**LAW IN ACTION**

**Judicial Notice**

Author Cliff Roberson, while serving as a marine judge advocate, prosecuted a desertion case in a military court located in the State of Hawaii. Roberson needed to enter sworn testimony from a previous trial of an unavailable witness to help establish that the defendant had deserted from his military unit. Under the then rules of evidence, Roberson needed to establish to the military court that the missing witness was not within the state and was at least 100 miles from the location of the courtroom. He entered evidence that the missing witness was presently located at an address in Alexandria, Virginia. But he failed to request the court to take judicial notice and he did not enter evidence of the fact that the address in Virginia was at more than 100 miles from the courtroom in Hawaii.

The case was appealed on the issue that the prior sworn testimony of the missing witness should not have been admitted by the military judge. The appellate court upheld (approved) the conviction by a 3-2 decision noting that as a matter of common knowledge that any location in the State of Virginia was more than 100 miles from the courtroom in Hawaii, but two members of the reviewing court contended that the admissibility of the prior testimony was not established.

## RIGHT OF DISCOVERY

The right of discovery, or inspection, is more closely related to the subject of evidence than to the procedures in the justice system. However, one of the responsibilities of the attorneys for both the prosecution and the defense is to exercise the right of discovery. The right of pretrial discovery in criminal matters is of comparatively recent origin. It was unknown at common law and still is not recognized in criminal matters in some states. The right of discovery is the pretrial right of the adversary to inspect, review, and copy certain materials held by the opposition that are anticipated to be introduced as evidence during the trial.

### Defendant's Right of Discovery

The right of pretrial discovery was created primarily for the benefit of the defendant. The theory was that the right would assist the defendant in case preparation and aid in getting a fair trial. The right would also enable the defense attorney to better cross-examine the witnesses for the prosecution and assist in impeaching witnesses who have questionable credibility. The purpose of a trial is to determine the truth of what happened in a particular case. The parties involved in a trial are not to play games or create surprises.

The right of pretrial discovery may come into being either by legislative action or by appellate court decisions and may be exercised in two ways. The defense may make an oral request to the prosecuting attorney or to the law enforcement agency involved for permission to examine the material held in the case. The alternative method consists of a written request by the defendant's attorney in the form of a motion to produce the evidence held by the prosecution.

In *United States v. Jordan*, (2010) a federal trial judge was presented with a motion by defense to require that the prosecution turnover certain evidence. The discovery was seeking to defendant is seeking "credibility information" relating to a confidential informant. The prosecutor not wishing to identify the informant opposed the motion.

The court held that the defendants had no general constitutional right to discovery in criminal proceeding, but noted that the Supreme Court held in *Brady v. Maryland*

## COURTS IN ACTION

**Should the defendant prior to trial be allowed to inspect the tangible physical objects that the prosecutor may offer into evidence?**

### State ex rel. Mahoney v. Superior Court, 78 Ariz. 74, 75-79 (Ariz. 1954)

The County Attorney of Maricopa County sought a writ in this court directed to the Superior Court of Maricopa County and the presiding judge thereof (hereinafter designated respondent), to restrain the court from enforcing an order requiring the county attorney to provide certain tangible physical objects in his possession for the inspection by the defendant in a criminal proceeding then pending in Superior Court.

The record discloses the following situation: One William Demand had been held to answer to the superior court on a homicide charge. The case having been set for trial on October 19, 1954, upon an information charging murder, counsel for defendant filed a motion for production and the opportunity to inspect certain documents, papers and tangible objects then in the possession of the prosecutor, asserting that this was necessary in order for him to properly prepare his defense in the case. The defendant wanted to inspect included tangible physical objects such as pistols, a lead slug taken from the body of the man whom he was accused of killing; a shirt, car keys, etc. The trial court entered an order compelling the State to produce the items for the defendant's inspection upon his compliance with certain conditions.

The county attorney contends that under the common law the right of discovery and inspection did not exist in the field of criminal law, and hence in the absence of an authorizing statute or court rule the trial court was wholly without jurisdiction to make the order in question. We agree that the common law as it came to us from England recognized no right of discovery or inspection prior to trial in criminal cases. The right of discovery in criminal cases was not recognized at common law.

The leading English case is Rex v. Holland cited in most American cases on the problem. Therein it was held there was no principle or precedent to warrant the granting of an application to inspect evidence contained in a report of a board of inquiry of the East India Company. However, this rule has since been radically changed in England as an incident to the adoption of pre-trial procedure before a committing magistrate. England now allows all of the evidence in the possession of the Crown to be inspected by the counsel for the defendant. Defendant knows all that the Crown knows. He has all the evidence in his possession before the witness goes on the stand. He has all the evidence that can be presented in that court at trial, before the trial begins.

Concededly, at present there is no rule of court or statute in Arizona expressly authorizing inspection and discovery in criminal cases prior to trial . . .

We believe that the order in question [to allow inspection] can be sustained under the inherent powers of the court necessary to the due administration of justice. The "inherent powers" of a court are an unexpressed quantity and undefinable term, and the courts have indulged in more or less loose explanations concerning it. Undoubtedly, courts of justice possess powers which were not given by legislation and which no legislation can take away. These are "inherent powers" resident in all courts of superior jurisdiction. These powers spring not from legislation but from the nature and constitution of the tribunals themselves.

The inspection was limited to the demonstrative evidence heretofore enumerated; furthermore the order expressly prescribed safeguards against any possible substitution or trickery.

We do not share the fears of the petitioner that the whole system of criminal law will be subverted by allowing an order of inspection such as this to stand. The State does not want to secure convictions by any unfair concealment or surprise. It is the duty of the State to concern itself as much in having the innocent acquitted as in securing the conviction of the guilty, and the State is desirous of giving every accused person a fair and reasonable opportunity to make his defense.

We are not unmindful that there are constitutional privileges granted a defendant in a criminal case which place upon the prosecution a heavy burden in the preparation and presentation of its case, but we cannot see how permitting the defendant an inspection at his expense, where a proper showing is made, adds to that burden. It seems apparent that there are times when to deny this privilege prior to trial might result in the hearing itself being delayed—at a considerable expense to the State—while such an examination or tests are made. We believe justice dictates that the defendant be entitled to the benefit of any reasonable opportunity to prepare his defense and to prove his innocence.

We are of the opinion that such a rule is in the interest of justice, and that it is left to the sound discretion of a trial court when a proceeding is pending therein as to whether such inspection and examination should be allowed or not.

(1963) that "the suppression by the prosecution of evidence favorable to an accused upon request violates due process where the evidence is material either to guilt or to punishment, irrespective of the good faith or bad faith of the prosecution." The court noted that the government's obligation to disclose exculpatory information includes evidence that may be used to substantially impeach the credibility of a government witness. The court concluded that the touchstone of the government's disclosure obligations is the "materiality" of the information, that is, evidence for which there is a reasonable possibility that, had the evidence been disclosed to the defense, the result of the proceeding would have been different.

The court noted that the defendant in the instant case was seeking information relating to the reliability of the confidential informant (CI) who provided information in connection with the search warrant. The court concluded that there was no question that in analyzing a warrant's validity, a court may assess a source's reliability or personal background. [The court then ruled that a motion for discovery was not the proper procedure to attach the sufficiency of a search warrant.] The court then held that the defendant's request for reliability information concerning the CI who provided information in connection with the search warrant was denied, subject to renewal if the defendant submits evidence that the search warrant affidavit contained false information and that absent such evidence the court lacked probable cause for the warrant.

## Prosecution's Right of Pretrial Discovery

Rule 16 of the Federal Rules of Criminal Procedure grants to the government (the prosecution) almost the identical rights of pretrial discovery that are granted to the defendant. More states in the future may follow the precedent set by the federal government in granting the right of pretrial discovery to the prosecution.

Most states that recognize the right to pretrial discovery have granted little pretrial right of discovery to the prosecution. This trend supports the contention that the right of pretrial discovery is a one-way street. The most convincing argument against allowing pretrial discovery by the prosecution is that the right would compel the defendant to be a witness against himself or herself. Many legal scholars are at a loss to understand how furnishing the names and addresses of witnesses or the defense to be used—such as an alibi or **insanity** defense—would be self-incrimination, but there are state courts that have prohibited the prosecution from exercising the right of pretrial discovery upon the self-incrimination claim.

In addition to the self-incrimination allegation, the supreme court of one state has held that the prosecution must prove the defendant guilty beyond a reasonable doubt and that any discovery by the prosecution that would lessen that burden is not permissible. It is almost impossible to imagine any discovery that would not, in some respect, lessen the burden of the prosecution. This holding by that court has been highly criticized in legal circles as being too restrictive and without merit.

Many states, however, do require pretrial notice and a list of witnesses in those cases where the defendant will be using an alibi defense. This notice rule is based on the concept that alibi defense evidence is considered as easy to falsify.

## MENTAL STATUS OF DEFENDANT

In a criminal trial, there are two separate issues regarding the mental state of the defendant, insanity and **competency** to stand trial. Note both are legal, not medical definitions. The defense of insanity refers to the defendant's mental state at the time that the alleged crime was committed. Competency to stand trial refers to the defendant's mental state at the time of the trial. The due process clauses of the Fifth and Fourteenth Amendments of the U.S. Constitution prohibit the trial of an individual who is incompetent. A defendant is considered incompetent if he or she lacks the capacity to understand the nature and object of the proceedings against him or her, or lacks the ability to consult with the defense counsel or to assist the defense counsel in preparing a defense (Roberson and Wallace 2009).

If no issue is raised as to the competency of the defendant to stand trial, then it is assumed that he or she is competent. If the defendant's competency is at issue, the burden of presenting the evidence as to his or her competency is on the defense. The U.S. Supreme Court in *Cooper v. Oklahoma* (1996) held that it was permissible for a state to place the burden on the defendant to establish his or her lack of competency, but that Oklahoma's requirement that the defense establish the incompetency by clear and convincing evidence was too much of a burden on the defense. Most states require that the defendant establish incompetency by the preponderance of the evidence, a lower level of proof.

If the defendant is determined to be incompetent, the state may detain him or her for a reasonable period of time necessary to determine whether there is a substantial probability that he or she will attain competency in the near future (*Jackson v. Indiana*, 1972). Unlike the insanity defense, if the defendant regains his or her competency, he or she may then be prosecuted.

## PRESENTATION OF EVIDENCE

The trial judge exercises reasonable control over the mode and order of interrogating witnesses and presenting evidence so as to (1) make the interrogation and presentation effective for the ascertainment of the truth, (2) avoid needless consumption of time, and (3) protect witnesses from harassment or undue embarrassment (Roberson and Wallace 2009).

### Witnesses

Before testifying, a witness is required to declare that he or she will testify truthfully by oath or affirmation. The purpose of the oath or affirmation requirement is to preserve the integrity of the judicial process by awakening the witness's conscience and making the witness amenable to perjury prosecution for false testimony (*United States v. Zizzo*, 1997).

Cross-examination should be limited to the subject matter of the direct examination and matters affecting the credibility of the witness. A court may, in the exercise of discretion, permit inquiry into additional matters as if on direct examination.

Leading questions should not be used on the direct examination of a witness except as may be necessary to develop the witness's testimony. Ordinarily leading questions should be permitted on cross-examination. When a party calls a hostile witness, an adverse party, or a witness identified with an adverse party, interrogation may be by leading questions.

A witness may be cross-examined on any matter relevant to any issue in the case, including credibility. In the interests of justice, the judge may limit cross-examination with respect to matters not testified to on direct examination.

## LAW IN ACTION

### Cross-examination of a witness at a trial

On December 11, 1991, William Kennedy Smith, the nephew of President John F. Kennedy and Senators Robert F. Kennedy and Ted Kennedy, was acquitted of rape by a Florida trial jury that had deliberated for 77 minutes after hearing an impassioned closing argument by his attorney who said the sexual encounter that prompted the allegation was "right out of a romance novel."

William Smith was represented by noted attorney Roy Black. Following is an excerpt of Attorney Black's cross-examination of a prosecution witness

| | |
|---|---|
| BLACK: | You say you went to the Kennedy home on the early morning hours of March thirtieth? Is that correct? |
| WITNESS: | Yes. |
| BLACK: | Your friend says that she was raped. Is that right? |
| WITNESS: | Yes. |
| BLACK: | But what she tells you is that she wants her shoes, is that correct? |
| WITNESS: | Yes. |
| BLACK: | Several times she was worried about her shoes? |
| WITNESS: | Yes |
| BLACK: | So you went into the house, is that correct? |
| WITNESS: | Yes |
| BLACK: | Into the house where the rapist is right? |
| WITNESS: | I guess you could say that yes |
| BLACK: | It's dark in there? |
| WITNESS: | Yes |
| BLACK: | You go through the kitchen right? |
| WITNESS: | Yes |
| BLACK: | Into the little hallway. |
| WITNESS: | Yes |
| BLACK: | It's dark in this hallway, isn't it. |
| WITNESS: | Right |
| BLACK: | You meet up with this man who your friend says is a rapist isn't that correct? |
| WITNESS: | I was unafraid of him. No. I was not afraid. |
| BLACK: | That is not my question . . . my question is did you meet this may who your friend says is the alleged rapist? |
| WITNESS: | Yes |
| BLACK: | In this dark hallway is that right? . . . |

[For an excellent treatment of the case see Gregory M. Matoesian (2001) *Law and the Language of Identity* New York: Oxford University Press]

> **Question:** Why is the counsel allowed to use leading questions (questions that imply an answer) when cross-examining the witness?

## Expert Testimony

If scientific, technical, or other specialized knowledge will assist the jury or the judge in trials without juries to understand the evidence or to determine a fact in issue, a witness qualified as an expert by knowledge, skill, experience, training, or education may testify thereto in the form of an opinion or otherwise if (1) the testimony is based upon sufficient facts or data, (2) the testimony is the product of reliable principles and methods, and (3) the witness has applied the principles and methods reliably to the facts of the case.

The fields of knowledge which may be drawn upon are not limited to the scientific and technical but extend to all specialized knowledge. Similarly, the expert is viewed not in a narrow sense, but as a person qualified by knowledge, skill, experience, training, or education. Thus, within the scope of the rule are not only experts in the strictest sense of the word, such as, physicians, physicists, and architects, but also the large group sometimes called skilled witnesses, such as bankers or landowners testifying to land values.

## Opinion Testimony by Non-expert Witnesses

Generally a non-expert witness is required to testify only as to facts within the knowledge of the witness. A non-expert witness's testimony in the form of opinions or inferences is limited to those opinions or inferences which are (1) rationally based on the perception of the witness, (2) helpful to a clear understanding of the witness's testimony or the determination of a fact in issue, and (3) not based on scientific, technical, or other specialized knowledge. For example, it is generally permissible for a non-expert witness to testify that she thought that the defendant's behavior was odd as long as the witness can testify to facts that would logically lead to that conclusion.

The facts or data in the particular case upon which an expert bases an opinion or inference may be those perceived by or made known to the expert at or before the hearing. If they are of a type reasonably relied upon by experts in the particular field in forming opinions or inferences upon the subject, the facts or data need not be admissible in evidence in order for the opinion or inference to be admitted.

## Relevant Evidence

Relevant evidence is where it has some tendency as a matter of logic and human experience to make the proposition for which it is advanced more likely than that proposition would appear to be in the absence of that evidence. To identify logically irrelevant evidence, ask, "Does the evidence assist in proving the fact that one party is trying to prove?" Problems of relevancy call for an answer to the question of whether an item of evidence possesses sufficient probative value to justify receiving it in evidence. For example, evidence that a person purchased a revolver shortly prior to a fatal shooting with which he is charged is considered relevant because it may prove that the person was guilty of the fatal shooting if the gun used in the shooting is the same gun that was purchased.

Although relevant, evidence may be excluded if its probative value is substantially outweighed by the danger of unfair prejudice, confusion of the issues, or misleading the jury, or by considerations of undue delay, waste of time, or needless presentation of cumulative evidence. Case law recognizes that certain circumstances call for the exclusion of evidence which is of unquestioned relevance. These circumstances entail risks which range all the way from inducing decision on a purely emotional basis, at one extreme, to nothing more harmful than merely wasting time, at the other extreme. Situations in this area call for balancing the probative value of and need for the evidence against the harm likely to result from its admission.

**LAW IN ACTION**

**Nebraska Press Ass'n v. Stuart, 427 U.S. 539 (U.S. 1976)**

**May a trial judge legally order the press not to publish information regarding a criminal trial?**

A Nebraska state trial judge, in anticipation of a trial for a multiple murder which had attracted widespread news coverage, entered an order which restrained petitioner newspapers, broadcasters, journalists, news media associations, and national newswire services from publishing or broadcasting accounts of confessions or admissions made by the accused to law enforcement officers or third parties, except members of the press, and other facts "strongly implicative" of the accused. The newspaper contested the order in the appellate court.

The Supreme Court held that based on the pretrial record the trial judge was justified in concluding that there would be intense and pervasive pretrial publicity concerning the case, and he could also reasonably conclude, based on common human experience, that publicity might impair the accused's right to a fair trial. His conclusion as to the impact of such publicity on prospective jurors was of necessity speculative, however, dealing as he was with factors unknown and unknowable.

The Court noted that there was no finding that measures short of prior restraint on the press and speech would not have protected the accused's rights and that it was not clear that prior restraint on publication would have effectively protected the accused's rights, in view of such practical problems as the limited territorial jurisdiction of the trial court issuing the restraining order, the difficulties inherent in predicting what information will in fact undermine the jurors' impartiality, the problem of drafting an order that will effectively keep prejudicial information from prospective jurors, and the fact that in this case the events occurred in a small community where rumors would travel swiftly by word of mouth.

The Court held that to the extent that the order prohibited the reporting of evidence adduced at the open preliminary hearing held to determine whether the accused should be bound over for trial, it violated the settled principle that there is nothing that proscribes the press from reporting events that transpire in the courtroom and the portion of the order restraining publication of other facts "strongly implicative" of the accused is too vague and too broad to survive the scrutiny given to restraints on First Amendment rights.

## PLEA BARGAINING

Plea negotiating, or plea bargaining, as it is more commonly known, is nothing more than agreement between the prosecuting attorney and the defense to reduce a charge to a lesser crime, to drop certain charges, or to receive a lessened sentence in return for a guilty or nolo contendere plea. Plea negotiating usually takes place shortly after the initial appearance or the arraignment of a defendant. In most jurisdictions, the negotiating can continue up to the time that the verdict is rendered. Plea negotiating is often discussed during the pretrial conference. Although it has been held that the judge should not be a part of the negotiation, he or she should be made aware of it, and in many instances must, by law, accept the conditions of the plea bargaining before the guilty or nolo contendere plea is acceptable.

Plea bargaining has been both praised and criticized. Some allege that plea bargaining is important in the administration of criminal law and is advantageous to the state by saving time and money, and it also increases efficiency and flexibility in the criminal process. The advantage to the defendant is reduced punishment. Plea bargaining has been criticized, particularly by some law enforcement officers, because it allows a criminal to take advantage of the justice system by not being convicted and sentenced for the crime actually committed. The result is a much lighter penalty.

## Benefits of Plea Bargaining

Although the practice of accepting negotiated pleas has been criticized, many prosecuting attorneys state that the acceptance of a negotiated plea often is for more justifiable reasons than lightening caseloads and clearing crowded court calendars. Sometimes, an offender is initially charged on a *more serious* crime than is warranted by the evidence. Or an offender may be charged with a more serious crime so that a higher bail will be set. Reducing the number of charges in exchange for a negotiated plea may be justified on the grounds that many judges tend to give concurrent sentences. There would be little advantage in going to trial on a larger number of charges over accepting a plea on a reduced number. As for accepting a negotiated plea on the promise of a lighter sentence, prosecutors point out that they have little or no control over the sentence that may be given one convicted of a crime. Even if the accused were convicted as a result of a trial, the sentence could be the same as that which was agreed to in the negotiated plea.

In the past, plea bargaining was not discussed openly since it was considered to be unethical, if not illegal. Judges seldom were aware of any agreements made by plea bargaining because, to be valid, a guilty or nolo contendere plea had to be freely and voluntarily given. If the plea was induced upon a promise of leniency, there was a question of its being freely and voluntarily given. The secrecy of plea bargaining was eliminated by legislative action and court decisions, and today plea bargaining is openly engaged in as part of the justice system.

## COURTS IN ACTION

**Does the trial judge have a right to refuse a plea bargain based on the fact that it was not agreed to until the day of trial?**

**People v. Reynaldo Pedro Cuenca, 2008 Cal. App. Unpub. LEXIS 7251, 5-8 (Cal. App. 1st Dist. Sept. 3, 2008)**

On April 10, 2007, defendant Cuenca and codefendant Wolf were charged with: (1) possession of methamphetamine for sale in violation of Health and Safety Code section 11378, and (2) child abuse likely to cause great bodily harm or death in violation of section 273a, subdivision (a). The child abuse charge was based on the prosecution's allegation that defendant endangered his four minor children by possessing methamphetamine for sale in the apartment he shared with them. The information also alleged that defendant had a prior conviction for possession for sale of a controlled substance

On May 29, 2007, the date set for trial, defendant's trial counsel and the prosecutor presented a proposed plea agreement to the trial judge. The parties initially presented the proposed agreement in a discussion off the record, in which the trial judge stated that he would not approve the agreement because it was untimely.

The trial judge and the parties later continued this discussion on the record. In that colloquy, the prosecutor stated that he and defendant's counsel both understood that the court had a "general rule" that plea bargains would not be approved on the day of trial. The prosecutor, however, asked the trial judge to make an exception to the court's policy based on considerations of fairness and judicial economy. In support of this request, the prosecutor stated that he was aware of "multiple" instances in which trial judges had not followed the policy and had approved plea bargains that were presented on the day of trial. The prosecutor also stated that the parties had not delayed in trying to resolve the case. He stated that the reason the parties had not presented the proposed agreement earlier was that the case originally had been assigned to a different judge and that the prosecutor and defendant's trial counsel had both been out of town and unable to meet with the newly-assigned trial judge on the Friday before the trial date. Finally, the prosecutor argued that approval of the plea agreement would not unduly inconvenience the potential jurors who had appeared that morning.

Defendant's trial counsel joined in the prosecutor's request that the trial court accept the plea agreement and stated that she had been out of town the previous Friday to try to serve a subpoena on one of the witnesses in defendant's case. Defendant's counsel also stated that it was her understanding that the trial court's decision not to accept the plea agreement was based on the inconvenience to the potential jurors, and she argued that the court had not stated any "legal ground" for its decision.

After hearing the parties' arguments, the trial judge explained his decision not to approve the plea agreement. Initially, the court noted that Napa County had a policy that had been in place for many years, of which both counsel were "well aware," that "there are no plea bargains on the morning of trial." The court then explained the reasons for this policy, including the need to know in advance of the trial date which cases are resolved so that potential jurors will not waste their time appearing for jury service and so that the court can plan effectively for the trials that actually will go forward. The court noted that 42 potential jurors had come to court that morning for defendant's trial, which was the only one set for that day.

On June 1, 2007, the jury found defendant guilty as charged on count one, possession of methamphetamine for sale. As to count two, the jury acquitted defendant of child abuse likely to cause great bodily harm or death, but convicted him of the lesser included offense of child abuse. The trial court found true the special allegation that defendant had a prior conviction for possession for sale of a controlled substance.

## Excerpts from appellate court decision

Defendant contends that the trial court, by applying the Napa County policy against accepting plea agreements on the morning of trial, improperly refused to exercise its discretion to approve the agreement and thus violated defendant's due process rights. We disagree.

The trial court has "exclusive discretion" as to whether to approve such a proposed agreement. Accordingly, this court reviews a trial court's decision to accept or reject a proposed plea agreement only for abuse of discretion. However, a trial court may not "arbitrarily refuse to consider" a proposed agreement; such an arbitrary refusal is an improper failure to exercise discretion. As defendant notes, courts have held that an improper refusal to exercise discretion as required by law can violate due process or other procedural rights.

In exercising its discretion, a trial court properly may impose reasonable time limitations on the presentation of proposed plea agreements and may decline to approve proposed agreements that are untimely. It appears that the competing interests of accurately scheduling court calendars and judiciously taking pleas to avoid trial can be accommodated while reasonably restricting pleas to certain time periods. The purpose of improving calendar management justifies the setting of deadlines beyond which no conditional plea may be taken.

The trial court here did not "arbitrarily" refuse to consider the proposed plea agreement, either because of hostility to the statute governing plea bargains or for any other improper reason. Instead, the trial court properly based its decision on the Napa County Superior Court policy against the submission of plea bargains on the morning of trial. Moreover, the record shows that the trial court considered the issue and made a thoughtful decision. The court heard and considered the parties' arguments, both off and on the record, and then explained the reasons for the Napa County policy.

## Questions in Review

1. What constitutes a public trial?
2. Explain the rights established by the Sixth Amendment.
3. What is the purpose of the rules of evidence?
4. Under what conditions may a non-expert witness express his or her opinions while testifying?

5. What is the difference between competency to stand trial and insanity?
6. Should the prosecutor engage in plea bargaining with the defense? Justify your opinions.

## Practicum

**Is it constitutional for a state to establish a higher standard of mental capacity when deciding if a defendant is mentally competence than the standard it uses to determine if the defendant has sufficient mental capacity to be prosecuted? After reading the following case, provide your opinion and justify it.**

The issue was examined in Indiana v. Edwards, 128 S. Ct. 2379 (U.S. 2008). Justice Breyer wrote the opinion of the Court, in which Chief Justice Roberts, and Justices Stevens, Kennedy, Souter, Ginsburg and Alito joined. Justice Scalia and Thomas dissented.

Ahmad Edwards tried to steal a pair of shoes from an Indiana department store. After he was discovered, he drew a gun, fired at a store security officer, and wounded a bystander. He was caught and then charged with attempted murder, battery with a deadly weapon, criminal recklessness, and theft. His mental condition subsequently became the subject of three competency proceedings and two self-representation requests, mostly before the same trial judge.

At his first competency hearing in August 2000, five months after Edwards' arrest, his court-appointed counsel asked for a psychiatric evaluation. After hearing psychiatrist and neuropsychologist witnesses, the trial court found Edwards incompetent to stand trial and committed him to Logansport State Hospital for evaluation and treatment.

In March 2002 doctors found that Edwards' condition had improved to the point where he could stand trial. The trial judge held a competency hearing, considered additional psychiatric evidence, and found that Edwards, while "suffering from mental illness," was "competent to assist his attorneys in his defense and stand trial for the charged crimes."

In April 2003, Edwards' counsel sought yet another psychiatric evaluation of his client. And, in April 2003, the court held another competency hearing. Edwards' counsel presented further psychiatric and neuropsychological evidence showing that Edwards was suffering from serious thinking difficulties and delusions. A testifying psychiatrist reported that Edwards could understand the charges against him, but he was "unable to cooperate with his attorney in his defense because of his schizophrenic illness"; "his delusions and his marked difficulties in thinking make it impossible for him to cooperate with his attorney." In November 2003, the court concluded that Edwards was not then competent to stand trial and ordered his recommitment to the state hospital.

In June 2005, the hospital reported that Edwards' condition had again improved to the point that he had again become competent to stand trial. Just before trial, Edwards asked to represent himself. He also asked for a continuance, which, he said, he needed in order to proceed pro se [as his own attorney]. The court refused the continuance. Edwards then proceeded to trial represented by an appointed counsel. The jury convicted him of criminal recklessness and theft but could not reach a verdict on the charges of attempted murder and battery.

The State decided to retry Edwards on the attempted murder and battery charges. Just before the retrial, Edwards again asked the court to permit him to represent himself. Referring to the lengthy record of psychiatric reports, the trial court noted that Edwards still suffered from schizophrenia and concluded that "with these findings, he's competent to stand trial but I'm not going to find he's competent to defend himself." The trial court denied Edwards' self-representation request. Edwards was represented by appointed counsel at his retrial. The jury convicted Edwards on both of the remaining counts.

Edwards subsequently appealed to Indiana's intermediate appellate court. He argued that the trial court's refusal to permit him to represent himself at his retrial deprived him of his constitutional right of self-representation. The appellate court agreed and ordered a new trial. The state appealed to the Indiana

Supreme Court which affirmed the appellate court's decision on the belief that the U.S. Supreme Court's precedents, namely, Faretta v. California, required the State to allow Edwards to represent himself. At Indiana's request, the U.S. Supreme Court agreed to consider whether the Constitution required the trial court to allow Edwards to represent himself at trial.

Justice Breyer stated in the majority:

This case focuses upon a criminal defendant whom a state court found mentally competent to stand trial if represented by counsel but not mentally competent to conduct that trial himself. We must decide whether in these circumstances the Constitution forbids a State from insisting that the defendant proceed to trial with counsel, the State thereby denying the defendant the right to represent himself. . . . We conclude that the Constitution does not forbid a State so to insist.

The Court noted that the Constitution does not permit trial of an individual who lacks "mental competency." And defined the competency standard as including both (1) whether the defendant has a rational as well as factual understanding of the proceedings against him and (2) whether the defendant has sufficient present ability to consult with his lawyer with a reasonable degree of rational understanding.

The Court concluded that its foundational "self-representation" case, Faretta, held that the Sixth and Fourteenth Amendments includes a constitutional right to proceed without counsel when a criminal defendant "voluntarily and intelligently elects to do so." The Court implied that right from: (1) a "nearly universal conviction," made manifest in state law, that forcing a lawyer upon an unwilling defendant is contrary to his basic right to defend himself if he truly wants to do so; (2) Sixth Amendment language granting rights to the "accused;" (3) Sixth Amendment structure indicating that the rights it sets forth, related to the fair administration of American justice, are personal to the accused; (4) the absence of historical examples of forced representation; and (5) respect for the individual.

Justice Breyer concluded:

The nature of the problem before us cautions against the use of a single mental competency standard for deciding both (1) whether a defendant who is represented by counsel can proceed to trial and (2) whether a defendant who goes to trial must be permitted to represent himself. Mental illness itself is not a unitary concept. It varies in degree. It can vary over time. It interferes with an individual's functioning at different times in different ways. The history of this case illustrates the complexity of the problem. In certain instances an individual may well be able to satisfy the mental competence standard, for he will be able to work with counsel at trial, yet at the same time he may be unable to carry out the basic tasks needed to present his own defense without the help of counsel . . .

Indiana has also asked us to overrule Faretta. We decline to do so. We recognize that judges have sometimes expressed concern that Faretta, contrary to its intent, has led to trials that are unfair. But recent empirical research suggests that such instances are not common . . .

Justice Scalia with whom Justice Thomas joined stated in dissent:

The Constitution guarantees a defendant who knowingly and voluntarily waives the right to counsel the right to proceed pro se at his trial. Faretta v. California, 422 U.S. 806, 95 S. Ct. 2525, 45 L. Ed. 2d 562 (1975). A mentally ill defendant who knowingly and voluntarily elects to proceed pro se instead of through counsel receives a fair trial that comports with the Fourteenth Amendment. . . . The Court today concludes that a State may nonetheless strip a mentally ill defendant of the right to represent himself when that would be fairer. In my view the Constitution does not permit a State to substitute its own perception of fairness for the defendant's right to make his own case before the jury–a specific right long understood as essential to a fair trial. . . .

Because I think a defendant who is competent to stand trial, and who is capable of knowing and voluntary waiver of assistance of counsel, has a constitutional right to conduct his own defense, I respectfully dissent.

## Key Words

**Competency:** Refers to an accused mental state at trial time. A defendant must be able to assist his or her counsel in defending the case.

**Declarant:** An individual making a statement generally in a legal document or while testifying at a trial or other legal hearing.

**Hearsay:** A statement, other than one made by the declarant while testifying at the trial or hearing, offered in evidence to prove the truth of the matter asserted.

**Insanity:** The abnormal mental state of an accused at the time the criminal offense was committed.

**Plain error rule:** The rule that an appellate court may only consider a judicial ruling on the evidence that was not objected to at trial, if the ruling was clearly wrong and prejudiced the defendant.

# References

## COURT CASES

*Brady v. Maryland*, 373 U.S. 83, 87, 83 S. Ct. 1194, 1196-97, 10 L. Ed. 2d 215

*Cooper v. Oklahoma*, 517 U.S. 348 (1996).

*Patton v. United States*, 281 U.S. 276 (1930).

*Jackson v. Indiana*, 406 U.S. 715 (1972).

*United States v. Jordan*, 2010 U.S. Dist. LEXIS 15761, 5-6 (D. Mass. Feb. 23, 2010)

*United States v. Pelullo*, 964 F.2d 193 (3d Cir. 1992).

*United States v. Zizzo*, 120 F.3d 1338 (7th Cir. 1997).

*United States v. Jordan*, 2010 U.S. Dist. LEXIS 15761, 5-6 (D. Mass. Feb. 23, 2010).

## BOOKS, ARTICLES, AND JOURNALS

Matoesian, Gregory M. *Law and the Language of Identity.* New York: Oxford University Press, 2001.

Roberson, Cliff, and Harvey Wallace. *Procedures in the Justice System*, 9th ed. Columbus, OH: Pearson, 2009.

# 4

# Federal Courts

**What you need to know about Federal Courts**

After you have completed this chapter, you should know:

- Article III, U.S. Constitution provides the authority for the establishment of a federal court system.
- Jurisdiction refers to the power of a court to hear and decide a controversy. Jurisdiction is divided into three components: jurisdiction over the parties, jurisdiction over the subject matter, and geographical jurisdiction.
- Venue refers to the geographical location of the trial court.
- A trial court hears evidence and finds facts whereas an appellate court only reviews the cases for legal issues.
- In the United States, there is a dual court system—state and federal. As a general rule state courts decide matters involving state issues and federal courts decide matters involving federal issues.
- Federal courts are courts of limited jurisdiction. Except in limited situations, this means that federal courts are limited to deciding only federal issues and that jurisdiction in federal court is not assumed but must be established.
- There are three levels of courts in the federal system: U.S. District Courts, U.S. Courts of Appeals, and the Supreme Court.
- Federal magistrate judges function under the supervision of U.S. district court judges.
- Generally cases come before the U.S. Supreme Court by a writ of certiorari.
- The writ of certiorari is an order from an appellate court, in this case the Supreme Court, to a lower court ordering the lower court to submit the case records so that the appellate court can review the decision.
- To appeal a decision, normally the losing party submits a petition for a writ of certiorari.
- The Supreme Court accepts only a small percentage of the petitions filed each year.

**Chapter Outline**

- Introduction
- Federal Magistrates
- Federal District Courts
- U.S. Courts of Appeals
- U.S. Supreme Court

## INTRODUCTION

U.S. Constitution, Article III, Section 1. Supreme Court and inferior courts—Judges and compensation.

> The judicial Power of the United States, shall be vested in one supreme Court, and in such inferior Courts as the Congress may from time to time ordain and establish. The Judges, both of the supreme and inferior Courts, shall hold their Offices during good Behaviour, and shall, at stated Times, receive for their Services, a Compensation, which shall not be diminished during their Continuance in Office.

Every court of United States must derive its jurisdiction and judicial authority from Constitution or laws of United States (*Jecker v. Montgomery*, 1852).

The court systems in both the federal and state courts are complicated and at times technical. The organization of American courts is based on three general principles:

- Jurisdiction, which refers to the power of a court to hear and decide a controversy. Jurisdiction is divided into three components: jurisdiction over the parties, jurisdiction over the subject matter, and geographical jurisdiction.
- Whether the court is a trial court or an appellate court—a trial court hears evidence and finds facts whereas an appellate court only reviews the cases for legal issues.
- Dual court system—state or federal issue

### Establishment of the Federal Judiciary

Prior to the U.S. Constitution, the central government was governed from 1781 to 1789 by the Articles of Confederation. The Articles did not provide for a federal court system and the federal government was forced to use state courts that proved to be unworkable. Accordingly, what is now Article III of the U.S. Constitution was accepted by the delegates at the Constitutional convention without debate (Harrell and Anderson 1982).

After the constitution was ratified, the first bill introduced in the U.S. Senate dealt with the issue of establishing a federal court system. After extensive debate, the Judiciary Act of 1789 was enacted. Like many other statutes enacted by Congress, the Act was a compromise between the Federalists who advocated for a strong central government and the Anti-Federalists who advocated for strong state governments and a weak federal government. The Federalists were successful in the establishment of a separate federal judicial system. The Anti-Federalists were successful in protecting state interests in three significant ways (Richardson and Vines 1970):

- Boundaries of district courts were drawn along state lines and no district court boundaries crossed stated lines. While the district courts were tasked with enforcing federal law, they were organized by states and each district court was responsible for its own state area.
- District court judges were to be selected from residents of the district. This provision ensured that district court judges were local residents.
- The Act provided that district courts were to be courts of limited jurisdiction. The jurisdiction of district courts is discussed later in this chapter.

The Judiciary Act of 1789 proved to be only a temporary compromise between those who advocated for a strong central government and those who advocated for a weak central government. In 1801, the Federalists were successful in passage of the Judiciary Act of 1801 (also known as The Midnight Judges Act). This Act created many new federal judges and extended the jurisdiction of the district courts. After Thomas Jefferson was sworn in as the third president in 1801, under his leadership Congress

**COURTS IN ACTION**

**Public Opinion of the U.S. Supreme Court**

According to a 2009 survey of public opinion almost one half of the public felt that the ideology of the Supreme Court in 2009 was about right. The question asked was: "Is the U.S. Supreme Court too conservative, too liberal, or about right. The results: 29 percent too liberal; 47 percent about right; and 22 percent too conservative. [Adam Liptak (2010, July 25) New York Times, A-1].

repealed the Act and returned the federal judiciary to its original status. The Judiciary Act of 1801 did, however, result in the famous case, *Marbury v. Madison* (1803). In the Marbury case, Chief Justice John Marshall originated the concept of judicial review, which empowered the Supreme Court with the authority to review acts legislative acts (Richardson and Vines 1970).

## Circuit Court of Appeals Act of 1891

Two major problems with the Judiciary Act of 1789 was the workload of the justices and the requirement that the justices "ride the circuits." The Act required that the Supreme Court justices also serve as judges of the circuit courts. The justices, most of whom were elderly, regularly complained that circuit riding caused serious physical hardships and diverted them from the far more important duties of a Supreme Court justice. For example, the justice assigned to the southern circuit was required travel of approximately 3,600 miles a year in an area that had poor roads. At one point, the justices agreed to take a reduction in salary if Congress would appoint separate circuit judges.

Most members of Congress, however, believed that circuit riding transformed the justices into schoolmasters, who brought federal authority and national political views to the distant states and that the circuit riding justices impressed on the citizenry the authority of the remote national government. It was also argued that circuit riding also exposed the justices to local political sentiments and legal practices.

Finally in 1869, congress established a separate circuit court judiciary, although the justices retained nominal circuit riding duties until the Circuit Court of Appeals Act of 1891. Congress officially ended the practice in 1911 (Hall 1992).

## Circuit Court of Appeals Act of 1891

The Circuit Court of Appeals Act of 1891 created nine new courts known as circuit courts of appeal (renamed U.S. Courts of Appeals in 1948). The Act of 1891 eliminated the need for Supreme Court justices to participate in deciding circuit court cases. The Act, however, retained the circuit courts, which were not eliminated until 1911, when their work was assigned to the federal district courts, the lowest level of the federal judicial system. The U.S. Courts of Appeals will be discussed later in this chapter.

## Judges Bill of 1925

The Judges' Bill of 1925 clarified the Supreme Court's role and responsibilities within the federal judiciary. The Bill repealed most of the mandatory jurisdiction requirements that required the Supreme Court to accept certain cases. The Bill limited the automatic right of appeal to the Supreme Court to only a limited number of cases and established in other areas cases that would come before the Court only when the justices granted a writ in response to a petition or motion from a party in a case before a lower court. As the result of the Bill, the Supreme Court became a forum for deciding questions of constitutional principle with the circuit courts of appeals issuing final decisions in most federal appeals cases.

The drafting of the Judges' Bill started in 1921 when Chief Justice Taft advocated the establishment of a judicial conference that would contribute to the more efficient administration of the lower federal courts. Taft and a committee of justices drafted legislation intended to ease the caseload of the Supreme Court. The Senate Judiciary Committee formally requested that Taft and the justices draft legislation that might remedy the backlog of cases. Justice Willis Van Devanter headed the committee that referred the draft to the full Court before submitting it to Congress in 1921.

The bill was called the "Judges' Bill" because it was drafted by the justices. The Bill eliminated direct appeals from the district courts to the Supreme Court except in cases related to interstate commerce and antitrust legislation, writs of errors by the United States in criminal cases, reviews of rulings of the Interstate Commerce Commission, and injunctions against state administrative agencies. In addition, appeals from the state courts of last resort to the Supreme Court were limited to cases in which the state court declared an act of the United States invalid or denied a claim that a state law was unconstitutional. Other appeals from the state courts were required to be submitted by petition. Only U.S. Courts of Appeals decisions regarding state constitutional rulings also could be taken to the Supreme Court. Other decisions of the courts of appeals could be taken to the Supreme Court only by certiorari, although an appellate court could certify a case for a ruling from the Supreme Court. Cases appealed to the Court by certiorari are not required to be taken by the Court and most writs of certiorari are denied by the Court. Congress did not act on the recommended bill until late 1924. It was enacted in February 1925 (Hall 1992). The present structure of the federal court system provides for four levels of courts; magistrates, district courts, courts of appeals, and the Supreme Court. Each of these levels and their relationship to each other will be discussed in the following sections of this chapter.

## Jurisdiction

As previously noted, jurisdiction refers to the power of a court to decide a controversy. Jurisdiction of a court may not be waived by the parties to the controversy and any decision made by a court without jurisdiction is void. Geographical jurisdiction is based on the concept that a court is generally authorized to hear and decide controversies within specified geographical areas. For example, an Ohio state court normally does not have the authority to decide a controversy in Illinois involving two citizens of Illinois.

As noted earlier in this chapter, federal courts are courts of limited jurisdiction. Except in limited situations, this means that federal courts are limited to deciding only federal issues and that jurisdiction in federal court is not assumed but must be established. The court must also have jurisdiction over the subject matter, for example, a bankruptcy court does not have authority in most situations to decide criminal matters.

Jurisdiction over the person is also a required element before the court has authority to decide the controversy. For the most part, jurisdiction of the person in a criminal case is obtained by having the person appear in open court before the judge.

## Venue

Venue refers to the geographical location of the trial court. Venue is governed by the U.S. Constitution, Sixth Amendment that provides:

> In all criminal prosecutions, the accused shall enjoy the right to a speedy and public trial, by an impartial jury of the state and district wherein the crime shall have been committed . . .

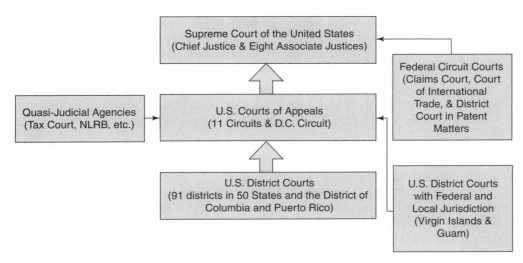

**FIGURE 4-1** Structure of Federal Court System.

A defendant may waive venue, but not jurisdiction. When a defendant requests, by a motion for change of venue, that his or her trial be moved to a different location in order to obtain a fair trial, the defendant is waving venue. Unless the defendant waives venue, he or she has the right to be tried in the district in which the crime was committed.

## U.S. MAGISTRATES

The Federal Magistrates Act provides that a magistrate may be assigned such additional duties as are not inconsistent with the Constitution and laws of the United States. 28 U.S.C. § 636(b)(3). Read literally and without reference to the context in which they appear, these words might encompass any assignment that is not explicitly prohibited by statute or by the Constitution. . . . The Federal Magistrates Act grants district courts authority to assign magistrates certain described functions as well as such additional duties as are not inconsistent with the Constitution and laws of the United States. . . .We recognized that Congress intended magistrates to play an integral and important role in the federal judicial system . . . the Constitution was not violated by the reference to a Magistrate of a motion to suppress evidence in a felony trial. . . . (*Peretz v. United States*, 1991, p. 932.)

The office of Magistrate Judge can be traced to the United States Commissioners who had served the federal judiciary since the 1790. During the 1960s, the congressional judiciary committees and judges on the Judicial Conference of the United States advocated for revisions to the commissioner system. At that time, U.S. Commissioners were paid by a fee system and the appointment process varied from court to court. There were no uniform criteria for selection. In addition, action was needed to relieve the congestion of the federal court dockets. Expanding the judicial responsibilities of the commissioners was one method of relieving the congestions in federal district court.

The Federal Magistrates Act of 1968 created the new title of "magistrate" and expanded the magistrates' authority to conduct misdemeanor trials with the consent of the defendants, to serve as special masters in civil actions, and to assist U.S. District Judges in pretrial and discovery proceedings as well as petitions for posttrial relief. The Act also authorized district judges on any court to assign to magistrates additional duties not inconsistent with the Constitution and laws of the United States.

In the federal court system, the U.S. Magistrate judges are equivalent to state trial judges in courts of limited jurisdiction, for example, county courts, municipal courts, or city courts. The magistrate judges operate under the supervision of district court judges. The broad goal of the Magistrates Act was stated in the House Report on the bill:

"... to cull from the ever-growing workload of the U.S. district courts matters that are more desirably performed by a lower tier of judicial officers." H.Rep. No. 1629, 90th Cong., 2d Sess. (U.S. Code Cong. and Admin. News, 1968, at 4255).

Originally the magistrate judges were called magistrates. Many magistrates were unhappy with their title and Congress modified the Act in 1990 by changing their official title to magistrate judge.

Magistrate judges are appointed by district court judges. Full-time magistrate judges are appointed for eight-year terms and part-time magistrates are appointed for four years. Magistrate judges can be removed for cause. In most cases, a magistrate judge must be an attorney and admitted to practice in the local federal district court. There are currently authorized over 500 full-time and 40 part-time magistrate judgeships. The part-time judges generally serve areas such as national parks were the work is seasonal.

While federal magistrate judges perform quasi-judicial duties and work within the federal judicial system, they are not considered as Article III judges in that they are not appointed by the president and confirmed by the Senate. In addition, they do not serve for life as do Article III judges. [Note: The Article III designation refers to Article III of the U.S. Constitution.]

The U.S. Supreme Court has issued several opinions limiting the power of the magistrate judges because they were not considered as Article III judges. Congress has on

## LAW IN ACTION
### *Peretz v. United States*, 501 U.S. 923 (U.S. 1991)

Peretz and a codefendant were charged with importing four kilograms of heroin. At a pretrial conference attended by Peretz and his counsel, the trial judge was advised by defense counsel that there was no objection to picking the jury before a magistrate. Neither defendant asked the district court to review any ruling made by the magistrate. Peretz was convicted and his codefendant was acquitted in the trial. Peretz appealed, contending that it was error to assign the jury selection to the magistrate and that the judgment should be reversed. The Court of Appeals disagreed and held that consent by defense counsel to a magistrate-supervised voir dire (questioning of potential jurors) waived any subsequent challenge on those grounds, and the conviction was affirmed. The U.S. Supreme Court affirmed the conviction. The Supreme Court held that the trial court could refer jury selection to a magistrate as long as the defense consented and that once consent was given defendant waived any subsequent challenge on those grounds.

The Supreme Court noted in a footnote to the opinion:

It can hardly be denied that the system created by the Federal Magistrates Act has exceeded the highest expectations of the legislators who conceived it. In modern federal practice, federal magistrates account for a staggering volume of judicial work. In 1987, for example, magistrates presided over nearly half a million judicial proceedings. As a recent State Report noted, in particular, magistrates in 1987 conducted over 134,000 preliminary proceedings in felony cases; handled more than 197,000 references of civil and criminal pretrial matters; reviewed more than 6,500 social security appeals and more than 27,000 prisoner filings; and tried more than 95,000 misdemeanors and 4,900 civil cases on consent of the parties. (*Peretz v. United States*, 1991, p. 5565)

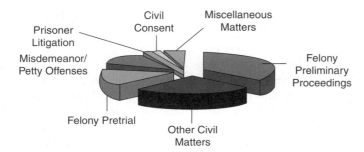

**FIGURE 4-2**    Matters disposed of by Magistrate Judges during a twelve month period. Based on data obtained from the Federal Magistrates' Association, http://www.fedjudge.org/ accessed March 29, 2009.

numerous occasions responded by amending the Magistrate Act. For example, in 2000, Congress amended the Act to specially empower the magistrate judges to enter a sentence for a petty offense that is a class B misdemeanor charging a motor vehicle offense, a class C misdemeanor, or an infraction; and the power to enter a sentence for a class A misdemeanor, or a class B or C misdemeanor in a case in which the parties have consented.

Presently, magistrate judges have the authority to perform a wide variety of judicial duties in felony cases including holding preliminary proceedings, conduction initial appearances, appoint counsel for indigent defendants, hold bail hearings, and issue warrants. In misdemeanor cases, the magistrate judges have the authority to preside over trials, accept guilty pleas, and impose sentences.

U.S. Magistrate Judges have assumed an important role in the federal court system. Each year magistrate judges review approximately 26,000 court filings involving prisoner litigation matters. In fiscal year 2008, U.S. magistrate judges disposed of a total of 948,086 matters in the courts. As noted in Figure 4-1, magistrate judges are significantly involved in both civil and criminal litigation in the federal court system. [Third Branch, 2008]

**What is the role of magistrate judges today in the federal court system? How has it changed in 40 years?**

The following material is an excerpt from interview with U.S. District Court Judge Dennis Cavanaugh. Judge Cavanaugh has chaired the Judicial Conference Committee on the Administration of the Magistrate Judges System since 2006. He was a U.S. magistrate judge for the District of New Jersey from 1993 to 2000. In 2000, he was appointed to the federal bench as a U.S. District Judge in the District of New Jersey.

## LAW IN ACTION

### Public Notice Appointment of United States Magistrate Judge El Paso, Texas

The United States District Court for the Western District of Texas is accepting applications for the position of full-time United States Magistrate Judge at El Paso, Texas. The term of office is eight years and the current annual salary for the position is $155,756.

A full public notice for the magistrate judge, application forms, and application submission procedures are posted on our web site at: www.txwd.uscourts.gov/jobs/default.asp Applications must be received no later than May 30, 2009. Questions may be directed to Director of Human Resources, (210) 249-4034 x505.

The above notice was announced by the clerk, U.S. District Court, Western District of Texas on March 25, 2009.

**Question: What is the role of magistrate judges today in the federal court system? How has it changed in 40 years?**

**Judge Cavanaugh:** The role of magistrate judges has evolved in a number of ways. First of all, Congress has acted repeatedly to enhance the authority of magistrate judges, to clarify their judicial status, and to improve the system's overall effectiveness. In response to early challenges to the authority of magistrate judges to handle various types of proceedings, Congress amended the 1968 Act a number of times: in 1976 to explicitly authorize magistrate judges to conduct evidentiary hearings, and then in 1979, to expressly authorize them to enter final orders disposing of civil cases with the consent of the parties. Also, limited contempt authority was authorized in 2000.

In addition to the direct effect of legislation specifically enhancing and clarifying the scope of magistrate judges' authority, the federal courts have responded to the overall growth in caseload by using magistrate judges to meet the particular demands of their changing caseloads. For example, in recent years many courts have assigned an increasing number of felony guilty plea proceedings to magistrate judges.

Congress also has acted to improve the salary and retirement benefits of magistrate judges and to promote the recruitment and appointment of highly qualified individuals. In 1990, Congress changed the title from magistrate to United States magistrate judge, making it clear that these are judicial officers to be addressed as judge or magistrate judge.

Magistrate judges are adjuncts to the Article III district judges. Full-time magistrate judges serve an eight-year term and they may be reappointed for successive terms. They are appointed by the district judges in each district.

**Question: What do you see for the future of the magistrate judges system?**

**Judge Cavanaugh:** Within statutory and constitutional parameters, I believe that magistrate judges will continue to be authorized to exercise a broad range of authority. Innovations in the utilization of magistrate judges will probably, and hopefully, continue. It will be driven by increasing caseloads and the need to maximize the effectiveness of magistrate judge utilization overall.

I'm hopeful that we can make strides towards greater diversity in the magistrate judge system, which the Magistrate Judges Committee strongly encourages. I also believe the stature and responsibilities of the office of magistrate judges will continue to attract very high-caliber applicants. And I expect that magistrate judges will continue to play an important role as an effective and flexible judicial resource in addressing critical workloads and challenges, as for example, the way magistrate judges have been heavily utilized to meet the massive influx of criminal cases in the southwest border courts that we just discussed.

Reprinted by permission of the Third Branch, *Newsletter of the Federal Courts* 40, no. 10 (October 2008).

## FEDERAL DISTRICT COURTS

### The Role of Federal Courts

In the United States, there are 89 federal district courts located among the 50 states plus 5 additional district courts in the District of Columbia, Puerto Rico, and the territories of Virgin Islands, Guam, and the Northern Mariana Islands. Some states, such as Alaska, have a single judicial district. Most states, depending upon their population, such as New York, Illinois, California, Texas, Pennsylvania, Florida, and Georgia have additional districts bearing such geographical names as the "Southern," "Middle," or "Northern" Districts. Both the number of federal court divisions and judgeships are specified by Title 28 of the United States Code.

District Courts are further divided into **divisions** among major centers of population. For example, the Southern District of Georgia is composed of the divisions of Augusta, Brunswick, Statesboro, Dublin, and Waycross, each a city within the state of

**COURTS IN ACTION**

**Fair Sentencing Act of 2010**

For three decades, individuals convicted of crack offenses faced far harsher penalties than defendants convicted of similar offenses involving cocaine powder. A person in possession of 500 grams of powder cocaine would face a five-year mandatory minimum sentence. Crack offenders would face the same penalty for a mere 5 grams. The Fair Sentencing Act of 2010 [Public Law No: 111–220] reduces the sentencing disparity to 18 to 1, meaning that a person convicted of selling 28 grams of crack would face the same five-year mandatory minimum as someone with 500 grams of cocaine. The law also eliminates mandatory minimum sentencing for simply possessing crack cocaine. The U.S. Sentencing Commission says that between 5,500 and 6,000 offenders are sentenced for crack offenses each year. The law will reduce by up to 27 months sentences for about 3,000 offenders each year.

According to the Washington Post, for the past three decades most of those arrested for crack offenses were mostly young, African American men and they faced far harsher penalties than the white and Hispanic suspects most often caught with powder cocaine. A person found holding 500 grams of powder cocaine would face a five-year mandatory minimum; crack offenders would have to be in possession of a mere 5 grams to face the same obligatory sentence. Crack offenders faced a 10-year mandatory minimum for carrying 10 grams of the drug; the same penalty would not kick in for a powder-cocaine suspect unless caught with 1,000 grams. ["Editorial: The Fair Sentencing Act corrects a long-time wrong in cocaine cases" Washington Post, August 3, 2010, p. A-18]

Georgia. Each division may have a federal courthouse and is the location for the trial of cases arising from among select counties assigned to that division.

District courts are among the busiest in the nation. Not only do district courts hear civil cases involving large sums of claimed damages involving personal injury and contracts, but also they hear criminal cases. The number of criminal cases continues to grow.

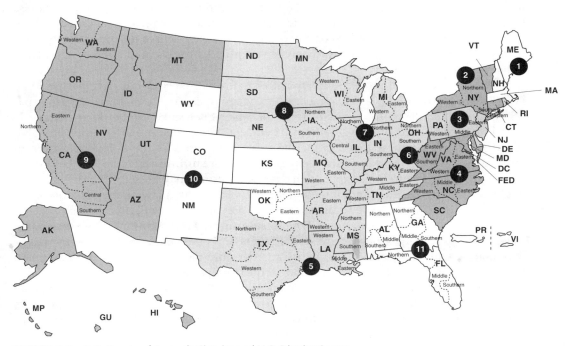

**FIGURE 4-3**    U.S. Courts of Appeals Circuits and U.S. District Courts

**LAW IN ACTION**

**The Role of the Federal Judge—Judicial Ethics**

For the judiciary to be effective, the public must have confidence in the integrity and impartiality of its judges. Since a judge hears controversies, renders judgment, and administers justice, scrupulous adherence to the judicial canon of ethics is required. A judge's participation in community events, political affairs, and financial activities may result in the public's perception that the judge may be biased or otherwise showing favoritism while sitting on the bench. As a result, a judge must prudently disqualify or recuse herself from participating in decisions where she is unable to act impartially or the perception is that the judge has a stake in the outcome of the case. Ethics committees provide guidance to judges to help them make appropriate decisions and to conform their behavior. Since federal judges are appointed for life by the president of the United States with the advice and consent of the United States Senate, a federal judge's removal from office may only be accomplished through congressional impeachment proceedings.

For instance, in 2008, there were over 70,896 cases involving over 90,000 defendants prosecuted in federal district court for violations of federal statutes involving such cases as drug offenses, firearms offenses, income tax cases, immigration violations, terrorism, and white-collar crimes. In addition, federal courts hear cases brought by state prisoners asserting claims of deprivation of constitutional rights. Such cases involving the **writ of habeas corpus** may allow the defendant's conviction and the conditions of confinement to be reviewed by a federal judge.

In most cases, a federal district court is the court of first impression. This simply means that the trial and other evidentiary hearings are conducted in the district court. It is the federal judge's responsibility to conduct jury trials, hear evidence, and render judgments based upon the facts proven in court and the applicable law. In this forum, witness testimony is presented, documentary evidence is admitted, counsel's arguments are made to the jury, and jurors are instructed on the law so they may deliberate and arrive at a verdict. On average, it takes approximately seven months for a criminal case to go from indictment to sentencing.

A federal criminal prosecution typically begins with an **indictment** that has been issued by a **grand jury**. The indictment is the charging document that sets forth in separate **counts** the alleged violations of federal statutes committed by the defendants. The grand jury, composed of between 16 to 24 citizens, sits to determine whether probable cause exists to determine that a crime has been committed by the defendant. After an indictment is issued, the defendant is either arrested or **summoned** to appear before the magistrate judge for an initial appearance so that a **bond** may be set if the defendant is eligible for pretrial release and, if the defendant is **indigent**, a lawyer may be appointed to defend him at trial. Depending upon local practice, the arraignment is conducted shortly after the initial appearance. The **arraignment** is a hearing during which the indictment is formally presented to the defendant and enters a plea of "not guilty" to the indictment. At this stage, a not guilty plea is the only plea that a defendant can enter, because the magistrate judge is not authorized to accept guilty pleas in felony cases; this authority is vested in the federal district judge alone. After the arraignment, in appropriate cases, the magistrate judge will order a motions' hearing where evidence and arguments are presented concerning the seizure of evidence, the admissibility of the defendant's statements, and other issues in preparation for trial.

As the case is prepared for trial, the government shares with the defendant's counsel discovery of the case agent reports, the defendant's statements, and evidence that is both incriminating and exculpatory. Notably, if the United States Attorney or any assistant fails to disclose information to the defense that could be used to attack the credibility of a government witness, the charges may be dismissed. A prominent example of failing to provide the defense of conflicting information about a witness's testimony is the federal prosecution of former Alaska United States Senator Ted Stevens where the judge dismissed the charges after a jury found Stevens guilty of providing false information to the Senate about gifts he received. The dismissal was based, in part, upon the government's failure to disclose critical information to the defense about a witness's prior statements that contradicted his trial testimony.

The production of discoverable items to the defense is just one of the ethical obligations that rest upon the federal prosecutor. The Assistant United States Attorney who represents the government must not bring vindictive or selective prosecutions based upon a person's race, religion, status, or other constitutional grounds. In addition, the prosecutor has a duty to preserve evidence, which must also assure that the court is made aware of any witness testimony that the prosecutor believes is untrue. The prosecutor's duty in a criminal prosecution is to seek justice. As the Supreme Court has stated, an Assistant United States Attorney may "prosecute with earnestness and vigor," but may not use "improper methods calculated to produce a wrongful conviction." If the use of such methods "so [infects] the trial with unfairness as to make the resulting conviction a denial of due process," the conviction should be overturned. The prosecutor's role as a member of the Court Group is further discussed in Chapter 6.

When the case is called for trial, a jury is empanelled by first randomly selecting names from a pool of residents within the district. Before a panel of 12 jurors plus usually two alternates are finally selected, the trial judge and attorneys conduct the **voir dire**, a process of asking questions regarding the juror's background, to exclude jurors who may be biased for or against one side or the other based upon financial or personal interests as well as prior knowledge of the case through media reports. In federal court, the voir dire is typically conducted by the federal judge with suggestions for questions submitted by counsel. The voir dire process assures that the evidence will be heard by a fair and impartial group of the defendant's peers.

As the trial proceeds after a jury is empanelled, counsel are called open to provide an opening statement. Counsels' opening statements should not be argument. Rather, opening statements are intended to provide roadmaps to the jurors as to how the case will be presented and what counsel expect the evidence will be. In complicated cases, counsel will outline for the jurors what they will hear from the witness stand and how the evidence will be presented through such means as case agents, police, expert witnesses, and documentary evidence. The counsel for the defendant may waive his opening until the beginning of the defense case after the government has presented its evidence.

As the government presents evidence, the prosecutor must be mindful that the evidence must be relevant to proving beyond a **reasonable doubt** the **elements of the offenses**. The elements of the offenses are the component parts, often defined by statute, which must be proven to establish a violation of the criminal code. For instance, in an **embezzlement** case involving wrongfully taking government money or property, the elements are: (1) that the money or property belonged to the United States or an agency thereof and had a value in excess of $1,000; (2) that the property lawfully came into the possession or care of the defendant; (3) that the defendant fraudulently appropriated the money or property to his own use or the use of others; and (4) that the defendant did so knowingly and willfully with the intent either temporarily or permanently to deprive the owner of the use of the money or property so taken. Failure to prove beyond a reasonable doubt any of the elements of the offense results in the **acquittal** of the defendant.

During the trial, the Federal Rules of Evidence are applied to determine the admissibility of evidence such as testimony, documents, and exhibits. Adopted by the United States Congress in 1975, the rules regulate the foundations required for the admissibility of evidence and the type of evidence that can be considered by the jury. The rules promote such vital interests as efficiency in presenting evidence, reliability in the quality of evidence, and fairness in the adversary process. As an example of reliability concerns, the rules specify the type of out-of-court statements that are admissible. Some out-of-court statements, considered to be **hearsay**, are admissible only under limited conditions since the defendant is unable to cross-examine the person making the out-of-court statement. An example of hearsay is when a witness attempts to testify that he was told something by another person who is not a witness to the trial. Such testimony, when offered to prove a relevant fact, is inadmissible since the defendant is unable to cross-examine the person who is not a witness to the trial. Although the general rule is that hearsay is inadmissible, there are over 20 exceptions to this hearsay rule that permit certain types of hearsay, such as statements made to a treating physician, to be admitted as reliable evidence and still maintain the fairness of the proceedings.

As the government proceeds with its evidence, witnesses are called to the stand to provide testimony. The prosecutor begins the questioning with the **direct examination** of a witness that involves the use of nonsuggestive questions to present the witness's testimony. Direct examination questions are open-ended and establish answers to the "who,

## LAW IN ACTION

### Example of Direct Examination of Prosecutor's Questioning of Undercover Agent about Drug Transaction and the Defendant's Intent

Q:  Detective Witness, do you know the defendant?
A:  Yes, I do.
Q:  How do you know him?
A:  I was working undercover, and I bought some drugs from him on three occasions.
Q:  Do you know Mr. Co-conspirator?
A:  Yes, I do.
Q:  How do you know him?
A:  He was with the defendant on several occasions when I met with him.
Q:  Directing your attention to March 10, 20XX, did you see the defendant and Mr. Conspirator that day?
A:  Yes, I did.
Q:  Please describe the circumstances under which you saw them.
A:  I was supposed to meet the defendant at Joes' Bar to buy some drugs, and I saw the defendant and Mr. Co-conspirator in the parking lot. They called me over to Mr. Co-Conspirator's car and we were standing under a lamp post. Mr. Co-conspirator popped his trunk and the defendant pulled a small bag of leafy marijuana from a large backpack which contained several other small bags that were just like the one I was buying. Later we discovered that there were 22 small bags like the one I got.
Q:  Did the defendant say anything to you?
A:  Yes, he handed me the bag and said "That will be 200 bucks."
Q:  Did Mr. Co-conspirator say anything?
A:  He said to the defendant, "Ask your buddy if he knows any more customers. We need to move this stuff by payday."

what, how, when, and why" of the prosecution's case. Typically, police officers or federal case agents testify regarding evidence that was seized, their observations of the criminal activities conducted by the defendant, and any statements that the defendant may have provided during interrogation. Other witnesses may also testify as to their pertinent observations related to the offense. Such witnesses are called "**fact witnesses**" because they are limited to providing testimony regarding what they saw and heard and other relevant sensory perceptions.

Another type of witness who may be called to the stand is the **expert witness.** For a person to testify as an expert witness, the witness must be qualified with having knowledge of the technical subject matter through special training or experience in that field. After the court has accepted the witness as an expert, he may provide an opinion concerning technical matters. For example, an expert witness may be a laboratory examiner who, through scientific tests and analysis, was able to conclude certain facts about items involved in a crime. More specifically, a firearms expert would likely be able to testify that a round of ammunition was fired from a particular firearm as a result of the markings left on a round after it was discharged from the barrel of the firearm. Such a witness may provide important testimony during the trial but such evidence may be rebutted by other experts called by opposing counsel. In addition, the jury is instructed that merely because an expert witness has expressed an opinion, the jury need not accept that opinion.

As each witness is called and after the government's direct examination of the witness, the defense counsel is given an opportunity to cross-examine the witnesses. This process permits the defendant to confront "the witnesses against him" as guaranteed by the Sixth Amendment to the United States Constitution. **Cross-examination** allows counsel to bring out favorable facts to support later argument, to diminish the impact of unfavorable facts, and to attack the credibility of the witness. During cross-examination, counsel asks **leading questions** that suggest the answer for the witness. For example, on cross-examination, a proper question is: "You saw the knife in John's hand, correct?" as opposed to an open-ended or non-leading question used during direct examination, such as "What did you see?"

After the government has presented the testimony of its witnesses and other evidence, the government rests. At this point in the trial, the defendant may proceed with presenting his case, although under the **Fifth Amendment to the United States Constitution**, the defendant is not required to testify. The defendant may present witnesses' testimony through direct examination and the government may cross-examine the defendant's witnesses by attacking their credibility by presenting, for example, felony convictions of such witnesses. At the end of the defendant's case, the government may present **rebuttal witnesses** to address any evidentiary points elicited during the defendant's case.

At the end of the evidence, counsel for the government and the defense present their **closing arguments** to provide a summary of the evidence. Most importantly, however, closing arguments are a persuasive and argumentative statement, based upon the facts presented during the trial, designed to convince the jury how to vote during their deliberations on the evidence. Prior to jury retiring to deliberate, the trial judge provides instructions as to the law and the process to be followed during the jury's deliberations.

Among the instructions provided to the jury, the judge will define **reasonable doubt** for the jurors. In the Eleventh Circuit, which comprises the states of Alabama, Georgia, and Florida, and similarly in other circuits, the trial judge instructs the jury about reasonable doubt in the following manner:

[W]hile the Government's burden of proof is a strict or heavy burden, it is not necessary that a Defendant's guilt be proved beyond all possible doubt. It is only required that the Government's proof exclude any "reasonable doubt" concerning the Defendant's guilt.

A "reasonable doubt" is a real doubt, based upon reason and common sense after careful and impartial consideration of all the evidence in the case. Proof beyond a reasonable doubt, therefore, is proof of such a convincing character that you would be willing to rely and act upon it without hesitation in the most important of your own affairs. If you are convinced that the Defendant has been proved guilty beyond a reasonable doubt, say so. If you are not convinced, say so.

The judge will also instruct the jury regarding the definitions of terms used in the indictment, the elements of the offenses, as well as the law regarding any defenses, such as self-defense, **alibi**, and **good faith**, which may have been raised by the defendant.

The juror's verdict must be **unanimous**. That is, for the defendant to be found guilty, all jurors must agree that the government proved beyond a reasonable doubt all elements of the offense charged. Likewise, a finding of not guilty must also be reached by unanimous agreement. If the jurors fail to reach a unanimous agreement, then the result is a **hung jury** that may result in a **retrial**.

After the jury reaches their verdict, a judge sets a later hearing to determine the defendant's sentence. Usually, at least 45 days transpire before a sentencing hearing is held. Before the sentencing hearing, the judge refers the case to a United States probation officer to conduct a presentence investigation into the defendant's background, family history, work history, and criminal background. In addition, the United States Sentencing Guidelines are used to calculate a sentencing range to be considered by the judge and the parties. During the sentencing hearing, the government may present information about the impact of the crime upon victims and the defendant may present character witnesses and mitigating information. The judge pronounces sentence and enters a judgment of conviction. After the hearing, the defendant has 10 days to file a notice of appeal to the Circuit Court of Appeals.

## U.S. COURTS OF APPEALS

The 94 federal judicial districts are organized into 11 regional circuit courts of appeal plus the Federal Circuit Court of Appeals. A court of appeals hears appeals from the district courts located within its circuit, as well as appeals from decisions of federal administrative agencies. The geographic boundaries for the 11 circuits are depicted in the following diagram. The Court of Appeals for the Federal Circuit has nationwide jurisdiction to hear appeals in specialized cases such as those involving patent laws, international trade, and federal claims.

In an effort to relieve a burdening caseload in the United States Supreme Court and to handle a dramatic increase in federal filings, Congress, in the Judiciary Act of 1891, established nine courts of appeals, one for each judicial circuit. The circuit judge and the district judges in the circuit sat on the three-person courts of appeals panels.

In 1893, Congress created a Court of Appeals of the District of Columbia. In 1922, the forerunner of the Judicial Conference of the United States was established and gave the senior judge in each circuit some formal administrative authority over the district courts in each circuit. By the 1920s, each U.S. court of appeals had at least three assigned judgeships, thereby eliminating the need for the regular service of district judges on court of appeals panels.

Two additional courts of appeals were created with the establishment of new regional circuits, the tenth in 1929 and the eleventh in 1980. The thirteen appellate courts (including the federal circuit) have approximately 180 judges.

**LAW IN ACTION**

The United States Constitution gives Congress the power to create federal courts other than the Supreme Court and to determine their **jurisdiction**. Significantly, it is Congress, rather than the judiciary, that controls the type of cases that may be heard in the federal courts.

In addition to establishing the courts' jurisdiction, Congress determines how federal courts will operate in three significant ways. "First, it decides how many judges there should be and where they will work. Second, through the confirmation process, Congress determines which of the president's judicial nominees ultimately become federal judges. Third, Congress approves the federal courts' budget and appropriates money for the judiciary to operate." Notably, the judiciary's budget is less than one percent of the entire federal budget.

www.uscourts.gov/understand03/content_2_1.html

As intermediate courts between the district courts, in which trials are held, and the U.S. Supreme Court, the Circuit Courts of Appeal review questions of law and fact and rule on any legal errors that may have occurred during the pretrial and trial phase of the prosecution. The Circuit Courts of Appeal wield much influence upon the enforcement of laws in the United States. As a measure of the influence of the circuit courts, in 2008, 61,104 appeals were filed in the circuit courts including 13,667 criminal appeals and 16,853 prisoner petitions. On the other hand, in the United States Supreme Court, the court averages around 70 decided cases in recent years. Practically speaking, for most criminal defendants, the Circuit Court of Appeal is the court of last resort since very few cases are accepted for consideration by the Supreme Court.

Each case in the Circuit Court is heard originally by a three-judge panel. Their decision and written opinion becomes binding precedent within the geographical area served by the circuit court.

To start an appeal, the defendant must file an appellate brief by typically hiring or having appointed counsel. Procedural steps including filing a notice of appeal, appearance of counsel, and an appellate brief meeting the court's specifications must be followed to perfect an appeal. On appeal, the defendant is referred to as the

**COURTS IN ACTION**

**Chief Justice John G. Roberts, U.S. Supreme Court on the role of judges**

Chief Justice John G. Roberts stated that he views the role of judges as "limited" and that they "do not have a commission to solve society's problems, as they see them, but simply to decide cases before them according to the rule of law." In responding to a question by a Washington Post reporter about judicial activism, Roberts said, "When the other branches of government exceed their constitutionally-mandated limits, the courts can act to confine them to the proper bounds. It is judicial self-restraint; however, that confines judges to their proper constitutional responsibilities." [Mike Allen and R. Jeffrey Smith (2005, August 5) "Judges Should Have 'Limited' Role, Roberts Says." Washington Post, A-1]

## COURTS IN ACTION

### The Smallest U.S. Circuit

The United States Court of Appeals for the First Circuit, which encompasses Maine, New Hampshire, Massachusetts, Rhode Island, and Puerto Rico, is small not only in terms of the geographic area it encompasses, but more important, it is the regional circuit with the smallest number of judgeships. Indeed, for many years, it had only three judgeships the same size as regular United States court of appeals panels. That was changed when the Omnibus Judgeship Act of 1978 which added judgeships to all of the circuits. The First Circuit now has six active-duty judges' positions.

In addition to the use of its senior judges, the First Circuit, like all but one other court of appeals (the Seventh Circuit), makes use of district judges from within the circuit sitting by designation, and it also avails itself of the services of visiting judges—court of appeals judges and district judges from outside the circuit, almost all of whom are senior judges.

The First Circuit hears oral argument primarily at one location, Boston, while also sitting twice a year in San Juan, Puerto Rico, but not all the judges are in residence at Boston. Like other circuits (except for the D.C. and Federal Circuits), the judges have their principal chambers at various locations—some at circuit headquarters but, as noted above, some elsewhere, with the latter coming to Boston for oral argument.

Because of its small size and caseload, the First Circuit has not received much attention. Receiving far more attention have been the "old" Fifth Circuit before it was divided, because of its importance in the implementation of school desegregation; the District of Columbia Circuit (D.C. Circuit), considered by many to be the nation's preeminent administrative law court; the Seventh Circuit, because the University of Chicago law professors on the court have brought a law-and-economics approach to it; and the Ninth Circuit, the nation's largest, because of efforts to divide it and because of the Supreme Court's reversal of its decisions. [Stephen L. Wasby (2010) Suffolk University Law Review, vol 43(4) pp. 417–418.]

**appellant**. The government is referred to as the **appellee**. The appellant's brief must assert errors made by the trial court or the government during the course of the prosecution and the legal authority supporting the appellant's argument. In reply, the appellee's brief sets forth contrary arguments seeking to support the verdict and sentence of the defendant.

At the circuit court's discretion, some cases are chosen for the parties to present oral arguments to the judges. During oral argument, the parties debate the application of the controlling legal authority as well as the interpretation of statutes and case law as they apply to the issues on appeal. The judges question counsel seeking clarification of written arguments and a deeper understanding of the case, its issues, and the parties' positions. During the entire proceedings at the appellate level, the circuit court does not hear evidence or witness testimony but instead relies entirely upon the record and transcript of the trial proceedings.

The circuit court judges decide the case, in many instances, by issuing a written opinion that describes the facts of the case, the decision, and the judges' rationale for the decision. Since the cases are heard by a panel of three judges, depending upon the complexity and viewpoints of the judges, the court may issue a **majority opinion**, that is, the decision in the case; a **dissenting opinion**, that is, a judge's opposing views from the majority; and a **concurring opinion**, that is, a judge's agreement with the majority's conclusion but for different reasons.

## U.S. SUPREME COURT

The first session of the Supreme Court was on February 2, 1790, in the Royal Exchange building in New York City (Hall 1992).

Jimmy Carter was the only U.S. President to serve a full term in office without appointing any justices to the Supreme Court (Hall 1992).

The U.S. Supreme Court is the highest court in the federal system. It is the only court specifically established by the Constitution. It is composed of one chief justice and eight associate justices. As Article III judges, the justices of the U.S. Supreme Court are appointed by the president and confirmed by the U.S. Senate. The Constitution does not specify the number of justices on the Supreme Court. Article III of the Constitution gives

### COURTS IN ACTION

### Original Jurisdiction by U.S. Supreme Court

When two states have a legal conflict, the U.S. Supreme Court has original jurisdiction. The term original jurisdiction refers to the court where the action is initially started. One such case was New Jersey v. New York, 523 U.S. 767 (1998). The State of New Jersey had filed suit against State of New York, concerning state ownership of a portion of an island in New York harbor, claiming that because New Jersey owned all of the submerged land surrounding Ellis Island, it owned the portion of the island that was later expanded through landfill operations.

An 1834 compact between New York and New Jersey, approved by U.S. Congress pursuant to the Compact Clause of the U.S. Constitution, set the boundary line between the two states as the middle of the Hudson River, but provided that Ellis Island, then three acres, was part of New York, despite its location on the New Jersey side of the river.

Ellis Island lies in New York Harbor 1,300 feet from Jersey City, New Jersey, and one mile from the tip of Manhattan. At the time of the first European settlement it was mostly mud, sand, and oyster shells, which nearly disappeared at high tide. The Mohegan Indians called it "Kioshk," or Gull Island, while the Dutch of New Amsterdam, after its thrifty acquisition, renamed it (along with two other nearby specks) for the oyster, in recognition of the rich surrounding beds. England seized it from the Dutch in 1664, the same year that Charles II included the Island in a grant to his brother, the Duke of York, of the land and water of the present States of New York and New Jersey. The Duke in turn granted part of this territory to Lord Berkeley and Sir George Carteret, the proprietors of New Jersey, whose domain was described as bounded on the east part by the main sea, and part by Hudson's river.

After 1891, when the United States decided to use the Island to receive immigrants, the National Government began filling around the Island's shoreline and over the next 42 years added some 24.5 acres to the original Island. The Island also turned out to be too small, and by the time the new Ellis Island immigration station opened in January 1892, the United States had already added enough fill to the surrounding submerged lands to double the original three acres. By 1897, the Island was up to 14 acres and would go on growing for almost 40 years more.

After the original wood and stucco depot burned in 1897, the United States expanded the land for even larger quarters. Although the new depot, which opened in 1900, sat on approximately the same spot on the original island as the prior main immigration building, it was joined by a hospital placed on a separate island created by landfill in 1899. The National Government often referred to the latter as Island No. 2, which covered about three acres on the southwestern side of a ferry slip. A covered gangway built on piles connected the two islands, which were soon to be joined by one more, though not before the occurrence of another step in the boundary dispute.

Because the hospital of 1900 could not provide sufficiently isolated wards for patients with contagious diseases, these patients were sent to New York City for care and treatment. When, in 1902,

*(Continued)*

the City Health Department announced it would no longer receive such immigrants, the United States had to provide its own contagious disease hospital, which it planned to build on a third island to be joined to Island No. 2 by another gangway. Construction stopped, however, when New Jersey challenged the National Government's appropriation of the submerged lands surrounding the Island.

The dispute was not resolved until December 1904, when New Jersey's Riparian Commissioners conveyed to the United States "all the right, title, claim and interest of every kind, of the State of New Jersey" to 48 acres of territory that included and surrounded Ellis Island, in exchange for $ 1,000. Deed from the State of New Jersey to the United States of America, Recorded, County of Hudson, State of New Jersey, Dec. 23, 1904. The United States then pressed on with construction and in 1906 completed the new island of 4.75 acres, often called Island No. 3. Here the new contagious disease hospital was constructed in 1909 and occupied by 1911.

In 1954, immigration was diverted from the Island. Since then, the Island has been developed as a national historic site, but New York and New Jersey have asserted rival claims of sovereign authority over its filled land.

The U.S. Supreme Court stated that since New Jersey owned the submerged land, it also owned that portion of the island later expanded through the landfill, while New York still owned rights over the original land that was subject to their agreement. The court also concluded that New York did not obtain ownership over New Jersey's portion by possession. Finally, the court ruled that the boundary was the same as in the original agreement, and could not be changed for convenience.

Congress the power to fix the number of justices. Originally, the Judiciary Act of 1789 provided that the Court would have one chief justice and five associate justices. As the nation grew geographically and in population, Congress increased the number of justices to correspond with the growing number of judicial circuits: the Court was expanded to seven members in 1807, nine in 1837. Except for a short period of time when the Congress authorized ten justices, the Court has remained at nine since 1837.

When the Court met for the first time on February 1, 1790, only the chief justice and two of the five associate justices were present. The Judiciary Act required that at least four justices must be present to constitute a quorum. Since the Court was unable to conduct any business that day, Chief Justice John Jay adjourned until the next day. On February 2, 1790, a fourth justice joined the proceeding and thus the Court held its first official session. The court crier opened the proceedings with the cry:

> Oyez! Oyez! Oyez! Oyez! All person having business before the honorable, the Supreme Court of the United States, are admonished to draw near and give their attention, for the Court is now sitting. God save the United States and this Honorable Court. (Irons 2006, 85)

This same invocation has remained unchanged for more than 200 years. Because the Supreme Court is basically an appellate court and had no appeals pending for the first session no one had any business before the court. The four justices spent the first session drafting court rules and procedures for the admission of lawyers to practice before the Court (Irons 2006).

### Selection of Supreme Court Justices

As Article III judges, the Supreme Court justices are nominated by the president and confirmed by the U.S. Senate. According to Dorsen (2008), the selection process for Supreme Court justices in recent years has become very complex. He noted that while presidents have the constitutional power to nominate justices, and, in doing so, they have employed several criteria at different times, including professional merit, ideological compatibility, and political support by the president and his advisers.

**LAW IN ACTION**

**Chief Justice John Jay (1745–1829)**

**Appointed September 9, 1789 and resigned on June 29, 1795**

John Jay was appointed by President Washington as the first chief justice. Jay's forefathers were wealthy having made their fortune in mercantile and he married into the Livingston family, which at that time was considered as the richest family in the country. Apparently his favorite statement was: "Those who own the country should govern it." At the time of his appointment, Jay had a lucrative legal practice and little judicial experience. His only judicial experience was that he had served as New York State's chief justice for less than two years. Jay was more interested in national politics than he was in legal disputes.

At the first Continental Congress in 1775, Jay advocated against the colonies separating from Great Britain, but once Congress adopted the Declaration of Independence, he supported the colonies. He received national acclaim for negotiating a treaty of peace, the Jay Treaty, between the United States and Great Britain in 1795. After he resigned from the Court, he was elected governor of New York. (Iron 2006)

In recent years, the Senate has used public hearings to ascertain a nominee's qualifications and, within certain limitations, the nominee's ideological attitudes. Dorsen contends that this process is now intensely political because the Supreme Court's broad authority as the final interpreter of the Constitution. He also notes that many of the constitutional issues, such as abortion, raise highly contestable problems that have great political significance (Dorsen, 2008).

## Writ of Certiorari

Except for minor exceptions, the Supreme Court's jurisdiction is discretionary. Under the U.S. Constitution, the Supreme Court is the court of original jurisdiction in only a few limited situations. For the most part, the Court reviews decisions from state courts of last resort and federal courts. Generally cases come before the U.S. Supreme Court by a writ of certiorari. Certiorari is a Latin word meaning "to be informed of, or to be made certain in regard to." The writ is an order from an appellate court, in this case the Supreme Court, to a lower court ordering the lower court to submit the case records so that the appellate court can review the decision. In appellate cases, the Supreme Court only reviews legal issues. Accordingly, the question before the Court is generally considered to be whether the law has been correctly applied by the lower court.

Before the Court issues a writ of certiorari, a losing party in the case in the lower court will file a petition for a writ of certiorari (informally called "Cert Petition") asking the Supreme Court to review the decision of a lower court. The petition includes a list of the parties, a statement of the facts of the case, the legal questions presented for review, and arguments as to why the Court should grant the writ. The phrase "Cert. Denied" is informally used in legal citations to indicate that the Supreme Court has denied a petition for writ of certiorari in the case being cited. Review on writ of certiorari is not a matter of right, but a judicial discretion. The Supreme Court will grant a petition for writ of certiorari only for compelling reasons.

The "rule of four" refers to the process by which four justices must vote to accept a writ before the Court will accept the case. If any four justices do not vote to grant the writ, then a denial of certiorari is issued.

## LAW IN ACTION

## Strange Case of Robert Lee Tarver

In re Tarver, 528 U.S. 1152 (U.S. 2000)

The petition for a writ of habeas corpus is denied. Justice Stevens, Justice Souter, Justice Ginsburg, and Justice Breyer would set the case for oral argument. The order of Court heretofore entered February 3, 2000, is vacated, and the application for stay of execution of sentence of death is denied.

### Rule of Four?

In the early hours of April 14, 2000, Robert Lee Tarver died in Alabama's electric chair, even though four Justices of the United States Supreme Court had voted to review the merits of his case. Each year, practitioners and pro se litigants alike file petitions to the U.S. Supreme Court without fully knowing the rules pursuant to which the Court will decide their client's or their own, fate. The reason, according to Ira P. Robbins, is that the Supreme Court operates under two sets of rules those that are published and those that are not. The former specify some Court procedure and purport to guide lawyers and litigants seeking review and relief from the Court. The unpublished set of rules guides the internal decision-making processes of the Court. The Court uses these rules to determine which cases to accept and to manage its docket. According to Ira Robbins, the Court closely guards information concerning these rules. Robbins contends that the very existence of internal rules, as well as the manner in which they function, can be inferred only from an examination of dissenting opinions and from published statistics on how Justices voted in particular cases. This lack of information on the Supreme Court's internal workings leaves litigants and lawyers, as well as the media, at a loss when attempting to understand the judicial process.

In the Tarver opinion, set forth earlier in this box, four justices voted to hear oral argument which apparently should have delayed the execution, but the writ to stay [delay] the execution was denied. [Ira P. Robbins (2002) "Justice by the Numbers: The Supreme Court and the Rule of Four—Or Is It Five?" Suffolk University Law Review, vol. 36(1), pp. 1–2]

The current justices (in 2009), except for Associate Justice John Paul Stevens, participate in what is known as the "cert pool." The law clerks for the eight justices are randomly assigned cert petitions. The clerks then analyze and evaluate in a memorandum on each petition that describes what the case is about, what the arguments are for and against review, and what action the law clerk recommends the Court take on the request for review on the merits. The memorandum is then distributed the clerks of the eight justices who participate in the pooling arrangement. Justice Stevens and his clerks individually review each petition without receiving input from the cert pool. A common criticism of the cert pool arrangement is that places too much power into the hands of a single recent law school graduate who may have no preexisting familiarity with the complex subject matter of a given area of law that a case involves. (Bashman 2009).

The Court receives approximately 8,000 petitions each year and normally only grants between 80 and 140. Of those granted, generally about 15 pertain to criminal justice issues. A denial of certiorari does not mean that the Court believes that the lower court or state court of last resort correctly decided the case. It only means that the Court did not wish to address the issue presented in the case.

**LAW IN ACTION**

**Popular Myths about the U.S. Supreme Court**

According to Edward Lazarus (2009), some of the conventional wisdom about the U.S. Supreme Court is wrong. To justify his opinion, he discusses the following myth:

*Myth:* Justices often surprise the presidents who appoint them.

*Fact:* Lazarus claims that while a few appointees have not met the expectations of the president that appointed them, it is only a few. According to him, history shows that justices tend to perform very much as they might have been expected to perform. If some justices seem to undergo a shift during the several decades the justices serve, it is usually because the court's ideological balance changes around them. Often, Justice David Souter is pointed out as a justice who did not meet the conservative expectations of his appointer, President George H.W. Bush. Lazarus points out that this should not have been a surprise because Souter's brand of moderate New England Republicanism was at odds with the pro-states'-rights, pro-prayer-in-school, pro-life, anti-affirmative-action views that make for a judicial conservative on the modern court.

*Myth:* The most influential justices are consensus builders.

*Fact:* According to Lazarus, it is only a very few justices who have been able to use their political skills to build bridges and meaningfully influence a court decision. He cites Chief Justice Earl Warren as one of the few exceptions. According to Lazarus generally the most influential justices attain their power not based on their consensus building abilities, but because of simple arithmetic that five votes beat four. He uses the 2008-2009 Supreme Court as an example in which the most powerful justice was Anthony Kennedy because he was the swing vote on most split decisions.

*Myth:* Supreme Court Justices are umpires.

*Fact:* Lazarus contends that they are not umpires. Since there is no rule book for the application of the constitution to fact situations, the justices make subjective judgments that are influenced by their individual views about right and wrong.

## Court of Limited Jurisdiction

> The power to review cases from both state and federal courts gives the Supreme Court a unique position in the American judicial firmament (Meador 2000, 25).

Although decisions by the U.S. Supreme Court are the "supreme law of law of the land," the Court is considered as a court of limited jurisdiction. For the most part, the Supreme Court reviews a case only after a state court of last resort or a federal court of appeals have rendered an opinion. The Court does have the authority to issue a writ of certiorari before the lower court has reached a decision, this authority is rarely used. As noted earlier in this chapter, the Supreme Court has original jurisdiction in only a few areas. Original jurisdiction refers to the court in which the action is initiated. The Supreme Court has jurisdiction [power] to review all decisions of federal appellate courts. It also has jurisdiction to review state court decisions on matters involving federal issues, for example, whether the defendant's conviction violated his or her right under the U.S. Constitution. State courts of last resort, generally the state supreme courts, have final authority on state issues that do not involve a federal question. For example, a question of whether or not police conduct violated the accused rights under the U.S. Constitution would involve a federal issue, but if the question was whether or not the conduct violated only a state constitution the state court would have final authority. As stated by Meador: "The Supreme Court's jurisdiction over state courts is confined to reviewing decisions of the highest court of a state involving a controlling question of federal law" (Meador 2000, 27).

The Supreme Court also has jurisdiction to accept a petition for an "extraordinary writ" such as mandamus, prohibition, or habeas corpus. The extraordinary writs are rarely granted by the Supreme Court, but are more frequently granted by lower courts. Often the Court will review a lower court's ruling on an extraordinary writ (Bashman 2009).

## Court Procedures

If the Court grants a writ, the case is then scheduled for hearing and briefs are required to be filed by opposing parties. The briefs provide each party's statement of facts, view of the law as applied to the facts, and written argument as to why the party should prevail in the case. After briefs are submitted and oral argument is presented, the Court hands down a written opinion.

The Court starts a new term the First Monday in October each year and generally concludes the term in August. The Court hears oral argument on Mondays, Tuesdays, and Wednesdays in seven two-week sessions during October to April. Generally, conferences are held on Wednesday afternoon and Fridays. Opinions are generally announced and issued on Mondays.

After oral arguments, the justices vote. Often several rounds of voting take place because justices may change their votes during the decision making process, often turning a minority into a majority and vice versa. The first vote on a case is taken during the week of oral arguments. For cases heard on Monday, the justices vote on it on Wednesday afternoon. For oral arguments heard on Tuesday and Wednesday, the justices vote on Friday. After the vote, the most senior justice in the majority assigns the task of writing the majority opinion to one of the justices voting in the majority. If the decision is not unanimous, the senior justice in the minority assigns a member of the minority to write the dissenting opinion. Often individual justices will write his or her individual opinion either concurring in the majority or dissenting opinion. The majority opinion speaks, however, as the final decision of the court.

## COURTS IN ACTION

### Frequently Asked Questions Regarding Federal Judges and Federal Courts

*Source*: http://www.uscourts.gov/Common/FAQS.aspx accessed August 8, 2010

### Q: Who appoints federal judges?

Supreme Court justices, court of appeals judges, and district court judges are nominated by the President and confirmed by the United States Senate, as stated in the Constitution. The names of potential nominees are often recommended by senators or sometimes by members of the House who are of the President's political party. The Senate Judiciary Committee typically conducts confirmation hearings for each nominee. Article III of the Constitution states that these judicial officers are appointed for a life term. The federal Judiciary, the Judicial Conference of the United States, and the Administrative Office of the U.S. Courts play no role in the nomination and confirmation process.

**Q: What are the qualifications for becoming a federal judge?**

The Constitution sets forth no specific requirements. However, members of Congress, who typically recommend potential nominees, and the Department of Justice, which reviews nominees' qualifications, have developed their own informal criteria.

**Q: How is a chief judge selected?**

One is not nominated or appointed to the position of chief judge (**except for the Chief Justice of the United States**); they assume the position based on seniority. The same criteria exist for circuit and district chiefs. The chief judge is the judge in regular active service that is senior in commission of those judges who are (1) 64 years of age or under; (2) have served for one year or more as a judge; and (3) have not previously served as chief judge.

**Q: What is a senior judge?**

The "Rule of 80" is the commonly used shorthand for the age and service requirement for a judge to assume senior status, as set forth in Title 28 of the U.S. Code, Section 371(c). Beginning at age 65, a judge may retire at his or her current salary or take senior status after performing 15 years of active service as an Article III judge (65 + 15 = 80). A sliding scale of increasing age and decreasing service results in eligibility for retirement compensation at age 70 with a minimum of 10 years of service (70 + 10 = 80). Senior judges, who essentially provide volunteer service to the courts, typically handle about 15 percent of the federal courts' workload annually.

**Q: What are federal magistrate judges?**

A U.S. magistrate judge is a judicial officer of the district court and is appointed by majority vote of the active district judges of the court to exercise jurisdiction over matters assigned by statute as well as those delegated by the district judges. The number of magistrate judge positions is determined by the Judicial Conference of the United States, based on recommendations of the respective district courts, the judicial councils of the circuits, and the Director of the Administrative Office of the U.S. Courts. A full-time magistrate judge serves a term of eight years. Duties assigned to magistrate judges by district court judges may vary considerably from court to court.

**Q: How are new judgeships created?**

Court of appeals and district court judgeships are created by legislation that must be enacted by Congress. The Judicial Conference (through its Judicial Resources Committee) surveys the judgeship needs of the courts every other year. A threshold for the number of weighted filings per judgeship is the key factor in determining when an additional judgeship will be requested. Other factors may include geography, number of senior judges, and mix of cases. The Judicial Conference presents its judgeship recommendations to Congress.

**Q: How many courts of appeals are there?**

There are 13 judicial circuits, each with a court of appeals. The smallest court is the First Circuit with six judgeships, and the largest court is the Ninth Circuit, with 28 judgeships. A list of the states that compose each circuit is set forth in Title 28 of the U.S. Code, Section 41. The number of judgeships in each circuit is set forth in Title 28 of the U.S. Code, Section 44.

**Q: How many district courts are there?**

There are 89 districts in the 50 states, which are listed with their divisions in Title 28 of the U.S. Code, Sections 81–144. District courts also exist in Puerto Rico, the Virgin Islands, the District of Columbia, Guam, and the Northern Mariana Islands. In total there are 94 U.S. district courts. Some states, such as Alaska, are composed of a single judicial district. Others, such as California, are composed of multiple judicial districts. The number of judgeships allotted to each district is set forth in Title 28 of the U.S. Code, Section 133.

**Q: How do I file a criminal case?**

Individuals do not file criminal charges in U.S. district courts. A criminal proceeding is initiated by the government, usually through the U.S. attorney's office in coordination with a law enforcement agency. Allegations of criminal behavior should be brought to local police, the FBI, or other appropriate law enforcement agency.

### Q: How are judges assigned to cases?

Judge assignment methods vary. The basic considerations in making assignments are to assure equitable distribution of caseloads and avoid judge shopping. By statute, the chief judge of each district court has the responsibility to enforce the court's rules and orders on case assignments. Each court has a written plan or system for assigning cases. The majority of courts use some variation of a random drawing. One simple method is to rotate the names of available judges. At times judges having special expertise can be assigned cases by type, such as complex criminal cases, asbestos-related cases, or prisoner cases. The benefit of this system is that it takes advantage of the expertise developed by judges in certain areas. Sometimes cases may be assigned based on geographical considerations. For example, in a large geographical area it may be best to assign a case to a judge located at the site where the case was filed. Courts also have a system to check if there is any conflict that would make it improper for a judge to preside over a particular case.

### Q: How do I file a complaint against a judge?

The complaint process is not intended to address complaints related to the merits of a case or a court's decision. Any person alleging that a judge of the United States has engaged in conduct prejudicial to the effective and expeditious administration of the business of the courts, or that such officer cannot discharge all the duties of the office because of physical or mental disability, may file a complaint with the clerk of the court of appeals for that circuit or applicable national court. The statute governing this complaint mechanism is set out at Title 28, U.S. Code, Section 351(a). Each circuit court of appeals web site has information about how to file a complaint in that circuit.

### Q: How are jurors contacted for service in federal court?

Before potential jurors are summoned for service, their names are randomly drawn from voters lists (and sometimes drivers lists) to receive a questionnaire to determine whether they meet the legal qualifications for jury service. Individuals who receive questionnaires are required to complete and return them to the clerk's office, which then screens the completed questionnaires to determine eligibility for jury service. (In some courts, qualification questionnaires and summonses are mailed together.)

### Q: Must I respond to my jury duty notice?

Yes, it is legally required, and there are penalties for noncompliance. Jurors perform a vital role in the American system of justice. Jury service is an important civic function that supports one of the fundamental rights of citizens the right to have their cases decided by a jury of their peers.

### Q: Who may serve as a juror?

The Jury Act, which is set out at Title 28, U.S. Code, Sections 1861–1878, calls for random selection of citizens' names from voters lists or combined voters and drivers lists. (Because random selection is required, individuals may not volunteer for service.)

The act states that individuals are legally disqualified from service:

- if they are not a citizen of the United States 18 years old, who has resided for a period of one year within the judicial district;
- if they are unable to read, write, and understand the English language with a degree of proficiency necessary to fill out a qualification form;
- if they are unable to speak the English language;
- if they are incapable by reason of mental or physical infirmity to render jury service; or
- if they have felony charges pending against them or they have been convicted of a felony and their civil rights have not been restored.

In addition, the Jury Act lists three groups that are exempt from federal jury service:

- members of the armed forces on active duty;
- members of professional fire and police departments; and

- "public officers" of federal, state or local governments, who are actively engaged in the performance of public duties.

**Q: Will I be paid for jury service?**

Yes, federal jurors are paid $40 a day. (Employees of the federal government are paid their regular salary in lieu of this fee.) In most courts, jurors also are reimbursed for reasonable transportation expenses and parking fees.

Your employer may continue your salary during all or part of your jury service, but is not required to do so. Nonetheless, the Jury Act forbids any employer from firing, intimidating, or coercing any permanent employee because of their federal jury service.

**Q: What if the distance to the courthouse is too far or too difficult for me to travel?**

The Jury Act allows courts to permanently excuse a juror from service at the time he or she is summoned on the grounds of "undue hardship or extreme inconvenience" if the distance to the courthouse makes it difficult for the juror to travel. The juror should write a letter to the chief judge of the court requesting an excuse with an explanation of hardship. As with temporary deferrals, whether to grant an excuse is a matter of discretion for the court and cannot be reviewed or appealed to Congress or any other entity.

**Q: What if the dates of my jury service conflict with my work or vacation schedule?**

The Jury Act allows courts to grant temporary deferrals of service on the grounds of "undue hardship or extreme inconvenience." The qualification questionnaire and juror summons provides specific information on how to request a deferral from your individual court. Whether to grant a deferral is a matter of discretion for the court and cannot be reviewed or appealed to Congress or any other entity.

**Q: Why have some people never been called for jury duty?**

Eligibility for federal jury service is dependent both upon an individual meeting the legal qualifications for service and upon the random chance of having one's name drawn from the source lists.

Each judicial district must have a formal written plan for the selection of jurors, which provides for random selection from a fair cross-section of the community in the district, and which prohibits discrimination in the selection process. Voter records either voter registration lists or lists of actual voters are the required source of names for federal court juries. Some courts supplement voter lists with other sources, such as lists of licensed drivers. A copy of a district's jury plan is available for review in the clerk's office.

In addition, many courts offer excuses from service, on individual request, to designated groups of persons or occupational classes. Such groups may include persons over age 70; persons who have, within the past two years, served on a federal jury; and persons who serve as volunteer fire fighters or members of a rescue squad or ambulance crew.

## Questions in Review

1. What were some of the issues involved in creating a federal court system?
2. What are the functions of a U.S. magistrate judge?
3. Define "jurisdiction."
4. Why aren't U.S. magistrate judges considered to be Article III judges?
5. How is evidence presented in district court?
6. How is a jury instructed about "reasonable doubt?"
7. What is the process of sentencing a criminal defendant in federal court?
8. Where is the circuit court of appeal located for your state?
9. Why do circuit courts of appeal more broadly influence the body of law than the Supreme Court of the Untied States?
10. What are jury instructions?
11. Generally how are cases brought before the Supreme Court?
12. What does a writ of certiorari command of a lower court?
13. Why is the U.S. Supreme Court considered as a court of limited jurisdiction?

# References

## COURT CASES

*Berger v. United States*, 295 U.S. 78, 88 (1935) overruled on other grounds by Stirone v. United States, 361 U.S. 212 (1960).

*Jecker v. Montgomery* (1852) 54 U.S. 498, 13 How 498, 14 L Ed 240.

*Marbury v. Madison*, 5 U.S. 137 (U.S. 1803)

*Peretz v. United States*, 501 U.S. 923 (U.S. 1991)

*United States v. Burton*, 871 F.2d 1566 (11th Cir. 1989)

## STATUTES

Federal Court of Appeals act of 1891 (Act March 3, 1891, c. 517, 26 Stat. 828 [U.S. Comp. St. 1901, p. 550])

Federal Judiciary Act of 1789, 28 U.S.C.S. § 725

Federal Judiciary Act of 1801; 2 Stat. 89

Federal Judiciary Act of 1891; 26 Stat. 826, also known as the Evarts Act after its primary sponsor, Senator William M. Evarts.

Federal Judges' Bill of 1925: "An Act to amend the Judicial Code, and to further define the jurisdiction of the circuit courts of appeals and of the Supreme Court, and for other purposes." 43 Stat. 936

Federal Magistrates Act: 28 U.S. Code § 636

## JUDICIAL RULES

*Eleventh Circuit Pattern Jury Instructions (Criminal Cases) 2003.* www.ca11.uscourts.gov/documents/jury/crimjury.pdf (accessed April 12, 2009)

Federal Rules of Evidence

## SECONDARY REFERENCES

*2008 Year-End Report on the Federal Judiciary.* www.supremecourtus.gov/publicinfo/year-end/2008year-endreport.pdf (accessed June 13, 2009).

Bashman, Howard J. *Demystifying the U.S. Supreme Court's Cert Granted Process.* 2009. www.law.com/jsp/article.jsp?id=1192179811865 (accessed on April 2, 2009).

Cross, Frank B. *Decision Making in the U.S. Courts of Appeals.* Stanford University Press, 2007.

Dorsen, Norman. "The selection of U.S. Supreme Court justices." *International Journal of Constitutional Law* 4 no. 4 (October 2008): 652–663.

Federal Magistrates' Association. http://www.fedjudge.org/ (accessed March 29, 2009).

Irons, Peter. *A People's History of the Supreme Court*, rev. ed. New York: Penguin Books, 2006.

Harrell, Mary Ann, and Burnett Anderson. *Equal Justice Under Law: The Supreme Court in American Life*, rev. ed. Washington, DC: National Geographic Society, 1982.

Hall, Kermit L. *The Oxford Companion to the Supreme Court of the United States*. Oxford, GB: Oxford University Press, 1992.

Lazarus, Edward. "Four Myths about the Supreme Court." *Time Magazine* (June 8, 2009): 30–32.

Meador, Daniel John. *American Courts*, 2nd ed. St. Paul, MN: West, (2000).

Richardson, Richard and Kenneth Vines. *The Politics of Federal Courts*. Boston: Little, Brown, 1970.

The Third Branch. "A Look at the Duties of a U.S. Magistrate Judge." *Newsletter of the Federal Courts* 40 no. 10, October 2008. (accessed on March 31, 2009 at www.uscourts.gov/ttb/2008-10/article02_3.cfm).

# 5

# State and Commonwealth Courts

**What you need to know about State and Commonwealth Courts**

After you have completed this chapter, you should know:

- Most criminal trials are tried in state criminal courts.
- Most states have trial courts, intermediate appellate courts, and a court of last resort.
- Most state court judges are elected.
- The courts of limited jurisdiction try most criminal cases.
- All but two states criminal courts are based on English common law.
- The major trial courts handle serious criminal crimes.
- In order for an individual to be tried by a state court for a criminal offense, the defendant must be charged with a violation of that state's criminal code.
- As a general rule, states adjudicate state issues and the federal courts adjudicate federal issues.
- The colonial courts were strongly influence by their religious beliefs.
- There are about 1,400 courts of limited jurisdiction in states. They are generally called municipal, county, city, or justice courts.
- Because the number of traffic, petty, and misdemeanor cases far outnumber serious criminal cases, the lower courts constitute the first and, in most instances, the only contact that most citizens have with our criminal court system.
- Limited jurisdiction courts vary across the United States and often within a single state.
- In criminal cases tried before limited jurisdiction courts, the appeals are to the state's major trial courts.
- In most states, if the criminal case is appealed from a lower court, the case is tried "de novo" in the major trial court.
- The office of the justice of peace was copied from the English.
- Today, in many states the justice of the peace is a judge of a court of limited jurisdiction. In other states the justice of peace has been replaced by a magistrate, or a quasi-judicial official with certain statutory judicial powers.
- The major trial courts are more formal in their proceedings than the lower courts. They are courts of record in that a formal record is made of their proceedings and most of the proceedings are recorded verbatim.
- There is no requirement in the U.S. Constitution for an appellate court system. Almost every legal system, however, has developed procedures to address grievances about initial judicial determinations.

■ State courts of last resort (COLRs) are the final decision makers for matters involving the interpretations of state law not involving a federal issue.

■ The court reform movement, initiated early in the twentieth century, was aimed at reducing the fragmentation and disparity inherent in many state court systems.

**Chapter Outline**
■ Introduction
■ Jurisdiction of State Courts
■ History of State Courts
■ National Center for State Courts
■ Courts of Limited Jurisdiction
■ Major Trial Courts
■ Intermediate State Courts of Appeals
■ Court Reform Movements
■ Questions in Review

## INTRODUCTION

> Justice, though due to the accused, is due to the accuser also. The concept of fairness must not be strained till it is narrowed to a filament. We are to keep the balance true.
> —Justice Cardozo in *Snyder v. Massachusetts*, 291 U.S. 97 (1934)

In this chapter, state and commonwealth courts are examined. For purpose of economy of words, the phrase "state courts" will include the commonwealth courts in those states like Kentucky, Virginia, and Pennsylvania who use the term "commonwealth" to describe their courts and the courts in the District of Columbia, Virgin Islands, and Puerto Rico, which handle local issues. In Chapter 4, federal courts were examined. While all federal courts are considered as courts of limited jurisdiction because of the U.S. Constitution, the major state trial courts are considered as courts of general jurisdiction. This distinction will be explored later in this chapter.

Most criminal trials are conducted in state courts. It is estimated that 95 percent of the criminal trials each year in the United States take place in state courts. For example, there are at least four counties in the United States in which the state courts in each county try more criminal cases than are tried in the entire federal system. Those counties include Cook County, Illinois (Chicago); Los Angeles County, California; New York County, New York; and Harris County, (Houston) Texas. For example, the Superior Courts of Los Angeles County California provide services to over 9.5 million residents who live and work throughout the 4,080 square miles of Los Angeles County.

While no two state court systems are exactly alike, there are striking similarities. Most states have a three-tiered court system with courts of limited jurisdiction, general jurisdiction, and appellate courts. The major trial courts in the states have general trial jurisdiction. It is in the major trial courts that serious crimes are tried. Jurisdictional levels of state courts vary widely, but each state uses some or all of the following four jurisdictional levels.

- *Courts of last resort (COLR)*—Courts with final authority over all appeals. These courts exercise both mandatory and discretionary review.
- *Intermediate appellate courts*—Courts that hear appeals from general jurisdiction and limited jurisdiction trial courts as well as administrative agencies. These courts exercise both mandatory and discretionary review, depending on the state.

**COURTS IN ACTION**

**Crime in the United States**

**Felony Defendants**

- In the nation's 75 largest counties, an estimated 58,100 defendants were charged with a felony offense in 2006.
- More than three-fourths of felony defendants had a prior arrest history, with 69% having multiple prior arrests.
- Fifty-eight percent of felony defendants in the nation's 75 largest counties were released prior to adjudication and about a third of the released defendants committed some form of pretrial misconduct.
- About two-thirds of felony defendants were eventually convicted and more than 95% of these convictions occurred through a guilty plea.
- Seventy percent of defendants convicted were incarcerated in a state prison or local jail.

**Felony Convictions**

- State and federal courts convicted a combined total of nearly 1,145,000 adults of felonies in 2004. Of these felony convictions, an estimated 1,079,000 adults were convicted in state courts and 66,518 were convicted in federal courts, accounting for 6% of the national total.
- In 2004, 70% of all felons convicted in state courts were sentenced to a period of confinement in a state prison (40%) or a local jail (30%). Jail sentences are short-term confinement (usually less than 1 year) in a county or city facility. Prison sentences are long-term confinement (usually 1 year or more) in a state facility.
- Prison sentences handed down by state courts in 2004 averaged almost 5 years.

Source: U.S. Bureau of Statistics web site: http://bjs.ojp.usdoj.gov/index.cfm?ty=tp&tid=22 accessed on August 12, 2010

- *General jurisdiction trial courts*—Major trial courts hearing serious criminal or civil cases. Cases are designated to general jurisdiction courts based on the severity of punishment or the allegation/dollar value of the case.
- *Limited jurisdiction trial courts*—Trial courts with primary jurisdiction over lesser criminal and civil manners, including misdemeanors, small claims, traffic, parking, and infractions. These courts can also handle the preliminary stages of felony cases.

## JURISDICTION OF STATE COURTS

In order for an individual to be tried by a state court for a criminal offense, the defendant must be charged with a violation of that state's criminal code. While we may use the term common law crimes, in all states to be a crime the act must be prohibited by a statute, code, ordinance, or other binding rule.

Often the same criminal conduct constitutes crimes in more than one state. For example, in *Simpson v. State* (1893), the defendant shot at the victim from a riverbank in the State of South Carolina. Savannah River is the boundary between the two states and at the point where the act occurred, the river was only 75 yards wide. The victim was in a boat upon the river, within the State of Georgia. Defendant Simpson was convicted assault with intent to murder. His motion for a new trial was denied. The court held that although the victim was not injured, the balls shot from defendant's gun struck the river in close proximity to him,

## COURTS IN ACTION

### Victims of Crime

The National Criminal Victimization Survey (NCVS) collects information from victims on nonfatal violent and property crimes, reported and not reported to the police, against persons age 12 or older from a nationally representative sample of U.S. households. It produces national rates and levels of personal and property victimization.

- In 2008, U.S. residents age 12 or older experienced approximately 21 million crimes, according to findings from the National Crime Victimization Survey.
  - o 77% (16.3 million) were property crimes
  - o 23% (4.9 million) were crimes of violence
  - o 1% (136,700) were personal thefts
- In 2008, for every 1,000 persons age 12 or older, there occurred
  - o 1 rape or sexual assault
  - o 2 robberies
  - o 3 aggravated assaults
  - o 13 simple assaults.
- Murders were the least frequent violent victimization—about 6 murder victims per 100,000 persons in 2007.

and therefore it was certain that they took effect in Georgia. The court held that a crime was committed in the place where defendant's criminal act took effect. Hence, he was liable to punishment in Georgia, even though he was in another state when he fired his gun. Consequently, if one shooting from another state is considered to have committed an act in the other, in a legal sense, where his bullet went, the fact that he missed the person at which he aimed would not alter the legal principle. This would be considered constructive presence in the state where the bullet struck. Whether the attempt was successful or not, the crime was perpetrated in Georgia. In addition, the shooter probably committed a crime in South Carolina by discharging a weapon in that state with the intent to hit someone.

In another case, Robert Thomas was deputy sheriff in Dade County Florida. He appealed his conviction of first degree murder in a Commonwealth of Pennsylvania arguing that the trial court lacked jurisdiction to try him for murder even though the felony murder took place in Pennsylvania because the proof of the commonwealth was that a conspiracy which resulted in the felony murder was formed and plotted entirely outside the Commonwealth of Pennsylvania. The court ruled that when one put in force an agency for the commission of crime, he, in legal contemplation, accompanied the same to the point where it became effectual. Further, the court held that one did not have to be physically present in a state to be guilty of a criminal offense there. Also, the court found that acts done outside a jurisdiction, but intended to produce and producing detrimental effects within it, justified a state in punishing the cause of the harm as if he was present at the effect, if the state should succeed in getting him within its power. The court affirmed the judgment, concluding that criminal responsibility attached to defendant even though he was not physically present in the Commonwealth when the crime occurred.

A classic example used in law schools involves the scenario where an ex-husband lived in New York. His ex-wife lived in the State of New Jersey. The ex-husband takes a vacation in Las Vegas. There he purchases poison and inserts it into some candy. He then mails the candy from Nevada to his ex-wife in New Jersey. At the time, the ex-wife has taken an extended vacation in Florida. The candy received in New Jersey and forwarded to Florida where the ex-wife's husband died from eating the candy. In this convoluted fact situation, the ex-husband committed a federal crime by putting the poisoned candy in the U.S. Mails, a crime in the State of Nevada by sending the poisonous candy to New Jersey, a crime in New Jersey when the candy arrived in New Jersey, and finally the murder in Florida where the new husband died.

## Subject Matter Jurisdiction

As noted earlier, there are separate state and federal court systems. As a general rule, states adjudicate state issues and the federal courts adjudicate federal issues. Criminal statutes enacted by the U.S. Congress are known as federal criminal laws and are enforced by federal officers. Criminal laws passed by the state legislatures are generally enforced by city police departments or sheriffs and their deputies, and are assisted by state officers where they have the authority to do so. Although most of the criminal laws within a state are state enacted, the violators are generally prosecuted in the county court or local system, since that is where the trial courts are located.

When a crime is committed, the violator may have broken either a federal law or a state law, depending upon the act. For example, a person may rob a liquor store, an act that would be a violation of a state statute, since all states have laws making robbery a crime. If a person, however, violated the federal Sherman Antitrust Law, the violation would be a federal violation.

It is possible for a person to commit both a federal and a state violation with a series of acts arising out of a sequence of events. For example, a person may steal an automobile in one state and transport it to another state. Such an individual could be prosecuted in the local courts for the theft of the vehicle and prosecuted in the federal courts because it is a federal crime to transport a vehicle from one state to another knowing that it has been stolen. In this example, the offender has actually committed two violations as a result of two different acts—one being the theft and the other the transportation of the vehicle while knowing that it has been stolen. He or she may have committed a violation in the state in which the vehicle was transported. In these examples, each state or federal court system has its own trial jurisdiction exclusive of the other.

As noted earlier, it is possible for an individual to violate both a federal and a state law by the same act. For example, an individual may kill a federal officer, thereby violating a federal statute, and the killing if it was within a state would be a violation of the state homicide statute. Under these circumstances, concurrent jurisdiction would exist. The question then would be whether the accused could be prosecuted in both the federal and the state courts. Where an act violates both federal and state statutes, the federal government can always take jurisdiction and prosecute the violation. In some states, like California, if the federal government prosecutes, the state prosecutor is barred by state statute from prosecuting for the same criminal act. Although most crimes committed on government reservations are also local or state violations, the federal courts may have exclusive jurisdiction to try those matters because they were committed on government reservations. It should be pointed out that government reservations with exclusive jurisdiction are comparatively few in number. In order for a territorial area to be a government reservation, the land must have always been U.S. property, with the title still retained by the United States, or property acquired from a state for which all right and title was relinquished. Most military installations and national parks are government reservations; most post offices are not. Scattered throughout the United States are many national forests, but most of these are not government reservations, so that any crimes committed in these forests are within the jurisdiction of the local courts. However, any theft of the trees from these forests is a theft of government property, which would be a federal violation.

## Koon v. United States

The *Koon v. United States* case (1996) involves a situation where both the state and federal courts tried several Los Angeles police officers for criminal acts. In this situation, the officers were acquitted in state court and were convicted in federal court. In federal court, they were tried for violation of federal law and in state court for violation of California law.

On the evening of March 2, 1991, Rodney King and two of his friends sat in King's wife's car in Altadena, California, a city in Los Angeles County, and drank malt liquor for a number of hours. Then, with King driving, they left Altadena via a major freeway. King was intoxicated.

California Highway Patrol officers observed King's car traveling at a speed they estimated to be in excess of 100 mph. The officers followed King with red lights and sirens activated and ordered him by loudspeaker to pull over, but he continued to drive. The highway patrol officers called on the radio for help. Units of the Los Angeles Police Department joined in the pursuit, one of them manned by Officer Laurence Powell and his trainee, Timothy Wind.

King left the freeway, and after a chase of about eight miles, stopped at an entrance to a recreation area. The officers ordered King and his two passengers to exit the car and to assume a felony prone position—that is, to lie on their stomachs with legs spread and arms behind their backs. King's two friends complied. King, too, got out of the car but did not lie down. Officer Stacey Koon arrived, at once followed by Officers Ted Briseno and Roland Solano. All were officers of the Los Angeles Police Department, and as sergeant, Koon took charge. The officers again ordered King to assume the felony prone position. King got on his hands and knees but did not lie down. Officers Powell, Wind, Briseno, and Solano tried to force King down, but King resisted and became combative, so the officers

retreated. Koon then fired taser darts (designed to stun a combative suspect) into King.

The events that occurred next were captured on videotape by a bystander. As the videotape begins, it shows that King rose from the ground and charged toward Officer Powell. Powell took a step and used his baton to strike King on the side of his head. King fell to the ground. From the eighteenth to the thirtieth second on the videotape, King attempted to rise, but Powell and Wind each struck him with their batons to prevent him from doing so. From the thirty-fifth to the fifty-first second, Powell administered repeated blows to King's lower extremities; one of the blows fractured King's leg. At the fifty-fifth second, Powell struck King on the chest, and King rolled over and lay prone. At that point, the officers stepped back and observed King for about ten seconds. Powell began to reach for his handcuffs.

At one-minute-five-seconds (1:05) on the videotape, Briseno, in the District Court's words, "stomped" on King's upper back or neck. King's body writhed in response. At 1:07, Powell and Wind again began to strike King with a series of baton blows, and Wind kicked him in the upper thoracic or cervical area six times until 1:26. At about 1:29, King put his hands behind his back and was handcuffed.

Officers Stacey C. Koon and Laurence M. Powell were acquitted on state charges of assault and excessive use of force in the beating of a Rodney King, a suspect during an arrest. After the acquittal in state court of violating the state laws, they were convicted in federal district court under 18 U.S.C. § 242 for violating King's constitutional rights under color of law. The protection against double jeopardy did not apply to the officers because they were tried for different offenses in different jurisdictions, that is, California and federal.

## HISTORY OF STATE COURTS

Kent's *Commentaries on American Law* (1830) was the first general legal treatise based exclusively on the common law of the United States. James Kent was Chancellor of New York and Chief Justice of the New York Supreme Court.

—O'Hara 2009

Most prosecutions in colonial courts were for moral offenses.

—Lamm 2002, 532

With the exception of the State of Louisiana and Puerto Rico, the state courts are based on English common law concepts as they existed when the various colonies were founded. Because Louisiana was settled by the French and Puerto Rico was settled by the Spanish, these two states are organized under the civil law model that exists in most countries in continental Europe including Spain and France. When the new nation was founded and became the United States of America, the original states adapted the system that was being used at the time in the colonies and in England (Glick and Vines 1973).

According to Hall (2002), the colonial lawmakers and colonial judges shared two key assumptions with their English counterparts. The first was that there was no clear dividing line between sin and crime. The pious person was a law abiding person and the sinner was a criminal. Many of the colonial prosecutions were for drunkenness, fornication, and failure to attend church. The second key assumption was that sinful misconduct led to more serious criminal misconduct.

As noted by Alan Rogers, the colonial courts were strongly influence by their religious beliefs. For example Rogers (2008, 2) stated:

> Justice in Massachusetts in the seventeenth century was shaped by two Puritan beliefs—**magistrates** ruled in the name of God and residents of the community held common moral values—and was tempered by the reality that because men and women were inherently imperfect they sometimes permitted their passions to lead them to commit murder.

The colonial courts replicated the English courts, but the complicated and sophisticated procedures that existed in the English courts were not well suited for the needs of the colonists who were trying to survive in the new world. In both England and in the colonies, the criminal courts had the dual function of keeping peace and determining guilt or innocence. When there was civil unrest, the courts in both England and the colonies used the criminal justice system to suppress dissent. During those times, the determination of guilt or innocence was secondary to the goal of defending the interests of the existing governments (Hall, 2002).

The colonial courts quickly modified and simplified many of their procedures to better fit the needs of the people living in the colonies. For example, in the seventeenth century, the English courts were focused on controlling the surplus of wandering poor. In the colonies, however, the labor supply was scarce and the courts could not afford to limit the labor force. Both the English and the colonial courts tended to define crimes as felonies and misdemeanors. Generally, in England, the punishment for felonies, being a serious crime, was death. The punishment in the colonies was less severe. In the colonies, murderers were generally hanged while those convicted of lesser crimes were shamed, fined, sold into forced labor, whipped, or incarcerated for short terms (Hall 2002).

In England, the criminal trial was more straightforward. Defendant's life generally depended on his or her influencing a judge or a jury that he or she was not guilty. In the colonies, petty offenses were generally summarily tried before only a judge. Defendants in colonial courts were required to pay jury costs if they were found guilty. In cases of serious crimes, colonial juries tended to play a greater role in the trial than the English juries. Pleas bargaining appeared play an important rule even in the colonial area. The process of determining guilt or innocence in the colonial trial often was influenced by the status of the defendant or victim. In the colonial courts, defendants in criminal cases had fewer rights and court decisions were generally quicker than in present-day criminal trials. Prior to the eighteenth century, lawyers rarely appeared in criminal courts on behalf of defendants (Nelson 1979).

As the towns and villages grew, so did the justice system. The colonial courts were not as elaborate as those of England and the judges were less well trained. Unlike the English courts, the pleadings in the colonial courts were in English and not Latin. A larger proportion of the colonial male adult population participated in the operation of the local courts than was the case in England. The lowest-level court in the colonies was the justice of peace (JP). The JP handled petty offenses and minor disputes. While a JP was not required to keep records of the court proceedings, many did. The personal records that survived indicate that the JPs relied on a system of fines and bonds that bound defendants to obey the law and keep peace. Often the defendant was required to post a surety or bond that would be forfeit if the defendant repeated the offense (Hall 2002).

It was also during the colonial period that the concept of separation of power emerged and was drafted into the federal and state constitutions. State governments, like the federal government, each consist of three sections: the legislative branch to make laws, the executive branch to carry out the laws, and the judicial branch to resolve legal disputes and administer justice. The three branches of government, however, did not develop equally after the U.S. Constitution was adopted in 1787. The judicial branches, including criminal courts, were the last parts of the government to develop (Carp and Stidham 2001).

After the Declaration of Independence, the structure and procedures in state courts were influenced differently by economic interests, the debate over state versus national power, and political partisanship. Despite the common starting place, the state courts quickly changed to meet the individual needs of the states. As noted by Glick and Vines, diversity was the hallmark of the colonies. Each colony changed the court system according to its variations in local conditions and customs. Many of the differences that emerged during the early days still exist today in our various state courts (Glick and Vines 1973).

Currently, most county or judicial districts have at least one **court of general jurisdiction**. In most states it is a superior or district court consisting of one or more judges. The more populated counties may have several superior or district courts. The county clerk is ex-officio clerk of the superior or district court. Superior or district court judges normally serve four- or six-year terms. In most states they are elected. Each county is divided into courts of limited jurisdiction generally called municipal court districts and/or justice court districts as provided by statutes. Usually, if the judicial district has more than the specified number of residents, it will have at least one municipal court. If the district has less than the specified number of residents, it will have a justice court.

## LAW IN ACTION

### Individual Differences Between States

- In two states, Maryland and New York, the Court of Appeals is the highest state court, and in New York the Supreme Court, Civil Court, and Criminal Court collectively are lower courts.
- The States of Delaware, Mississippi, New Jersey, and Tennessee have both "courts of law" and "courts of equity" (chancery courts). While there is a distinction between law and equity lawsuits and some legal consequences as to each, most states do not maintain separate court systems.
- In Texas and Oklahoma, the state supreme courts do not handle criminal cases. Both states use a criminal court of appeals as the court of last resort for criminal cases. In other states, there is a single court of last resort for both criminal and civil matters, but the court may not be named the Supreme Court. Collateral attacks on criminal convictions, such as state-level habeas corpus petitions, are generally considered to be civil cases because they are not brought by a prosecutor and do not seek to convict someone of a crime, these suits are in both Texas and Oklahoma are appealed to the state court of criminal appeals rather than to the state supreme courts.
- The courts of Louisiana and the Commonwealth of Puerto Rico are organized under a civil law model with different procedures from those of the courts in all other states.
- The District of Columbia courts which handle local cases are organized on an American version of the common law system established originally in England.

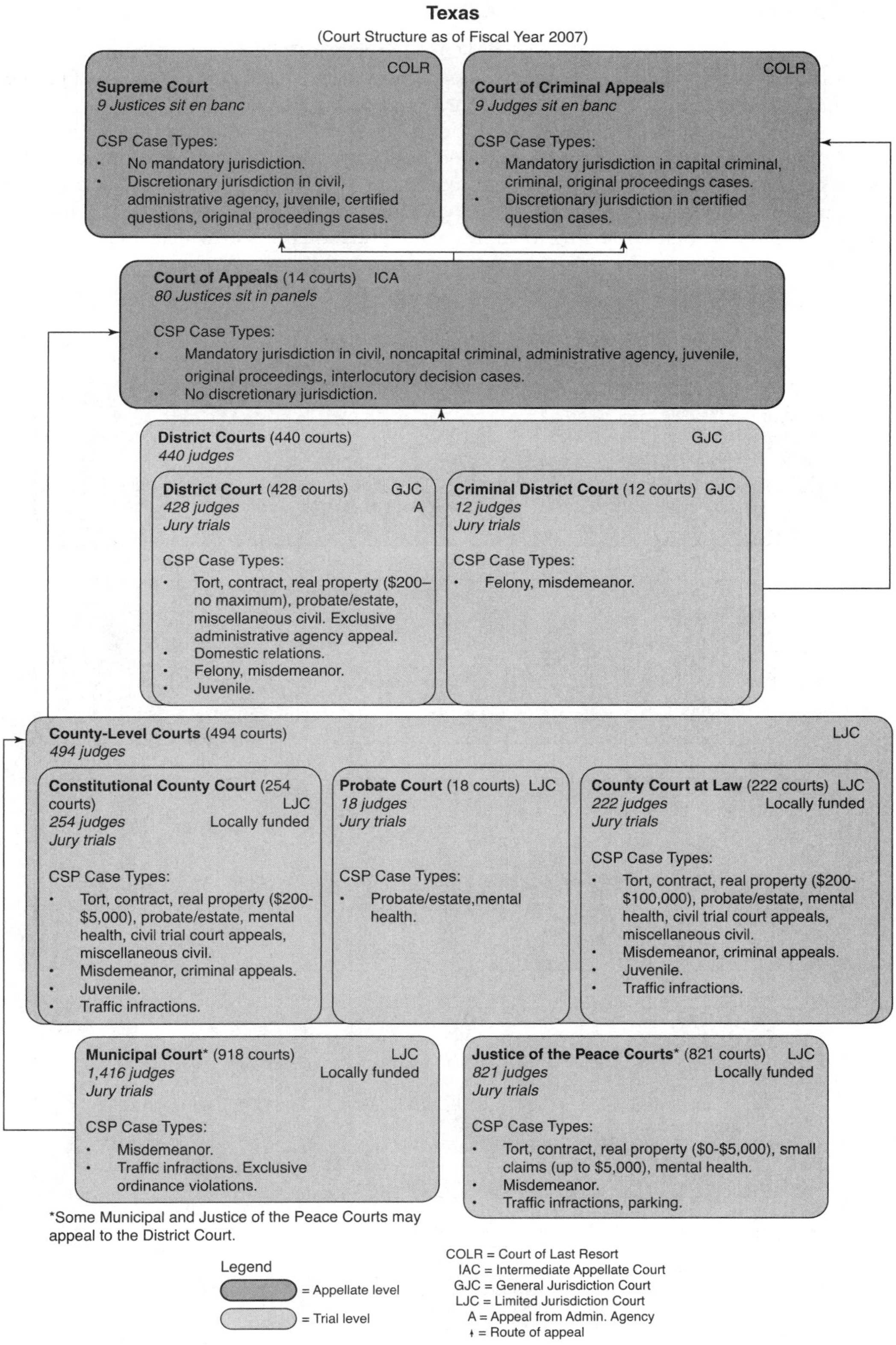

**Texas**
(Court Structure as of Fiscal Year 2007)

**Supreme Court**                                    COLR
*9 Justices sit en banc*

CSP Case Types:
• No mandatory jurisdiction.
• Discretionary jurisdiction in civil, administrative agency, juvenile, certified questions, original proceedings cases.

**Court of Criminal Appeals**                        COLR
*9 Judges sit en banc*

CSP Case Types:
• Mandatory jurisdiction in capital criminal, criminal, original proceedings cases.
• Discretionary jurisdiction in certified question cases.

**Court of Appeals** (14 courts)    ICA
*80 Justices sit in panels*

CSP Case Types:
• Mandatory jurisdiction in civil, noncapital criminal, administrative agency, juvenile, original proceedings, interlocutory decision cases.
• No discretionary jurisdiction.

**District Courts** (440 courts)                     GJC
*440 judges*

**District Court** (428 courts)    GJC
*428 judges*    A
*Jury trials*

CSP Case Types:
• Tort, contract, real property ($200–no maximum), probate/estate, miscellaneous civil. Exclusive administrative agency appeal.
• Domestic relations.
• Felony, misdemeanor.
• Juvenile.

**Criminal District Court** (12 courts)  GJC
*12 judges*
*Jury trials*

CSP Case Types:
• Felony, misdemeanor.

**County-Level Courts** (494 courts)                 LJC
*494 judges*

**Constitutional County Court** (254 courts)    LJC
*254 judges*    Locally funded
*Jury trials*

CSP Case Types:
• Tort, contract, real property ($200-$5,000), probate/estate, mental health, civil trial court appeals, miscellaneous civil.
• Misdemeanor, criminal appeals.
• Juvenile.
• Traffic infractions.

**Probate Court** (18 courts)  LJC
*18 judges*
*Jury trials*

CSP Case Types:
• Probate/estate,mental health.

**County Court at Law** (222 courts)  LJC
*222 judges*    Locally funded
*Jury trials*

CSP Case Types:
• Tort, contract, real property ($200-$100,000), probate/estate, mental health, civil trial court appeals, miscellaneous civil.
• Misdemeanor, criminal appeals.
• Juvenile.
• Traffic infractions.

**Municipal Court*** (918 courts)                    LJC
*1,416 judges*    Locally funded
*Jury trials*

CSP Case Types:
• Misdemeanor.
• Traffic infractions. Exclusive ordinance violations.

**Justice of the Peace Courts*** (821 courts)    LJC
*821 judges*    Locally funded
*Jury trials*

CSP Case Types:
• Tort, contract, real property ($0-$5,000), small claims (up to $5,000), mental health.
• Misdemeanor.
• Traffic infractions, parking.

*Some Municipal and Justice of the Peace Courts may appeal to the District Court.

Legend
 = Appellate level
 = Trial level

COLR = Court of Last Resort
IAC = Intermediate Appellate Court
GJC = General Jurisdiction Court
LJC = Limited Jurisdiction Court
A = Appeal from Admin. Agency
↑ = Route of appeal

**FIGURE 5-1**  Texas State Court System.

## NATIONAL CENTER FOR STATE COURTS

The National Center for State Courts (NCSC) is located in Williamsburg, Virginia. NCSC's web address is www.ncsconline.org. Its mission is to improve the administration of justice through leadership and service to state courts, and courts around the world.

At the First National Conference of the Judiciary, held in Williamsburg, Virginia, in 1971, then Chief Justice Warren Burger called for the creation of a central resource for the state courts—a "national center for state courts." The National Center for State Courts began operations in the same year at the headquarters of the Federal Judicial Center in Washington, D.C., before moving to its permanent headquarters in Williamsburg in 1978.

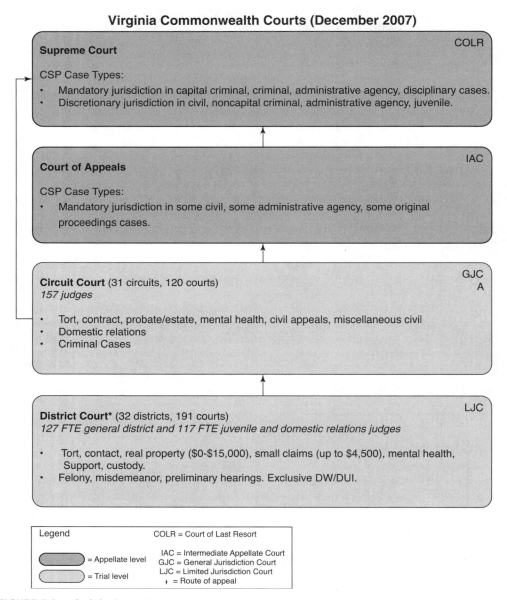

**Virginia Commonwealth Courts (December 2007)**

**Supreme Court** — COLR

CSP Case Types:
- Mandatory jurisdiction in capital criminal, criminal, administrative agency, disciplinary cases.
- Discretionary jurisdiction in civil, noncapital criminal, administrative agency, juvenile.

**Court of Appeals** — IAC

CSP Case Types:
- Mandatory jurisdiction in some civil, some administrative agency, some original proceedings cases.

**Circuit Court** (31 circuits, 120 courts) — GJC A
*157 judges*

- Tort, contract, probate/estate, mental health, civil appeals, miscellaneous civil
- Domestic relations
- Criminal Cases

**District Court*** (32 districts, 191 courts) — LJC
*127 FTE general district and 117 FTE juvenile and domestic relations judges*

- Tort, contact, real property ($0–$15,000), small claims (up to $4,500), mental health, Support, custody.
- Felony, misdemeanor, preliminary hearings. Exclusive DW/DUI.

Legend
= Appellate level
= Trial level

COLR = Court of Last Resort
IAC = Intermediate Appellate Court
GJC = General Jurisdiction Court
LJC = Limited Jurisdiction Court
↑ = Route of appeal

**FIGURE 5-2** Virginia Court System.

Initially, the National Center concentrated on helping courts to reduce backlogs and delay. This work included the publication of the groundbreaking *Justice Delayed: The Pace of Litigation in Urban Trial Courts* in 1978. The National Center also gave judges and court administrators a vital national perspective on court operations through its Court Statistics Project which it started in 1978; the work of its Knowledge Information Service, which handled more than 1,000 requests for court-related information during its first year of operation (1979); and the holdings of its Library, the largest collection of court administration-related materials in the world. Since its founding in 1971, the National Center for State Courts has played a key role in the development of court administration worldwide. Important National Center initiatives include:

- Developing the skills of more than 1,000 court leaders through the Court Executive Development Program of the Institute for Court Management.
- Improving how courts treat jurors through the work of its Center for Jury Studies and the promotion of innovations in jury system management.
- Promoting the use of technology to improve court operations through National Court Technology Conferences (starting in Chicago in 1984), original research, and direct technical assistance.
- Developing in partnership with courts standards for evaluating how well courts serve the public, such as the Trial Court Performance Standards.
- Working with court associations, such as the Conference of Chief Justices and National Association for Court Management, to improve public trust and confidence in the courts by conducting and building upon the first National Conference on Public Trust and Confidence in the Judiciary.

Information provided by NCSC, at www.ncsconline.org (accessed on May 18, 2009).

## COURTS OF LIMITED JURISDICTION

There are about 1,400 courts of limited jurisdiction in the states. They are generally called municipal, county, city, or justice courts. Because the number of traffic, petty, and misdemeanor cases far outnumber serious criminal cases, the lower courts constitute the first and, in most instances, the only contact that most citizens have with our criminal court system. Limited jurisdiction courts vary across the United States and often within a single state. These courts, also referred to as lower courts, are also more of a reflection of the community and community standards than any other type of court. Lower courts are generally not considered as **courts of record** and therefore do not keep formal written records of the proceedings. Generally, the lower courts are considered as courts of limited jurisdiction because their jurisdiction is limited and they may decide only those issues and controversies specifically delineated by state statutes or state constitutions.

In criminal cases tried before limited jurisdiction courts, the appeals are to the state's major trial courts. In most states, if the criminal case is appealed from a lower court, the case is tried "de novo" in the major trial court. In a trial de novo, the case is completely retried as if it were a new case.

In many states, the limited jurisdiction courts conduct the first appearance of the accused in felony trials. At the first appearance, the accused is advised of the charges against him or her assigned an attorney if the defendant does not already have one, and bail is set.

In almost all states, the lower court judges are elected. In some states, they are appointed by the governor but are subject to voter confirmation at the next general election. In those states where they are appointed by the governor, normally they must also be confirmed by a judicial appointment committee which contains representatives from the state legislatures and the judiciary.

## Justice of Peace

The office of the justice of peace (JP) was copied from the English. At the time the colonies were settled, the English JPs were usually not trained in law and were members of the local gentry who served as judges in cases involving minor matters and transgressions. The title "Justice of the Peace" can be traced back to 1361during the reign of King Edward III of Plantagenet with the passage of the Justice of the Peace Act. The peace to be guarded was the King's peace, the maintenance of which was the duty of the Crown under the royal prerogative. English Justices of the Peace still use the power conferred on them in 1361 to bind over unruly persons "to be of good behaviour" (Smith 1927). The bind over is not considered punishment, but a preventive measure, intended to ensure that people thought likely to offend will not do so. Currently in England, the Lord Chancellor nominates candidates with local advice, for appointment by the Crown (Friedman 1998).

Today, in many states the JP is a judge of a **court of limited jurisdiction**. In other states the JP has been replaced by a magistrate, or a quasi-judicial official with certain statutory judicial powers. In those states that still have JP; the justices normally preside over misdemeanor cases, traffic violations and minor civil law matters. A primary duty of the JP in many states is officiating at weddings (Justices of Peace 2008).

In Arizona, a JPs has the same jurisdiction as a municipal magistrate with respect to traffic and misdemeanor cases and restraining orders. Additionally, an Arizona JP court hears civil law suits up to a limit of $10,000, small claims cases, and issues evictions. The JPs are elected in Arizona by partisan elections for four year terms from specific districts called precincts. They have the same authority and responsibility as all other judges in the state with respect performing marriages, administrating oaths, adhering to the code of judicial conduct, and all aspects of justice administration (Justices of Peace 2008).

Other states have abolished the office of JP and transferred the duties and responsibilities to other limited jurisdiction courts such as police courts, city courts, and magistrate courts. In some cities, the JP has been replaced by municipal court and in urban areas by county courts. The American Bar Association has for years led an effort to abolish the office of JP (Justices of Peace, 2008).

## Nonlawyer Judges

A few states permit the appointment or election of no-lawyers as lower-court judges or JPs. In *North v. Russell* (1976), North was charged in city police court of driving while under the influence of alcohol. He pled not guilty and requested a jury trial. His request for a jury trial was denied, and he was tried before a city police court by a judge who was not a lawyer. North was found guilty and sentenced to thirty days in jail. He did not appeal his conviction to the court of intermediate appeal, a Kentucky circuit court for a trial de novo, to which he was entitled pursuant to Kentucky statues; instead, he filed a writ of habeas corpus with the Kentucky Court of Appeals, which affirmed his conviction. North claimed in his writ that his sentence to jail violated his due process rights under the Fourteenth Amendment to the U.S. Constitution because the judge in the police court was not an attorney and had no special legal training. He then petitioned the U.S. Supreme Court which accepted his writ and denied his contention that his due process rights were violated.

The Supreme Court concluded that The Kentucky two-tier trial court system with lay judicial officers in the first tier in smaller cities and an appeal of right with a de novo trial before a traditionally law-trained judge in the second did not violate either the due process or equal protection guarantees of the Constitution of the United States. The Court noted that the right to a new trial was absolute for a defendant tried in a city police court in Kentucky. A defendant need not allege error in the inferior court proceeding. And if he or she had sought a new trial by the second tier court, the Kentucky statutory scheme contemplates that the slate be wiped clean. Prosecution and defense would begin anew (trial de novo).

A second major issue in the North case involved the fact that Kentucky's constitutional provisions required that judges be attorneys in larger cities and but not in the smaller cities violated the unequal protection clause of the constitution. The Kentucky Court of Appeals in *Ditty v. Hampton*, (1972) articulated reasons for the differing qualifications of police court judges in cities of different size with the following rationale:

- The greater volume of court business in the larger cities requires that judges be attorneys to enable the courts to operate efficiently and expeditiously (not necessarily with more fairness and impartiality).
- Lawyers with whom to staff the courts are more available in the larger cities.
- The larger cities have greater financial resources with which to provide better qualified personnel and better facilities for the courts.

The Supreme Court in *North v. Russell* (1976) concluded that population and area factors may justify classifications within a court system and held that each state may establish one system of courts for cities and another for rural districts, one system for one portion of its territory and another system for another portion as long as all people within a classified area are treated equally. Convenience, if not necessity, often requires this to be done, and it would seriously interfere with the power of a State to regulate its internal affairs to deny to it this right.

The *North v. Russell* case was concerned with the issue of whether a trial before a nonlawyer judge violated federal constitutional rights. What happens when a state court of last resort determines that under its state constitution, municipal courts judges are required to be licensed to practice law in the state? This issue being a state constitutional question, the state high court makes the final decision.

In *City of White House v. Whitley* (1998), a Tennessee city passed an ordinance establishing a municipal court, but did not require the municipal judge to be licensed to practice law in the state. The district attorneys general argued that nonattorney judges

## COURTS IN ACTION
### Public Defenders Offices in the United States

- In 2007, 957 public defender offices across the nation received more than 5.5 million indigent defense cases.
- Misdemeanor cases accounted for about 40% of all cases received by state-based public defender offices and about 50% of the cases received by county-based offices.
- Half of all state-based public defender offices had formal caseload limits in place in 2007.
- Total expenditures in public defender offices exceeded $2.3 billion in 2007.
- More than 15,000 full-time equivalent litigating attorneys were employed by public defender offices in 2007.
- State-based public defender programs employed more than 4,000 full-time equivalent litigating attorneys, with a median of 163 per state-based program.
- County-based offices employed about 11,000 full-time equivalent litigating attorneys, with a median of seven per office.
- In addition to attorneys, public defender offices nationwide employed nearly 9,700 full-time equivalent support staff, including investigators, paralegals, and administrative staff.

could not preside over hearings where the defendants faced the possibility of incarceration. The Tennessee Supreme Court agreed and held that the municipal judges must be licensed to practice law if they presided over trials for defendants who might be incarcerated. The state court stated that a criminal defendant had a constitutional right to representation by a legally qualified attorney. To require a lesser standard of a judge presiding over the trial of a criminal offense punishable by incarceration would defeat the constitutional purpose of the right to counsel. The Tennessee court held that the failure to provide a judge qualified to comprehend and utilize counsel's legal arguments was a denial of due process protections of the state constitution which guaranteed to a criminal defendant on trial for an offense punishable by incarceration the right to be tried before an attorney judge. As this case illustrates, a state may provide additional individual rights to an accused in a criminal case than are required by the federal constitution and the U.S. Supreme Court decisions.

### County and Municipal Courts

County courts in the early English system of justice were under the jurisdiction of the sheriff and these courts were administrated by the suitors of the county, that is, the freeholders. The suitors were the real judges and the sheriff was the ministerial officer (Black's Law Dictionary 1957, 422).

In a few states like Texas, the county courts serve also as county administrators. In Texas, the county judge is generally considered the chief administrator of the county government. In the most populous counties, county courts of law are the actual county trial courts that serve as limited jurisdiction trial courts. In some states that have county and municipal courts, the county courts handle minor criminal matters in rural areas and the municipal courts in urban. In other states, the municipal courts are the first-level trial courts in all areas of the state. Some states also use police courts and city courts as first-level trial courts to handle misdemeanor cases. In addition, in many states, the municipal courts handled preliminary matters in felony cases such as arraignments, bail setting, and first appearances.

### Subordinate Judicial Officers

The state legislatures are permitted by state constitutions to provide for the appointment of officers, such as commissioners and referees, to perform subordinate judicial duties. Commissioners of municipal or justice courts usually may adjudicate infractions. For example, in many counties a traffic court commissioner is appointed to adjudicate traffic infractions. In many states, a commissioner may hold hearings in a criminal case and forward his or her recommendations to a trial judge for approval. In some states, with consent of the defendant and the prosecutor, the actual trial may be held before a court commissioner.

## MAJOR TRIAL COURTS

> The task of the trial court is to reconstruct the past from what are, at best, second-hand reports of the facts.
> —Justice Jerome Frank, U.S. Court of Appeals

The major trial courts are more formal in their proceedings than the lower courts. They are courts of record in that a formal record is made of their proceedings and most of the proceedings are recorded verbatim. They are also courts of general jurisdiction in that they have the authority to hear and determine all criminal cases. The major trial courts usually have exclusive jurisdiction over felonies; they are generally the only trial courts which have the authority to try felony cases. All states require that the judges of the major

**LAW IN ACTION**

**State Major Criminal Trial Courts**

***Circuit Court:*** Alabama, Arkansas, Florida, Hawaii, Illinois, Indiana, Kentucky, Maryland, Michigan, Mississippi, Missouri, Oregon, South Carolina, South Dakota, Tennessee, Virginia, West Virginia, and Wisconsin

***Court of Common Pleas:*** Ohio and Pennsylvania

***District Court:*** Colorado, Idaho, Kansas, Louisiana, Minnesota, Montana, Nebraska, Nevada, New Mexico, North Dakota, Oklahoma, Texas, Utah, and Wyoming

***Superior Court:*** Alaska, Arizona, California, Connecticut, Delaware, District of Columbia, Georgia, Maine, Massachusetts, New Hampshire, New Jersey, North Carolina, Rhode Island, Vermont, Washington, and New York

***Supreme Court:*** New York (New York also uses county courts and superior courts)

*Source:* David Rottman, Carol Flango, and R. Shedine Lockley, *State Court Organizations* (Washington DC: U.S. Department of Justice, Bureau of Justice Statistics, GPO), 1995.

trial courts be lawyers. For the most part, state trial courts are either district or superior courts. In New York State, the major trial courts are the supreme courts.

It is estimated that there are about 2,000 major state trial courts in the United States with approximately 11,000 judges. Often in a judicial district, the major trial court will have more than one trial judge assigned or appointed with each judge sitting as the court trial judge for that judicial district. In 2002, there were over 7.4 mission civil court filings and 4.8 million criminal cases filed in the state major trial courts (Ostrum, Kauder, and LaFountain 2003).

## How Busy are the Major State Trial Courts?

The latest data available is for May 2004. It is estimated that between May 2004 and May 2007, the case loads increased by 27 percent.

- An estimated 57,497 felony cases were filed in the state courts of the nation's 75 largest counties during May 2004.
- About a fourth of these felony defendants were charged with a violent offense, usually assault (12%) or robbery (5.4%). Those charged with murder (0.6%) or rape (0.9%) accounted for a small percentage of defendants overall.
- About three-fourths of defendants were charged with a nonviolent felony. The most frequently charged nonviolent offenses were drug trafficking (15%), other drug offenses (21.6%), burglary (7.9%), and theft (7.8%).
- 39 percent of defendants had an active criminal justice status at the time of the current charged offense, including 16 percent who were on probation, 11 percent on pretrial release, and 5 percent on parole.
- 59 percent of all defendants were convicted of a felony, and 9 percent were convicted of a misdemeanor.
- The highest felony conviction rates were for defendants charged with motor vehicle theft (74%), a driving related offense (73%), murder (70%), burglary (69%), or drug trafficking (67%).
- The lowest felony conviction rates were found among assault defendants (45%).

- 97 percent of convictions occurring within 1 year of arrest were obtained through a guilty plea. About 9 in 10 guilty pleas were to a felony.
- Murder defendants (25%) were the most likely to have their case adjudicated by trial.
- Overall, 75 percent of the defendants whose most serious conviction charge was a felony were sentenced to incarceration. Nearly all of the remaining convicted defendants received a probation sentence.

*Source:* Langton, Lynn and Thomas H. Cohen, *State Court Organization*, Special Report NCJ 217996 (Washington, DC: U.S. Department of Justice, Office of Justice Programs, October 2007).

## INTERMEDIATE STATE COURTS OF APPEALS

There is no requirement in the U.S. Constitution for an appellate court system. Almost every legal system, however, has developed procedures to address grievances about initial judicial determinations. As familiar as the word "appeal" is to us, the procedure was a surprising procedure for the American colonists to have adopted. Three hundred years ago, the term "appeal" referred to a legal procedure which was available only in the separate system of English courts governed by canon and civil law—and not in the common law system with which the Puritan settlers were so enamored (Bilder 1997, 913).

The right to appeal trial court decisions was present in most of the colonies. For example, Tymann (2000) noted that beginning in 1639, the Massachusetts Bay Colony formally chartered the Court of Assistants and entrusted it with appellate authority. This act established one of the first appellate systems in the colonies and according to Tymann became the bedrock of American justice systems (Tymann 2000, 126).

Like the structures of other state courts, the structure of the intermediate courts of appeals also varies. In 11 states, there are no intermediate courts of appeals. These states are the states that have relatively small population bases. In 24 states, the ICAs are organized on a statewide basis. In 15 states, the state legislatures have divided their states into appellate districts, each containing a court of appeals with one or more divisions. Each division normally has a presiding justice and at least two associate justices.

Appellate justices are elected or appointed. Many of the appointed justices are subject to voter confirmation after a specified period of time. Court of appeals are appellate courts and do not try cases. Their decisions are based on record of trial in the trial court, appellate briefs submitted by the parties, and oral argument (some appeals are decided without oral argument) before the appellate court.

Only about 20 percent of state criminal convictions are appealed to an ICA. When a court of appeals reverses a serious criminal conviction, the press frequently provides extensive coverage of the results. This leads to the conclusion that numerous criminal cases are reversed on appeal. It is estimated that appellate courts reverse less than one in 15 of the criminal convictions they review. In the 37 states that have the death penalty as a legal punishment, 35 of them bypass the ICAs in capital cases and provide for direct appeal to the court of last resort (Hoffman and Mahoney 2001).

### Why Intermediate Appellate Courts?

Richard Hoffman and Barry Mahoney (2001) conducted research on this question. They conclude that the state intermediate appellate courts ("IACs") are the courts in which the great bulk of appellate cases are resolved. Unlike state COLRs, IACs have limited power to control their caseloads. Most receive and dispose of far greater numbers of cases than do state supreme courts. In a few states, the court of last resort exercises great control over the intermediate appellate court or courts by sifting through appeals to select those that should proceed to direct review in the highest court and sending others to the intermediate court.

In addition, the highest courts may decide which intermediate appellate court opinions are approved for publication. Indeed, in some states, the issuance of a highest-court opinion even results in the expunging of the intermediate court ruling. While state COLRs often play a leadership role through their exercise of general superintendence authority over the court system, intermediate appellate courts normally have no other assignment other than to resolve the appeals brought to them for decision. Hoffman and Mahoney (2001) call them the "work horses" of appellate litigation in most states. They noted that there were almost 200,000 cases filed yearly in state intermediate appellate courts.

## COURTS OF LAST RESORT

For purposes of this text, the term "courts of last resort" is used to refer to the highest state court handling criminal appeals. As noted earlier, in most states, this is the state supreme court. In the State of New York, it is the court of appeals and in Texas and Oklahoma it is the court of criminal appeals.

State COLRs are the final decision makers for matters involving the interpretations of state law not involving a federal issue. As the final decision maker, they are very influential in state governments. The COLRs have original jurisdiction in only a few cases. Original jurisdiction means that a case may be brought directly in or started in the state COLR. For the most part, the original jurisdiction is limited to cases involving attorney discipline and matters involving state court judges. Except in capital cases, COLRs have discretionary jurisdiction in most criminal cases. Discretionary jurisdiction means that the COLR has the right to select only those cases that it wishes to decide. As a general rule, COLRS are very selective in the cases that they select to hear. When a COLR refuses to hear or decide a case that does not mean that the lower court decision was correct. It only means that the COLR determined that the case did not warrant hearing or a decision by the COLR.

**LAW IN ACTION**

**How long does it take for a death penalty case appeal to be decided by the state high court?**

Professors Latzer and Cauthen (2007) conducted a study of appellate time in state capital cases. Their results are summarized below:

- The frequency of state courts of last resort (COLR) decisions by year reflects national homicide trends. The number of capital appeals resolved annually rose steadily from 1992 to 1997 and declined thereafter.
- Three-quarters (.737) of the appeals upheld the capital conviction and sentence.
- The reversal rate was 26.3 percent.
- Six out of ten reversals overturned the sentence alone.
- In only 11 percent of the cases the conviction was overturned.
- Measuring from date of death sentence to appeal decided by the COLR, it took a median 966 days to complete direct appeal.
- Petitioning the U.S. Supreme Court added 188 days where certiorari was denied, and a median 250 days where certiorari was granted and the issues were decided on the merits.
- Virginia was the most efficient of all states in the study, with a median processing time from sentence to COLR ruling of 295 days. Measuring from notice of appeal to COLR decision, Georgia, at 297 days, is the fastest court of last resort.
- Ohio, Tennessee, and Kentucky were the least efficient COLRs, consuming respectively, 1,388, 1,350 and 1,309 days.
- Ohio reduced its time consumption by 25 percent by eliminating intermediate appeals court review. (Latzer and Cauthen 2007)

Judicial compensation for justices on COLRs varies widely. In 2007, the median income of high court judges was $149,200, and ranged from $106,185 to $209,521. The employment conditions of judges differ in other ways as well. Judges enjoy different levels of secretarial and clerical support. Roughly speaking, elected judges are paid less than appointed judges; they are also more likely to have graduated from a local law school (National Center for State Courts, 2007).

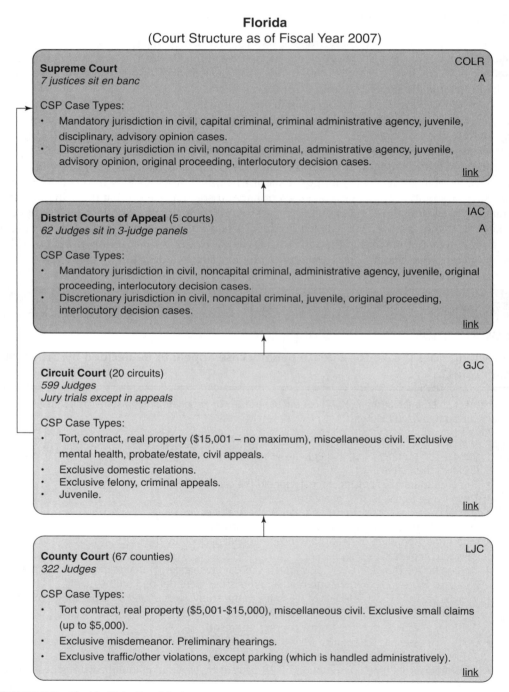

**Florida**
(Court Structure as of Fiscal Year 2007)

**Supreme Court**                                                          COLR
*7 justices sit en banc*                                                      A

CSP Case Types:
- Mandatory jurisdiction in civil, capital criminal, criminal administrative agency, juvenile, disciplinary, advisory opinion cases.
- Discretionary jurisdiction in civil, noncapital criminal, administrative agency, juvenile, advisory opinion, original proceeding, interlocutory decision cases.

link

**District Courts of Appeal** (5 courts)                                    IAC
*62 Judges sit in 3-judge panels*                                             A

CSP Case Types:
- Mandatory jurisdiction in civil, noncapital criminal, administrative agency, juvenile, original proceeding, interlocutory decision cases.
- Discretionary jurisdiction in civil, noncapital criminal, juvenile, original proceeding, interlocutory decision cases.

link

**Circuit Court** (20 circuits)                                             GJC
*599 Judges*
*Jury trials except in appeals*

CSP Case Types:
- Tort, contract, real property ($15,001 – no maximum), miscellaneous civil. Exclusive mental health, probate/estate, civil appeals.
- Exclusive domestic relations.
- Exclusive felony, criminal appeals.
- Juvenile.

link

**County Court** (67 counties)                                              LJC
*322 Judges*

CSP Case Types:
- Tort contract, real property ($5,001-$15,000), miscellaneous civil. Exclusive small claims (up to $5,000).
- Exclusive misdemeanor. Preliminary hearings.
- Exclusive traffic/other violations, except parking (which is handled administratively).

link

**FIGURE 5-3** Florida State Court System.

**LAW IN ACTION**

**Early Judicial Selection Methods for State Judges**

*Prior to 1776:* The earliest judge appointments were made by the king.

*Prior to 1800:* The judges were selected by the governor.

*1800s:* States begin shifting from gubernatorial appointments to popular elections to counter the political spoils system.

*1980s:* States begin to shift from partisan to nonpartisan election of judges. In nonpartisan system, the judges are elected without political party designations.

*1940:* Voters amended the Missouri constitution by adopting the "Nonpartisan Selection of Judges Court Plan," commonly known as the "Missouri Plan." Under this plan, judges were selected by hybrid appointive-merit retention.

### Missouri Nonpartisan Court Plan

During the 1930s, the public became increasingly dissatisfied with the increasing role of politics in judicial selection and judicial decision making. Judges were subject to political influences due to the election process. Judges spent campaigning rather than performing their duties. In November 1940, voters amended the Missouri constitution by adopting the "Nonpartisan Selection of Judges Court Plan," which was placed on the ballot by initiative petition. The adoption of the plan was caused by public unhappiness against the widespread abuses of the judicial system by the "Boss Tom" Pendergast political machine in Kansas City and by the political control exhibited by ward bosses in St. Louis. The Missouri nonpartisan court plan, commonly called the Missouri Plan, since has served as a national model for the selection of judges and has been adopted in more than 30 other states.

*Source:* Missouri Courts Web page at www.courts.mo.gov (accessed on May 11, 2009).

## COURT REFORM MOVEMENTS

The court reform movement, initiated early in the twentieth century, was aimed at reducing the fragmentation and disparity inherent in many state court systems. The movement focused on consolidating state trial courts, creating state-centralized court administrations for budgetary and regulatory purposes, and increasing professionalism among court judicial, clerical, and administrative staff (Langton and Cohen 2007).

In 1964, Illinois became the first state court system to become unified. All trial courts in Illinois were consolidated into a unified circuit court with one chief judge overseeing the operations and procedures in each division (Baum 2001). Illinois state court system presently includes one court of last resort, one intermediate appellate court divided into five districts, and one court of general jurisdiction sectioned into numerous trial court divisions (Langton and Cohen 2007).

In contrast to the Illinois judicial system is that of New York's state court system which includes one court of last resort, two intermediate appellate courts, two types of general jurisdiction trial courts divided into 69 divisions, and eight types of limited jurisdiction trial courts separated into 1,695 divisions. In New York's numerous town and village justice courts most expenses, including salaries, travel, building, and property expenses, are funded at the county level.

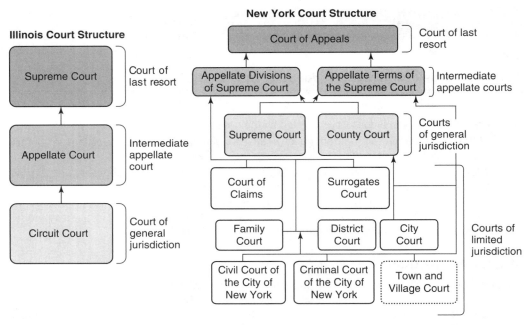

Two contrasting state court systems: Illinois and New York. Illinois has unified their courts and New York has not.

By 2007, at least 10 states have consolidated their court systems by merging general and limited jurisdiction trial courts. In addition, many of the responsibility for trial court expenses were also shifted from the county judicial districts to the state. An example of a unified court is the Superior Court of Los Angeles County, California.

## LAW IN ACTION

### The Superior Courts of Los Angeles County

#### Unification Movement

To maximize the use of judicial resources, Los Angeles County Municipal Courts and the Superior Court began in 1988 to cross-assign cases. This program involved having judges at each court level hear court matters that were normally not within the jurisdiction of their court, thereby assisting in reducing case backlogs. Eventually the municipal courts and the superior courts in Los Angeles County were unified into a unified superior court with the stated goal of providing excellence of service and responsible and effective use of resources in providing fair and timely disposition and accurate recording of its legal proceedings. The unified superior court is the trial court of general and limited jurisdiction.

#### General jurisdiction cases include:

- *Criminal*—felony offenses punishable by death or imprisonment in state prison.
- *Civil*—cases involving all types of civil disputes with claims of damages of more than $25,000, including personal injury, contract and business disputes, and condemnation of property through eminent domain proceedings.
- *Juvenile*—cases involving dependent minors who have been abused or neglected, and minors who are accused of crimes, infractions, or incorrigible behavior. The juvenile court also handles adoption proceedings.

- *Family Law*—cases involving divorce, legal separation and paternity.
- *Mental Health*—cases involving the treatment and custody of mentally ill persons.
- *Probate*—cases involving the estates of deceased persons as well as the guardianship and conservatorship of estates for those unable to care for themselves.
- *Appellate Department*—appealed cases from lower courts.

## Limited jurisdiction cases include:

- *Criminal*—misdemeanor offenses punishable by a maximum fine of $1000 and a county jail term of one year or less, infractions punishable by fine only, preliminary hearings in felony cases to determine whether felony prosecution shall be held in the Superior Court.
- *Civil*—cases involving civil disputes with claims of damages up to and including $25,000.
- *Small Claims*—cases involving civil disputes with claims of damages no more than $7,500 for individuals, $5,000 for corporations and other entities; a serve-yourself court, with no attorney permitted for either party, and appeals permitted only from defendants where there is a new trial before a judge. Each party may have a lawyer, if desired, in a new trial on appeal.
- *Traffic*—citations issued by law enforcement agencies in Los Angeles

*Source:* Web site of the Los Angeles Courts www.lasuperiorcourt.org/aboutcourt (accessed on May 13, 2009).

## Questions in Review

1. How important are state courts in our criminal justice system?
2. Under what circumstances a person could be tried in both a state and a federal court for the same criminal act?
3. What type of court system does your state utilize?

4. If an individual is tried in a municipal court, which court would generally decide the appeal and what would the appellate court consider in deciding the appeal?
5. Explain the differences between a court of limited jurisdiction and a court of general jurisdiction.

## Practicum

According to Norman Lefstein, guaranteeing the right of legal representation to indigent defendants in state felony prosecutions was a movement that launched what might be called this country's "right to counsel revolution" in criminal and juvenile proceedings. [Norman Lefstein, (2004) "In Search of Gideon's Promise: Lessons from England and the Need for Federal Help," Hastings Law Journal vol. 55. 835–845]. The following In re Edwards case looks at a state's obligation in this area. Should the states be required to meet federal standards in establishing public defenders offices? Why?

### IN RE EDWARD S., 173 CAL. APP. 4TH 387, 390 (CAL. APP. 1ST DIST. 2009)

**Excerpts from court's opinion:** A public defender's office is considered to be the equivalent of a law firm, and responsibility for handling a case falls upon the office as a whole. The ethical obligations of public defenders and other publically funded attorneys who represent indigent persons charged with crimes are no

different from those of privately retained defense counsel. A deputy public defender whose excessive workload obstructs his or her ability to provide effective assistance to a particular client should, with supervisorial approval, attempt to reduce the caseload, as by transferring nonrepresentational responsibilities to others, refusing new cases, and/or transferring cases to another lawyer with a lesser caseload. If the deputy public defender is unable to obtain relief in that manner, he or she must file a motion with the trial court requesting permission to withdraw from a sufficient number of cases to allow the provision of competent and diligent representation to the remaining clients. In support of the motion, counsel should provide the court with information necessary to justify the withdrawal, while being mindful of the obligations not to disclose confidential information or information as to strategy or other matters that may prejudice the client.

The American Bar Association's (ABA) interest in this issue is long-standing. (ABA Standing Com. on

Legal Aid & Indigent Defendants, Gideon Undone: The Crisis in Indigent Defense Funding (Moran ed. 1983) [rep. of 1982 conference hearing]; In 2004, after extensive hearings on the issue, the ABA found that forty years after Gideon v. Wainwright, indigent defense in the United States remains in a state of crisis, resulting in a system that lacks fundamental fairness and places poor persons at constant risk of wrongful conviction and that, as a result, the integrity of the criminal justice system is eroded and the legitimacy of criminal convictions is called into question. The ABA emphasized that funding for indigent defense services is shamefully inadequate, so that lawyers frequently are burdened by overwhelming caseloads and essentially coerced into furnishing representation in defense systems that fail to provide the bare necessities for an adequate defense, specifically including investigative resources, resulting in routine violations of the Sixth Amendment obligation to provide effective assistance of counsel. This view, hardly confined to the ABA, is shared not just by the United States Department of Justice, which has long been concerned about the problem.

We conclude that the representation provided appellant by the Mendocino County Public Defender's Office was deficient, in that it fell below an objective standard of reasonableness under prevailing professional norms.

## Key Terms

**Court of General Jurisdiction:** A court in which the jurisdiction of the court is assumed and its jurisdiction does not need to affirmatively appear in the pleadings. General jurisdiction courts have broad subject-matter jurisdiction and are the courts that hold felony trials.

**Court of Limited Jurisdiction:** A court in which jurisdiction of the court is not assumed, but must affirmatively appear in the pleadings. A limited jurisdiction court handle specific and limited types of cases. Generally misdemeanors cases are tried in such courts.

**Court of Record:** A court whose acts and judicial proceedings are enrolled or recorded for permanent record.

**Magistrate.** Includes magistrates, district judges, superior court judges, and any other judicial officer authorized by law to conduct a preliminary examination of a person accused of a crime or issue a warrant.

**Subject Matter Jurisdiction:** Pertains to the types of cases that a court has the authority to decide.

**Subpoenas:** Orders issued by the clerk of the court in which a criminal proceeding is pending at any time for such witnesses as any party may require for attendance at trial and at hearings, for taking depositions, or for any other lawful purpose.

**Venue:** Venue refers to the geographical location of the trial; the judicial district or county in which the trial should be conducted.

## References

### CASES

*City of White House v. Whitley*, 979 S.W.2d 262 (Tenn. 1998)
*Commonwealth v. Thomas*, 410 Pa. 160 (Pa. 1963)
*Ditty v. Hampton*, 490 S.W.2d 772 (Ky. 1972)
*Koon v. United States*, 518 U.S. 81 (U.S. 1996)
*North v. Russell,* 427 U.S. 328 (1976)
*Simpson v. State*, 92 Ga. 41 (Ga. 1893)

### BOOKS, JOURNALS AND ARTICLES

Baum, Lawrence. *American Courts: Process and Policy.* Boston: Houghton Mifflin, 2001.
Bilder, Mary. "The Origin of Appeal in America." *Hasting Law Journal* 48 (July 1997): 913–919.
Black's Law Dictionary 4th ed. St. Paul, MN: West, 1957.

Carp, Robert A., and Ronald Stidham. *Judicial Process in America*, 5th ed. Washington, DC: CQ Press, 2001.
Friedman, Lawrence. *American Law: An Introduction*. New York: Norton, 1998.
Glick, Henry, and Kenneth Vines. *State Court Systems* Englewood Cliffs, NJ: Prentice-Hall, 1973.
Hall, Kenneth. *The Oxford Guide to American Law*. New York: Oxford University Press, 2002.
Hoffman, Richard B., and Barry Mahoney. *Managing Caseflow in State Intermediate Appellate Courts*. Denver: Justice Management Institute, 2001.
"Justice of the peace." *The Columbia Encyclopedia*, 6th ed. (2008). http://www.encyclopedia.com/doc/1E1-justicep.html (accessed on May 17, 2009).
Kent, James. *Commentaries on American Law,* Volume1–4 (Novi, MI: LawMart, 1830, reprinted 2006).

Lamm, Richard. "Privacy and Public Policy" *Denver University Law Review* 79 (2002): 532–538.

Langton, Lynn and Thomas H. Cohen. *State Court Organization.* Special Report NCJ 217996. Washington, DC: U.S. Department of Justice, Office of Justice Programs, October, 2007.

Latzer, Barry and James N. G. Cauthen. "Justice Delayed? Time Consumption in Capital Appeals: A Multistate Study." Williamsburg, VA: National Center for State Courts, 2007.

National Center for State Courts. *Survey of Judicial Salaries,* 2007. www.ncsconline.org/WC/Publications/KIS_JudComJudSal070107Pub.pdf (accessed on May 18, 2009).

Nelson, William E. *Americanization of the Common Law: The Impact of Legal Change on Massachusetts Society, 1760–1830.* Cambridge, MS: Harvard Univ. Press, 1979.

O'Hara, James. "Trivia Quiz." *Supreme Court Historical Society Quarterly Newsletter* 31, no. 2 (2009)

Ostrom, Brian, Neal Kauder, and Robert LaFountain. *Examining the Work of State Courts, 2002.* Williamsburg, VA: National Center for State Courts, 2003.

Rogers, Alan. *Murder and the Death Penalty in Massachusetts.* Amherst :University of Massachusetts Press, 2008.

Smith, Chester H. "The Justice of the Peace System in the United States." *California Law Review* 15 (1927): 118–141.

Tymann, Benjamin. "Populism and the Rule of Law." *Suffolk University Law Review* 34 (2000): 125–140.

# 6

# Courtroom Work Group

**What you need to know about Courtroom Work Group**

- Courtroom work group participants include the judge, the prosecutor, the defense counsel, witnesses, the jury, and the court's professional staff.
- The judge's role at trial is to preside over the proceedings and see that order is maintained.
- The judge decides whether any of the evidence that the parties want to use is admissible.
- Before the jury begins its deliberations about the facts in the case, the judge gives the jury instructions about the law that applies to the case.
- Once a defendant is convicted, the judge or the jury will determine the sentence.
- A prosecutor has special ethical obligations in criminal cases.
- A prosecutor must disclose to the defense any exculpatory evidence and evidence that may be used to attack the credibility of a witness.
- A prosecutor must seek justice in each case, which may include dismissing charges when the evidence is insufficient to convict.
- A defendant who is unable to afford a lawyer to represent him at trial may have a court-appointed lawyer if the defendant is subject to confinement.
- Before testifying, an obligation to tell the truth is imposed on the witness by an oath or an affirmation.
- A witness must answer the questions of the trial counsel unless a privilege exists such as the privilege against self-incrimination.
- When a defendant chooses to testify, he or she waives the privilege against self-incrimination.
- Generally lay (non-expert) witnesses must testify to only matters within one's personal knowledge and may not testify as to opinions, inferences, or conclusions.
- Generally only expert witnesses may testify about their opinions after they have been qualified as an expert based upon their specialized knowledge or experience.
- The courtroom deputy clerk administers oaths to witnesses, marks exhibits, and helps the judge keep the trial running smoothly.
- The court reporter compiles the official record of the trial, which includes everything that is said or introduced into evidence.

**Chapter Outline**

- Introduction
- Judges
- Prosecutors

- Defense Counsel
- Witnesses
- Jury
- Professional Staff
- Questions In Review

## INTRODUCTION

According to a recent survey of the Bureau of Justice Statistics, approximately 66 percent of the nation think that the criminal justice system is fair in its treatment of people accused of committing crime. This confidence and faith in our criminal justice system is the result of the efforts and dedication of not only the law enforcement officer on the streets but also the professionals who serve in our courtrooms. The courtroom work groups assure that cases are tried expeditiously because justice delayed is often justice denied. These groups assure that fairness and impartiality exist in the fact finders, that counsel provide effective representation, and that prosecutors act ethically. The professional staff assures that a complete **record** is made of the proceedings so that appellate courts and the public can review the proceedings and form their own conclusions about the fairness of the trial.

This chapter describes the roles that judges, prosecutors, defense counsel, witnesses, juries, and the professional staff have in criminal cases. The diligent interaction among these groups assures that continued confidence and trust in our criminal justice system exists.

## JUDGES

At a trial, facts are established through the testimony of witnesses and the admission into evidence of exhibits, such as documents. The judge supervises this process and determines according to the rules of evidence which information can legitimately be considered. The judge assures that the parties are treated fairly and that their positions are duly considered.

The judge should ensure that the witnesses speak from their own knowledge and do not rely upon the statements of other witnesses. A **witness** should be precluded from

### COURTS IN ACTION
### Courtroom Work Group

Samuel Walker contends that working together every day, members of the courtroom work group reach a general consensus about how different kinds of cases should be handled. This involves shared understanding about how much cases are "worth." There are "heavy" cases (that is, serious violent crimes) and "garbage" cases (relatively minor cases). This valuation allows them to move cases along quickly. Conflict between prosecution and defense is the exception rather than the rule. Although in theory we have an adversarial process, in which truth is to be determined through conflict between the prosecution and defense, the reality is that an administrative system is in effect, with a high degree of consensus and cooperation. [Samuel L. Walker (2001) Sense and nonsense about crime and drugs 5th ed. Belmont, CA. Wadsworth, p. 53.]

changing her story based upon what another witness has testified to. To prevent witnesses from changing their stories, they are kept out of the courtroom until they are called to testify on the stand. Either party may request that this rule be invoked to avoid an improper influence on witness testimony.

In criminal cases, this rule is often invoked and enforced by the judge. In federal criminal cases, however, the investigating agent, such as a special agent of the Federal Bureau of Investigation, may sit at counsel table with the prosecutor during the trial to assist the prosecutor, may listen to all witnesses testify, and then may testify herself. This is an exception to the general rule of keeping witnesses out of the courtroom.

## LAW IN ACTION

### Time Management in the Courts

Judges must assure that cases are tried efficiently so that the court's limited resources are best used to reduce the growing backlog of cases. Steven Wallace, a retired judge from Orange County, Florida, offers these rules for time management in courts.

1. ***"Hire the best judicial assistant you can get."*** The judicial assistant or judge's clerk maintains the calendar for the court. The judge's assistant makes decisions about the setting of hearings that impact the lives of counsel, witnesses, and parties.
2. ***"Start on time."*** Respect for the court's time and the litigants' time by starting promptly will make the entire hearing process efficient. Starting late has a ripple effect that will affect other judicial hearing in which counsel may be involved.
3. ***"Set priorities for completion."*** A judge should establish what work is most important to complete. Because a defendant's liberty is at stake, and legislatures have imposed time limits for the processing of criminal cases, criminal prosecutions have precedence over civil cases. Decisions made on motions also must be prioritized. For example, a motion to suppress evidence must be decided before the government's case begins and sufficiently in advance so that the counsel can adjust the evidence they rely upon in court.
4. ***"Work a full day."*** The judge "works for the community, is paid to perform a fulltime job, and cheats if unwilling to perform as the work requires." The backlog of criminal cases impacts the welfare of society and leads to the further overcrowding of county jails with prisoners awaiting trial.
5. ***"Don't talk too much."*** A judge should "recognize the purpose of the proceeding and head inexorably toward the goal of completing it" The judge should only say what is essential to accomplish the purpose at hand. As Judge Wallace stated: "[P]eople don't come to the courtroom to listen to the judge talk. They come because they have to be there and they all want to leave as soon as possible. So a judge ought to be succinct. The judge and the record will be better off as a result."
6. ***"Don't let the lawyers or litigants run the show."*** It is the judge's responsibility to control the amount of time that lawyers argue and present evidence. Cases need to move along so that more parties have access to the courtroom. Lawyers who ramble, repeat, and just keep talking need to be reined in by the judge.
7. ***"Minimize continuances."*** The judge should have a strict policy that allows continuances only for "good cause." In many cases, the judge's decision not to grant a continuance results in the case being resolved by the parties without a trial.
8. ***"Make decisions."*** A judge should preside over hearings by being prepared, listening attentively to the parties, and when called upon render a decision. A judge should avoid taking matters "under advisement" and delaying a decision.

# PROSECUTORS

In the federal criminal system, the government is represented by a prosecutor, known as the Assistant United States Attorney who works for one of the 94 United States Attorneys, appointed by the president. In the state system, the government is represented by assistant district attorney, assistant state's attorney or assistant county prosecutor who works for the district attorney, state's attorney, or county prosecutor, typically of a county, who is an elected official.

In both systems, the prosecutor screens the cases to determine if there is sufficient evidence that can be properly admitted for the **jury** to find beyond a reasonable doubt that the defendant committed the crime charged. The prosecutor may also decide to enter into a plea agreement with the defendant that requires the defendant to plead guilty to certain crimes in exchange for a dismissal of some charges, a lighter sentence, or other perceived benefit. Typically, the prosecutor has unreviewable discretion to enter into a plea agreement.

A prosecutor has unreviewable discretion in determining what charges to file against the accused. For instance, a prosecutor has the discretion, depending upon the facts, to charge an aggravated assault instead of an attempted murder which may lead to a more lenient sentence.

The prosecutor's close relationship with the police and criminal investigating agencies allows the prosecutor to use law enforcement resources to gather evidence. The prosecutor also can use the grand jury to subpoena witnesses to testify and to require the production of documents that further the criminal investigation. Typically, the prosecutor has access to more funds than the defendant to investigate and prepare for trial.

An important responsibility of the prosecutor is to disclose to the defendant evidence that is favorable to the defense. The Supreme Court has said that the prosecutor "remains responsible for gauging [the cumulative effect of all exculpatory evidence] regardless of any failure by the police to bring favorable evidence to the prosecutor's attention." If there is a reasonable probability that the disclosure of exculpatory evidence would have produced a different result at trial, the defendant's conviction should be reversed, and the defendant is entitled to a new trial. In *Kyles v. Whitley*, the prosecutor failed to disclose to the defense evidence that could be used to cross-examine one of the state's witnesses to impeach or

## LAW IN ACTION

### Duty of a Prosecutor

Should the prosecutor only be an advocate for the government in seeking a conviction? Should a prosecutor seek a conviction at all costs? The Supreme Court of the United States has commented on these questions and has set forth the law regarding the role of the prosecutor in the American criminal justice system. In *Berger v. United States*, the Supreme Court said:

> [The prosecutor] is the representative not of an ordinary party to a controversy, but of a sovereignty whose obligation to govern impartially is as compelling as its obligation to govern at all; and whose interest, therefore, in a criminal prosecution is not that it shall win a case, but that justice shall be done. As such, he is in a peculiar and very definite sense the servant of the law, the twofold aim of which is that guilt shall not escape or innocence suffer. He may prosecute with earnestness and vigor—indeed, he should do so. But, while he may strike hard blows, he is not at liberty to strike foul ones. It is as much his duty to refrain from improper methods calculated to produce a wrongful conviction as it is to use every legitimate means to bring about a just one."

undermine the witness's credibility. Kyles was granted a new trial as a result of the prosecutor's failure to comply with the law to disclose favorable evidence.

Despite the presumption of innocence applied to the defendant, during a trial jurors may be predisposed to believe that "where there's smoke, there's fire" and the prosecutor should have a "presumption of good faith" based upon her standing and public office in the community. These unspoken predilections may influence jurors to be inclined to find a defendant guilty. Concern about an uneven playing field during a trial between the government and the defendant has resulted in establishing ethical standards applied to prosecutors.

A critical phase of the trial is when counsel speak to the jurors in their closing arguments. This singular opportunity provides counsel the time to advocate their positions, explain the testimony and evidence in favorable terms, and persuade jurors to make conclusions and render a verdict that upholds counsels' contentions. The American Bar Association, a national group of lawyers interested in assuring professionalism and ethical conduct, has established standards for prosecutors relating to closing arguments. The standards for closing argument provide:

1. The prosecutor may argue all reasonable inferences from evidence in the record. It is unprofessional conduct for the prosecutor to intentionally misstate the evidence or mislead the jury as to the inferences it may draw.

## COURTS IN ACTION

### Discretion of a Prosecutor in Sexual Assault Cases

AI1 of the decision makers in the American criminal justice system have a significant amount of unchecked discretionary power: but the one who stands apart from the rest is the prosecutor. The prosecutor decides who will be charged, what charge will be filed, who will be offered a plea bargain, and the type of bargain that will be offered, The prosecutor also may recommend the sentence the offender should receive. As Supreme Court Justice Jackson noted in 1940. "the prosecutor has more control over life, liberty, and reputation than any other person in America."

None of the discretionary decisions made by the prosecutor is more critical than the initial decision to prosecute or not, which has been characterized as "the gateway to justice." Prosecutors have wide discretion at this stage in the process; there are no legislative or judicial guidelines on charging and a decision not to file charges ordinarily is immune from review.

### Victim Characteristics and Sexual Assault Case Outcomes

There is a substantial body of research examining case processing decisions in sexual assault cases. This research reveals that sexual assault case outcomes, like outcomes in other types of cases, are strongly influenced by legally relevant factors such as the seriousness of the crime and the offender's prior criminal record. A number of studies also document the influence of victim characteristics. These studies reveal that sexual assault case processing decisions are affected by the victim's age, occupation, and education, by "risk-taking" behavior such as hitchhiking, drinking, or using drugs, and by the reputation of the victim. Sexual assault case outcomes also are affected by the relationship between the victim and the offender; reports of rape by strangers are investigated more thoroughly than reports of rape by someone the victim knows. Stranger rapes also are less likely to be unfounded by the police or rejected by the prosecutor, but are more likely to result in a conviction or a prison sentence. [Internal citations omitted.]

[Excerpts from: Cassia C. Spohn Ph.D.; Dawn Beichner; Erika Davis Frenzel; and David Holleran (2001) "Prosecutors' Charging Decisions in Sexual Assault Cases: A Multi-Site Study, Final Report" NCJ 197048; Rockville, MD: National Criminal Justice Reference Service., pp. 2–13]

2. It is unprofessional conduct for the prosecutor to express his or her personal belief or opinion as to the truth or falsity of any testimony or evidence or the guilt of the defendant.

3. The prosecutor should not use arguments calculated to inflame the passions or prejudices of the jury.

4. The prosecutor should refrain from argument which would divert the jury from its duty to decide the case on the evidence, by injecting issues broader than the guilt or innocence of the accused under the controlling law, or by making predictions of the consequences of the jury's verdict.

These ethical standards restrain prosecutors from abusing their influential position in a courtroom. They also contribute to the jury deciding the case based upon the evidence admitted during the trial and the law as instructed by the trial judge. The overarching standard for prosecutors is to be "an administrator of justice," while performing "[t]he duty . . . to seek justice, not merely convict."

Historically, prosecutors were seen as mostly advocates processing cases and were not closely involved in proactive way fighting crime. In the late twentieth century, however,

**LAW IN ACTION**

**Excerpts from *People v. Dehle*, 166 Cal. App. 4th 1380 (Cal. App. 3d Dist. 2008)**

The importance, to the public as well as to individuals suspected or accused of crimes, that discretionary functions [of a prosecutor] be exercised with the highest degree of integrity and impartiality, and with the appearance thereof, cannot easily be overstated. The public prosecutor is the representative not of any ordinary party to a controversy, but of a sovereignty whose obligation to govern impartially is as compelling as its obligation to govern at all; and whose interest, therefore, in a criminal prosecution is not that it shall win a case, but that justice shall be done. As such, he is in a peculiar and very definite sense the servant of the law, the twofold aim of which is that guilt shall not escape or innocence suffer.

The nature of the impartiality required of the public prosecutor follows from the prosecutor's role as representative of the People as a body, rather than as individuals. The prosecutor speaks not solely for the victim, or the police, or those who support them, but for all the People. That body of "The People" includes the defendant and his family and those who care about him. It also includes the vast majority of citizens who know nothing about a particular case, but who give over to the prosecutor the authority to seek a just result in their name. Thus the district attorney is expected to exercise his or her discretionary functions in the interests of the People at large, and not under the influence or control of an interested individual.

While the district attorney does have a duty of zealous advocacy, both the accused and the public have a legitimate expectation that his zeal will be born of objective and impartial consideration of each individual case. Of course, a prosecutor need not be disinterested on the issue whether a prospective defendant has committed the crime with which he is charged. If honestly convinced of the defendant's guilt, the prosecutor is free, indeed obliged to be deeply interested in urging that view by any fair means. True disinterest on the issue of such a defendant's guilt is the domain of the judge and the jury—not the prosecutor. It is a bit easier to say what a disinterested prosecutor is not than what he is. He is not disinterested if he has, or is under the influence of others who have, an axe to grind against the defendant, as distinguished from the appropriate interest that members of society have in bringing a defendant to justice with respect to the crime with which he is charged.

prosecutors began to recognize that both inside and outside of the courtroom, they were able to form partnerships with criminal investigation agencies and law enforcement units to design strategies to fight crime. Crime prevention became a shared goal among prosecutors and police. According to the National District Attorneys Association's National Center for Community Prosecution, "the proactive, collaborative, problem-solving approach is distinguished by certain key principles: (1) recognizing the community's *role* in public safety; (2) engaging in problem solving; (3) establishing and maintaining partnerships; and (4) evaluating outcomes of activities." The American Bar Association (ABA) has recognized this unique function of the prosecutor "to seek reform and improve the administration of criminal justice."

---

*The primary responsibility of a prosecutor is not to prosecute—but to seek justice.*

---

## DEFENSE COUNSEL

The Sixth Amendment of the United States Constitution provides that "[i]n all criminal prosecutions, the accused shall enjoy the right . . . to have the Assistance of Counsel for his defense." This right to counsel applies to all federal and state criminal prosecutions in which the defendant is accused of a felony or of a misdemeanor if a sentence of incarceration is actually imposed. In a few states, the right to counsel is extended to all criminal defendants. In criminal cases, the government also provides a lawyer without cost for any defendant who is unable to afford one.

It is important to note that in the context of judicial proceedings, the right to a defense lawyer arises after the initiation of proceedings including an arraignment. Prior to the start of judicial proceedings, the defendant may request counsel during interrogation and should be appointed counsel during an identification lineup.

The Sixth Amendment requires that a defense lawyer do more than just be present at a hearing, instead the defense lawyer should zealously represent the defendant. The United States Supreme Court has stated: "[I]f counsel entirely fails to subject the prosecution's case to meaningful adversarial testing, then there has been a denial of Sixth Amendment rights that makes the adversary process itself presumptively unreliable."

The foundations of the American criminal justice system are the presumption of innocence afforded a defendant and the burden of proof standard imposed upon the government to prove each element of the offense beyond a reasonable doubt. The notion of protecting the unjustly accused can be traced back to both Roman law and English common law. Living in the first century, Emperor Trajan decreed that there should be certainty in determining guilt and innocence. He said: "[I]t was better to let the crime of a guilty person go unpunished than to condemn the innocent."

The reasonable doubt standard was established common law at the time that the Bill of Rights, including the Sixth Amendment, was adopted. The Supreme Court articulated the standard in the following statement: "No man should be deprived of his life . . . unless the jurors who try him are able, upon their consciences, to say that the evidence before them . . . is sufficient to show beyond a reasonable doubt the existence of every fact necessary to constitute the crime charged."

Justice William O. Douglas depicted proof beyond a reasonable doubt as "the great barricade." Defense lawyers argue that this "formidable barricade" is the highest standard of certainty in the law. The argument continues that an assault or a breach upon this barricade is insufficient under the law. Instead, for the government to convict, it "must scale the very top of the barricade to prevail."

## COURTS IN ACTION

### Indigent Defendants 18 U.S. Code § 3006A

Each United States district court, with the approval of the judicial council of the circuit, shall place in operation throughout the district a plan for furnishing representation for any person financially unable to obtain adequate representation in accordance with this section. Representation under each plan shall include counsel and investigative, expert, and other services necessary for adequate representation. Each plan shall provide the following:

1.  Representation shall be provided for any financially eligible person who—
    A.  is charged with a felony or a Class A misdemeanor;
    B.  is a juvenile alleged to have committed an act of juvenile delinquency as defined in section 5031 of this title [18 USCS § 5031];
    C.  is charged with a violation of probation;
    D.  is under arrest, when such representation is required by law;
    E.  is charged with a violation of supervised release or faces modification, reduction, or enlargement of a condition, or extension or revocation of a term of supervised release;
    F.  is subject to a mental condition hearing under Chapter 313 of this title [18 USCS §§ 4241 et seq.];
    G.  is in custody as a material witness;
    H.  is entitled to appointment of counsel under the sixth amendment to the Constitution;
    I.  faces loss of liberty in a case, and Federal law requires the appointment of counsel; or
    J.  is entitled to the appointment of counsel under section 4109 of this title [18 USCS § 4109].

2.  Whenever the United States magistrate [United States magistrate judge] or the court determines that the interests of justice so require, representation may be provided for any financially eligible person who—
    A.  is charged with a Class B or C misdemeanor, or an infraction for which a sentence to confinement is authorized; or
    B.  is seeking relief under section 2241, 2254, or 2255 of title 28.

3.  Private attorneys shall be appointed in a substantial proportion of the cases. Each plan may include, in addition to the provisions for private attorneys, either of the following or both:
    A.  Attorneys furnished by a bar association or a legal aid agency.
    B.  Attorneys furnished by a defender organization established in accordance with the provisions of subsection (g).

### United States v Rountree (1966, SD NY) 254 F Supp 1009

Purpose of 18 USCS § 3006A is to provide adequate legal representation to defendants otherwise unable to employ counsel, and to insure that experienced and capable members of bar could be called upon without causing undue financial sacrifice.

---

In 1972, the Supreme Court recognized that our courts are not perfect. Persons are unjustly convicted for a various reasons: prejudice, ignorance, mistake, judicial indifference, police ineptitude, prosecutorial vindictiveness, or defense counsel underzealsousness. Despite all of the procedural safeguards in the criminal justice system, it is still a system designed and administered by human beings who inevitably err and make mistakes. Defense lawyers are the prominent person in the courtroom who brings reasonable doubt to life to assure that the system is renders a fair and certain verdict.

### LAW IN ACTION

### At What Point Must the State Appoint an Indigent Defendant Counsel?

In Rothgery v. Gillespie County, 2008 U.S. LEXIS 5057, 13-14 (U.S. June 23, 2008), Justice David Souter delivered the majority opinion.

In Rothgery, a criminal background check wrongly disclosed that he had a record of a felony conviction. The local police officers relied on this record to arrest him as a felon in possession of a firearm. The officers lacked a warrant, and so promptly brought Rothgery before a magistrate judge, as required by Tex. Crim. Proc. Code Ann., Art. 14.06(a). Texas law has no formal label for this initial appearance before a magistrate, but it is commonly known as the "article 15.17 hearing." Texas combines the Fourth Amendment's required probable-cause determination with the setting of bail, and is the point at which the arrestee is formally apprised of the accusation against him, Tex. Crim. Proc. Code Ann., Art. 15.17(a).

Rothgery's article 15.17 hearing followed routine. The arresting officer submitted a sworn "Affidavit Of Probable Cause" that described the facts supporting the arrest and charged that Rothgery committed the offense of unlawful possession of a firearm by a felon—3rd degree felony [Tex. Penal Code Ann. § 46.04]. After reviewing the affidavit, the magistrate judge determined that probable cause existed for the arrest. The magistrate judge informed Rothgery of the accusation, set his bail at $ 5,000, and committed him to jail, from which he was released after posting a surety bond.

Rothgery had no money for a lawyer and made several oral and written requests for appointed counsel, which went unheeded. The following January, he was indicted by a Texas grand jury for unlawful possession of a firearm by a felon, resulting in his rearrest the next day, and an order increasing bail to $ 15,000. When he could not post it, he was put in jail and remained there for three weeks. On January 23, 2003, six months after the article 15.17 hearing, Rothgery was finally assigned a lawyer, who promptly obtained a bail reduction (so Rothgery could get out of jail), and assembled the paperwork confirming that Rothgery had never been convicted of a felony. Counsel relayed this information to the district attorney, who in turn filed a motion to dismiss the indictment, which was granted.

In Justice Souter's opinion, he noted that the Sixth Amendment right of the "accused" to assistance of counsel in "all criminal prosecutions" is limited by its terms: "it does not attach until a prosecution is commenced." He stated that the Court has for purposes of the right to counsel, pegged commencement to the initiation of adversary judicial criminal proceedings—whether by way of formal charge, preliminary hearing, indictment, information, or arraignment. And that the rule is not mere formalism, but recognition of the point at which the government has committed itself to prosecute, the adverse positions of government and defendant have solidified, and the accused finds himself faced with the prosecutorial forces of organized society, and immersed in the intricacies of substantive and procedural criminal law.

The Court held that Texas's article 15.17 hearing marks that point, with the consequent state obligation to appoint counsel within a reasonable time once a request for assistance is made. The Court stated that it was irrelevant that the presence of counsel at a Tex. Code Crim. Proc. Ann. art. 15.17 hearing, say, may not be critical, just as it is irrelevant that counsel's presence may not be critical when a prosecutor walks over to the trial court to file an information. The question whether arraignment signals the initiation of adversary judicial proceedings is distinct from the question whether the arraignment itself is a critical stage requiring the presence of counsel. Texas's article 15.17 hearing plainly signals attachment, even if it is not itself a critical stage. A criminal defendant's initial appearance before a judicial officer, where he learns the charge against him and his liberty is subject to restriction, marks the start of adversary judicial proceedings that trigger attachment of the Sixth Amendment right to counsel.

Defense lawyers begin to test the government's case by filing motions to suppress evidence. The Fourth Amendment protects personal liberty and security from unfettered police practices such as unreasonable searches and seizures. If evidence is seized without a warrant and outside of the complex exceptions to the warrant requirement, then the evidence will be excluded from trial. A defense counsel's motion to suppress starts the court's review of the police practices leading to the seizure of evidence.

At trial, defense lawyers chiefly use cross-examination to raise doubts about the witnesses credibility and factual statements. Cross-examination is posing questions to an adverse witness to test, inspect, and evaluate what the witness is really saying. Cross-

## COURTS IN ACTION

### Effective Assistance of Counsel

### *McFarland v. State,* 928 S.W.2d 482 (Tex. Crim. App. 1996)

George McFarland was convicted of the offense of capital murder, specifically murder in the course of a robbery. He received the death penalty. On appeal, the Texas Court of Criminal Appeals [court of last resort for criminal cases in Texas] affirmed his conviction despite the fact that his attorney slept through much of his trial in 1992. As noted by a reporter attending the trial, the counsel's mouth kept falling open and his head lolled back on his shoulders. According to the trial judge, the defendant has a right to counsel and the "constitution doesn't say the lawyer has to be awake." The record shows that the counsel was 72 years old at the time of trial and was prone to take afternoon naps. The U.S. Supreme Court denied review.

In the Strickland v. Washington case, the Supreme Court has recognized the importance of an attorney to the trial process:

> . . . Even the intelligent and educated layman has small and sometimes no skill in the science of law. If charged with crime, he is incapable, generally, of determining for himself whether the indictment was good or bad. He is unfamiliar with the rules of evidence. Left without the aid of counsel he may be put on trial without a proper charge, and convicted upon incompetent evidence, or evidence irrelevant to the issue or otherwise inadmissible. He lacks both the skill and knowledge adequately to prepare his defense, even though he may have a perfect one. He requires the guiding hand of counsel at every step in the proceedings against him. Without it, though he may not be guilty, he faces the danger of conviction because he does not know how to establish his innocence.

#### Excerpts from the Texas Court's Decision:

The standard for testing claims of ineffective assistance of counsel was announced in Strickland v. Washington, 466 U.S. 668 (1984). A claimant must prove that counsel's representation so undermined the proper functioning of the adversarial process that the trial cannot be relied on having produced a just result. Appellant must prove: (1) that his counsel's representation was deficient; and (2) that the deficient performance was so serious that it prejudiced his defense. This means appellant must prove by a preponderance of the evidence that counsel's representation fell below the standard of prevailing professional norms, and that there is a reasonable probability that but for counsel's deficiency the result of the trial would have been different.

The review of counsel's representation is highly deferential. The court indulges in a strong presumption that counsel's conduct falls within a wide range of reasonable representation. The burden is on appellant to overcome that presumption. Appellant must identify the acts or omissions of counsel that are alleged to constitute ineffective assistance and affirmatively prove that they fall below the professional norm for reasonableness. After proving error, appellant must affirmatively prove prejudice. Appellant must prove that counsel's errors, judged by the totality of the representation, not by isolated instances of error or by only a portion of trial, denied him a fair trial. It is not enough for appellant to show that the errors had some conceivable effect on the outcome of the proceedings. He must show that there is a reasonable probability that, but for counsel's errors, the fact finder would have had a reasonable doubt respecting guilt and/or the sentence of death.

**LAW IN ACTION**

**Florida Rules of Criminal Procedure Rule 3.111(B)**

Counsel shall be provided to indigent persons in all prosecutions for offenses punishable by incarceration, including appeals from the conviction thereof. In the discretion of the court, counsel does not have to be provided to an indigent person in a prosecution for a misdemeanor or violation of a municipal ordinance if the judge, at least 15 days prior to trial, files in the cause a written order of no incarceration certifying that the defendant will not be incarcerated in the case pending trial or probation violation hearing, or as part of a sentence after trial, guilty or nolo contendere plea, or probation revocation. This 15-day requirement may be waived by the defendant or defense counsel.

examination, through the use of questions that suggest the answer, known as leading questions, may expose witness bias, lack of recollection, or other vulnerability. A famous law professor, John Henry Wigmore, stated that "[c]ross-examination is the greatest legal engine ever invented for the **discovery** of truth."

Defense lawyers also use objections to limit the government's evidence or to assure that the each piece of evidence is admitted only in accordance with the rules of evidence. Chapter 3 covered the rules of evidence.

## WITNESSES

Witnesses play a vital role during a hearing. It is through witness testimony that evidence is received, facts are established, and ultimately, the guilt or innocence of a defendant is determined. During a criminal trial, witnesses are sequestered from the courtroom proceedings so that they do not hear the testimony of other witnesses. Before a witness testifies, she is administered an oath or affirmation to tell the truth.

The jury as the fact finder determines the credibility of each witness and the weight that is placed on the witness's testimony. For instance, the jury may place little weight on the testimony of a witness who was present at the scene and had the opportunity to see the defendant's actions but, nonetheless, has difficulty recollecting the details of what occurred.

Witnesses testify by responding to questions of the attorneys during both direct examination and cross-examination. The party that calls the witness conducts direct examination by asking open-ended questions to reveal the relevant facts and circumstances known by the witness. On direct examination, the use of leading questions is prohibited. The essential test of whether a question is leading is whether the phrasing of the question suggests the answer desired by the questioner. For instance, a leading question may be as simple as, "The light was red, correct?" to the more complex leading question as, "After conducting your laboratory analysis, you concluded that the defendant's DNA matched the blood that was found at the scene of the robbery, right?" Both questions suggest the answer and would be objectionable for being leading questions.

Cross-examination is conducted by the opposing party who did not call the witness. During cross-examination, counsel may use leading questions. Generally, cross-examination is limited to the scope of the questions asked during direct examination, but the witness may also be cross-examined on such matters as: (1) the capacity of the witness to observe and remember, (2) the bias or interests of the witness that may affect the witness's truthfulness, and (3) additional facts that relate to those testified to on direct examination.

In a criminal trial, the right to fully cross-examine the witnesses within the scope of the subjects raised during direct examination is a right guaranteed by the United States

Constitution. Specifically, the Sixth Amendment provides that an accused has a right to confront witnesses against him. This right of confrontation is viewed as a fundamental right to assure a fair criminal trial. Although the judge may, in his sound discretion, limit cross-examination when the subject is considered exhausted, it is reversible error if the defendant is not afforded the absolute right to cross-examine a witness.

Recently, the United States Supreme Court extended the right to cross-examine a lab analyst who has completed a lab report upon a scientific analysis of a substance relevant to a criminal prosecution. Prior to 2009, prosecutors used laboratory reports in nearly all prosecutions involving illegal drugs, fingerprint identifications, blood alcohol tests, and DNA analysis. In *Massachusetts v. Melendez-Diaz*, the Court reversed a conviction for trafficking in cocaine, because the state relied upon a crime lab report that certified that the cocaine was in plastic bags found in the car which the defendant was riding. Although the Court considered requiring lab analysts to testify would be a costly and time consuming process, which may cause delay and increased criminal case backlogs, the Court determined that a failure to have the lab analyst subject to cross-examination violated the defendant's right to confront the witnesses against him.

## Children as Witnesses

Children may testify as witnesses who observed the commission of a crime, but many times they testify as victims of a crime. Although generally witnesses are presumed to be competent to testify, before a child witness may testify, the judge must determine the competency of the child to testify.

The judge considers the child's age, intelligence, and sense of moral and legal responsibility of the duty to tell the truth. To be determined competent, the child must have the capacity to observe events so that she could later recollect the events and communicate in response to questions about the events. It need not be shown that a child understands the oath to tell the truth but the child must realize that a punishment will follow if the truth is not told.

As an example, in a South Dakota case, a four-and-a-half-year-old female eyewitness to her mother's kidnapping was permitted to testify. The young girl, who had been three years old at the time of the kidnapping, demonstrated sufficient ability to observe, recollect, communicate, and tell the truth to satisfy the minimal standards of competence to testify according to the court. The trial judge observed the girl in a play setting and heard the testimony of a child psychologist and then determined that the girl had the ability to recollect certain facts, her communications skills were appropriate to her age, and she had the knowledge of the difference between right and wrong. The young girl's testimony was instrumental in obtaining a conviction.

## Opinion Testimony by Lay (Non-expert Witness)

If a witness is not testifying as an expert, the witness's testimony in the form of opinions or inferences is limited to those opinions or inferences which are (1) rationally based on the perception of the witness; (2) helpful to a clear understanding of the witness's testimony or the determination of a fact in issue; and (3) not based on scientific, technical, or other specialized knowledge. Lay witnesses often find it difficult to express themselves in language which is not that of an opinion or conclusion. For example, law enforcement agents could testify that the defendant was acting suspiciously without being qualified as experts; however, the rules on experts are applicable where the agents testify on the basis of extensive experience that the defendant was using code words to refer to drug quantities and prices.

## Expert Witnesses

In a criminal case, a witness's testimony is generally restricted to the facts within the personal knowledge, observation, or recollection of the witness. A lay witness, as opposed to an expert witness, generally, cannot testify to opinions, inferences, impressions, or conclusions. Conclusions are within the domain of the jury sitting as the fact finder in a criminal prosecution.

An expert witness, on the other hand, may testify as to her opinion. There are several qualifications to this general rule. First, the expert witness must be qualified as an expert by specialized knowledge, skill, experience, training, or education to the extent that her opinion would probably aid the jury to determine the facts. It is sufficient that the expert be qualified on only one of these grounds. This means that an expert witness need not be a formally educated scientist or physician, although some are, but may be a tradesman, such as a plumber or carpenter, or other professional, such as a policeman. What is

## LAW IN ACTION

### Eyewitness Identifications

Eyewitness identification is vital to the prosecution of many criminal cases. When the victim of a crime is called upon to testify about the identification of her attacker, the jury takes special notice about the certainty and verification of the perpetrator's identity. The victim is asked: "Do you see the person who committed the crime in the courtroom?" When the answer is a point of the witness's finger to the defendant seated at counsel table with the confident words, "It is him," the evidence is difficult to rebut.

Recent research, however, has begun to question how accurate is visual memory. The CBS News Show "60 Minutes" reported on a 1984 case in which 22-year-old college student Jennifer Thompson was raped in her off campus apartment.

She studied her attacker's face the best that she could and identified the perpetrator three days later in a photo array and later in a physical lineup. At a trial, based upon Thompson's in-court identification, Ronald Cotton was convicted and sentenced to prison.

After 11 years, Cotton was released because his DNA did not match the DNA at the crime scene. It was a case of mistaken identity and an innocent man was convicted. Now Thompson and Cotton speak together at conferences as advocates for the reform of the eyewitness identification process. To see more about this fascinating case, view the video and read the report, go to this link: www.cbsnews.com/stories/2009/03/06/60minutes/main4848039_page3.shtml?tag=contentMain;contentBody

### Excerpts from *Jones v. State*, 273 Ga. 213 (Ga. 2000)

When a trial court concludes that an identification procedure is impermissibly suggestive, the issue becomes whether, considering the totality of the circumstances, there was a substantial likelihood of irreparable misidentification. If not, then both the pretrial and in-court identifications are admissible. Factors to be considered in determining whether there was a substantial likelihood of misidentification include: (1) the witness's opportunity to view the accused at the time of the crime; (2) the witness's degree of attention; (3) the accuracy of the witness's prior description of the accused; (4) the witness's level of certainty at the confrontation with the accused; and (5) the length of time between the crime and the confrontation. The ultimate question is, whether under the totality of the circumstances, the identification is reliable.

The admission of expert testimony regarding eyewitness identification is in the discretion of the trial court. Where eyewitness identification of the defendant is a key element of the State's case and there is no substantial corroboration of that identification by other evidence, trial courts may not exclude expert testimony without carefully weighing whether the evidence would assist the jury in assessing the reliability of eyewitness testimony and whether expert eyewitness testimony is the only effective way to reveal any weakness in an eyewitness identification. However, the admission or exclusion of this evidence lies within the sound discretion of the trial court, whose decision will not be disturbed on appeal absent a clear abuse of discretion.

important is that the expert witness has peculiar knowledge or experience of which the jury would not be generally aware.

The second qualification is that the scientific, technical, or specialized knowledge offered by the expert witness will assist the jury to understand the evidence or determine a fact in issue at trial. Decisions concerning the qualifications of the expert witness and the admissibility of her testimony are left to the sound discretion of the trial judge. The weight to be attached to the expert testimony, however, is left to the discretion of the jury.

Several procedural steps must be satisfied before an expert is allowed to testify. The prosecutor must disclose in discovery the identity of the expert, her qualifications, the basis for her testimony, and the opinion to which she will testify. The report prepared by the expert witness must be provided to the defense, too. At trial, the prosecutor must lay a foundation, which establishes that the expert witness is qualified. The witness must testify as to her credentials, such as her education, experience, certifications from professional organizations, and scholarly work that she has authored. After the defense counsel has had an opportunity to cross-examine the witness as to her expert qualifications, the trial judge decides whether to allow the witness to testify as to an expert opinion. These steps may occur outside of the jury's presence. Once the witness is received as an expert, she is allowed to testify as to opinions, inferences, and conclusions within her field of expertise.

## JURY

According to the National Center for State Courts, "each year in the United States, nearly 32 million people are randomly selected and summonsed to serve as jurors in the approximately 150,000 jury trials that take place in state and federal courts." About 1.5 million will ultimately be sworn as trial jurors in both civil and criminal trials. More members of the public are exposed to the American justice system as jurors rather than as defendants, witnesses, or any other way.

In a criminal trial, the jury is a group of lay citizens who are sworn to faithfully listen and judge the evidence according to the law given by the judge and render a verdict to the best of their ability. Jurors are told that they are the judges of the facts in the case in accordance with the law as instructed by the judge. They are advised that they cannot follow their own notion or opinion as to what the law is or ought to be. Instead, they must apply the law as explained by the judge, regardless of the consequences. They must also base their verdict solely upon the evidence, without prejudice or sympathy.

Potential jurors are chosen from a jury pool chosen randomly by the **clerk of court** from a list generated from lists of registered voters and people with drivers' licenses who reside in a judicial district. The selection method employed by judicial districts helps ensure that jurors represent a cross section of the community without regard to race, gender, national origin, age or political affiliation.

**LAW IN ACTION**

**Florida Rules of Criminal Procedure Rule 3.270. Number of Jurors**

Twelve persons shall constitute a jury to try all capital cases, and six persons shall constitute a jury to try all other criminal cases.

The general qualifications to be a juror are that the person must be: (1) United States citizen; (2) at least 18 years of age; (3) residing in the judicial district for one year; (4) proficient in the English language; (5) without any disqualifying mental or physical condition; and (6) not currently subject to felony charges or convicted of any felony. Certain groups of persons are exempt from jury service. They are: (1) active duty members of the armed forces; (2) members of police and fire departments; (3) others who work with emergency services or those who have recently served on a jury. Lastly, the court in its discretion may grant a temporary deferral of service on the grounds of "undue hardship or extreme inconvenience."

At a criminal trial, before a jury is empaneled, the selection process includes both **peremptory challenges** and **challenges for cause**. This selection process is known as **voir dire**.

Challenges for cause are based upon establishing that a potential juror is unable to sit fairly and impartially to judge the facts in the case. To strike a juror for cause, counsel must establish to the satisfaction of the judge that the prospective juror does not have an open mind to fairly consider only the evidence introduced during the trial.

Peremptory challenges are granted at the general discretion of counsel so long as the peremptory challenge is on grounds that are racially neutral. Counsel need not provide any justification for striking a juror with a peremptory challenge. In federal criminal cases, the defense counsel is allowed ten peremptory challenges and the government is allowed six.

At a criminal trial, the jury is instructed to presume that the defendant is innocent. They are also told that the burden of proof rests with the government and that each element of the offense must be proven beyond a reasonable doubt in order to render a verdict of guilty. Jurors are cautioned that they must not discuss the evidence in the case until they are instructed to begin their deliberations by the trial judge. The greatest reward to a juror is the knowledge that they have performed the duty of maintaining law and order and upholding justice among their fellow citizens.

## LAW IN ACTION

### Excerpts from Appellate Decision in *State v. Adams*, 406 Md. 240 (Md. 2008)

It is the most sacred constitutional right of every party accused of a crime, that the jury should respond as to the facts, and the court as to the law. It is the duty of the court to instruct the jury as to the law; and it is the duty of the jury to follow the law, as it is laid down by the court. This is the right of every citizen; and it is his only protection. If the jury were at liberty to settle the law for themselves, the effect would be, not only that the law itself would be most uncertain, from the different views, which different juries might take of it; but in case of error, there would be no remedy or redress by the injured party; for the court would not have any right to review the law as it had been settled by the jury. Indeed, it would be almost impracticable to ascertain, what the law, as settled by the jury, actually was. On the contrary, if the court should err, in laying down the law to the jury, there is an adequate remedy for the injured party, by a motion for a new trial, or a writ of error, as the nature of the jurisdiction of the particular court may require. Every person accused as a criminal has a right to be tried according to the law of the land, the fixed law of the land; and not by the law as a jury may understand it, or choose, from wantonness, or ignorance, or accidental mistake, to interpret it.

## THE COURT'S PROFESSIONAL STAFF

The professional staff in a criminal court is made of trained and skilled persons to assure that a complete record is made of the proceedings and that the court is assisted in conducting its business.

A **court reporter** trained in stenography and in audio recordings makes a complete record of the entire trial proceedings. The court reporter is present at each session and the record includes the verbatim words spoken by the judge, counsel, witnesses, and other participants. The record also includes the actual exhibits that have been received into evidence.

Court reporters have the training and skills to taking the words that have entered the reporters' ears and leaving his fingertips an instant later in a stenography machine. Instead of typing actual words, court reporters record words as "outlines" which are limited-alphabet abbreviations. "WAURM," for example, commonly means "What is your name?" It may take 40 months of training for a court reporter to become proficient.

With computer aided recording, court reporters are able to easily provide attorneys with daily **transcripts** to aid them for cross-examination of witnesses. Judicial clerks can copy and paste the judge's exact language from the bench into a written text for a minute order issued by the judge.

A deputy clerk of court creates a record listing each person who testifies and marks any documents, photographs, or other items introduced as exhibits into evidence.

On appeal, the appellate judges and parties rely upon the complete record, including the transcript of the proceedings and the exhibits to determine whether there were procedural errors or legal mistakes committed during the trial.

At a criminal trial, the court's **bailiff** serves to bring the courtroom to order, open the court session, and assure that proper decorum is maintained according to the court's order. The bailiff also maintains custody of the jury assuring that the jury's needs are cared for while it is sitting.

## Questions in Review

1. What is the role of the judge in criminal trials?
2. How can judges reduce the backlog of criminal cases?
3. What ethical obligations does the prosecutor have in a criminal case?
4. Should the prosecutor seek a conviction in every case? Why or why not?
5. Why are indigent defendants provided counsel?
6. What does zealous representation by counsel mean?
7. What are lay witnesses allowed to testify to?
8. What are expert witnesses allowed to testify to?
9. What are the necessary qualifications for a witness to be declared by the court to be an expert witness?
10. Under what circumstances can a child witness testify?
11. How is a transcript prepared of the courtroom proceedings?
12. Who is responsible for assembling the record of trial for an appeal?

## Key Terms

**Bailiff:** A court attendant whose duties are to keep order in the courtroom and to have custody of the jury.

**Clerk of Court:** An officer appointed by the judges of the court to assist in administratively managing the processing of cases, in maintaining court records, in handling financial matters, and in providing other logistical support to the court.

**Challenge for Cause:** The privilege of striking a juror from the panel during voir dire based upon an articulated reason that the juror may be prejudiced or biased.

**Court Reporter:** A person hired by the court who makes a word-for-word record of what is said in court, generally by using a stenographic machine, shorthand, or audio recording, or a combination of those, and then produces a transcript of the proceedings.

**Discovery:** The process by which lawyers learn about their opponent's case in preparation for trial.

Typical items of discovery in criminal cases include grand jury transcripts, depositions, investigative reports, witnesses' statements, and laboratory reports. All of these items provide the defense counsel information about the relevant facts underlying the prosecution.

**Indigent Defendant:** A criminal defendant who lacks the financial means to pay for his own defense including the services of a defense lawyer. When a defendant is determined to be indigent, he is entitled to a court-appointed lawyer.

**Jury:** The group of citizens selected to hear the evidence in a trial and render a verdict on matters of fact. Also known as a petit jury or a trial jury.

**Jury Instructions:** A judge's directions to the jury before it begins deliberations regarding the factual questions it must answer and the legal rules that it must apply.

**Opinion Evidence:** Evidence of what the witness thinks, believes, or infers in regards to the facts in dispute at a trial, as opposed to testimony based upon the witness's own personal knowledge of the facts generally gained from his sensory perceptions.

Opinion evidence from lay witnesses is generally not admissible at trial.

**Peremptory Challenge:** The privilege of striking a juror from the panel during voir dire without providing a reason for the challenge. Each counsel is provided a limited number of peremptory challenges in a criminal case.

**Record:** A written account of the proceedings in a case, including the indictment, motions, pleadings, evidence, witness testimony, and exhibits admitted or considered during the course of the prosecution.

**Transcript:** A written, word-for-word record of what was said, either in a proceeding such as a criminal trial, or during some other official hearing, such as an arraignment or hearing on a motion to suppress.

**Voir Dire:** The process by which judges and lawyers select a trial jury from among those eligible to serve, by questioning them to make certain that they would fairly decide the case. "Voir dire" is a phrase meaning "to speak the truth."

**Witness:** A person called upon by either side in a lawsuit to give testimony before the court or jury.

## List of References

### STATUTES

Jury Selection and Service Act, 28 U.S.C. §§ 1861, et seq.,

### CASES

*Argersinger v. Hamlin*, 407 U.S. 25 (1972)
*Batson v. Kentucky*, 476 U.S. 79 (1986)
*Berger v. United States*, 295 U.S. 78 (1935)
*Chambers v. Mississippi*, 410 U.S. 287 (1973)
*Crawford v. Washington*, 541 U.S. 36 (2004)
*Davis v. United States*, 160 U.S. 469 (1895)
*Gideon v. Wainwright*, 372 U.S. 335 (1963)
*Johnson v. Louisiana*, 406 U.S. 356 (1972)
*Johnson v. Zerbst*, 304 U.S. 458 (1938)
*Kyles v. Whitley*, 514 U.S. 419 (1995)
*Miles v. United States*, 103 U.S. 304 (1881)
*Melendez-Diaz v. Massachusetts*, 557 U.S. __, 129 S. Ct. 2527 (2009)
*Pointer v. Texas*, 380 U.S. 400 (1965)
*State v. Anderson*, 2000 SD 45, 608 N.W.2d 644 (S.D. 2000)
*United States v. Cronic*, 466 U.S. 648 (1984)

### BOOKS, JOURNALS AND ARTICLES

American Bar Association. *ABA Standards for Criminal Justice: Prosecution and Defense Function*, 3d ed. 1993. www.abanet.org/crimjust/standards/pfunc_toc. html (accessed April 24, 2010).

*Black's Law Dictionary* 4th ed. St. Paul, MN: West, 1957.
Conom, Tom P. "Bulwarks of Liberty: Presumption of Innocence and Reasonable Doubt." *The Champion* (December 1991): 18–23. www.nacdl.org/public.nsf/ GideonAnniversary/Index1/$FILE/PresumeInnocence. pdf (accessed April 25, 2010).
Dedel, Kelly. "Witness Intimidation." U.S. Department of Justice, Office of Community Oriented Policing Services, 2006. www.cops.usdoj.gov/files/RIC/ Publications/e07063407.pdf (accessed April 24, 2010)
DeBenedictis, Don J. "Excuse Me, Did You Get All That?" *ABA Journal* 79 (1993): 84.
Deitz, Laura, et al. "Witnesses." *American Jurisprudence*, 2nd ed. vol. 81, section 208 (2010).
*Eleventh Circuit United States Court of Appeals, Pattern Jury Instructions (Criminal Cases)* 2003. www.ca11. uscourts.gov/documents/jury/crimjury.pdf (accessed May 8, 2010).
Gershman, Bennett. "The New Prosecutors." *University of Pittsburg Law Review* 53 (1992): 393–407.
*Handbook for Trial Jurors Serving in the United States District Courts*. www.uscourts.gov/jury/trialhandbook. pdf (accessed May 8, 2010).
Hynes, Charles J. "The Evolving Prosecutor: Broadening the Vision, Expanding the Role." *Criminal Justice* 24 (2009): 1.

Kamisar, Yale. "The Fourth Amendment and Its Exclusionary Rule" *The Champion* (September–October, 1991): 20–25. www.nacdl.org/public.nsf/GideonAnniversary/Index1/$FILE/4ExclusionaryRule.pdf (accessed April 25, 2010).

National Center for State Courts, Center for Jury Studies. http://www.ncsc-jurystudies.org (accessed May 9, 2010).

Posner, Richard A. *How Judges Think*. Cambridge: Harvard University Press, 2008.

Shinall, Jennifer Bennett. "Slipping Away from Justice: The Effect of Attorney Skill on Trial Outcomes." *Vanderbilt Law Review* 63 (2010): 267–306.

"Respondents Reporting Whether They Think the Criminal Justice System Is Fair in Its Treatment of People Accused of Committing Crime." *Sourcebook of Criminal Justice Statistics* (2003), page 139. www.albany.edu/sourcebook/pdf/t245.pdf (accessed May 10, 2010).

Understanding the Federal Courts, www.uscourts.gov/understand03/content_1_0.html (accessed May 9, 2010).

Wallace, Steven. "Eight Rules For Judicial Time Management." *Judicature* 91, no. 2 (2007): 87–92.

Wright, Charles Alan, and Gold, Victor James. "Opinions and Expert Testimony." *Federal Practice and Procedure* vol. 29, section 6265 (2010).

# 7

# Extraordinary Writs

**What you need to know about Extraordinay Writs**

After you have completed this chapter, you should know:

- A writ is a mandatory precept, under seal, issued by a court, and commanding the person to whom it is addressed to do or not to do some act.

- An extraordinary writ is a judicial order issued generally by an appellate court to make available the remedies not regularly within the powers of lower courts; for example, writ of habeas corpus, mandamus, or prohibition.

- Extraordinary writs provide an alternative to the typical appeal process to contest a lower court's order.

- An extraordinary writ allows an appellate court to review an issue that could not adequately be addressed through the typical appeals process.

- Generally an extraordinary writ can only be used when there is no adequate remedy at law or in other words, the issue cannot be reviewed meaningfully on appeal from a final order or judgment.

- The primary rationale for the use of extraordinary writs is to allow review by the appellate courts when an ordinary appeal would be meaningless.

- The difference between writs of mandamus and writs of prohibition is that the writ of mandamus orders a judicial body, generally a trial court, to perform a duty, which the law clearly and positively requires, while the writ of prohibition prevents a judicial body from exercising its power in a manner unauthorized by law.

- A writ of prohibition is appropriate in the context where a court is ordering something that falls outside the scope of its jurisdiction or authority.

- A writ of prohibition is used as a preventative, not a corrective measure.

- The writ of habeas corpus is literally a request for the court to order the warden or jailor to produce the prisoner and justify why he or she is being detained in prison or other confinement.

- The writ of habeas corpus is normally used by prisoners to attack their prison sentences.

- Many legal scholars have called this writ of habeas corpus the most important human right in the U.S. Constitution

**Chapter Outline**

- Introduction
- Extraordinary Writs
- Writ of Habeas Corpus
- Writ of Certiorari
- Briefs

# INTRODUCTION

> **The writ of habeas corpus** enjoys an extremely important place in the history of this state and this nation. often termed the "great writ," it 'has been justifiably lauded as "the safe-guard and the palladium of our liberties."
> —*People v. Villa* (2009) 45 Cal.4th 1063, 1068.
> The writ is "a critical check on the executive, ensuring that it does not detain individuals except in accordance with law."
> —*Hamdi v. Rumsfield* (2004) 542 U.S. 507, 525.

A writ defies simple definition. Legally, a **writ** is defined as a mandatory precept, under seal, issued by a court, and commanding the person to whom it is addressed to do or not to do some act. One might think of a writ as a written order issued by a court directing some other court officer to do or not to do a particular act. An **extraordinary writ** is a judicial order issued generally by an appellate court to make available the remedies not regularly within the powers of lower courts; for example, writ of habeas corpus, mandamus, or prohibition.

# EXTRAORDINARY WRITS

Extraordinary writs provide an alternative to the typical appeal process to contest a lower court's order. An extraordinary writ allows an appellate court to review an issue that could not adequately be addressed through the typical appeals process. For example, as noted by the Minnesota Battered Women's Legal Advocacy Project (2003), there are a variety of circumstances where extraordinary writs are important to battered women due to the urgency and safety concerns of many proceedings involving battered women. The urgency of these issues combined with a legal system that does not always respond appropriately to the needs of battered women make extraordinary writs a valuable resource.

In Minnesota, similar to most states, there are four circumstances where either a writ of mandamus or writ of prohibition may be obtained. These include:

- When no adequate remedy at law exists, or in other words the issue cannot be reviewed meaningfully on appeal from a final order or judgment;
- When the court is about to exceed its jurisdiction resulting in irreparable harm;
- When the trial court's action may effectively decide the case; or
- When review of the trial court decision will settle or establish a new rule of practice affecting other litigants (Herr and Vasaly 1993).

The primary rationale for the use of extraordinary writs is to allow review by the appellate courts when an ordinary appeal would be meaningless. There is no right to an extraordinary writ because it is discretionary, which means that the appellate court has discretion in whether to consider the extraordinary writ.

An additional restriction is that the reviewing court cannot control judicial discretion, An appellate court may force the lower court to perform its duties, exercise its judgment, perform its judicial functions, follow the clear statement of the law, or prevent the lower court from exceeding its authority or jurisdiction but can not force the lower court to make a discretionary judgment. (Minn. Stat. sec 586.01).

## Writ of Mandamus or Writ of Prohibition

The difference between writs of mandamus and writs of prohibition is that the writ of mandamus orders a judicial body, generally a trial court, to perform a duty that the law

**LAW IN ACTION**

**A federal issue must be present before a federal court can issue a writ of habeas corpus.**
Norris v. Schotten, 146 F.3d 314, 328-329 (6th Cir. Ohio 1998)

A claim based solely on an error of state law is not redressable through the federal habeas process. It is especially inappropriate for a federal habeas court to set aside a state court's ruling on an issue of state law where, as in the present situation, Ohio's appellate courts on direct appeal have already found appellant's claim of a violation of his statutory right to a speedy trial to be meritless. Although this principle does not prohibit federal habeas relief where a state court's error in interpreting or applying its own law has rendered the trial that convicted the appellant so fundamentally unfair as to have deprived appellant of substantive due process in violation of the U.S. Constitution. This is not our situation here. In requesting federal habeas relief, appellant did not claim and offered no proof that the Ohio court system as a whole was arbitrary and lacked a rational mechanism/process for remedying errors.

The U.S. Court of Appeals also noted that it was not the job of a habeas court to reweigh trial testimony and to reevaluate the credibility of witnesses; such responsibilities are those of a trial jury. On either habeas review or direct appeal to the Ohio Court of Appeals, an insufficiency of the evidence claim is reviewed with the evidence viewed in the light most favorable to the prosecution.

### Allaway v. McGinnis, 301 F. Supp. 2d 297 (S.D.N.Y. 2004)

Pro se petitioner [without assistance of a counsel] state inmate was convicted of assault in the second degree. The conviction was affirmed on direct appeal. The inmate filed the present petition for a writ of habeas corpus arguing that an evidentiary ruling at his trial deprived him of his due process right to a fair trial under the Fourteenth Amendment to the United States Constitution and that the length of his sentence was excessive.

**Facts:** The trial court admitted evidence that earlier in the day in which the inmate stabbed another resident of a homeless shelter, he also hit a third resident with a bottle or pipe. The trial court determined that the evidence was relevant to completing the narrative of the events of the day and to establish the identity of the inmate. The appellate division determined that the evidence at issue was properly admitted as a matter of state law. The present court could grant habeas relief only if the trial court's decision to admit evidence of the inmate's prior bad act rendered his trial so fundamentally unfair that it denied him his right to due process of law as guaranteed by the Constitution of the United States. There was nothing to indicate that the decisions of the state courts met the requirements. The inmate could not establish that the testimony made his trial fundamentally unfair. The inmate did not argue that his sentence was imposed in violation of the United States Constitution, which was the only basis on which the present court could grant habeas relief for a state court sentencing determination.

**Decision:** The inmate's petition for a writ of habeas corpus was denied. No federal constitutional issue is presented where the sentence is within the range prescribed by state law. On habeas review, it is not a federal court's duty to balance the probative value against the unfair prejudice because the Due Process Clause does not permit federal courts to engage in a finely tuned review of the wisdom of state evidentiary rules. A federal district court may grant habeas relief to a state prisoner whose claims were decided on the merits by a state court only if the state court's decision was contrary to, or involved an unreasonable application of, clearly established federal law, as determined by the United States Supreme Court.

**LAW IN ACTION**

**Examples of the Use of Extraordinary Writs in Battered Women Cases**

Provided by the Minn. Battered Women's Legal Advocacy Project

- In divorce/custody proceedings, when a family court judge inappropriately orders a family into mediation when domestic abuse is present, a battered woman could seek a writ of prohibition to prevent the family court judge from making the inappropriate order to mediation;
- In a harassment restraining order proceedings, when the court or court administrator inappropriately orders the petitioner to pay filing fees or fees for service of process, the battered woman could seek a writ of prohibition preventing the court from requiring her to pay these fees because they are contrary to what the law clearly states or she may seek a writ of mandamus compelling the court to follow the law which clearly states that petitioners are exempt from these fees. (See Minn. Stat. sec. 518B.01 subd. 3a).

clearly and positively requires, while the writ of prohibition prevents a judicial body from exercising its power in a manner unauthorized by law.

The **writ of mandamus** commands or orders a lower court to do something that it has failed to do, which is clearly a duty required of them. To obtain a writ of mandamus a petitioner must show:

- The lower court failed to fulfill an official duty clearly imposed by law;
- The failure resulted in a public wrong specifically injurious to petitioner; and
- There is no other adequate legal remedy.

For example, a writ of mandamus could be issued to compel a lower court to waive the filing fees for a petitioner who seeks to obtain a family protection order (OFP) when the court refuses to proceed unless the petitioner pays a filing fee in cases where the state statutes required the waiver of fees. Failure to waive the fee could give rise to a petitioner filing a writ of mandamus to compel the lower court to follow its duty clearly stated in the law. A writ of mandamus may be an appropriate remedy because there is no other specific legal remedy for a petitioner who is prevented from obtaining an OFP because she cannot afford the filing fee.

There are two general types of writs of mandamus: peremptory and alternative writs of mandamus. Peremptory writs of mandamus may be issued when the right to require the performance of the act is clear, and it is apparent that no valid excuse for nonperformance can be given. Alternative writs of mandamus allow for the defendant to answer the petition for the writ of mandamus to show cause why they should not be compelled to comply with the writ. The basic differences between the two is that with a peremptory writ, there is no valid excuse for nonperformance of the act clearly required by law, while for an alternative writ of mandamus the law may be unclear and there may be some valid excuse for not complying.

For the most part, the difference is mainly procedural because if the reviewing court decides the writ is an alternative writ of mandamus, then the body being compelled to comply with the writ may have an opportunity to answer and show cause why it should not have to comply with the writ. If the reviewing court finds that the writ is peremptory, then it will not allow the opposing party to answer and will issue the writ of mandamus, because the law so clearly states the duty required by the opposing party.

A **writ of prohibition** is appropriate in the context where a court is ordering something that falls outside the scope of its jurisdiction or authority. There are three requirements before a writ of prohibition will be granted:

- An inferior court or tribunal must be about to exercise judicial or quasi-judicial power;
- The exercise of such power must be unauthorized by law; and
- The exercise of such power must result in injury for which there is no adequate remedy.

A writ of prohibition is used as a preventative, not a corrective measure. The higher court is preventing or prohibiting the lower court from doing something that it has no authority to do. For example, a writ of prohibition may be appropriate is if a judge is exceeding her/his authority by ordering a couple into mediation in a dissolution proceeding when domestic violence has occurred, and a state law provides that mediation will not be ordered for dissolution when a court has found probable cause that domestic abuse has occurred and there is no available remedy to address the injury to a battered woman caused by ordering her into mediation with her abuser, the court would be exceeding its authority by ordering mediation.

There are two methods for requesting writs of mandamus or prohibition. The usual process is by written petition to the court with jurisdiction over issuing the writ. An emergency mechanism is generally provided by state statutes, which allows for an "emergency" oral petition for extraordinary writs when factors or time issues would prevent the normal procedures.

## LAW IN ACTION

### Process of review of state court proceeding by inferior federal courts in habeas corpus proceedings is not unconstitutional.

*United States ex rel. Elliott v. Hendricks,* 213 F.2d 922 (3d Cir. Pa. 1954)

Elliott, a state prison inmate, appealed from a judgment of the United States District Court that dismissed his petition for habeas corpus. Elliott claimed that his sentence was unconstitutionally fixed at death instead of life imprisonment because the psychiatrist appointed by the state trial court to render an opinion on his mental condition was so mentally impaired as to render the psychiatrist's report and opinion worthless.

**Facts:** A state court found Elliott guilty of murder and sentenced him to death. At sentencing, a psychiatrist appointed by the state court provided a report that was unfavorable to him. Later, the psychiatrist was found to be suffering from a mental condition, and was committed to an institution. Claiming that the psychiatrist was so mentally impaired at the time that his report was worthless, and that the report caused the sentence to be fixed at death instead of life imprisonment, Elliot petitioned the state court for habeas corpus. After that petition was denied, Elliot asserted the same claims in a petition to the district court for habeas corpus. The court rejected the state's argument that a federal court could not constitutionally review Elliot's conviction and sentence. The U.S. Constitution gave federal courts power to use habeas corpus to test whether a state prison inmate was deprived of constitutional rights. The court affirmed the denial of habeas corpus because the state court was not misguided by the psychiatrist's testimony, the sentence was not based on erroneous assumptions, and Elliot had received due process from the state courts. The court noted that the psychiatric examination of Elliot during sentencing process was discretionary, not mandatory. When it imposed sentence the state court was not misguided by the psychiatrist's testimony, and did not impose its sentence on any erroneous set of assumptions. The issue raised by Elliot had been fairly decided on his prior petition for habeas corpus to the state court.

**LAW IN ACTION**

**Constitution of the United States, Article I, Section 9**

The Privilege of the Writ of Habeas Corpus shall not be suspended, unless when in Cases of Rebellion or Invasion the public safety may require it.

Generally district or superior courts have original jurisdiction over all cases of mandamus, unless the writ is to be directed at a district or superior court judge, in which case the court of appeals has jurisdiction over the mandamus case.

A filing fee is required to petition for either an oral or written extraordinary writ. The filing fee is not required if a petition for an oral writ is denied. To proceed without prepaying these fees, a person may apply to proceed "in forma pauperis" that basically allows a person who cannot afford to pay the fees to proceed without paying.

## WRIT OF HABEAS CORPUS

The writ of habeas corpus is literally a request for the court to order the warden or jailor to produce the prisoner and justify why he or she is being detained in prison or other confinement. The writ is normally used by prisoners to attack their prison sentences. Many legal scholars have called this writ the most important human right in the U.S. Constitution. In 1769, Samuel Johnson wrote about the greatness of the British form of government, stating: "The Habeas Corpus is the single advantage our government has over other countries."

Scholars have traced the origins of the writ of habeas corpus as a protection against illegal imprisonment back to at least the New Testament time when Festus the Roman sought justice for Paul's imprisonment in Palestine. Festus is reported to have stated: "For it seemeth to me unreasonable to send a prisoner, and not withal to signify the crimes against him."

The writ of habeas corpus was adopted in England by the Habeas Corpus Act of 1679 as a weapon against tyranny. This act passed by the House of Lords provided: "No man may be accused, arrested, or detained except in cases fixed by the law. . . ."

**LAW IN ACTION**

**The Folklore of Habeas Corpus**

At the time that the Habeas Corpus Act of 1679 was being debated in the English House of Lords, the act received strong support from an exceedingly portly member of the house. When the lords lined up to be counted, the parliamentary monitor (person who records the votes), as folklore has it, jokingly counted the portly lord's vote as ten votes. The monitor allowed the vote to stand when no one noticed his joke. The act passed by two votes.

The first federal habeas corpus act was passed by the United States in 1789. This act stated that judges "shall have power to grant writs of habeas corpus for the purpose of an inquiry into the cause of commitment." All 50 states have enacted similar provisions in either the state constitution or by statutes.

The writ must be filed in a court with jurisdiction over the person holding the prisoner or detainee. For example, if a prison sentence is given by a federal court, the writ may only be filed in a federal court, since the prisoner would be held in a federal prison or under the direction of a federal official. If the conviction is in a state court, the individual may appeal to a state court or to a federal court (if a violation of a federally protected right is concerned).

There is no limit to the number of writs that a prisoner may file as long as each pertains to a different subject or issue. For example, a prisoner may appeal to a state court of appeals contending that his or her state court conviction was in violation of the state's constitutional protections against unreasonable searches. He or she also can file in federal court a writ contending that the state court conviction was in violation of the U.S. Constitution's protections against unreasonable searches.

If a prisoner or detainee submits a writ to a federal district court contending that his or her state court conviction was in violation of the rights guaranteed by the federal constitution and the federal district court denies his or her writ, then he or she may appeal the denial of the writ to a federal court of appeals. Many decisions of the U.S. Supreme Court regarding state convictions reach the Supreme Court via the writ. The U.S. Supreme Court in *Stone v. Powell* (1976) attempted to limit federal habeas corpus petitions of state court convictions if the accused had a full and fair review in state court. This limitation has had only limited effect on the number of writs filed.

A writ is started by the prisoner (petitioner) filing a petition for habeas corpus with the appropriate court, naming the warden or head of the penal institution as the defendant. If the court orders a hearing after reviewing the petition, the defendant (warden) may be called to provide evidence in resistance to the petition. Habeas corpus also may be used in limited noncriminal situations and where the accused is in custody prior to trial.

The courts have used many grounds for granting habeas corpus relief. Some of the more popular grounds are listed below:

- The denial of counsel at various stages of trial proceedings.
- The failure of the state to disclose evidence favorable to the defendant.
- Prejudicial pretrial publicity prevented the defendant from obtaining a fair trial.
- Insanity of defendant at time that he entered a guilty plea.
- The use of evidence seized in violation of the defendant's constitutional rights.
- Questions regarding the use of confessions or admission by the defendant.

Most writs involving state cases are filed in state courts. The federal courts sit to ensure that individuals are not imprisoned in violation of their federal constitutional rights. As a general rule, a federal court will not grant the writ in cases originally tried in state courts unless it is established that (1) state remedies have been exhausted, and (2) the prisoner or detainee makes a claim that his or her state trial or appeal involved a denial of federal constitutional rights.

The U.S. Supreme Court held in the *Rose v. Lundy* (1982) case that a petition containing both exhausted and unexhausted claims must be dismissed. ("Exhausted" refers to the fact that the petitioner has no further state remedies to redress a specific claim.) The Court reasoned that since there were claims that had not been exhausted, the petitioner had not exhausted all his state remedies.

The writ of **habeas corpus** has been termed the great writ because its purpose is to obtain the prompt release of one who is being unlawfully detained. The right to this writ is embodied in the U.S. Constitution and in the laws of all the states. The statutes of the states read similarly to the following: Every person unlawfully imprisoned or restrained of liberty,

**LAW IN ACTION**

**In reviewing a state prisoner's writ of habeas corpus, should a federal court use federal law or state law?**

*Santos v. Laurie, 433 F. Supp.* 195, 196-200 (D.R.I. 1977)

Petitioner Ricardino Santos seeks a writ of habeas corpus. He contends that his convictions for second degree murder of his wife and assault with a deadly weapon on his brother-in-law were illegal because the guilty pleas on which they were entered were not knowingly and voluntarily made. He alleges that he relied on a statement made by his attorney that the state had promised to recommend a sentence of not more than 15 years incarceration, a recommendation which was never in fact made.

The guilty pleas were entered on November 23, 1970. On January 7, 1971, Santos received a twenty-five year sentence on the second degree murder charge, and a deferred sentence on the assault count. The available state remedies have since been exhausted in three separate proceedings raising the same claims. Rhode Island Superior Court Justice Bulman, who took the plea, denied a writ, after oral argument but without an evidentiary hearing. After acquiring new counsel, Santos then sought habeas corpus in the Rhode Island Superior Court, and this was denied by Justice Gallant on July 3, 1974 after a full evidentiary hearing.

After hearing testimony and considering the transcripts of earlier proceedings, the judge of the state superior court, Justice Gallant stated: On the basis on the credible evidence, I find that:

1.  No commitment was made by any responsible State official that the State would recommend a sentence of 10 to 15 years contingent upon the petitioner's plea of guilty to a reduced charge of second degree murder.
2.  Petitioner's counsel represented to him that the Attorney General would recommend, and he would receive a 10 to 15 year sentence if he pleaded guilty to a reduced charge of second degree murder, and that if the court did not follow the recommendation he would be allowed to reinstate his not guilty plea.
3.  The petitioner was induced to plead guilty in a bona fide reliance on the foregoing representations.
4.  When Mr. Santos pleaded on November 23, 1970, he told the court that there had been no inducements offered and that he was willing to take his chances on whatever sentence the court saw fit to impose.

The superior court judge stated that he was satisfied that Santos believed that his attorney had an agreement as to a recommendation by the Attorney General; that the court almost always followed such a recommendation; and that if it did not, he could reinstate his not guilty plea. Justice Gallant nevertheless denied Santos' habeas petition. He believed himself bound by Rhode Island decisional law, which precludes relief unless any assurances given a defendant by defense counsel can be objectively corroborated by the acts of state officials. Thus, under Rhode Island case law, a plea is voluntary even if it is entered in reliance on defense counsel's representation of prosecutorial promises, provided that state officials have not corroborated those promises by word or deed.

**Decision by U.S. District Court Judge Raymond J. Pettine, Chief Judge:** A federal court must apply federal constitutional law in habeas corpus proceedings, although it may apply that law to reliably found state facts. Here, Santos was definitely told by his attorney that the state had agreed to recommend a specific sentence, a recommendation that was not in fact later made. It is of no constitutional difference to Santos whether the promise was made and not kept. The critical question is whether or not the defendant's plea was knowingly and voluntarily made, not whether or not the conduct of responsible state officials has been blameless. It is not only the misconduct of state officials which effectively deprives the defendant of rights of

*(Continued)*

due process of law and effective assistance of counsel. On the basis of the facts established by Justice Gallant, Santos is entitled to relief.

Here, it is established that Santos' counsel told him (1) that the state had promised to recommend a sentence of from ten to fifteen years if he pleaded guilty to second degree murder, (2) that he would in all probability receive a sentence of not more than fifteen years, and (3) that if anything went wrong and the court refused the plea, the State had agreed to permit a withdrawal of the plea.

Justice Gallant's findings incorporate two alleged state promises: (1) a promise of a recommendation by the state of a 10–15 year sentence; and (2) a promise that the plea could be withdrawn if the Court did not accept the recommendation. I do not understand Justice Gallant to have found any promise that Santos would definitely receive a 10–15 year sentence. Such a promise would be inconsistent with the promise to allow the plea to be withdrawn if the recommendation was not accepted.

Santos believed, and relied on, the representations of his court-appointed counsel that the state had promised a recommendation. That recommendation was not in fact ever made. His plea was therefore not knowingly and voluntarily entered, and it may not stand. The facts noted by Judge Gallant also establish that the conviction was a product of ineffective assistance of counsel to such an extent as to render the proceedings a "sham", and to deprive Santos of his right to counsel. Indeed, the state concedes that if a defense counsel is found to have assured Santos of a non-existent agreement by the prosecuting attorney, the ineffective assistance of counsel claim is made out.

In an unusual reversal of roles, the state vigorously contends that this Court should not accept Justice Gallant's findings. Instead, the Court is urged to examine the entire record and make its own findings of fact. This argument is without merit. Only in the Superior Court habeas corpus proceedings was any factual hearing held, with witnesses called, the rules of evidence observed, and credibility weighed in person by the fact finder. The petition was denied without an evidentiary hearing. Although the habeas corpus petition before the Rhode Island Supreme Court was technically a de novo proceeding, that court took no testimony, made no findings of fact, and denied the petition on the record below without opinion.

Ordinarily, when a habeas corpus petitioner prevails on a claim that the promise on which he relied in pleading guilty was not kept, he is given a choice of withdrawing the plea or specific enforcement. Specific enforcement cannot be required of the state here, because the state may not be compelled to honor a promise it never made. Nevertheless, the state may decide that justice would be served by a kind of specific enforcement. If the Attorney General can in good conscience recommend a sentence of 10–15 years, and if the Superior Court is willing to allow Santos to withdraw his plea in the event that it chooses not to accept the non-binding recommendation, the plea may stand and Santos may be resentenced under it. If the State adopts this course of action, Santos will have obtained everything which he relied on in entering the plea and will have no right to withdraw it. If the Attorney General or the state judge do not believe that justice would be served by this course, Santos must either be released or be tried or permitted to plead anew. The state, of course, would then be free to make a different recommendation, or none at all.

A writ of habeas corpus shall issue, unless within sixty days petitioner is retried or is resentenced in accordance with this opinion.

---

under any pretense whatever, may request a writ of habeas corpus to inquire into the cause of the imprisonment or restraint. The person who believes that he or she is being unlawfully imprisoned, or someone in that person's behalf, may petition the appropriate court to have a writ of habeas corpus issued. Generally, a writ of habeas corpus may be issued by a judge of the superior court or its equivalent, or by a justice of an appellate court. In most states, the judge of the inferior court has no authority to issue a writ of habeas corpus.

The petition must state the place of confinement, the officer or person doing the confining, and the facts explaining why the petitioner feels unlawfully imprisoned. If the reason is valid, the writ will be issued and served on the person holding the prisoner, commanding that the prisoner be brought before the issuing court for a hearing to determine whether there is sufficient cause to confine the prisoner. A copy of the writ is furnished to the local prosecuting attorney in order that evidence may be presented endeavoring to prove the legality of the imprisonment. But the burden of proof is on the imprisoned person to prove by a preponderance of evidence that the imprisonment is unlawful. If the offense for which the person is imprisoned is a bailable one, the person may be entitled to post bail pending the habeas corpus hearing.

If, after hearing the evidence presented by the prisoner and the prosecuting attorney, the judge concludes that the prisoner is being unlawfully detained, an order for the prisoner to be set free is issued. The prisoner may not be charged further on that offense, unless additional evidence is developed showing reasonable cause for an arrest and commitment by a legal process. If the judge concludes that the imprisonment was lawful, the prisoner will remain in custody to await the appropriate judicial processes.

The early use of the writ of habeas corpus was limited to obtaining the immediate release of one unlawfully restrained. But in recent years, the use of this writ has been broadened materially to make it applicable in a number of situations. For example, if an offender believes that the bail set for release is excessive, a writ of habeas corpus may be filed in an effort to get a reduction in bail. Further, if a convicted person believes that the sentence is excessive, the writ may be filed to have a determination made on this issue. This writ has also been used to determine the effectiveness of counsel. One of the more extensive uses made of the writ in recent years has resulted from some appellate court decisions, particularly those of the U.S. Supreme Court, which affect the rights of one convicted. For example, in *Witherspoon v. Illinois*, 391 U.S. 510 (1968), the U.S. Supreme Court held that a prospective juror could not be challenged for cause just because the juror had reservations against the death penalty. This decision caused writs of habeas corpus to be filed by all those convicted and given the death penalty in trials in which prospective jurors had been excused for cause as being against the death penalty. These writs requested that the sentence of death be reduced to life imprisonment. This action was possible, since the U.S. Supreme Court made the *Witherspoon* decision retroactive. When a decision is made retroactive, it is effective even though a trial is completed and the appeal period has passed. If a decision is not made retroactive, only those offenders whose trial or appeal has not been completed may take advantage of it.

The writ is also the way that the death penalty in state criminal trials is often attacked in federal court. In the past, convictions were voided years after the defendants were found guilty. The process has also been used to delay the imposition of the death penalty. To eliminate this possibility, in 1996 the U.S. Congress passed the Antiterrorism and Effective Death Penalty Act. This act establishes limitation periods for the bringing of habeas actions and requires that federal courts generally defer to state courts' determinations. Under the act, a habeas corpus petitioner will normally have one year in which to seek relief. If the claim has been adjudicated in state court, relief will not be available unless the state court's adjudication resulted in a decision that is either contrary to or has involved an unreasonable application of clearly established federal law as determined by the U.S. Supreme Court, or was based on an unreasonable determination of the facts in light of the evidence presented in the state court proceedings. The presumption of correctness accorded state courts' factual findings was also strengthened. Second or successive habeas corpus actions presenting new claims must be dismissed unless the claim is shown to rely on a new, previously unavailable rule of constitutional law or unless the factual predicate for the claim could not have been discovered previously through due diligence and the new facts would be sufficient to establish by clear and convincing evidence that, except for the error, no reasonable fact finder would have convicted.

## LAW IN ACTION

Do the detainees in Guantanamo Bay have the right to contest their confinement in federal court by use of the Writ of Habeas Corpus?

This issue was examined in the case of Boumediene v. Bush, 2008 U.S. LEXIS 4887 (U.S. 2008). Justice Kennedy delivered the opinion of the Court in which Justices Stevens, Souter, Ginsburg, and Breyer joined. Chief Justice Roberts filed a dissenting opinion, in which Justices Scalia, Thomas, and Alito joined. The Court was bitterly divided in this decision. Justice Scalia in an opinion concurring with Chief Justice Roberts's dissent stated: "The Nation will live to regret what the Court has done today. I dissent."

Petitioners are aliens designated as enemy combatants and detained at the United States Naval Station at Guantanamo Bay, Cuba. The issue before the Court was whether petitioners have the constitutional privilege of habeas corpus. The Court in a 5–4 decision held that they do have the habeas corpus privilege. The Court noted that Congress had enacted the Detainee Treatment Act of 2005 (DTA), 119 Stat. 2739, that provides certain procedures for review of the detainees' status. The Court held that those procedures were not an adequate and effective substitute for habeas corpus.

The Court noted that some of the individuals were apprehended on the battlefield in Afghanistan, others in places as far away from there as Bosnia and Gambia. All are foreign nationals, but none is a citizen of a nation now at war with the United States. Each denies he is a member of the al Qaeda terrorist network that carried out the September 11 attacks or of the Taliban regime that provided sanctuary for al Qaeda. Each petitioner was determined to be an enemy combatant; and has sought a writ of habeas corpus in the United States District Court for the District of Columbia.

In the first actions commenced in February 2002, the District Court ordered the cases dismissed for lack of jurisdiction because the naval station is outside the sovereign territory of the United States. The Supreme Court granted certiorari and reversed, holding that 28 U.S.C. § 2241 extended statutory habeas corpus jurisdiction to Guantanamo.

The Court concluded that Art. I, § 9, cl. 2, of the Constitution has full effect at Guantanamo Bay. And if the privilege of habeas corpus is to be denied to the detainees, Congress must act in accordance with the requirements of the Suspension Clause. The Court stated that:

This Court may not impose a de facto suspension by abstaining from these controversies. Abstention is not appropriate in cases in which the legal challenge turns on the status of the persons as to whom the military asserted its power. . . . Petitioners, therefore, are entitled to the privilege of habeas corpus to challenge the legality of their detention. . . .

Where a person is detained by executive order, rather than, say, after being tried and convicted in a court, the need for collateral review is most pressing. A criminal conviction in the usual course occurs after a judicial hearing before a tribunal disinterested in the outcome and committed to procedures designed to ensure its own independence. These dynamics are not inherent in executive detention orders or executive review procedures. In this context the need for habeas corpus is more urgent. The intended duration of the detention and the reasons for it bear upon the precise scope of the inquiry. Habeas corpus proceedings need not resemble a criminal trial, even when the detention is by executive order. But the writ must be effective. The habeas court must have sufficient authority to conduct a meaningful review of both the cause for detention and the Executive's power to detain. . . . The laws and Constitution are designed to survive, and remain in force, in extraordinary times. Liberty and security can be reconciled; and in our system they are reconciled within the framework of the law. The Framers decided that habeas corpus, a right of first importance, must be a part of that framework, a part of that law.

**LAW IN ACTION**

**The Antiterrorism and Effective Death Penalty Act of 1996 (AEDPA)**

Pub. L. No. 104-132, 110 Stat. 1214

Signed into law on April 24, 1996 was designed to "deter terrorism, provide justice for victims, provide for an effective death penalty, and for other purposes." The AEDPA had a significant impact on the writ of habeas corpus. One provision of the AEDPA limited the power of federal judges to grant relief unless the state court's adjudication of the claim resulted in a decision that was contrary to, or involved an unreasonable application of clearly established federal law as determined by the Supreme Court of the United States; or based on an unreasonable determination of the facts in light of the evidence presented in the state court proceeding.

28 USCS § 2254

(a) The Supreme Court, a Justice thereof, a circuit judge, or a district court shall entertain an application for a writ of habeas corpus in behalf of a person in custody pursuant to the judgment of a State court only on the ground that he is in custody in violation of the Constitution or laws or treaties of the United States.

(b) (1) An application for a writ of habeas corpus on behalf of a person in custody pursuant to the judgment of a State court shall not be granted unless it appears that—

(A) the applicant has exhausted the remedies available in the courts of the State; or

(B) (i) there is an absence of available State corrective process; or

(ii) circumstances exist that render such process ineffective to protect the rights of the applicant.

(2) An application for a writ of habeas corpus may be denied on the merits, notwithstanding the failure of the applicant to exhaust the remedies available in the courts of the State.

(3) A State shall not be deemed to have waived the exhaustion requirement or be estopped from reliance upon the requirement unless the State, through counsel, expressly waives the requirement.

**Excerpts rom Petitioner's Brief in *Gomez v. Superior Court of Lassen County*, 2010 CA S. Ct. Briefs 79176.**

Petitions for writs of habeas corpus typically implicate weighty federal and state constitutional rights, including the guarantee that the state will not take life or liberty without due process of law (Cal. Const., art. I, § 7; U.S. Const. Amend XIV) or impose cruel and/or unusual punishment. (Cal. Const., art. I, § 17; U.S. Const. Amends. VIII & XIV.) This Court has long emphasized that habeas corpus concerns matters of the greatest importance: It is well to remember that this case involves fundamental rights, and is of universal interest. Around those rights the English have waged their great battle for liberty. Without the narration of the conflicts to which they have given rise, the history of the English people would be a dull affair. The right of the government with reference to persons accused of crime has been, and is yet, a matter of great consideration. It led to the agitation that wrung from power the Great Charter, the Petition of Right, and the Habeas Corpus Act. All the great achievements in favor of individual liberty, of which the English people are so justly proud, may be said to have come through contests over the rights of persons imprisoned for supposed crime. And justly it is deemed a matter of the utmost importance.

# Ex Parte Merryman

## (U.S. Circuit Court, 1861; 17 Fed. Cases 145)

The case of Ex Parte Merryman discusses the suspension of the Writ of Habeas Corpus. The writ is normally issued to determine if a person held in custody is being unlawfully detained or imprisoned. As noted earlier, it has been termed the great writ because its purpose is to obtain the immediate release of someone being unlawfully detained. The Constitution places limits on when the writ may be suspended. This case provides a look at how the Supreme Court can interfere with presidential actions.

### Facts of the Case

On May 25, 1861, Union troops entered the home of petitioner John Merryman, located outside of Baltimore, Maryland. The petitioner was a prominent local citizen and a state legislator. He also was noted for his strong Confederate sympathies. He was taken into custody by the military and detained at Fort McHenry. His attorney filed a writ of habeas corpus with the U.S. Circuit Court (then the name of the federal trial court). The presiding judge Roger Taney (also a Supreme Court justice who "rode circuit") issued the writ ordering the commanding general of Fort McHenry to appear and justify the detention. The general did not appear; instead he sent a letter explaining that the petitioner was guilty of treason and that the president had authorized the general to suspend the writ of habeas corpus.

### Excerpts from Majority Opinion—Chief Justice Taney delivered the opinion of the Court.

As the case comes before me . . . I understand that the President not only claims the right to suspend the writ of habeas corpus himself, at his discretion, but to delegate that discretionary power to a military officer. . . . Congress is, of necessity, the [only] judge of whether the public safety does or does not require it [suspension of writ]; and their judgment is conclusive. . . . The introduction of these words [Article I, Section 9] is a standing admonition to the legislative body of the danger of suspending it, and of the extreme caution they should exercise, before they give the government of the United States such power over the liberty of a citizen.

## WRIT OF CERTIORARI

The writ of certiorari is discussed in this chapter as a matter of convenience, but it is not normally considered as an extraordinary writ, this writ is the normal route an appeal should take from the trial court. This writ is issued by an appellate court to permit the review of a decision or judgment by a lower court. It is often issued when other means of appeal are not possible. The writ of **certiorari** is often granted by a state supreme court to review a lower court's decision in order to establish guidelines to be followed in future cases by either trial judges or lower appellate courts. This is particularly the case if there is some doubt concerning a law or procedure. This writ is automatically issued in most jurisdictions to review a case when the death penalty is imposed to determine whether the facts warrant a conviction and the imposition of the death penalty. The U.S. Supreme Court frequently issues this writ to review the decision of a state appellate court when there may be a possible denial of a U.S. constitutional guarantee. The U.S. Supreme Court decision *Coker v. Georgia*, 433 U.S. 584 (1977) is a good example. Coker was convicted of forceful rape and sentenced to death in a trial court in Georgia. The Georgia Supreme Court affirmed both the conviction and the death penalty. The U.S. Supreme Court granted Coker a writ of certiorari in order to determine whether the death penalty was excessive for the conviction of rape and, thus, a violation of the Eighth Amendment.

## BRIEFS

When a party applies to a court for a writ or when a party appeals a court decision, the party is generally required to submit a "brief," which is essentially a written argument as to why the court action requested should be granted. The brief is considered as the "Petitioner's Brief." The other party then submits a "respondent's brief," which generally contends that the requested court action should not be granted. Then the petitioner, person requesting the relief, may file a reply brief. To provide the reader with a favor of a brief, excerpts from a respondent's brief is contained in the following Law in Action. In this case, the original defendant and other defendants were the petitioners and the City of Chicago was the respondent. Note: The complete brief is 41 pages in length. So, portions of the brief were deleted for the purposes of this text. If the reader is interested, he or she may read the entire brief by using either Westlaw or Lexis-Nexis and using the following citation.

## LAW IN ACTION

*OTIS MCDONALD, et al., Petitioners, v. CITY OF CHICAGO, Respondent.*
No. 08-1521
SUPREME COURT OF THE UNITED STATES
2008 U.S. Briefs 1497; 2009 U.S. S. Ct. Briefs LEXIS 1893

**December** 30, 2009
On Writ of Certiorari to the United States Court of Appeals for the Seventh Circuit.
Initial Brief: Appellee-Respondent

**COUNSEL:** JAMES A. FELDMAN, Special Assistant Corporation Counsel, 5335 Wisconsin Avenue, N.W., Suite 440, Washington, D.C. 20015, (202) 730-1267.

MARA S. GEORGES, Corporation Counsel of the City of Chicago, BENNA RUTH SOLOMON,* Deputy Corporation Counsel, MYRIAM ZRECZNY KASPER, Chief Assistant Corporation Counsel, SUZANNE M. LOOSE, Assistant Corporation Counsel, ANDREW W. WORSECK, Assistant Corporation Counsel, 30 N. LaSalle Street, Suite 800, Chicago, Illinois 60602, (312) 744-7764.

*Counsel of Record.
Counsel for the City of Chicago.
RAYMOND L. HEISE, Village Attorney of Oak Park, 123 Madison Street, Oak Park, Illinois 60302, (708) 358-5660.
Counsel for the Village of Oak Park.
HANS GERMANN, RANJIT HAKIM, ALEXANDRA SHEA, MAYER BROWN LLP, 71 South Wacker Drive, Chicago, Illinois 60606, (312) 782-0600.
QUESTION PRESENTED
Whether the Second Amendment right to keep and bear arms is incorporated against the States by the Fourteenth Amendment's Due Process or Privileges or Immunities Clause.
View Table of Contents
View Table of Authorities

STATEMENT

In 1982, Chicago enacted a handgun ban, along with other firearms regulations, because "the convenient availability of firearms and ammunition has increased firearm related deaths and injuries" and

*(Continued)*

handguns "play a major role in the commission of homicide, aggravated assaults and armed robbery." Chicago City Council, Journal of Proceedings, Mar. 19, 1982, at 10049. Under Chicago's ordinance, "[n]o person shall . . . possess . . . any firearm unless such person is the holder of a valid registration certificate for such firearm," and no person may possess "any firearm which is unregisterable." Municipal Code of Chicago, Ill. § 8-20-040(a) (2009). Unregisterable firearms include most handguns, but rifles and shotguns that are not sawed-off, short-barreled, or assault weapons are registerable. *Id.* § 8-20-050. Registerable firearms must be registered before being possessed in Chicago (*id.* § 8-20-090(a)), and registration must be renewed annually (*id.* § 8-20-200(a)). Failure to renew "shall cause the firearm to become unregisterable." *Id.* § 8-20-200(c).

Otis McDonald, several other individual plaintiffs, the Illinois State Rifle Association, and the Second Amendment Foundation (collectively "petitioners") filed a lawsuit against Chicago, challenging the handgun ban and certain registration requirements. J.A. 16–31. The individual petitioners allege that they legally own handguns they wish to possess in their Chicago homes for self-defense; that they applied for permission to possess the handguns in Chicago; and that their applications were refused. J.A. 19–21. Petitioners allege in count I that Chicago's handgun ban violates the Second Amendment, as allegedly incorporated into the Fourteenth Amendment's Due Process Clause and Privileges or Immunities Clause. J.A. 26. Counts II, III, and IV raise Second and Fourteenth Amendment claims against the requirements of annual registration of firearms, registration as a prerequisite to possession in Chicago, and the penalty of rendering firearms unregisterable for failure to comply with either requirement. J.A. 27–29. Count V is an equal protection challenge to the unregisterability penalty. J.A. 30. . . .

### TITLE: BRIEF FOR RESPONDENTS CITY OF CHICAGO AND VILLAGE OF OAK PARK
### SUMMARY OF ARGUMENT

To address the problem of handgun violence in their communities, Chicago and Oak Park have enacted stringent firearms regulations prohibiting the possession of handguns by most individuals. The Court should reaffirm that the Second Amendment does not bind state and local governments. Neither the Court's selective incorporation doctrine under the Due Process Clause nor the Privileges or Immunities Clause provides a basis for imposing the Second Amendment on the States and establishing a national rule limiting arms regulation.

I. Bill of Rights provisions are incorporated into the Due Process Clause only if they are implicit in the concept of ordered liberty. That is an exacting standard that appropriately protects federalism values at the root of our constitutional system and is particularly appropriate when addressing firearms regulation. Firearms are designed to injure or kill; conditions of their use and abuse vary widely around the country; and different communities may come to widely varying conclusions about the proper approach to regulation. Thus, Chicago and Oak Park may reasonably conclude that in their communities, handgun bans or other stringent regulations are the most effective means to reduce fear, violence, injury, and death, thereby enhancing, not detracting from, a system of ordered liberty. Although other approaches are possible and may be effective elsewhere, it cannot be concluded that easy and widespread availability of firearms everywhere is necessary to ordered liberty.

The practice in the States throughout our history does not support incorporating the Second Amendment. While many States have adopted firearms rights in one form or another, the nature of these rights differs substantially from the Second Amendment right. The Second Amendment precludes an "interest balancing" approach and a ban on weapons in common use. But the States have generally adopted a "reasonable regulation" approach under which even stringent restrictions or outright bans of particular firearms are ordinarily upheld.

The Court has sometimes consulted the Framingera history of a provision in considering incorporation. For the Second Amendment, that history does not support incorporation. Although a right to firearms for personal use was recognized in a variety of sources of law that pre-existed the Constitution, *District of Columbia v. Heller,* 128 S. Ct. 2783 (2008), makes clear that it was not included in the Bill of Rights for its own sake or to protect it against the political process; rather, it was codified to protect the militia by eliminating the threat that the federal government would take away the arms necessary for militia service. Nothing in the congressional debate over the Amendment suggests any view that a private arms right unconnected to preservation of the militia was thought implicit in the concept of ordered liberty. The scope of the Second Amendment right—weapons in common use–also reflects its purpose of protecting the militia, rather than an individual right related to self-defense, since the Second Amendment protects weapons regardless of whether they are useful for self-defense. . . .

## ARGUMENT

### I. THE DUE PROCESS CLAUSE DOES NOT INCORPORATE THE SECOND AMENDMENT RIGHT TO KEEP AND BEAR ARMS.

#### A. A Provision Of The Bill Of Rights Applies To The States Under The Due Process Clause If It Is "Implicit In The Concept Of Ordered Liberty."

This Court held long ago that the provisions of the Bill of Rights, of their own force, apply only to the federal government and do not limit state or local governments. *Barron v. Mayor of Baltimore,* 32 U.S. (7 Pet.) 243 (1833). That continues to be the law. See *Virginia v. Moore,* 128 S. Ct. 1598, 1603 (2008); *United States v. Balsys,* 524 U.S. 666, 675 (1998). In a series of cases beginning in the late 19th century, the Court has recognized that the Due Process Clause of the Fourteenth Amendment incorporates—and therefore applies to the States—fundamental rights included in the Bill of Rights that are "implicit in the concept of ordered liberty." *Palko v. Connecticut,* 302 U.S. 319, 325 (1937), overruled on other grounds by *Benton v. Maryland,* 395 U.S. 784 (1969). As the Court explained in *Thornhill v. Alabama,* 310 U.S. 88 (1940), First Amendment rights were incorporated because they are "essential to free government." *Id.* at 95; see also *Schneider v. New Jersey,* 308 U.S. 147, 161 (1939) ("at the foundation of free government by free men"). Likewise, incorporation of the Fourth Amendment's protection against unreasonable search and seizure rested on the Court's conclusion that "the 'security of one's privacy against arbitrary intrusion by the police' is 'implicit in the concept of ordered liberty.'" *Mapp v. Ohio,* 367 U.S. 643, 650 (1961) (quoting *Wolf v. Colorado,* 338 U.S. 25, 27 (1949)).

    1. To be "implicit in the concept of ordered liberty," a right must be "implicit"—that is, essential—to the very "concept" of ordered liberty. As the Court has explained, that means that "neither liberty nor justice would exist if [the right] were sacrificed." *Palko,* 302 U.S. at 326; see also NRA Br. 8 ("a fundamental principle of liberty that is basic to a free society"). In what is regarded as the first selective incorporation case, the Court described such a right as "a principle of natural equity, recognized by all temperate and civilized governments, from a deep and universal sense of its justice." *Chicago, B. & Q. R.R. v. City of Chicago,* 166 U.S. 226, 238 (1897) (incorporating Takings Clause); see *Duncan v. Louisiana,* 391 U.S. 145, 149 n.14 (1968) ("[I]f a civilized system could be imagined that would not accord the particular protection," incorporation is not appropriate); see also *Malloy v. Hogan,* 378 U.S. 1, 4 (1964) (selective incorporation originated with *Chicago* case); *Twining v. New Jersey,* 211 U.S. 78, 106 (1908) ("a fundamental principle of liberty and justice which inheres in the very idea of free government"), overruled on other grounds . . .

### II. THE COURT SHOULD ADHERE TO PRECEDENT REJECTING INCORPORATION UNDER THE PRIVILEGES OR IMMUNITIES CLAUSE.

#### A. This Court Has Repeatedly Held That The Privileges Or Immunities Clause Does Not Incorporate Any Provisions Of The Bill Of Rights.

Petitioners devote the bulk of their brief to urging this Court to overrule a long line of precedent holding that the Privileges or Immunities Clause does not incorporate any or all of the provisions of the Bill of Rights. Pet. Br. 9-65. The *stare decisis* considerations that this Court examines overwhelmingly support continued adherence to those precedents. At the same time, the historical record on which petitioners rely does not nearly establish that such incorporation was understood by members of Congress, the ratifiers, or the public as a consequence of adopting the Clause; certainly an intent to incorporate under the Clause is not clear enough to upset settled precedent.

    1. The Privileges or Immunities Clause provides: "No State shall make or enforce any law which shall abridge the privileges or immunities of citizens of the United States." U.S. Const. amend. XIV. The Court first construed this clause in the seminal *Slaughter-House Cases,* ruling that it includes only those rights that "are dependent upon citizenship of the United States, and not citizenship of a State." 83 U.S. at 80. The Court noted that the immediately prior Citizenship Clause makes "persons

*(Continued)*

born or naturalized in the United States and subject to the jurisdiction thereof . . . citizens of the United States and of the State in which they reside"; if the Privileges or Immunities Clause "was intended as a protection to the citizen of a State against the legislative power of his own State," it was "remarkable . . . that the word citizen of the State should be left out" when the distinction from "citizens of the United States" had appeared elsewhere. *Id.* at 73-74. Accordingly, the Court construed the "privileges or immunities of citizens of the United States" to be those that "owe their existence to the Federal government, its National character, its Constitution, or its laws." *Id.* at 78-79. They did not include those derived from other sources. . . .

**CONCLUSION**

The judgment of the court of appeals should be affirmed.

Respectfully submitted,

JAMES A. FELDMAN, Special Assistant Corporation Counsel, 5335 Wisconsin Avenue, N.W., Suite 440, Washington, D.C. 20015, (202) 730-1267

MARA S. GEORGES, Corporation Counsel of the City of Chicago, BENNA RUTH SOLOMON,* Deputy Corporation Counsel, MYRIAM ZRECZNY KASPER, Chief Assistant Corporation Counsel, SUZANNE M. LOOSE, Assistant Corporation Counsel, ANDREW W. WORSECK, Assistant Corporation Counsel, 30 N. LaSalle Street, Suite 800, Chicago, Illinois 60602, (312) 744-7764

*Counsel of Record
*Counsel for the City of Chicago*

RAYMOND L. HEISE, Village Attorney of Oak Park, 123 Madison Street, Oak Park, Illinois 60302, (708) 358-5660

HANS GERMANN, RANJIT HAKIM, ALEXANDRA SHEA, MAYER BROWN LLP, 71 South Wacker Drive, Chicago, Illinois 60606, (312) 782-0600

*Counsel for the Village of Oak Park*
December 30, 2009

## Questions in Review

1. Article I of the U.S. Constitution provides, inter alia, that "the privilege of the Writ of Habeas Corpus shall not be suspended unless when in Cases of Rebellion or Invasion the public Safety may require it." How important to our justice system is the writ of habeas corpus?

2. In August 1861, Congress gave President Lincoln retrospective approval to suspend the writ of habeas corpus. Were Lincoln's actions in delegating this authority now legal?
**Note:** A grand jury indicted Merryman for conspiracy to commit treason. He was released on bail. He was never tried. For more background on this case, see Carl Swisher, The Taney Period, 1836–1864 (New York, Macmillan, 1974).

3. Should a prisoner be allowed to delay his execution by the late filing of a writ of habeas corpus? The following case discusses that issue. Presently, the writ is used in many cases to attack state criminal convictions.
**Note:** The Federal Civil Rights of Institutional Persons Act of 1980 requires that state prisoners exhaust all state remedies before going to the federal courts on a civil rights issue. The 1996 Antiterrorism and Effective Death Penalty Act placed time limits on the filing of habeas corpus petitions. In most cases, prisoners now have only one year from the time their state convictions are final to file their writs.

## Practicum

**The following case discusses some limits that have been placed on the use of writs. What are the limitations noted in the Daniels case? Explain your position as to the need for each limitation.**

**Daniels v. United States, 532 U.S. 374 (U.S. 2001)**
Earthy Daniels, who had four previous California state convictions for a violent felony, was convicted of being a felon in possession of a firearm in violation of federal law (18 U.S. Code 922(g)(1)) and received a

sentence that was enhanced under the Armed Career Criminal Act of 1984 (ACCA)—which imposed a mandatory minimum sentence on anyone who was convicted of a serious felony and had three previous violent felony convictions–to exceed the maximum sentence that the accused would have received had he not been adjudged an armed career criminal.

A federal prisoner may file a motion to vacate, set aside, or correct a sentence that was imposed allegedly in violation of the Constitution or laws of the United States. After the accused's federal sentencing proceedings concluded, the accused moved to have his sentence set aside on the alleged basis that the sentence violated the Federal Constitution because two of the prior convictions on which the sentence was in part based were unconstitutional, in that (1) one such conviction allegedly was (a) based on a guilty plea that was not knowing and voluntary, and (b) the product of ineffective assistance of counsel; and (2) the other such conviction allegedly was based on a guilty plea that was not knowing and voluntary.

The United States District Court for the Central District of California denied the motion. The United States Court of Appeals for the Ninth Circuit, affirming, expressed the view that federal habeas review of the validity of a prior conviction used for federal sentencing enhancement is available only with respect to a claim of failure to appoint counsel for an indigent defendant.

The United States Supreme Court affirmed and held that (1) the accused's federal sentence was properly enhanced pursuant to the ACCA on the basis of his four facially valid prior state convictions; and (2) in view of a concern an accused had no right under the ACCA or the Constitution to collaterally attack prior convictions in the course of the accused's federal sentencing proceeding–for ease of administration and for the finality of judgments, the accused, because he had failed to pursue remedies that were otherwise available to him to challenge the two state convictions in question, could not now use a motion to collaterally attack those convictions.

# References

## CASES

*Rose v. Lundy*, 455 U.S. 509 (1982)
*Stone v. Powell* , 428 U.S. 465 (1976)
*Witherspoon v. Illinois*, 391 U.S. 510 (1968)

## BOOKS, ARTICLES, AND JOURNALS

Herr, David F. and Mary R. Vasaly. "Appellate Practice in Minnesota: A Decade of Experience with the Court of Appeals." *William. Mitchell Law Review* 19 (1993): 613; see page 628 .
Minnesota Battered Women's Legal Advocacy Project, "Extraordinary Writs: Writ of Mandamus and Writ Of Prohibition" (2003). www.bwlap.org/publication/stream?fileName=writs.pdf (accessed on April 7, 2010).

# 8

# International Courts
# and Tribunals

**What you need to know about International Courts and Tribunes**

After you have completed this chapter, you should know:

- The purpose of the International Criminal Court, International Court of Justice, and the Court of Justice of the European League.
- The international crimes of genocide, war crimes, and crimes against humanity.
- Jurisdiction of the three discussed courts.
- Issues involved with international crimes.
- Purpose and functions of International Criminal Tribunal.

**Chapter Outline**

- Introduction
- International Crimes
- International Criminal Court
- International Criminal Tribunal
- International Court of Justice
- Court of Justice of the European Communities

## INTRODUCTION

The three international courts are discussed in this chapter: International Criminal Court (ICC), International Court of Justice (ICJ), and the Court of Justice of the European Communities. The ICJ is also referred to as the World Court by many. The ICJ hears disputes between states and the ICC and the Court of Justice of the European Communities prosecute individuals involved in international crimes.

Generally international criminal tribunes consider cases involving **genocide, war crimes,** and **crimes against humanity.** In addition, the courts operate under a **rule of law** concept. The "Rule of Law" is generally understood to refer to a principle of governance in which all persons, institutions, and entities, including the state itself, are accountable to laws consistent with international human rights norms and standards.

According to Justice Hassan B. Jallow (2009), Chief Prosecutor, International Criminal Tribunal, the International Criminal Tribunals also serve as models of legal norms and standards and thereby lay the foundation for the restoration of the Rule of Law in a post-conflict society. International standards help establish the rule of law by entrenching certain fundamental principles in the judicial context, such as the independence and impartiality of judges, and certain guarantees of a fair trial, such as the right to be informed promptly and in detail in a language which the accused understands of the nature and cause of the charge against him or her, to have adequate time and facilities for the preparation of his or her defense and to communicate with counsel of his or her own choosing, and to be tried in public and without undue delay.

## INTERNATIONAL CRIMES

### Genocide

In 1944, Raphael Lemkin combined the Greek word *genos* (race) with the Latin root *cide* (killing) and developed the word "genocide." The United Nations defines genocide to mean any of the following acts committed with intent to destroy, in part or in whole, a national, ethic, racial, or religious group, including:

- killing,
- causing serious bodily or mental harm to members of a group,
- deliberately inflicting on the group conditions of life calculated to bring about its physical destruction in whole or in part, or
- forcibly transferring children of the group to another group (Roberson and Das 2008).

### War Crimes

War crimes are generally defined as violations of the laws or customs of war, including murder, the ill-treatment or deportation of civilian residents of an occupied territory to slave labor camps, the murder or ill-treatment of prisoners of war, the killing of hostages, the wanton destruction of cities, towns, and villages, and any devastation not justified by military, or civilian necessity (Werth et al. 1999).

German military leaders were tried for war crimes at the Nuremberg trials. The Nuremberg trials were a series of military tribunals most notable for the prosecution of prominent members of the political, military, and economic leadership of Nazi Germany after its defeat in World War II. The trials were held in the city of Nuremberg, Germany, from 1945 to 1946, at the Palace of Justice. The first and best known of these trials was the Trial of the Major War Criminals before the International Military Tribunal (IMT), which tried 22 of the most important captured leaders of Nazi Germany. It was held from November 21, 1945 to October 1, 1946 (Goodhart 1946).

### Crimes against Humanity

Crimes against humanity was described by the 1998 Rome Statute of the International Criminal Court Explanatory Memorandum as particularly odious offences in that they constitute a serious attack on human dignity or grave humiliation or a degradation of one or more human beings. They are not isolated or sporadic events, but are part either of a government policy (although the perpetrators need not identify themselves with this policy) or of a wide practice of atrocities tolerated or condoned by a government or a de facto authority.

Murder, extermination, torture, rape, and political, racial, or religious persecution and other inhumane acts are considered as crimes against humanity only if they are part of a widespread or systematic practice. Isolated inhumane acts of this nature may constitute grave infringements of human rights, or depending on the circumstances, war crimes, but may fall short of falling into the category of crimes under discussion (United Nations Treaty Collection, 1998).

## COURTS IN ACTION

### Law of Nations Excerpts from Abagninin v. AMVAC Chem. Corp.,

### 545 F.3d 733, 739 (9th Cir. Cal. 2008)

Plaintiffs, foreign nationals, sued defendants, a chemical company, distributors, and produce companies, alleging genocide and crimes against humanity. The United States District Court for the Central District of California dismissed the action. The nationals appealed.

The nationals resided and worked on banana and pineapple plantations in Ivory Coast villages. The nationals alleged that the chemical company knew of an agricultural pesticide's toxicity that caused male sterility and abnormally low sperm counts as early as the 1950 but continued to make, sell and use the pesticide on the plantations. The appellate court found that no treaty of the United States, no controlling act of the President or Congress, and no judicial decision indicated that genocide was a knowledge-based norm. The nationals failed to allege facts that were sufficient to constitute state or organization action as required for crimes against humanity. Defendants were not a state or state like organization for purposes of international law and crimes against humanity.

The law of nations is synonymous with "customary international law," and violations of international law must contravene a norm that is specific, universal, and obligatory. Genocide is defined as a specific intent crime. Genocide means acts committed with intent to destroy, in whole or in part, a national, ethnical, racial or religious group, as such. Decisions from international tribunals also reflect the specific intent requirement for genocide. The requirements—the demanding proof of specific intent and the showing that the group was targeted for destruction in its entirety or in substantial part—guard against a danger that convictions for this crime will be imposed lightly.

We will assume that the norm for crimes against humanity is specific, obligatory, and universal. An attack directed against any civilian population is a course of conduct pursuant to or in furtherance of a State or organizational policy to commit such attack. The district court properly concluded that Abagninin failed to allege facts sufficient to constitute State or organization action as required for crimes against humanity.

The appellate court upheld the district court's ruling dismissing the case.

## ✳THE INTERNATIONAL CRIMINAL COURT✳

The International Criminal Court (ICC) was established by the 1998 Rome Statue of the International Criminal Court. ICC came into being on July 1, 2002 after it was ratified by 90 nations. The (ICC), in The Hague in the Netherlands, is bestowed with the power to prosecute individuals responsible for committing crimes of genocide, crimes against humanity, and war crimes. It has complimentary jurisdiction, established to exercise its jurisdiction to complement national courts and only exercise its own jurisdiction where national courts have failed or are unwilling to exercise their jurisdiction. The ICC cannot act if a case is being considered by a country with jurisdiction over it. The ICC has such specific jurisdiction over crimes of genocide, crimes against humanity, and war crime. For other cases, the ICC must leave it up to the courts of individual nations to prosecute many crimes that have international ramifications. (Appenteng 2009).

In 2000, President Bill Clinton signed the ICC Statute. In May 2002, President George W. Bush signed a declaration stating that the United States would no longer be legally bound by the statute. In addition, the U.S. Senate in 2002 enacted two pieces of legislation that were designed to hinder the operation of the ICC. Bush's stated opposition to the ICC was based on preserving sovereignty of the U.S. government and a fear that the court could be used as a vehicle for other countries to criminalize and punish actions by U.S. citizens (Yacoubian 2003).

The ICC is designed to bring to trial those who commit large-scale political crimes—genocide, war crimes, and crimes against humanity. The ICC is based on the concept that it has universal jurisdiction on crimes involving genocide, war crimes, and crimes against humanity. The ICC is part of an effort by the United Nations to establish global accountability for all, including political and military leaders (Roberson and Das 2008). The ICC offers progress toward the long-held ideal of global justice.

## LAW IN ACTION

### Rome Statute of the International Criminal Courts (Part I)

#### PART 1. ESTABLISHMENT OF THE COURT

##### Article 1
##### The Court

An International Criminal Court ("the Court") is hereby established. It shall be a permanent institution and shall have the power to exercise its jurisdiction over persons for the most serious crimes of international concern, as referred to in this Statute, and shall be complementary to national criminal jurisdictions. The jurisdiction and functioning of the Court shall be governed by the provisions of this Statute.

##### Article 2
##### Relationship of the Court with the United Nations

The Court shall be brought into relationship with the United Nations through an agreement to be approved by the Assembly of States Parties to this Statute and thereafter concluded by the President of the Court on its behalf.

##### Article 3
##### Seat of the Court

1. The seat of the Court shall be established at The Hague in the Netherlands ("the host State").

2. The Court shall enter into a headquarters agreement with the host State, to be approved by the Assembly of States Parties and thereafter concluded by the President of the Court on its behalf.

3. The Court may sit elsewhere, whenever it considers it desirable, as provided in this Statute.

##### Article 4
##### Legal status and powers of the Court

1. The Court shall have international legal personality. It shall also have such legal capacity as may be necessary for the exercise of its functions and the fulfilment of its purposes.

2. The Court may exercise its functions and powers, as provided in this Statute, on the territory of any State Party and, by special agreement, on the territory of any other State.

The ICC faces difficult challenges before it becomes a viable force in combating crimes against humanity. Questions include:

- Will U.S. opposition and noninvolvement seriously weaken the Court?
- Will the Court become a political tool used by the rich countries to bully leaders of poor nations and rally domestic public opinion around holier-than-thou propaganda?
- Will disputes between national courts and ICC jurisdiction create a legal gridlock?
- Will the ICC have sufficient independence to dispense justice in a reasonably fair and even-handed way?

## Why an ICC is Needed

According to Mirceva (2004), an international criminal court was needed to combat the widespread violations of international humanitarian law that that are being practiced in the contemporary world. Mirceva noted the growing concerns of the international community resulted in a demand for international criminal prosecution in an international criminal tribunal for crimes recognized under customary international law as a threat to international peace and security.

## ICC Cases

Some of the recent cases that are pending in the ICC according to the Global Police (2010) Web site include:

- On May 22, 2007, the International Criminal Court opened an investigation into crimes committed in the Central African Republic. The government of the Central African Republic referred the case to the ICC on December 22, 2004. The office of the prosecutor will investigate allegations of serious crimes committed in the country since July 1, 2002. The prosecutor vowed to pay special attention to sexual violence, which appears to have been a central feature of the conflict.
- The UN panel investigating the rape, murder, and abuse committed by the Guinean military in September 2009 concludes that three leading figures should stand trial in the International Criminal Court (ICC). Guinea is signatory of the ICC Rome Treaty, and thus, the court does not have to wait for the Security Council to refer the case The Para-Uribe Regime, the extraditions and justice in Colombia.
- In 2008, the ICC prosecutor Luis Moreno Ocampo investigated crimes of Colombian paramilitaries.

## Relationship between the United Nations' Security Council and ICC

According to Gowlland-Debbas (2001), the relationship between the Security Council and the ICC is one of the most controversial aspects of the 1998 Statute adopted in Rome on July 17, 1998. The linkage between political and judicial organs is based on the recognition that the functions of the ICC and the Council are complementary in respect of the four crimes over which the Court has jurisdiction—genocide, crimes against humanity, war crimes, and aggression (Article 5(1))—crimes, which, in its recent practice, the Security Council has determined, under Article 39 of the Charter, to be constituent elements of threats to or breaches of international peace and security, hence falling under its primary responsibility under the Charter.

The link established between threats to international peace and security and the core crimes giving rise to individual criminal responsibility under international law was also underlined by the Security Council in establishing the International Criminal Tribunals for Yugoslavia and Rwanda. Criminal justice has therefore been seen as one means of contributing to the restoration and maintenance of peace and the Statute of the International Criminal Court adopted in Rome in July 1998 sustains this linkage in its preamble, in recognizing that such grave crimes threaten the peace, security, and well-being of the world.

The question of the links between the Security Council and the International Criminal Court appear to go beyond the Statute itself and raises general international law and policy issues. One issue is the relationship between political and judicial bodies when the former acts in other than a strict judicial capacity. Often the fields of operation of the Security Council and the Court overlap. There is concern that the role of the Council may serve to obstruct the judicial integrity of the Court.

In view of the Security Council's primary responsibility in international peace and security, it may be impractical to deny the Council any role at all in the forging of a system of individual criminal responsibility and its linkage with the ICC could contribute to the latter's authority.

## Darfur Case

One problem with the ICC is the time required for the court to take any action. For example, in 2008, it was almost three years after the Security Council formally referred the situation in Darfur to the International Criminal Court that the prosecutor for the Court filed war crimes charges against Sudan's president, Omar al-Bashir. According to Joseph (2008), one of the many issues now confronting the Darfur region is the systematic rape of women and children. Since the conflict's start, hundreds of thousands of women and children have been raped and murdered at the hands of rebel forces and government-backed militias. Joseph notes that in previous ethnic conflicts, international courts' abilities to prosecute all crimes of sexual violence have been restricted.

On December 22, 2008, Sudanese national Mohamed Alsary Ibrahim appeared in a Sudanese court on charges of helping overthrow the state by transmitting information about a Darfur war crimes suspect Ahmed Haroun, Sudan's state minister for humanitarian affairs, to the International Criminal Court. The case against Ibrahim in a Sudanese court indicates one of the problems that the ICC has in obtaining evidence in cases before the court. The ICC operates through the indirect method. It does not have its own marshals or enforcement officials who can enforce orders of the court. Instead, Part 9 of the Rome Statute contains obligations of international cooperation and judicial assistance. In particular, Article 86 imposes on states parties the obligation to "cooperate fully with the Court in its investigation and prosecution of crimes within the jurisdiction of the Court." Article 89(1) authorizes the ICC to transmit a request for the arrest and surrender of a person.

According to Joseph, for the first time in world history an international court may be able to grant important and necessary relief to these victims. The ICC has been empowered by statute to prosecute a wide range of sex crimes, offer specific protections to the victims, and potentially prosecute such crimes as crimes against humanity or even genocide.

Whether the situation in Darfur resulted in crimes against humanity is one of the decisions that must be made by the ICC. The Rome Statute (1998) details a variety of acts of sexual violence, which qualify as crimes against humanity. As noted by Joseph, Article 7 on crimes against humanity describes crime against humanity and includes many sexual violence acts which are committed as part of a widespread or systematic attack directed against any civilian population. The article enumerates a list of eleven acts, which constitute crimes against humanity. Article 7 focuses solely on the Statute's substantial enumeration of the gender-related crimes of rape, sexual slavery, enforced prostitution, forced pregnancy, enforced sterilization, or any other form of sexual violence of comparable gravity.

The ICC Statute defines the crime of rape as both a crime against humanity and a war crime. There are issues in determining what constitutes rape. Generally rape is defined as the invasion of a person's body by conduct resulting in penetration, however

## LAW IN ACTION

### United Nation's Resolution 1593 (2005)

Adopted by the Security Council at its 5158th meeting, on 31 March 2005

The Security Council,

Taking note of the report of the International Commission of Inquiry on violations of international humanitarian law and human rights law in Darfur (S/2005/60),

Recalling article 16 of the Rome Statute under which no investigation or prosecution may be commenced or proceeded with by the International Criminal Court for a period of 12 months after a Security Council request to that effect, Also recalling articles 75 and 79 of the Rome Statute and encouraging States to contribute to the ICC Trust Fund for Victims,

Taking note of the existence of agreements referred to in Article 98-2 of the Rome Statute,

Determining that the situation in Sudan continues to constitute a threat to international peace and security,

Acting under Chapter VII of the Charter of the United Nations,

1. Decides to refer the situation in Darfur since 1 July 2002 to the Prosecutor of the International Criminal Court;
2. Decides that the Government of Sudan and all other parties to the conflict in Darfur, shall cooperate fully with and provide any necessary assistance to the Court and the Prosecutor pursuant to this resolution and, while recognizing that States not party to the Rome Statute have no obligation under the Statute, urges all States and concerned regional and other international organizations to cooperate fully;
3. Invites the Court and the African Union to discuss practical arrangements that will facilitate the work of the Prosecutor and of the Court, including the possibility of conducting proceedings in the region, which would contribute to regional efforts in the fight against impunity;
4. Also encourages the Court, as appropriate and in accordance with the Rome Statute, to support international cooperation with domestic efforts to promote the rule of law, protect human rights and combat impunity in Darfur;
5. Also emphasizes the need to promote healing and reconciliation and encourages in this respect the creation of institutions, involving all sectors of Sudanese society, such as truth and/or reconciliation commissions, in order to complement judicial processes and thereby reinforce the efforts to restore long lasting peace, with African Union and international support as necessary;
6. Decides that nationals, current or former officials or personnel from a contributing State outside Sudan which is not a party to the Rome Statute of the International Criminal Court shall be subject to the exclusive jurisdiction of that contributing State for all alleged acts or omissions arising out of or related to operations in Sudan established or authorized by the Council or the African Union, unless such exclusive jurisdiction has been expressly waived by that contributing State;
7. Recognizes that none of the expenses incurred in connection with the referral including expenses related to investigations or prosecutions in connection with that referral, shall be borne by the United Nations and that such costs shall be borne by the parties to the Rome Statute and those States that wish to contribute voluntarily;
8. Invites the Prosecutor to address the Council within three months of the date of adoption of this resolution and every six months thereafter on actions taken pursuant to this resolution;
9. Decides to remain seized of the matter.

slight, of any part of the body of the victim or of the perpetrator with a sexual organ, or of the anal or genital opening of the victim with any object or any other part of the body. Generally the invasion must have been committed by force, or by threat of force or coercion, such as that caused by fear of violence, duress, detention, psychological oppression or abuse of power, against such person or another person or by taking advantage of a coercive environment, or the invasion was committed against a person incapable of giving genuine consent. It is understood that a person may be incapable of giving genuine consent if affected by natural, induced or age-related incapacity. There are issues regarding what the definition of rape is, who can consent, and what the force requirement is.

## INTERNATIONAL CRIMINAL TRIBUNALS

International Criminal Tribunals are ad hoc tribunals generally established after the cessation of arm conflict. As noted by Jallow (2009), there have been many approaches taken to doing justice and restoring communities after civil conflict. Recently there have been three International Criminal tribunals (the former Yugoslavia, Rwanda, and Sierra Leone) to national trials, variations on truth commissions, and panels of inquiry, what is clear is that seeking justice through institutions of the law is one of the best means of determining responsibility for acts of genocide, war crimes, crimes against humanity, and other gross violations of human rights.

Jallow (2009) contends that where possible in the aftermath of conflict, national trials ought to play a large role in determining accountability and restoring the state. National trials often can deal with a greater number of perpetrators, and having trials in states where the atrocities occurred helps to reestablish the state, helps to rebuild the judiciary, helps to restore peace and helps to introduce the Rule of Law. National trials make a significant contribution to the search for justice and in restoring peace, as individuals are able to participate in re-establishing the Rule of Law in their own societies. But, according to Jallow, it is unreasonable to assume that national systems will always be capable of bringing or willing to bring justice for atrocities in all cases.

The United Nations Security established an international criminal tribune to prosecute persons considered responsible for genocide and other war crimes that occurred in Rwanda in 1994. As of January 2010, the Rwanda tribunal had tried 46 high-level officials. Five were acquitted; 32 were convicted of genocide, crimes against humanity, and war crimes. The others are waiting judgment. In addition, others were prosecuted in domestic courts. (Jallow 2009).

## INTERNATIONAL COURT OF JUSTICE

The International Court of Justice (Cour internationale de justice) (ICJ) is also known as the World Court. The ICJ is the primary judicial organ of the United Nations. It holds court sessions in the Peace Palace in The Hague, Netherlands. The main functions of the ICJ are to settle legal disputes submitted to it by states and to give advisory opinions on legal questions submitted to it by duly authorized international organs, agencies, and the UN General Assembly. The ICJ like the ICC has "global" jurisdiction (Schwebel 1987).

The ICJ was established in 1945 in the United Nations' Charter. The Court began to function in 1946 as the successor to the Permanent Court of International Justice which had been established by the League of Nations. The Statute of the International Court of Justice is the main constitutional document constituting and regulating the Court and its procedures.

The ICJ is composed of fifteen judges elected to nine year terms by the UN General Assembly and the UN Security Council from a list of persons nominated by the national groups in the Permanent Court of Arbitration. Judges serve for nine year terms and may be re-elected for up to two additional terms. Elections take place every three years, with one-third of the judges each time, in order to ensure continuity within the court.

The Court is tasked with the responsibility to represent the main forms of civilization and of the principal legal systems of the world. The ICJ has had only a relatively few number of cases. Some of its most famous cases include:

- A complaint by the United States in 1980 that Iran was detaining American diplomats in Tehran in violation of international law.
- A dispute between Tunisia and Libya over the delimitation of the continental shelf between them.
- A complaint by Pakistan on behalf of the people of Kashmir over oppression against India and charged it with state terrorism directly continuing violations of the international law.
- A dispute over the course of the maritime boundary dividing the U.S. and Canada in the Gulf of Maine area.
- A complaint by the Federal Republic of Yugoslavia against the member states of the North Atlantic Treaty Organization regarding their actions in the Kosovo War.

## COURT OF JUSTICE OF THE EUROPEAN COMMUNITIES

The Court of Justice of the European Communities was set up under the ECSC Treaty in 1952. It is based in Luxembourg. Its primary purpose is to ensure that the European Union's legislation is interpreted and applied in the same way in all EU countries, so that the law is equal for everyone. It ensures, for example, that national courts do not give different rulings on the same issue.

The Court also makes sure that EU member states and institutions do what the law requires. The Court has the power to settle legal disputes between EU member states, EU institutions, businesses, and individuals.

The Court is composed of one judge per member state, so that all 27 of the EU's national legal systems are represented. For the sake of efficiency, however, the Court rarely sits as the full court. It usually sits as a "Grand Chamber" of just 13 judges or in chambers of five or three judges. To help the Court of Justice cope with the large number of cases brought before it, and to offer citizens better legal protection, a Court of First Instance was created in 1988. This Court is responsible for issuing rulings on certain kinds of case, particularly actions brought by private individuals, companies and some organizations, and cases relating to competition law. This court also has one judge from each EU country.

Cases are submitted to the registry and a specific judge and advocate-general are assigned to each case. The procedure that follows is in two stages: first a written and then an oral phase. At the first stage, all the parties involved submit written statements, and the judge assigned to the case draws up a report summarizing these statements and the legal background to the case. The second stage consists of a public hearing. Depending on the importance and complexity of the case, this hearing can take place before a chamber of 3, 5 or 13 judges, or before the full Court. At the hearing, the parties' lawyers put their case before the judges and the advocate-general, who can question them. The advocate-general then gives his or her opinion, after which the judges deliberate and deliver their judgment.

The advocates general are required to give an opinion on a case only if the Court considers that this particular case raises a new point of law. The Court does not necessarily follow the advocate-general's opinion. Judgments of the Court are decided by a majority and pronounced at a public hearing. Dissenting opinions are not expressed. Decisions are published on the day of delivery. The procedure in the Court of First Instance is similar, except that there is no opinion from an advocate-general.

## COURTS IN ACTION

### The Following Case Provides an Example of Using U.S. Federal Courts to Enforce International Law.

Almog v. Arab Bank, PLC, 471 F. Supp. 2d 257 (E.D.N.Y. 2007)

Plaintiffs, United States and foreign nationals, sued defendant bank for knowingly providing services to terrorist organizations sponsoring suicide bombings on civilians in Israel. The U.S. nationals asserted claims under the Anti-Terrorism Act (ATA), 18 U.S.C.S. § 2331 et seq. The foreign nationals asserted violations of the law of nations with jurisdiction under the Alien Tort Claims Act (ATS), 28 U.S.C.S. § 1350. The bank moved to dismiss the complaint.

**Facts:** Plaintiffs contended that the bank knowingly provided financial resources to terrorist organizations that were engaged in systematic and widespread campaigns designed to kill Jews and Israelis and to coerce Israel to cede them certain territory by means of suicide bombings. Relying on a prior ruling, the court found that the complaint sufficiently stated violations of the ATA. The court further found that the complaint sufficiently alleged violations of the law of nations and that jurisdiction was proper under the ATS. The court noted that the organized and systematic suicide bombings and other murderous acts intended to intimidate or coerce a civilian population violated an established norm of international law.

Contrary to the bank's contention, the right to self-determination could not be effectuated in violation of the law of nations. The conduct alleged in the complaint was sufficiently specific and well-defined to be recognized as a claim under the ATS. Although the bank did not directly perform the underlying acts, liability was properly imposed for its acts of financing and aiding and abetting terrorism.

**Court decision:** The court denied the bank's motions to dismiss in all other respects. Under Federal Rule Civil Procedure (Fed. R. Civ. P.) 8(a), a pleading sets forth a claim for relief if it contains: (1) a short and plain statement of the grounds upon which the court's jurisdiction depends, (2) a short and plain statement of the claim showing that the pleader is entitled to relief, and (3) a demand for judgment for the relief the pleader seeks. Under this simplified pleading standard, a court should not dismiss a complaint unless no relief could be granted under any set of facts that could be proved consistent with the complaint. When considering a motion to dismiss pursuant to Fed. R. Civ. P. 12(b)(6) for failure to state a claim upon which relief can be granted, a court must accept the factual allegations set forth in a complaint as true and draw all reasonable inferences in favor of the plaintiff. On the issue of subject matter jurisdiction, a court may look beyond the pleadings in determining international law.

18 U.S. Code § 2333 provides that any U.S. national may sue for an injury sustained "by reason of an act of international terrorism." International terrorism is defined as activities that: (A) involve violent acts or acts dangerous to human life that are a violation of the criminal laws of the United States or of any state, or that would be a criminal violation if committed within the jurisdiction of the United States or of any state; (B) appear to be intended–(i) to intimidate or coerce a civilian population; (ii) to influence the policy of a government by intimidation or coercion; or (iii) to affect the conduct of a government by mass destruction, assassination or kidnapping; and (C) occur primarily outside the territorial jurisdiction of the United States, or transcend national boundaries in terms of the means by which they are accomplished, the persons they appear intended to intimidate or coerce, or the locale in which their perpetrators operate or seek asylum.

18 U.S. Code § 2339A defines the term "material support or resources" to include the provision of any property, service, including currency or monetary instruments or financial securities, or financial services. 18 U.S. Code § 2339B(a)(1) prohibits knowingly providing material support or resources to a foreign terrorist organization. To violate this subsection, a person must have knowledge that the organization: (1) is a designated terrorist organization; (2) has engaged or engages in terrorist activity; or (3) has engaged or engages in terrorism. 18 U.S.C.S. § 2331(3) defines the

*(Continued)*

term "person" as any individual or entity capable of holding a legal or beneficial interest in property. 18 U.S. Code § 2339B(g)(6) defines the term "terrorist organization" as an organization designated as a terrorist organization under § 219 of the Immigration and Nationality Act.

The current law of nations is composed only of those rules that sates universally abide by,
or accede to, out of a sense of legal obligation and mutual concern. First, then, in order for a rule
to become a norm of international law, sates must universally abide by or accede to it. he question is not one of whether the rule is often violated, but whether virtually all states recognize its
validity. That a norm of international law is honored in the breach does not diminish its binding
effect as a norm of international law. Second, states must abide by or accede to the rule from a
sense of legal obligation and not for moral or political reasons. Whether states abide by or accede
to a rule out of a sense of legal obligation is shown by, among other things, state practice.

It is only where the nations of the world have demonstrated that a wrong is of mutual, and
not merely several, concern, by means of express international accords, that a wrong generally recognized becomes an international law violation. Matters of "mutual" concern are those involving
states' actions performed with regard to each other. Matters of "several" concern are matters in
which states are separately and independently interested. Offenses that may be purely intra-
national in their execution, such as official torture, extra-judicial killings, and genocide, do violate
customary international law because the nations of the world have demonstrated that such
wrongs are of mutual concern and capable of impairing international peace and security.

International law is part of U.S. law, and must be ascertained and administered by the
courts of justice of appropriate jurisdiction as often as questions of right depending upon it are
duly presented for their determination. For this purpose, where there is no treaty and no controlling executive or legislative act or judicial decision, resort must be had to the customs and
usages of civilized nations, and, as evidence of these, to the works of jurists and commentators
who by years of labor, research, and experience have made themselves peculiarly well
acquainted with the subjects of which they treat. Such works are resorted to by judicial tribunals, not for the speculations of their authors concerning what the law ought to be, but for
trustworthy evidence of what the law really is.

Treaties, also referred to as conventions or covenants, that create legal obligations on
the states party to them, constitute primary evidence of the law of nations. A state's ratification
of a treaty is evidence of its intent to be legally obligated by the principles embodied in the
treaty and therefore evidences the "customs and practices" of that state. Treaties ratified by at
least two states provide some evidence of the law of nations; if enough states ratify a treaty, a
norm of international law may be established. The more sates that have ratified a treaty, especially those sates with greater relative influence in international affairs, the greater a treaty's
evidentiary value. Likewise, a treaty's evidentiary value is increased if the state parties actually
implement and abide by the principles set forth in the treaty either internationally or within
their own borders. In addition to treaties, United Nations Security Council resolutions, which
are binding on all member states, are evidence of the law of nations.

A treaty is legally binding on a state only when it ratifies the treaty. In the United States,
a treaty that is self-executing, that is, immediately creates rights and duties that are enforceable by domestic tribunals, or that has been executed through implementation by an Act of
Congress, giving rise to legally enforceable rights in our courts, provides greater evidence of
the customs and practices of the United States than a treaty that has not been executed.

The Convention on the Prevention and Punishment of the Crime of Genocide defines
genocide as: any of the following acts committed with intent to destroy, in whole or in part, a
national, ethnical, racial or religious group, as such: (a) Killing members of the group; (b)
Causing serious bodily or mental harm to members of the group; (c) Deliberately inflicting on
the group conditions of life calculated to bring about its physical destruction in whole or in
part; (d) Imposing measures intended to prevent births within the group; (e) Forcibly transferring children of the group to another group.

Article 7 of the Rome Statute of the International Criminal Court defines crimes against
humanity as any of the following acts when committed as part of a widespread or systematic
attack directed against any civilian population, with knowledge of the attack: (a) Murder;
(b) Extermination; (h) Persecution against any identifiable group or collectivity on political, racial,
national, ethnic, cultural, religious, gender or other grounds that are universally recognized as
impermissible under international law, in connection with any act referred to in this paragraph

or any crime within the jurisdiction of the court; (k) Other inhumane acts of a similar character intentionally causing great suffering, or serious injury to body or to mental or physical health. "Attack directed against any civilian population" means a course of conduct involving the multiple commission of acts previously referred to against any civilian population, pursuant to or in furtherance of a state or organizational policy to commit such attack; (b) "Extermination" includes the intentional infliction of conditions of life, inter alia the deprivation of access to food and medicine, calculated to bring about the destruction of part of a population.

## Questions in Review

1. What is the difference between a court and a tribunal?
2. Explain the functions of the International Criminal Court.
3. What are the differences between the International Criminal Court and the International Court of Justice?

4. Why do we need international courts or tribunals?
5. What crimes are generally prosecuted in the International Criminal Court?

## Practicum

**Would you have granted asylum based on the following facts?**

**Djedovic v. Gonzales, 441 F.3d 547 (7th Cir. 2006)**

Petitioner aliens, a husband and wife who were citizens of Serbia and Montenegro, sought review of the Board of Immigration Appeals' denial of their asylum application. The husband contended that he would be persecuted because of his desertion from the military and his opposition to the use of force against fellow Muslims. The wife, a Christian, contended that she would be persecuted because of her marriage to her husband who was Muslim.

The immigration judge, who believed the husband's testimony, concluded that the events he described did not amount to persecution, and the Board of Immigration Appeals agreed. The court found that substantial evidence supported that decision. The husband faced was military conscription,

which was not a form of persecution, and comments by other soldiers not directed against him personally. Even if the court assumed that the husband would be imprisoned on return for his desertion that was not persecution unless the draft and military service were persecution. The husband did not contend that Muslim deserters were treated worse than Christian deserters. Further, the husband was unlikely to be punished at all. The ex-president had died and his successors announced an amnesty that appeared to cover the husband.

While the wife testified that she and her children had been disowned by her parents and shunned by their neighbors and that people called her "ugly words" and spat in her direction, such actions did not amount to persecution. Shunning was private activity, not one sponsored, approved, or enforced by the state.

The petition for review is denied.

## Key Terms

**Crimes against humanity:** Crimes that constitute a serious attack on human dignity or grave humiliation or a degradation of one or more human beings.

**Genocide:** The systematic killing of a religious, racial, national, or ethnic group of people.

**Rule of Law:** A principle of governance in which all persons, institutions, and entities, including the State itself, are accountable to laws consistent with international human rights norms and standards.

**War Crimes:** Crimes that are violations of the laws or customs of war; including murder, the ill-treatment or deportation of civilian residents of an occupied territory to slave labor camps, the murder or ill-treatment of prisoners of war, the killing of hostages, the wanton destruction of cities, towns and villages, and any devastation not justified by military, or civilian necessity.

# References

Appenteng, Kwabena (2009, April) "An International Perspective: Global-law-zation?" Chicago Lawyer, pp. 10025–10026. The **International Criminal Court** (ICC), in The Hague in the Netherlands, is bestowed with the power to prosecute individuals responsible for committing crimes of genocide, crimes against humanity, and war crimes. Established in 2002, the ICC has "complimentary" jurisdiction, established to exercise its jurisdiction to complement national **courts** and only exercise its own jurisdiction where national **courts** have failed or are unwilling to exercise their jurisdiction. The ICC cannot act if a case is being considered by a country with jurisdiction over it.

Global Policy Web site at www.globalpolicy.org/international-justice/the-international-criminal-court/icc-investigations/28658.html (accessed on January 20, 2010).

Goodhart, A. L. "The Legality of the Nuremberg Trials." *Juridical Review* (April 1946); Gowlland-Debbas, Vera. *The Relationship between the Security Council and ICC.* New York: Global Policy Forum, 2001.

Joseph, Joshua H. "Gender and International Law: How the International Criminal Court Can Bring Justice to Victims of Sexual Violence." *Texas Journal on Women & Law* 18 (Fall 2008): 61–74.

Jallow, Hassan B. "Justice and the Rule of Law: A Global Perspective." *The International Lawyer* 43 (Spring 2009): 77–84.

Mirceva, Stojanka. "Why the International Criminal Court is Different." *Peace and Conflict Monitor* (January 26, 2004).

Roberson, Cliff and Dilip Das. *An Introduction to Comparative Legal Models of Criminal Justice.* Boca Raton, FL: Taylor & Francis, 2008.

Rome Statute of the International Criminal Court, art. 5, U.N. Doc. A/CONF.183/9 (July 17, 1998).

Schwebel, S. "Ad Hoc Chambers of the International Court of Justice." *American Journal of International Law* 81 (1987): 831–862.

United Nations Treaty Collection. *Rome Statute of the International Criminal Court* (1998), at. (accessed on January 20, 2010).

Werth, Nicolas, Karel Bartošek, Jean-Louis Panné, Jean-Louis Margolin, Andrzej Paczkowski, and Stéphane Courtois. *The Black Book of Communism: Crimes, Terror, Repression.* Cambridge: Harvard University Press, 1999.

Yacoubian, G.S. Jr. "Should the subject matter jurisdiction of the International Criminal Court include drug trafficking?" *International Journal of Comparative Criminology* 3 (2003): 175–190.

# 9

# Controlling Courtroom Conduct

**What you need to know about Controlling Courtroom Conduct**

After you have completed this chapter, you should know:

- A trial is expected to be conducted in a clam, dignified atmosphere.
- It is the responsibility of the judge to ensure that the courtroom proceedings are conducted in that manner.
- A judge's primary tool to maintain the order is by use of contempt proceedings.
- Disorderly conduct by a defendant or by the spectators may cause the judge to exercise the right of contempt.
- A witness who refuses to be sworn in and testify could be held in contempt of court.
- These acts generally take place within the presence of the judge and are known as direct contempt.
- The judge may punish the offender summarily—that is, there and then—without a hearing or any other procedure taking place.
- Attorneys as well as others may be held in contempt more than once during a trial and may be punished for each time they are so held.
- The U.S. Supreme Court has held that under these circumstances, the offender is entitled to a trial on the contempt charge.
- If the judge waits until the conclusion of the trial to take the contempt action, the offender is entitled to a trial on the contempt charge.
- Defense counsels are held in contempt more frequently than prosecuting attorneys.
- The judge should uphold the independence and integrity of the judiciary, shall perform the duties of the office impartially, and shall avoid impropriety and the appearance of impropriety in all of the judge's activities.
- A judge shall avoid impropriety and the appearance of impropriety.
- A judge should not make public comment on the merits of a matter pending or impending in any court.
- A judge should require similar restraint by court personnel subject to the judge's direction and control.
- Every state has some commission or panel to serve as more or less a watchdog on its judges.
- What constitutes judicial misconduct is an often litigated question.
- The test for impropriety is whether the conduct compromises the ability of the judge to carry out judicial responsibilities with independence, integrity, impartiality, and competence.
- The attorney-client privilege basically means that information furnished to an attorney in confidence by his or her client may not be disclosed without the permission of the client.
- The attorney-client privilege normally shields only confidential communications from client to attorney.

- Communications from attorney to client are privileged only if they constitute legal advice, or tend directly or indirectly to reveal the substance of a client confidence.

- The Supreme Court of the United States has long recognized that the scope of the privilege is governed by common law principles as interpreted and applied by the federal courts in the light of reason and experience.

- There are several exceptions to attorney/client privilege rule. The most common exception is that the privilege does not apply to future criminal conduct.

- A similar privilege is recognized in communications between spouses.

- No person has a more demanding and misunderstood role in our legal system than the defense counsel.

- First, the defense counsel is an officer of the court and as such he or she must conform to the requirements of the law.

- The defense counsel is the only individual who speaks on behalf of the defendant.

- When considering the ethical obligations of a prosecutor or police officer, the reader must remember that the primary responsibility of a prosecutor is not to prosecute, but to promote justice.

- The duty of a defense counsel, however, is not to promote justice, but to represent his client zealously within the bounds of the law.

- In a criminal trial, the defense's duty is to his or her client within the bounds of the law.

- Our system of justice functions on the adversary system wherein the prosecutor represents the people and the defense represents the accused with the judge acting as the referee.

- There are at least three constitutionally permissible approaches for the court's handling of an obstreperous defendant: (1) bind and gag him as a last resort, thereby keeping him present; (2) cite him for criminal or civil contempt; or (3) remove him from the courtroom, while the trial continues, until he promises to conduct himself properly.

**Chapter Outline**
- Introduction
- Contempt
- Judicial Ethics
- Judicial Misconduct
- Attorney/Client Communications
- Defense Counsel Obligations
- Ethical Issues in Prosecution
- Defendant Misconduct


## INTRODUCTION

This chapter is an examination of judicial and counsel ethics. In addition, other issues concerning the control of conduct in the courtroom will be explored. Since the judge controls to courtroom, a judge's **contempt** power, judicial ethics, and judicial misconduct will be discussed first. Next, the concept of privileged communications between attorneys and defendants will be discussed. Then ethical obligations and duties of defense counsel will be explored and the chapter concludes with an ethical examination of a prosecutor's duties and allowable conduct.

## CONTEMPT

A trial is expected to be conducted in a clam, dignified atmosphere. It is the responsibility of the judge to ensure that the courtroom proceedings are conducted in that manner. A judge's primary tool to maintain the order is by use of contempt proceedings. Contempt is defined as an act that is disrespectful to the court or adversely affects the administration of justice. Accordingly, any act that embarrasses, hinders, or obstructs the court in the administration of justice may be declared by the judge as contempt of court. Typical acts falling within this category include contemptuous or insulting remarks made to the judge and counsel's persistent arguments with the judge after an admonition to desist has been given. A judge may not go so far as to hold a defense counsel in contempt when counsel is merely defending his client vigorously. Although veteran defense counsel will admit that they have been threatened with contempt many times by trial judges.

Disorderly conduct by a defendant or by the spectators may cause the judge to exercise the right of contempt. A witness who refuses to be sworn in and testify could be held in contempt of court. These acts generally take place within the presence of the judge and are known as direct contempt. The judge may punish the offender summarily—that is, there and then—without a hearing or any other procedure taking place. The punishment may be imprisonment and/or a fine.

Not only are insulting remarks made to judge possible contemptuous acts, but also such remarks between the prosecuting attorney and the defense counsel. For example, in *People v. Fusaro* (1971), a case in which the two attorneys had exchanged a series of acrimonious remarks, the judge held both in contempt of court. The defense counsel accused the prosecuting attorney of "indulging in crap," to which the prosecuting attorney, according to the judge, "sank to the occasion by voicing an epithet denoting fecal matter of a male bovine." On another occasion, a prosecuting attorney was held in contempt upon using an old southern colloquialism implying that the defendant was the incestuous son of a canine mother.

An interesting development arose out of the Fusaro case. The defense counsel was held in contempt and was imprisoned in the middle of the trial. The facts of the case reflect the following: "The record reveals an acrimonious five-day trial in which the attorneys mistook bickering and side remarks for vigorous advocacy. The prosecutor . . . was guilty of at least one act of misconduct," and the defense attorney in his turn cluttered and interrupted the trial with frivolous objections. He aroused the trial judge's ire by permitting a witness to remain in the courtroom despite an exclusion order. He was twice late in returning to the trial after a recess. On the afternoon of the third day he was 15 minutes late, apologized and explained that the judge of another court had detained him. Outside the jury's presence the trial court held him in contempt for tardiness and imposed a one-day suspended jail sentence.

The exchange of remarks between the prosecuting attorney and defense counsel "indulging in crap" took place thereafter. At that point the judge recessed the trial, rebuked the attorneys, indicated that he wanted to consider their behavior and put the matter over to the next morning. The next morning, outside the jury's presence, the court found both attorneys in contempt. The prosecuting attorney apologized, and the judge fined him $50. The defense counsel endeavored to justify the language. The judge imposed a 24-hour jail sentence on defense counsel, refused to stay the execution and committed him to jail immediately. In view of the jailing, defendant's trial was recessed until the following morning.

The defendant was convicted on four narcotics charges. The conviction was appealed on the grounds that the judge had abused discretion in holding the defense counsel in contempt and immediately imposing a jail sentence. The defendant alleged that the jailing of the counsel prejudiced the defendant in the eyes of the jury and that a speedy trial was denied because of the interruption. Although the appellate court upheld the conviction, the court took a dim view of jailing a defense counsel in the middle of a trial.

Attorneys as well as others may be held in contempt more than once during a trial and may be punished for each time they are so held. Offenders have been known to receive sentences lasting for years if the sentences are made to run consecutively. The U.S. Supreme Court has held that under these circumstances, the offender is entitled to a trial on the contempt charge. The Court stated that criminal contempt is a crime and that the offender is entitled to the same trial procedure as in any other crime. If the total sentence exceeds six months, the offender is entitled to a trial by jury. If the sentence is not more than six months, the offender may be tried by a judge sitting without a jury, but the Court stated that the trial should be conducted by a judge other than the one holding the offender in contempt because of the possible emotional involvement in the matter (*Taylor v. Hayes*, 1974). Some states grant a person accused of a crime a jury trial for all violations. The offender would then be entitled to a jury trial even though the sentence would not exceed six months.

The U.S. Supreme Court has considerably restricted the right of a trial judge to take summary contempt action and has restricted the action that may be taken. But the Court apparently did not eliminate the right entirely. The wording of the Court indicated that if it is necessary to preserve the calm atmosphere and the dignity of the court, a judge may exercise the contempt action at the time of the misconduct and may even sentence the person involved. However, if the judge waits until the conclusion of the trial to take the contempt action, the offender is entitled to a trial on the contempt charge.

The Supreme Court has issued the following guidelines for when a judge may use his or her direct contempt powers (*Taylor v. Hayes*, 1974):

- It should be clear from the identity of the offender and the character of his acts that disruptive conduct is willfully contemptuous.
- The conduct warranting the sanction is preceded by a clear warning that the conduct is impermissible and that specified sanctions may be imposed for its repetition.
- The trial judge, as soon as practicable after he or she is satisfied that courtroom misconduct requires contempt proceedings, should inform the alleged offender of his intention to institute contempt proceedings.
- Before imposing any punishment for contempt, the judge shall give the offender notice of the charges and an opportunity to adduce evidence or argument relevant to guilt or punishment.
- The judge, before whom courtroom misconduct occurs, may impose appropriate sanctions including punishment for contempt. If the judge's conduct was so integrated with the contempt that he contributed to it or was otherwise involved, or his objectivity can reasonably be questioned, the matter shall be referred to another judge.

Defense counsels are held in contempt more frequently than prosecuting attorneys. This is probably because the actions of the defense counsel cannot by imputed to the defendant, whereas, if a prosecuting attorney indulges in misconduct, the misconduct may be considered a prejudicial error and ground to reverse a conviction.

While acts not performed in the presence of the judge may also be declared as contempt. These acts are known as indirect or constructive contempt, and they are usually the result of failure to abide by court orders. For example, jurors may discuss the facts of the case during a recess—in violation of the judge's order not to discuss the case—a juror may refuse to appear in court without sufficient good reason after receiving a summons to appear, or a witness may not appear as directed. Since indirect contempt does not occur in the presence of the judge, a hearing is held to determine

**LAW IN ACTION**

**Excerpts from *Autry v. State of Oklahoma*, 2007 OK CR 41, 172 P.3d 212, 214.**

The power of the court to summarily impose significant punishment, including imprisonment, for direct contempt in the absence of those usual protections afforded an accused by statutes and constitutional guarantees of due process, rests upon the absolute necessity of maintaining structured order in our courts. In consideration of this extraordinary power placed in the judiciary, the Court of Criminal Appeals recognized in *Gilbert v. State of Oklahoma*, 1982 OK CR 100, 648 P.2d 1226, 1232, that it is a matter of "critical importance" that all acts or essential elements making up the alleged direct contempt must occur in the immediate presence of the court in session as required by statute, and there can be no finding of direct contempt where only some of those acts occur in the court's presence. That Court noted this requirement is in accord with Oklahoma's rejection of common law definitions of contempt, as well as the well-accepted rule that statutes imposing penal sanctions should be strictly construed and also in keeping with the trend in recent years toward viewing summary contempt with disfavor and narrowly restricting its use.

The power of the trial judge to summarily impose punishment for direct contempt is limited by the provisions of 21 O.S.2001 §565.1, as follows: The trial judge has the power to cite for contempt anyone who, in his presence in open court, willfully obstructs judicial proceedings. If necessary, the trial judge may punish a person cited for contempt after an opportunity to be heard has been given.

whether the alleged offender should be held in contempt. Prior to the hearing, the judge will issue an order requesting the offender to show cause why he or she should not be held in contempt of court. Witnesses both for and against will be questioned at the hearing to assist in determining whether the accused should be held in contempt. If the judge determines that the person should be held in contempt, it would appear that the offender is entitled to a trial on the contempt charge, since the act was not committed in the presence of the judge.

The right of contempt is a powerful weapon, and it is meant to be. It permits a judge to prohibit court proceedings from getting out of hand because of misconduct. It also protects those involved in the court proceedings. If a judge should abuse his or her power of contempt, appeals may be made to a higher court for review and possible remedy.

## JUDICIAL ETHICS

The American Bar Association Code of Judicial Conduct-Canon 1 provides that a judge shall uphold the independence and integrity of the judiciary, shall perform the duties of the office impartially, and shall avoid impropriety and the appearance of impropriety in all of the judge's activities. Rule 1.01, which implements the canon, provides that a judge shall act at all times in a manner that promotes public confidence in the independence, integrity, and impartiality of the judiciary.

The commentary that accompanies Rule 1.01 notes that adherence to the judgments and rulings of courts depends upon public confidence in the independence, integrity, and impartiality of judges, which in turn depends upon judges acting without fear or favoritism in a manner free from self-interest or bias. And that an independent judiciary is indispensable to justice in our society. A judge should comply with high standards of judicial conduct to promote the independence of the judiciary and to foster public confidence in the administration of justice. The commentary also states that judges should participate in activities that promote ethical conduct among judges and lawyers and judges should also implement and enforce codes of conduct, support professionalism within the judiciary and the legal profession, and promote access to justice for all.

Rule 1.02 provides that a judge shall avoid impropriety and the appearance of impropriety. The commentary notes that public confidence in the judiciary is eroded by improper conduct by judges. The prohibition against acting with impropriety or the appearance of impropriety applies to both the professional and personal conduct of a judge. A judge must expect to be the subject of public scrutiny. A judge must therefore accept restrictions on the judge's conduct that might be viewed as burdensome by the ordinary citizen, and should do so freely and willingly.

### Code of Conduct for United States Judges (Effective July 1, 2009)

**A JUDGE SHOULD PERFORM THE DUTIES OF THE OFFICE FAIRLY, IMPARTIALLY, AND DILIGENTLY** The duties of judicial office take precedence over all other activities. In performing the duties prescribed by law, the judge should adhere to the following standards:

**A.** Adjudicative Responsibilities.
1. A judge should be faithful to, and maintain professional competence in, the law and should not be swayed by partisan interests, public clamor, or fear of criticism.
2. A judge should hear and decide matters assigned, unless disqualified, and should maintain order and decorum in all judicial proceedings.
3. A judge should be patient, dignified, respectful, and courteous to litigants, jurors, witnesses, lawyers, and others with whom the judge deals in an official capacity. A judge should require similar conduct of those subject to the judge's control, including lawyers to the extent consistent with their role in the adversary process.
4. A judge should accord to every person who has a legal interest in a proceeding, and that person's lawyer, the full right to be heard according to law. Except as set out below, a judge should not initiate, permit, or consider **ex parte communications** or consider other communications concerning a pending or impending matter that are made outside the presence of the parties or their lawyers. If a judge receives an unauthorized ex parte communication bearing on the substance of a matter, the judge should promptly notify the parties of the subject matter of the communication and allow the parties an opportunity to respond, if requested. A judge may:
   a. initiate, permit, or consider ex parte communications as authorized by law;
   b. when circumstances require it, permit ex parte communication for scheduling, administrative, or emergency purposes, but only if the ex parte communication does not address substantive matters and the judge reasonably believes that no party will gain a procedural, substantive, or tactical advantage as a result of the ex parte communication;
   c. obtain the written advice of a disinterested expert on the law, but only after giving advance notice to the parties of the person to be consulted and the subject matter of the advice and affording the parties reasonable opportunity to object and respond to the notice and to the advice received; or
   d. with the consent of the parties, confer separately with the parties and their counsel in an effort to mediate or settle pending matters.

**LAW IN ACTION**

**The Constitution of The State of New York**

Article Vi. Judiciary

**NY CLS Const Art VI, § 22**

There shall be a commission on judicial conduct. The commission on judicial conduct shall receive, initiate, investigate and hear complaints with respect to the conduct, qualifications, fitness to perform or performance of official duties of any judge or justice of the unified court system, in the manner provided by law; and, in accordance with subdivision d of this section, may determine that a judge or justice be admonished, censured or removed from office for cause, including, but not limited to, misconduct in office, persistent failure to perform his or her duties, habitual intemperance, and conduct, on or off the bench, prejudicial to the administration of justice, or that a judge or justice be retired for mental or physical disability preventing the proper performance of his or her judicial duties. The commission shall transmit any such determination to the chief judge of the court of appeals who shall cause written notice of such determination to be given to the judge or justice involved. Such judge or justice may either accept the commission's determination or make written request to the chief judge, within thirty days after receipt of such notice, for a review of such determination by the court of appeals.

5. A judge should dispose promptly of the business of the court.
6. A judge should not make public comment on the merits of a matter pending or impending in any court. A judge should require similar restraint by court personnel subject to the judge's direction and control. The prohibition on public comment on the merits does not extend to public statements made in the course of the judge's official duties, to explanations of court procedures, or to scholarly presentations made for purposes of legal education. (Committee on Codes of Conduct, 2009)

Every state has some commission or panel to serve as more or less a watchdog on its judges. New York's Commission on Judicial Conduct is a representative type commission.

## JUDICIAL MISCONDUCT

What constitutes judicial misconduct is an often litigated question. As explained by the judge in *United States v. Abernathy*, (2009), the test for impropriety is whether the conduct compromises the ability of the judge to carry out judicial responsibilities with independence, integrity, impartiality, and competence. Examples of actual improprieties include violations of law, court rules, or other specific provisions of this code. The test for an appearance of impropriety is whether the conduct of the judge would be perceived by a reasonable person with knowledge of the circumstances to impair the judge's ability to carry out judicial responsibilities with independence, integrity, impartiality, and competence.

The State of Florida disciplined one judge who:

• Declined to release a defendant pursuant to the clear mandate of Florida Rule of Criminal Procedure 3.134, which required the defendant's release pursuant to a writ of habeas corpus.

**COURTS IN ACTION**

**For 15 Years, a State Law Against Judicial Corruption Has Never been Enforced**

According to the Birmingham News, a 15-year-old Alabama law meant to discourage big-dollar donations to judicial campaigns has never been enforced, and each of the three branches of government blames another for the failure. [Mary Orndorff, "A15 years, a state law against judicial corruption never enforced" The Birmingham News, August 01, 2010, p. A–1].

The attorney general (AG) in response to an query by the Birmingham News stated that the state court system is supposed to come up with rules for enforcement; and the state court system says the law first needs the blessing of the U.S. Justice Department, which the AG's office has not sought; and a legislative sponsor of the law says he'd be happy to rewrite it if someone would tell him what's wrong with it.

"Only the combined forces of the three branches of government could create such a confusing situation," said Mark White, a Birmingham lawyer who led the 1996 review of the law and found several problems that make it hard to enforce [as quoted by the Birmingham News on August 1, 2010]. A federal lawsuit filed in July 2010 requested that the law be formally blocked until the Justice Department can review it, contending that, as the situation stands now, the law could be haphazardly enforced. According to Mary Orndorff, the law itself is not complicated. The law provides that judges who accept significant campaign contributions from someone who has a case in their court would have to step down from hearing the case. The limits are $2,000 for circuit judges and $4,000 for appellate judges. If the law were enforced, it would be one of the most strict judicial campaign finance laws in the country and likely would have a dramatic effect on how judges in Alabama raise money for their campaigns. The law was passed in 1995 and has not been used in a single case according to Orndorff.

Soon after the law passed, then-Alabama Attorney General Jeff Sessions submitted it to the U.S. Justice Department, which reviews all election-related changes in Alabama to make sure they don't disenfranchise minority voters, a requirement of the Voting Rights Act. But Sessions' office withdrew its submission before the Justice Department could act, arguing that the law was not directly related to voting and therefore did not need to be reviewed. Apparently, the U.S. Justice Department wrote the AG stating that the law did need preclearance, but it was never resubmitted.

The law specifies that the Alabama Supreme Court is responsible for writing the rules for implementing the law, which would require attorneys to disclose their donations–as well as those of their employees and client–to the judge's last election within days after a case or appeal is filed. [The Birmingham News web site regarding the law is posted at http://blog.al.com/sweethome/2010/08/alabama_campaign_law_unenforce.html, Accessed on August 6, 2010.]

- The judge was rude, abrupt, and abusive in his treatment of the defendant, acting more like a prosecutor than a [county] court judge.
- The judge issued arrest warrants for approximately 11 traffic defendants who had not answered the docket call, but who were in fact, properly in an adjoining courtroom pursuant to their summonses or the direction of the judicial deputy sheriffs or bailiffs. When the judge was informed of the circumstances, he nevertheless proceeded to have the arrest warrants carried out. The defendants were arrested and the judge initially declined to release them. As a result, these traffic defendants remained in jail until their release was considered by another judge.

Inquiry Concerning a Judge (Sloop), 946 So. 2d 1046, 1050 (Fla. 2006)

The Florida Court in removing one judge noted that the object of disciplinary proceedings was not for the purpose of inflicting punishment, but rather to gauge a judge's

## COURTS IN ACTION

### Black Collar Crime

In the United States, white collar crime is those crimes committed in a professional environment or within a profession. In the United Kingdom, the term "black collar crime" is used to describe judicial misconduct that amounts to criminal behavior. For the years 2008-9, the United Kingdom's Office for Judicial Complaints received 1,339 complaints. Of these, the Lord Chancellor and Lord Chief Justice took action in 89 cases, removing 25 judges and magistrates and 20 others resigned while being investigated. The largest category of complaint was judicial decision-making and case management, but the main reason for removal was failure to fulfill judicial duty. In one group of cases, the judges were found to have been taking bribes to award child custody to wealthy ex-husbands. [Lynne Wrennall, "Confronting Judicial Misconduct," Criminal Justice Matters: The Magazine of the Center for Crime and Justice Studies. June 2010, pp. 10–12.]

fitness to serve as an impartial judicial officer. In making that determination, the Supreme Court of Florida has often pointed out that judges should be held to higher ethical standards than lawyers by virtue of their position in the judiciary and the impact of their conduct on public confidence in an impartial justice system. At the same time, the Supreme Court of Florida has recognized that the discipline of removal should not be imposed upon a judge unless the Supreme Court of Florida concludes that the judge's conduct is fundamentally inconsistent with the responsibilities of judicial office. [Inquiry Concerning a Judge (Renke), 933 So. 2d 482 (Fla. 2006)]

The authors in their prior occupation as attorneys were always careful to make sure that their cell phones were turned off prior to going to court. Nothing makes a judge madder than hearing a cell phone ring in court. In one New York trial court, the judge

## LAW IN ACTION

### Excerpt from the Constitution of the State of Mississippi

On recommendation of the commission on judicial performance, the Supreme Court may remove from office, suspend, fine or publicly censure or reprimand any justice or judge of this state for: (a) actual conviction of a felony in a court other than a court of the State of Mississippi; (b) willful misconduct in office; (c) willful and persistent failure to perform his duties; (d) habitual intemperance in the use of alcohol or other drugs; or (e) conduct prejudicial to the administration of justice which brings the judicial office into disrepute; and may retire involuntarily any justice or judge for physical or mental disability seriously interfering with the performance of his duties, which disability is or is likely to become of a permanent character. [Miss. Const. art. 6, § 177A.]

### New Jersey Statute § 2B:2A-2 (2010)

§ 2B:2A-2. Cause for removal:

A judge may be removed from office by the Supreme Court for misconduct in office, willful neglect of duty, or other conduct evidencing unfitness for judicial office, or for incompetence.

## COURTS IN ACTION

### Conflict of Interest

In United States v. Kadomsky, 2002 U.S. Dist. LEXIS 20319 (E.D. Pa. Oct. 15, 2002)

Defendant's counsel had previously represented three of the government's witnesses. The government considered the three witnesses to be essential to its case and planned to call each of them to testify at trial. Defense counsel represented to the court that defendant was willing to waive any possible conflict of interest. He also represented that he would not cross examine the witnesses at trial. In addition to the constitutional rights of defendant, the court found that it also had to balance those rights that belonged to defense counsel's former clients. The court found that defense counsel had several actual and/or potential conflicts of interest. Conflicts of interest arose whenever an attorney's loyalties were divided, and an attorney who cross-examined former clients inherently encountered divided loyalties. The court was compelled to conclude that defense counsel, at the very least, had a serious potential for a conflict of interest, if not an actual conflict. Defense counsel had divided loyalty between his current client and his former clients, and any choice to represent his current client zealously would have required the abandonment of his duties to his former clients.

presided over the domestic violence part of the city court. During a weekly proceeding, a cell phone rang at the back of the courtroom; the judge asked that the cell phone be brought to him with a warning that everyone could go to jail if the cell phone was not discovered. When the cell phone was not found, 46 defendants were committed to custody. The judge was charged with violating a rule of judicial conduct (22 NYCRR) §§ 100.1, 100.2(A), and 100.3(B)(1), (3), and (6). Upon consideration, the court accepted the Commission's recommendation and removed the judge from the bench. While mitigating factors existed, including (1) testimony from two psychiatrists—who had examined and treated the judge—that marital difficulties led to the incident, (2) an otherwise unblemished record, and (3) an expression of sincere remorse, because the judge had numerous opportunities during the incident to reconsider the enormity of his actions and acted without any lawful basis, his conduct was damaging to the reputation of the courts and was extremely egregious. [Matter of Restaino (State Commn. on Jud. Conduct), 2008 ]

## ATTORNEY/CLIENT COMMUNICATIONS

> "The first duty of an attorney is to keep the secrets of his clients."
>
> —*Taylor v. Blacklow,* (1836).

### Origins of the Attorney-Client Privilege

As noted by Norman Thompson (2000), the exact origins of the **attorney-client privilege** are somewhat foggy. Thompson contends that it may have origins reaching back to the Roman Empire. At least, fragments of the privilege date back to sixteenth century Elizabethan England, when evidentiary privileges arose as the testimony of witnesses became the principal basis of jury verdicts and compulsory process was introduced. One of the leaders in the development of the modern rules of evidence John Wigmore (1961) wrote:

> The history of this privilege goes back to the reign of Elizabeth I, where the privilege appears as unquestioned. It is therefore the oldest of the privileges for confidential communications. The English privilege did not arise to protect

the interests of the client, but from a desire to uphold the oath and the honor of the attorney to abide by his implied "solemn pledge of secrecy." Cases upholding the attorney-client privilege appear as early as 1577.

American courts also initially entrusted the privilege to the attorney and not the client, following in the English tradition. It was not until the mid-1800s that American courts fashioned the prevailing rule that the client is the holder of the privilege and the attorney is obligated to claim it on his behalf, unless it is waived. *King v. Barrett*, 11 Ohio St. 261, 263 (1860).

According to Thompson, American cases dealing with the attorney-client privilege did not appear until the 1820s, but several post-Revolutionary War courts found the privilege rooted in both the law of evidence (protecting disclosures) and the law of agency (where a fiduciary relationship between a lawyer and client exists). Early American criminal courts and legal scholars viewed the privilege as an outgrowth of the Fifth Amendment privilege against self-incrimination. [*Rochester City Bank v. Suydam Sage & Co.*, 1851]. Later, the Sixth Amendment right to effective assistance of counsel began to appear as an additional rationale.

Thompson (2000) notes that many courts and scholars also believed the privilege should be extended beyond the bounds of Fifth Amendment in order to facilitate frank communications between attorney and client on all matters, criminal and civil. He sees this "utilitarian" view is the prevailing majority view today.

As noted by the court in *King v. Barrett* (1860), the communications made by a party to an attorney for the purpose of obtaining his professional advice or assistance, are, by the rule of the common law, in general privileged. Courts will neither require nor permit such communications to be divulged, to the prejudice of the client, and without his consent. This, however, is the privilege of the client, and not of the attorney, and it may, of course, be waived by the client. In order to protect such communications, no formal retainer, or actual payment of fees is necessary.

## Attorney-Client Privilege Today

The attorney-client privilege basically means that information furnished to an attorney in confidence by his or her client may not be disclosed without the permission of the client. The attorney-client privilege normally shields only confidential communications from client to attorney. Communications from attorney to client are privileged only if they constitute legal advice, or tend directly or indirectly to reveal the substance of a client confidence. (In re Sealed Case, 1984).

### LAW IN ACTION
### Federal Rules of Evidence Rule 501

Except as otherwise required by the Constitution of the United States or provided by Act of Congress or in rules prescribed by the Supreme Court pursuant to statutory authority, the privilege of a witness, person, government, State, or political subdivision thereof shall be governed by the principles of the common law as they may be interpreted by the courts of the United States in the light of reason and experience. However, in civil actions and proceedings, with respect to an element of a claim or defense as to which State law supplies the rule of decision, the privilege of a witness, person, government, State, or political subdivision thereof shall be determined in accordance with State law.

The Supreme Court of the United States has long recognized that the scope of the privilege is governed by common law principles as interpreted and applied by the federal courts in the light of reason and experience.

## Exceptions

There are several exceptions to attorney/client privilege rule. The most common exception is that the privilege does not apply to future criminal conduct. For example, if the defendant tells her defense counsel that she is going to rob a bank to obtain the funds to pay her attorney this statement is not privileged because it refers to the future intent to commit a crime. In addition, there is a crime-fraud exception only where the attorney is being used to further a future or ongoing scheme of misconduct. It does not apply to communications seeking legal representation with respect to a past act of crime or fraud; such statements are at the heart of the protection provided by the privilege. Moreover, the exception will not apply if the client consulted with an attorney to determine whether a prospective course of conduct was lawful (*United States v. White*, 1989).

Consider the following fact situation: You are representing a defendant. Prior to trial, she tells you that she is going to commit perjury at trial. What do you do? The defense counsel cannot violate the law in defending the accused. If, for example, the accused tells the counsel that he is going to testify falsely at the trial, the counsel should encourage the accused not to. If the accused insists on testifying and indicates that he will commit perjury, the defense counsel should request that the judge relieve the counsel from the duties to represent the accused before the accused testifies. The problem in this case, is that the counsel cannot tell the judge why he or she wants to be relieved due to the rules of confidentiality. All the counsel can tell the judge is that there is a conflict between the accused and counsel. This problem could last indefinitely, because when new counsel is appointed, if the accused tells the new counsel that he intends to commit perjury, the new counsel should also be excused. What normally happens, however, is once a counsel has been excused, the accused realizes the problem and doesn't tell all to the new counsel.

Consider this situation: A young girl is missing; the girl's parents offer a reward for information regarding the missing girl's whereabouts. You are defending an accused on an unrelated murder charge. He informs you that he killed the young girl and buried her body in the local cemetery. If the police find the body, evidence on the body will lead the police to your client. What do you do? Information that an attorney receives from his or her client is privileged and cannot be divulged without the client's consent. Accordingly, if an accused tells his attorney that he committed a murder, the attorney cannot divulge this information without the client's consent. This privileged communication is based on the theory that the accused needs to be able to communicate with his or her attorney without fear of the communications being used against him or her. In the above situation, the New York Bar Association ruled that the communication was privileged and the attorney should not have revealed the information regarding the girl's death. [Confidentiality and the Case of Robert Garrow's Lawyers, 28 Buffalo Law Review 211, 213–214 (1974)]

In one Virginia case, the accused told his counsel that the money from a bank robbery was in a locker in a bus station. The counsel advised the accused to hide the money elsewhere. The attorney was convicted of being an accessory after the fact. While the communications as to the location of the money was privileged, the attorney went beyond that when he advised the accused to hide the money in a different location. This conversation was overheard by a nosey telephone operator who reported it to the police. [Note: The privileged communication extends to the attorney, attorney's secretary and paralegal, but not to a third person such as a telephone operator who overhears the conversation.]

Where the attorney is merely acting as a conduit for information, that is, as a messenger, the privilege is inapplicable. So for example, if the attorney is merely reporting information that has been received from a government official, the communication is not protected by the privilege. In one case, an attorney's report to the client about what an IRS agent told the attorney was unprivileged, because it did not reveal, either directly or implicitly, legal advice (*United States v. DeFazio*, 1990)

In the DeFazio case, the court noted that the attorney testified only to what the IRS agent said to him, and that he later relayed those statements to the defendant. The court held that the content of this testimony was unprivileged because it did not reveal, either directly or implicitly, legal advice given defendant or any client confidences.

## Communications between Spouses

A similar privilege is recognized in communications between spouses. In *Wolfle v. United States* (U.S. 1934) a criminal trial, the trial court admitted into evidence a statement contained in a letter written by defendant to his wife. The statement was proved by a stenographer's testimony, who read from her notes, to whom defendant had dictated the letter. The appellate court affirmed defendant's conviction, holding the evidence was properly admitted. Upon review, the court affirmed and held that the statement was a relevant admission by defendant because it was probative of his guilty purpose or intent to commit the crime. The statement was not within the husband-wife privilege excluding such communications from admission into evidence because defendant voluntarily disclosed the statement to a third person, the stenographer. The statement was not entitled to protection within the privilege because normally husbands and wives could conveniently communicate without the need for a stenographer.

## LAW IN ACTION

## What Constitutes Criminal Contempt of Court?

## Black v. Blount 938 S.W.2d 394; 1996 Tenn. LEXIS 807 (1996)

Steven Black, an attorney, sought review of a judgment which convicted him of criminal contempt. The attorney represented certain individuals in a personal injury action. After the jury returned a damages verdict that the attorney felt was too low, the attorney gave a thumbs down gesture in court and confronted the jury and the defense attorney in the hall. The trial court appointed the amicus curiae [friend of the court] to prosecute a contempt citation against the attorney. The trial court found the attorney guilty of two counts of criminal contempt. The lower court reversed holding that the evidence was insufficient. The court held that criminal contempt of court which obstructed the administration of justice included all willful misconduct which embarrassed, hindered, or obstructed a court in its administration of justice or derogated the court's authority or dignity, thereby bringing the administration of law into disrepute. Even conduct that did not occur in the course of a proceeding was actionable.

Criminal contempts are intended to preserve the power and vindicate the dignity and authority of the law, and the court as an organ of society. Therefore, sanctions for criminal contempt are generally both punitive and unconditional in nature. Criminal contempt of court that obstructs the administration of justice is defined as any willful misconduct which embarrasses, hinders, or obstructs a court in its administration of justice or derogates the court's authority or dignity, thereby bringing the administration of law into disrepute.

The court also found that because the attorney was responsible for creating the situation that prompted the appointment of the amicus curiae, the trial court was authorized to order the attorney to pay attorney's fees.

**LAW IN ACTION**

**Does the Defendant Have a Right to Testify if his or her Attorney Believes that the Defendant will Testify Falsely on the Witness Stand?**

People v. Johnson 62 Cal. App. 4th 608 (1998)

Defendant Johnson sought review of a decision of the Superior Court of San Diego County (California), which convicted him on numerous counts of kidnapping, rape and robbery. He contested his convictions on the grounds that he was not allowed to testify on his own behalf. Johnson's counsel refused to put defendant on the stand because he believed Johnson planned to offer perjured testimony. The court found that the trial court erred in not allowing defendant to testify because defendant had a fundamental right to do so and where, as here, the attorney did not want to place his client on the stand because, it would have been better to simply allow the defendant to testify in a narrative manner rather than bar him from testifying.

The guarantee of Fourteenth Amendment of the U.S. Constitution that no one shall be deprived of liberty without due process of law which includes the right to be heard and to offer testimony, necessarily includes the criminal defendant's right to testify in his own behalf. The narrative approach to allowing a defendant who may offer perjured testimony to testify best accommodates the competing interests of the defendant's constitutional right to testify and the attorney's ethical obligations

The criminal defendant's constitutional right to testify is unlike other matters of trial strategy that are in the control of defense counsel. A criminal defendant has the right to take the stand even over the objections of his or her trial counsel. The right to testify on one's own behalf is of such fundamental importance that a defendant who timely demands to take the stand contrary to the advice given by defense counsel has the right to give an exposition of his or her defense before a jury. The defendant's insistence upon testifying may in the final analysis be harmful to the case, but the right is of such importance that every defendant should have it in a criminal case.

Of the various approaches to the problem of a defendant's intended perjury, the narrative approach represents the best accommodation of the competing interests of the defendant's constitutional right to testify and the attorney's obligation not to participate in the presentation of perjured testimony, since it allows the defendant to tell the jury, in the defendant's own words, his or her version of what occurred, and allows the attorney to play a passive role. In contrast, the two extremes—fully cooperating with the defendant's testimony and refusing to present the defendant's testimony—involve no accommodation of the conflicting interests; the first gives no consideration to the attorney's ethical obligations, the second gives none to the defendant's right to testify. The other intermediate solutions—persuasion, withdrawal, and disclosure—often result in no solution, i.e., the defendant is not persuaded, the withdrawal leads to an endless chain of withdrawals, and disclosure compromises client confidentiality and typically requires further action. The danger that the defendant may testify falsely is mitigated by the fact that the defendant is subject to impeachment and can be cross-examined. Further, to preclude the defendant's testimony entirely based on a possibility that defendant may lie deprives the jury of making that assessment and may deprive the jury of hearing other, nonperjurious evidence to which the defendant would have testified about had he or she been given the opportunity.

## DEFENSE COUNSEL OBLIGATIONS

Would you defend a person charged with murdering a young child? No person has a more demanding and misunderstood role in our legal system than the defense counsel. First, the defense counsel is an officer of the court and as such he or she must conform to the requirements of the law. The defense counsel is the only individual who speaks on behalf of the defendant. He or she has a duty to defend the client within the best of his or her means within the limits of the law. This includes a duty to defend a person who has committed an atrocious crime. If the counsel can legally prevent the state from proving the accused's guilt, the counsel has the duty to do so.

As noted by Applegate (1989), an attorney enjoys extensive leeway in preparing a witness to testify truthfully, but the attorney crosses a line when she influences the witness to alter testimony in a false or misleading way.

## ETHICAL ISSUES IN PROSECUTION

> "In representing the United States, a federal prosecutor has a special duty not to impede the truth."
>
> —*United States v. Reyes*, 2009

When considering the ethical obligations of a prosecutor or police officer, the reader must remember that the primary responsibility of a prosecutor is not to prosecute, but to promote justice. Note: The duty of a defense counsel, however, is not to promote justice, but to represent his client zealously within the bounds of the law. In a criminal trial, the defense's duty is to his or her client within the bounds of the law. Our system of justice functions on the adversary system wherein the prosecutor represents the people and the defense represents the accused with the judge acting as the referee. As noted by the R. R. Kidston, former Senior Crown Prosecutor of New South Wales, (1958, p. 148)

> A prosecutor is a "minister of justice." The prosecutor's principal role is to assist the court to arrive at the truth and to do justice between the community and the accused according to law and the dictates of fairness.

The prosecutor must argue the State's case forcefully, but while the prosecutor may strike hard blows, he may not strike foul ones, for the prosecutor's primary duty is to seek justice, not to attain convictions (*Durmer v. Rogers, 2006*, p. 74612).

A prosecutor is not entitled to act as if representing private interests in litigation. A prosecutor represents the community and not any individual or sectional interest. A prosecutor acts independently, yet in the general public interest. The "public interest" is to be understood in that context as an historical continuum: acknowledging debts to previous generations and obligations to future generations.

## DEFENDANT MISCONDUCT

In *Easterday v. Kirby* (2008) the court warned a defendant that due to his prior incidents of courtroom misconduct, his right of self representation will be terminated and he will be removed from the courtroom if he engages in conduct that abuses the dignity of the courtroom. That includes, but is not limited to: (1) bullying, insulting, humiliating, abusing, shouting, yelling, talking over others, intimidating, harassing, disruptive behavior, interrupting, disrespecting and/or threatening the Judge, prosecutor, courtroom personnel, U.S. Marshals or other security officers, co-defendants, witnesses, jurors, and/or courtroom observers; (2) failing or refusing to comply with rules of procedure and courtroom protocol; and (3) failing or refusing to obey the Judge's orders.

In *Illinois v. Allen* (1970), the defendant while on trial for robbery was removed from the courtroom for repeated disruptive behavior and the use of vile and abusive language directed at the trial judge, notwithstanding the judge's prior warning that removal would follow another outburst. Appointed counsel represented Allen during the period Allen was not allowed in the courtroom, principally the presentation of the State's case. Having given some assurances of good conduct, Allen was allowed to return to the courtroom while appointed counsel presented his defense. Allen was convicted. He filed a petition for a writ of habeas corpus in federal court, contending that he had been deprived of his right under the Sixth and Fourteenth Amendments to confront the witnesses against him. The Supreme Court held:

1. A defendant can lose his right to be present at trial, if, following the judge's warning that he will be removed if his disruptive behavior continues, he nevertheless insists on conducting himself in such a disruptive manner that his trial cannot proceed if he remains in the courtroom. He can reclaim the right to be present as soon as he is willing to comport himself with decorum and respect. pp. 342–343.

2. A trial judge confronted by a defendant's disruptive conduct can exercise discretion to meet the circumstances of the case; and though no single formula is best for all situations, there are at least three constitutionally permissible approaches for the court's handling of an obstreperous defendant: (1) bind and gag him as a last resort, thereby keeping him present; (2) cite him for criminal or civil contempt; or (3) remove him from the courtroom, while the trial continues, until he promises to conduct himself properly. pp. 343–346.

3. On the facts of this case the trial judge did not abuse his discretion, respondent through his disruptive behavior having lost his right of confrontation under the Sixth and Fourteenth Amendments. pp. 345–347.

## Questions in Review

1. How do the duties of a prosecutor differ from those of a defense counsel?
2. What steps may a judge take to control an unruly defendant?
3. What contempt powers does a judge have?
4. What is a prosecutor's primary duty?
5. Explain the importance of the attorney/client privilege?

## Practicum

**Should an individual be charged with criminal contempt because of the following letter he wrote that criticized a judge's decision was published in a newspaper?**

Dear Editor:

I see in your columns that Judge Lloyd's ruling in behalf of the Tavern owner's petition makes it mandatory for Council to see that the matter is placed on the ballot for the voters to again determine whether or not such sales shall be permitted between 4:00 P.M. and midnight.

As one who was present at the hearing it is difficult to understand just why the Judge ruled as he did. At the point of recess without the Judge is given to double talk it certainly seemed that he would rule against the Tavern Association. What happened in between that time? Whatever it was it must have influenced the good Judge's decision to pass the buck and make the voters decide the issue.

Why do we pay these men such good salaries if they are not capable of deciding issues when they come before them?

Now the question really is this, not shall the taverns have these extra hours of sale alone, but shall they dominate the good men of our Council, our Mayor, our Legal adviser and Police Department. In other words, who is going to run the affairs of Gloucester City? The constituted authorities or the Tavern Association?

There is only one answer to this question if we desire a decent city. And that is for every self-respecting citizen to go to the poles on election day and vote against this referendum, and 'RULE BY THE TAVERN ASSOCIATION.'

Yours truly
(s) Rev. Loriot D. Bozorth

**Justify your answer before reading the court's decision.**

### In The Matter Of Contempt Of Court By Loriot D. Bozorth
38 N.J. Super. 184; 118 A.2d 430; (1955)

Defendant Bozorth was charged with criminal contempt after a letter in which he criticized a judge's decision was published in a newspaper. After consideration, the court found defendant not guilty. The court held that defendant's letter, which contained statements criticizing a past decision of the court, did not warrant a conviction for criminal contempt because it was not of such a nature as to occasion a clear and present danger to the fair administration of justice. Further, the court stated that inaccurate and even false comment on litigation no longer pending did not warrant criminal contempt, and stated that to impose criminal contempt for comment on a matter not then pending, absent an effect upon the honest, fair, impartial and dispassionate administration of justice, would amount to improper censorship in violation of state and federal constitution guarantees of freedom of speech.

A contempt of court has been defined as a disobedience to the court by acting in opposition to its authority, justice and dignity. Generally speaking, he whose conduct tends to bring the authority and administration of the law into disrepute or disregard, interferes with or prejudices parties during litigation, or otherwise tends to impede, embarrass, or obstruct the court in the discharge of its duties is guilty of contempt.

Contempts fall into two general categories or classes, civil contempt and criminal contempt. Although by their very basic nature the two are frequently, at least to some extent, merged in a given act and are sometimes confused, it may be stated that normally, a civil contempt is a contempt consisting in a failure to perform some act required or ordered to be done by a court for the benefit of the opposing party, and is therefore an offense against the party in whose behalf a violated order or judgment is made. The ultimate object of a civil contempt proceeding is the vindication of private rights. A criminal contempt, on the other hand, concerns itself with conduct directed against the authority or dignity of the court. It is an act tending to obstruct, hinder or hamper justice in its due course. The purpose of a criminal contempt is the vindication of public authority and the preservation of the dignity of the court. It involves the element of public injury or offense.

Criminal contempts have been as well subdivided into two general categories, which are commonly referred to as direct or indirect and constructive contempts. The former, as the designation signifies, are contempts committed in the physical presence of the court. An indirect or constructive contempt is an act committed not in the presence of the court, but at some distance therefrom.

To constitute the offense of criminal contempt of court for statements made or articles written, the statements or writings must have been made or written at a time when a particular matter was pending in court and prior to the disposition thereof by a judge. The publication of an article concerning the matter pending before the court, which attacks the character or integrity of the court, jury, parties to the action, attorneys or officers of the court, and which has a tendency to influence or prejudice the tribunal or jury before which such matter is pending, constitutes contumacious conduct. It must tend to intimidate, influence, impede, embarrass or obstruct courts in the administration of justice in a matter pending to be deemed a contempt.

Defamatory comments on the conduct of a judge with respect to particular cases or matters finally disposed of, even though they may be libellous, are not generally deemed criminally contumacious. Both the state and federal constitutions contain guarantees of the freedom of speech and press. It is the inherent and basic right of any citizen under our government to criticize the conduct of his public officials.

Absent any effect upon the honest, fair, impartial and dispassionate administration of justice resulting from criticism of the past acts of a judge in a matter not then pending, to hold such criticism a criminal contempt would amount to a censorship, and this is an untenable and abhorrent situation under our government. Even where matters are pending before the court, in order to constitute written utterances criminally contemptuous there must be a clear and present danger to the fair administration of justice arising from such publications.

## Key Terms

**Attorney-client privilege:** A rule, which states that information furnished to an attorney in confidence by his or her client may not be disclosed without the permission of the client.

**Contempt:** An act that is disrespectful to the court or adversely affects the administration of justice.

**Ex Parte Communications:** In legal terms it refers to communications by one party to a court without the presence of the other parties. Ex parte communications are generally prohibited by the courts.

# References

## LEGISLATION

Mississippi Constitution article 6, § 177A
New Jersey Statute § 2B:2A-2 (2010)
New York Constitution, Article VI, § 22:

## COURT DECISIONS

*Autry v. State of Oklahoma*, 2007 OK CR 41, 172 P.3d 212, 214
*Durmer v. Rogers*, 2006 U.S. Dist. LEXIS 48556 (D.N.J., July 18, 2006)
*Easterday v. Kirby*, 2008 OK 104 (Okla. 2008)
*Gilbert v. State of Oklahoma*, 1982 OK CR 100, 648 P.2d 1226
*Ibarra v. Baker*, 338 Fed. Appx. 457, 465-466 (5th Cir. Tex. 2009)
*Illinois v. Allen*, 397 U.S. 337 (U.S. 1970)
Inquiry Concerning a Judge (Sloop), 946 So. 2d 1046, 1050 (Fla. 2006)
Inquiry Concerning a Judge (Renke), 933 So. 2d 482 (Fla. 2006)
In re Sealed Case, 737 F.2d 94, 99 (D.C. Cir. 1984)
*King v. Barrett*, 11 Ohio St. 261, 263 (Ohio 1860)
Matter of Restaino (State Commn. on Jud. Conduct), 2008 NY Slip Op 4947, 1 (N.Y. 2008)
*People v. Fusaro*, 18 Cal.App.3rd 877 (1971)
*Rochester City Bank v. Suydam Sage & Co.*, 5 How. Pr. 254, 258-59 (N.Y. Sup. Ct. 1851)
*Taylor v. Blacklow*, 132 Eng. Rep. 401, 406 (C.P. 1836).
*Taylor v. Hayes*, 418 U.S. 488 (1974)
*United States v. Abernathy*, 2009 U.S. Dist. LEXIS 114068 (E.D. Mich. Dec. 8, 2009)
*United States v. DeFazio*, 899 F.2d 626 (7th Cir. 1990)
*United States v. Reyes*, 2009 U.S. App. LEXIS 24575 (9th Cir. Cal. Nov. 5, 2009)
*United States v. White*, 887 F.2d 267 (D.C. Cir. 1989)
*Wolfle v. United States*, 291 U.S. 7 (U.S. 1934)

## JOURNALS, ARTICLES AND OTHER MATERIALS

American Bar Association. *Code of Judicial Conduct*. Chicago: American Bar Association, 1990.
Applegate, John S. "Witness Preparation." *Texas Law Review* 68 (1989): 277.
Committee on Codes of Conduct. *Code of Conduct for United States Judges*. Washington, DC: Administrative Office of the United States Courts, (2009).
Thompson, Norman K. "The Attorney-Client Privilege: Practical Military Applications of a Professional Core Value." *Air Force Law Review* 49, no. 1 (2000): 1–19
Wigmore, John (1961). Evidence in Trials at Common Law § 2290, at 542. New York: (McNaughton rev. 1961), 542

# 10

# Drug and DWI Courts

**What you need to know about Drug Courts**

After you have completed this chapter, you should know:

- Drug courts are premised on principles of therapeutic justice.
- The first drug court was established in 1989 in Dade County, Florida.
- Presently there are drug courts in all states and U.S. territories that have U.S. courts.
- Drug courts are specialized courts or court calendars, which provide for intensive judicial supervision, treatment services, sanctions, and incentives to address the needs of drug offenders.
- A nonadversarial approach is used in the drug courts with the prosecution and defense working to promote public safety while still protecting the participants' due-process rights.
- Drug courts provide access to a continuum of alcohol, drug, and other related treatment and rehabilitation services.
- Participants' abstinence is monitored by frequent testing.
- The ultimate goal of drug addiction treatment is to enable the individual to achieve lasting abstinence, with the immediate goals to reduce drug abuse, improve the individual's ability to function, and minimize the medical and social complications of drug abuse and addiction.
- Drug treatment court must take into account that defendants in the early stages of recovery may resist treatment and most probably do not remember how to perform mundane tasks such as grocery shopping.
- Critics of drug court programs frequently contend that the drug court entry process is a type of forced plea bargain, which involves intimidation and threat of violent coercion.
- The treatment programs generally involve community supervision designed to help the participants combat their addiction, prevent relapse as well as to obey the law and comply with program conditions.
- In most states there is a treatment court hearing before an individual is assigned to the program. In addition, there are frequent conferences with the treatment court coordinators to monitor the individual's participation and progress and to alter case management plans as needed.
- Drug treatment programs frequently provide ancillary services in an attempt to provide effective rehabilitation for the participants.
- Drug court treatment programs generally conduct frequent and random substance abuse tests of participants.
- The testing is designed to deter future usage, to identify participants who are both maintaining abstinence or who have relapsed, and to guide treatment and sanction decisions.

- Conditions for unsuccessful termination of the treatment program include noncompliance with treatment recommendations, failure to attend scheduled court hearings, noncompliance with supervision guidelines, arrest on a new charge, and demonstrating violent behaviors towards self or others.

- Probably the most frequent grounds stated for treatment termination are based on the results of the substance abuse tests.

- An individual has a right to a due process hearing in open court before he or she is terminated from a treatment program and the case is referred to trial.

- While our juvenile justice system developed with a distinctly different philosophy from the adult criminal justice system, the juvenile drug courts evolved directly from the adult drug court model.

- DWI courts are increasing in number exponentially across the country.

- Modeled after the effective approach of drug courts, DWI court evaluations appear to show impressive results on reducing recidivism

**Chapter Outline**
- Introduction
- What are Drug Courts?
- Drug Court Goals
- Drug Court Procedures
- Community Supervision
- Substance Abuse Testing
- Graduation
- Termination
- Drug Court Alumni Groups
- Ethical Issues
- Juvenile Drug Courts
- Participants in a Drug Court Program
- DWI Courts

## INTRODUCTION

Drug courts are premised on principles of therapeutic justice. Therapeutic justice is the use of social science to study the extent to which a legal rule or practice promotes the psychological and physical well-being of the people it affects. More specifically, drug courts are part of the emerging development of problem-solving courts designed to address root causes of criminality (such as drug addiction) and to provide offenders with treatment in order to help them return to the community as responsible citizens (Oram and Gleckker 2006, p. 474).

In Miami (Dade County) in the 1980s, a large majority of criminals were incarcerated because of drug offenses and were revolving back through the criminal justice system because of their drug abuse or addiction. With the support of the Florida Supreme Court, several local judges decided that a more effective approach would be the delivery of treatment services coupled with more intensive oversight by the criminal justice system. As a result, the drug court concept was created.

Drug courts began in 1989 as an experiment by the Dade County, Florida Circuit Court. A single judge devised and proactively supervised an intensive, community-based, treatment, rehabilitation, and supervision program for felony drug defendants in Dade County's effort to halt the recidivism rates among offenders involved in substance abuse. By 1998, 48 of the 50 state court systems had established drug courts (Drug Program Office, 1999). By 2006, all 50 states and the district courts in the District of Columbia, Northern Marina Islands, Puerto Rico, Guam and many tribal courts had implemented drug courts (American University, 2006). By March 2008, Florida had 111 drug courts in operation with seven more in the planning stages (National Center for State Courts, 2008).

> The design of the Miami Drug Court was both innovative and pragmatic, the product of a yearlong, worldwide study that Deputy Chief Judge Herbert Klein undertook at the direction of Chief Judge Gerald Wetherington to identify strategies for dealing with drug addicts, which Miami might adapt to manage the court's rising caseload of drug-possession cases effectively in light of resource constraints. . . .
>
> —Caroline Cooper 2007, 1.

## WHAT ARE DRUG COURTS

The National Center for State Courts website defines drug courts as "specialized courts or court calendars that provide for intensive judicial supervision, treatment services, sanctions, and incentives to address the needs of drug offenders" (National Center for State Courts, 2009). The essential elements of a drug court had been reduced to ten key elements by the Drug Courts Program Office (1997). The office lists the following ten essential elements:

- Drug courts integrate alcohol and other treatment services with the justice system case processing.
- A nonadversarial approach is used with the prosecution and defense working to promote public safety while still protecting the participants' due-process rights.
- Early and prompt identification of eligible participants.
- Drug courts provide access to a continuum of alcohol, drug, and other related treatment and rehabilitation services.
- Participants' abstinence is monitored by frequent testing.
- The courts operate with a coordinated strategy that governs the responses to participants' compliance.
- An ongoing judicial interaction with each drug court participant is essential.
- Monitoring and evaluation measure the achievement of program goals and gauge effectiveness.
- Continuing interdisciplinary education which promotes effective drug court planning, implementation, and operations.
- Forging partnerships among drug courts, public agencies, and community-based organizations to generate local support and enhance effectiveness of drug courts.

## DRUG COURT GOALS

As noted by retired California Superior Court Judge Hora (2008, p. 717), the ultimate goal of drug addiction treatment is to enable the individual to achieve lasting abstinence, with the immediate goals to reduce drug abuse, improve the individual's ability to function, and minimize the medical and social complications of drug abuse and addiction. Using the medical model of treatment as a reference, Judge Hora notes that individuals with substance abuse problems are like people with diabetes or heart disease—these individuals in treatment for drug addiction need to change behaviors and to adopt more healthful lifestyles.

**COURTS IN ACTION**

**Magistrate Judge's Report and Recommendation in a Probation Revocation Case**

**United States v. Chandley, 2010 U.S. Dist. LEXIS 16570, 2-7 (E.D. Ky. Feb. 4, 2010)**

This matter is before the Court following a final revocation hearing on January 27, 2010, on a Probation Violation Report filed by the United States Probation Office. The Defendant was present and represented by appointed counsel, Michael Fox, Esq.; the United States was represented by Lindsay Hughes, Esq.; and United States Probation Officer Mike Jones was also present.

The Defendant waived his right to proceed before the United States District Judge, and consented to allow the undersigned to preside over the entire proceedings. In addition, the Defendant expressed his desire to stipulate to all violations contained in the report. The Court, being fully advised, and after determining the voluntariness and factual basis of his stipulation, makes the following proposed Findings of Fact and Conclusions of Law:

### Findings of Fact

1. On February 11, 2008, the Defendant was sentenced following his plea of guilty to Count 10 of Ashland Indictment 07-cr-15-DLB-4, charging him with Passing Counterfeit Currency/Aiding and Abetting, in violation of Title 18 U.S.C. § 472 and 18 U.S.C. § 2. He was sentenced to a five (5) year term of probation.
2. United States Probation Officer Michael Jones documented the following conduct resulting in the violations stated in a Probation Violation Report dated September 8, 2009: (1) the Defendant tested positive for oxycodone on December 13, 2008 and December 20, 2008, subsequently admitting to using controlled substances without a valid prescription; (2) the Defendant missed a scheduled drug test for a Drug Court program on May 13, 2009, and failed to report to his scheduled state court appearance on May 14, 2009.

At the hearing on January 27, 2010, Chandley was informed of his right to persist in a plea of not guilty, his right to remain silent and his right to a hearing on the alleged violations. The Defendant stated under oath that he understood both the nature of the charges, and the maximum possible penalties. He thereafter knowingly and voluntarily made an oral stipulation to the violations contained within the report as stated above. His stipulation was based upon a sufficient factual basis containing all essential elements of the crimes charged and was offered without evidence of coercion or duress.

### Conclusions of Law

The above stipulation and report prove, by clear and convincing evidence, that defendant has violated the following conditions of probation:

**Standard Condition No. 1:** The defendant shall not commit another federal, state or local crime.

**Standard Condition No. 7:** The defendant shall refrain from excessive use of alcohol and shall not purchase, possess, use, distribute, or administer any controlled substance or any paraphernalia related to any controlled substances, except as prescribed by a physician.

**Special Condition No. 4:** The defendant shall successfully complete the drug program in which he currently participates for state court.

The original guideline range at sentencing in the matter was 15 to 21 months based upon total offense level and criminal history. Considering the most significant violation is a Grade B, the guideline range of imprisonment for violation of probation is 6–12 months.

The defendant was fully informed of his right of allocution, and knowingly waived the right before the United States District Judge, choosing to speak on his own behalf before the undersigned.

## Recommendation

In making a recommendation regarding the imposition of sentence, the undersigned has considered the following factors set forth in 18 U.S.C. § 3553:

i.   The nature and circumstances of the offense. The instant offenses involve illegal possession and use of controlled substances, in addition to failure to appear for court appearances as required. The conduct resulting in the offenses was required by this Court as part of its conditions of Probation, and as part of a diversion program on unrelated state court proceedings.

ii.  The history and characteristics of the Defendant. The Defendant was convicted of Passing Counterfeit Currency in violation of 18 U.S.C. § 472. The Defendant was participating in the state Drug Court program as part of a diversion arising from 7 counts of Theft By Unlawful Taking/Disposition Over $ 300. As a result of the instant violations, his diversion program was terminated and on August 13, 2009, he was sentenced to 5 years in the custody of the Kentucky Department of Corrections. He was paroled on December 18, 2009. In addressing his conduct and his current violations, he indicated at allocution his remorse and explained his behavior as being a result of his addiction to narcotics.

iii. The need for the sentence to reflect the seriousness of the offense, to promote respect for the law, to provide just punishment for the offense; to afford adequate deterrence to future conduct; to protect the public from further crimes of the defendant; and to provide correctional treatment for the defendant in the most effective manner.

iv.  In the instant matter, the most serious violation is a Grade B violation. In light of the Defendant's criminal history, the revocation guidelines call for a range of imprisonment from six (6) to twelve (12) months.

## It Is Therefore Recommended As Follows:

1.   That the Defendant's Probation be revoked and the Defendant be re-sentenced to a period of incarceration of six (6) months, with 36 months supervised release to follow;

2.   Upon release from incarceration, the Defendant be required to complete an inpatient Drug Rehabilitation program at a facility to be designated by the United States Probation Office.;

3.   During the term of supervised release:
     a.   the Defendant shall abstain from the use of alcohol;
     b.   The defendant shall refrain from use or unlawful possession of a narcotic drug or other controlled substance defined in 21 U.S.C. § 802 unless prescribed by a licensed medical practitioner;
     c.   The defendant shall not obstruct or attempt to obstruct or tamper, in any fashion, with the efficiency and accuracy of any prohibited substance testing which is required as a condition of release; and
     d.   The defendant shall submit his person, residence and home, office or vehicle to a search, upon the direction and discretion of the United States Probation Office.

Specific objections to this Report and Recommendation must be filed within fourteen days from the date of service thereof or further appeal is waived. General objections or objections that require a judge's interpretation are insufficient to preserve the right to appeal. A party may file a response to another party's objections within fourteen days after being served with a copy thereof. 28 U.S.C. § 636(b)(1)(C); Fed. R. Crim. P. 59.

This the 4th day of February, 2010.
Signed By:
Edward B. Atkins
United States Magistrate Judge

Hora (2008) states that many researchers wrongly believe that drug courts are based on an inconsistency in ideology. According to her, these researchers content that the courts in relying on the disease model of addiction that drug treatment courts deny that drug abusers are exercising a free choice to use drugs. The drug courts then terminate individuals from the programs because they fail to control their behavior while in the treatment program.

She contends that this assertion of inconsistency is incorrect in two respects. First, drug courts do not consider defendants to be without the ability to make choices. Second, while the initial use of drugs may be a choice, subsequent addiction is not a choice. Hora (2008) contends that such factors as behavioral control or willpower may play a powerful role at the onset of drug use and that the participants differ as to the extent of control they have over their addictions. She noted that personal responsibility and choice work in conjunction with, and not to the exclusion of, genetic and cultural factors.

Another often stated goal of the treatment programs employed by drug treatment courts is to produce law-abiding individuals who maintain control over their behavior, thus eliminating the need to commit collateral crimes to sustain their supply of the drug (Bales 2006).

## DRUG COURT PROCEDURES

### Forced Participation in a Drug Treatment Program

Critics of drug treatment courts contend that defendants are forced to choose between two undesirable alternatives; a drug treatment program or possible incarceration. Proponents for the courts contend that when defendants are offered drug treatment court placement, they are given a true choice between therapeutic court enrollment and regular case processing (McColl 2000). The proponents point out that U.S. Supreme Court Associate Justice Potter Stewart noted in *Robinson v. California* (1962) that a state could establish a program of compulsory treatment for those addicted to narcotics, and that such a program of treatment might require periods of involuntary confinement. He also stated that penal sanctions could be imposed for failure to comply with established compulsory treatment procedures.

Judge Hora (2008) notes that a drug treatment court must take into account that defendants in the early stages of recovery may resist treatment and most probably do not remember how to perform mundane tasks such as grocery shopping. The individuals need be pressured to comply with the treatment requirements. As noted by Chappel (2007, p. 12): "Judges should coerce treatment until sobriety becomes tolerable."

### Role of Plea Bargaining

The treatment option provided by drug treatment courts is synonymous with the practice of plea bargaining. An individual offered an assignment to a drug court treatment program basically makes a choice to enter the program or to suffer the possible consequences of penal sentences in regular criminal court. The process of accepting a drug court program is a form of plea bargaining. In addition, to qualify for the program, a defendant must waive some of his or her constitutional rights in exchange for the opportunity to receive the treatment and possibly avoid a criminal conviction.

### Coercion in Drug Court Pleas

Critics of drug court programs frequently contend that the drug court entry process is a type of forced plea bargain that involves intimidation and threat of violent coercion. This contention is based on the concept that the defendant is forced to either volunteer for the drug treatment program or face a long prison term (Oram and Gleckker 2006). Proponents of drug courts argue that this coercion is warranted because of drug court's benefits far outweigh its disabilities.

Judge Bamberger (2003, p. 1091), a New York Supreme Court Judge, criticized the drug court entry process because it speeds up the process by eliminating the preliminary hearing and having the defendant volunteer at an early stage in the trial process the drug treatment program. Judge Bamberger explained this process in more detail:

> At the early stage in the proceedings, when the specialized court begins inter- vention, counsel often do not have very much information about the accusa- tions and the case, have virtually no discovery or police paperwork, and does not know what issues may be present in the case, as, for example, if there is any basis to challenge the admissibility of the evidence against the defendant, or if there is a defense to the charges.

In *Newton v. Rumery* (1987), the U.S. Supreme Court held that plea bargains did not violate the U.S. Constitution even though it does seem coercive in nature. While the issue of coercion in drug court pleas has not been addressed by the U.S. Supreme Court, it would appear that the Court would use the same logic in upholding the validity of the pleas.

Oram and Gleckker (2006) note that in normal court proceedings, judges, when sentencing a defendant, are allowed to consider whether a defendant has taken responsi- bility for his or her actions. They also note that in the drug court setting, a person is not only required to accept responsibility by acknowledging that he or she did something wrong, but the defendant is also asked to accept treatment for his or her problem.

Oram and Gleckker conclude that a judge can be excessively overbearing in con- vincing defendants to volunteer for drug court programs. According to them, a defendant may feel so overcome by a judge's comments that he or she will accept whatever the judge has said in order to please the judge. They contend that sometimes plea bargains are not really bargains, but sentences from judges. However, Oram and Gleckker con- clude that drug court programs offer less risk for defendants and that the defendant may want to choose this alternative rather than taking his or her chances in a traditional trial where the state would have the burden of proving guilt.

Oram and Gleckker (2006, p. 510) state that:

> Drug court practitioners should strive to ensure that defendants are voluntarily entering drug court without coercion. Defendants considering entering drug court have not yet been convicted of a criminal offense and deserve to have a legitimate choice about whether to enter drug court. Although coercion may work in some situations, it should not be used at the expense of a defendant's constitutional right to due process. Pleas must be entered voluntarily without coercion to uphold this right.

When a defendant pleads guilty in a criminal court, the trial judge is required to make certain findings regarding the voluntariness of the plea and if there are sufficient facts to sus- tain the plea. The U.S. Supreme Court in *Boykin v. Alabama* (1969) requires that before a trial judge may accept a guilty plea, the judge must inform the defendant of the significance of the guilty plea. The defendant must be informed that by pleading guilty, he or she waives all right against self-incrimination, the right to a trial by jury, and the right to be confronted by his or her accusers. In addition, the judge must make a finding on the record that the plea is voluntarily entered and that the accused understands the consequences of his or her plea. A similar requirement could help prevent coercive elections to drug court programs.

## Treatment Components

While there are some variations in the treatment components of drug treatment court pro- gram, the basic components include short jail terms, frequent court appearances, frequent testing, abstinence, and counseling. Frequently residential treatment programs are used.

These programs focus on transitioning defendants to a sober lifestyle. Many drug courts require the participants to attend twelve-step meetings. Most of popular twelve-step programs have a religious base. Accordingly, this religious connection makes such programs controversial.

## Common Drug Court Models

The most common models drug court models are listed below; however, a combination of them and others are also employed based upon the individual needs of the jurisdiction (Maryland's Office of Problem-Solving Courts, 2007).

- Diversion plea—the defendant pleads guilty as a requirement of participation in the program; however, the plea is withdrawn and the case is dismissed upon completion of the program.
- Deferred sentencing—a guilty plea is accepted and sentencing is deferred pending program participation. Upon successful completion of the program, an appropriate probationary sentence is imposed or the case is dismissed.
- Post-conviction probation—the defendant is placed on probation with the successful completion of the program as a condition of probation.
- Defendant waives his or her rights to a speedy trial and the trial is held in abeyance. If the defendant completes the drug treatment program, the prosecution moves to dismiss the pending criminal charges.

## Entry Process

Drug court candidates are assessed either before entry into the program or at treatment entry to develop individualized treatment plans to establish clinical appropriateness for the treatment provider. A clinically trained and qualified counselor, social worker, psychologist, or psychiatrist generally performs the assessment. Assessments normally culminate in a placement that is least intensive/restrictive at first and then intensify as clinically indicated. Ongoing assessments, pursuant to accepted clinical practices, are used to monitor progress, to change the treatment plan if necessary, and to identify relapse.

While there are some variances in specific eligibility requirements, generally individuals are considered based on two main components; offense qualifiers/disqualifiers and offender qualifiers/disqualifiers. Maryland's eligibility considerations follow the general pattern and are used to provide specific examples of the disqualifiers. The screening process determines whether individuals are appropriate and eligible for the program based upon the target population criteria (Maryland's Office of Problem-Solving Courts, 2007). It appears that in most programs, a trial judge has discretion to deviate from the stated considerations. Offense disqualifiers include:

- crimes involving violent offenses
- weapon offenses
- offenses involving personal injuries to a victim

Offender disqualifiers include individuals with/on:

- open warrants or pending cases
- probation or parole
- lengthy criminal records
- mental health issues
- prior drug court treatment

In most states there is a treatment court hearing before an individual is assigned to the program. In addition, there are frequent conferences with the treatment court coordinators to monitor the individual's participation and progress, and to alter case management plans as needed. The conferences generally occur every four to six weeks depending on the level of the person's participation, progress, and addiction. Generally, they are more frequent at the initial stages of program participation. If necessary, the treatment court coordinator will summons the individual to appear in open court before the trial judge for an accelerated hearing.

### Right to Equal Protection and Access to Drug Court Programs

Judicial districts within a state are not required to establish drug court programs even though such programs may be available in adjoining judicial districts within the same state (*State v. Little*, 2003). In the Little case, defendant Little was arrested in Gray County, Washington, in one of the few counties in that state, which had not yet adopted a drug court program. Little claimed that having drug courts in some counties and not in others was a violation of the constitutional right of equal protection and access. The State of Washington Appellate Court held that the state statute that provided for discretionary creation of drug courts did not create a discriminatory or suspect classification of drug offenders. The court based its findings on the fact that all offenders within the same county either have or do not have access to drug court programs.

It would appear that individuals within the same judicial district should have equal access to a drug program. While admission to a drug court treatment program is discretionary with the trial judge. A judge may not arbitrarily deny an individual from participation in such programs. For example, a judge may not deny individuals of certain cultures or racial backgrounds from drug court programs based only on those criteria.

## COMMUNITY SUPERVISION

The treatment programs generally involve community supervision designed to help the participants combat their addiction, prevent relapse, as well as to obey the law and comply with program conditions. The community supervision agents maintain close contact with participants through frequent office and home visits. Agents will also interact with the treatment team, family members, employers, and social services agencies to implement the approach to each participant's recovery. They also routinely coordinate, refer, monitor, and help manage daily activities to compliance and promote well-being. They often act as the liaison between local agencies and the treatment court program, striving to incorporate the community into each participant's treatment plan. In many programs, probation officers act as the agents, and, in some, treatment or court coordinators are used as agents.

The ranges of treatment modalities to treat alcohol and substance abuse addicts include:

- *Early Intervention Services*—to treats patients who may be in the early stages of alcohol or drug use. Services may include assessment, treatment planning, case management, group or individual counseling, and family services.
- *Detoxification Services*—monitor the decreasing amount of alcohol and other drugs in the body, manages withdrawal symptoms, and motivates the individual to participate in an appropriate treatment program for alcohol or other drug dependence.
- *Outpatient detoxification services*—include physical examination, medical evaluation, assessment, treatment planning, administering and monitoring medication, monitoring vital signs, discharge or transfer planning, and referral services.
- *Inpatient detoxification services*—include nursing assessment at admission, physical examination, addiction assessment, treatment planning, discharge or transfer planning, monitoring of vital signs, administering of medication, family services, alcohol and drug education, motivational counseling, and referral services.

- *Intensive Outpatient*—provides structured outpatient evaluation and treatment of patients who require programming nine or more hours weekly. Services include assessment, treatment planning, case management services, individual counseling at least once monthly, and leisure and recreational activities.
- *Halfway Houses*—offers a living space, plus treatment services directed toward preventing relapse, applying recovery skills, promoting personal responsibility, and reintegration. Services include case management, individual counseling at least once every month, and leisure and recreational activities.
- *Long Term Residential Care*—provides structured environment in combination with medium intensity treatment and ancillary services to support and promote recovery. Services include assessment, treatment planning, alcohol and drug education, individual counseling, leisure and recreation counseling, referral services, and assistance with vocational issues.
- *Therapeutic Community*—provides a highly structured environment in combination with moderate to high intensity treatment and ancillary services to support and promote recovery, and uses the treatment community as a key therapeutic agent. Services include medical assessment, physical examination, assessment, treatment planning, medication monitoring, therapeutic activities that may include individual and group counseling, alcohol and drug education, career counseling, nutrition education, and family services.
- *Medically Monitored Intensive Inpatient Treatment (Intermediate Care)*—provides a planned regimen of 24-hour, professionally directed evaluation, care and treatment in an inpatient setting. Services include weekly individual counseling, treatment planning, group counseling, alcohol and drug education, nutrition education, weekly family sessions, case management, medical evaluation, physical examination, medication monitoring, sub-acute detoxification, medical services, diagnostic services, and referral services.
- *Medication-Assisted Treatment*—uses pharmacological interventions such as an abuse to provide treatment, support and recovery services to alcohol-addicted patients. Services include medical assessment, physical examination, counseling, drug and alcohol testing, medication administration and monitoring, and referral services. (The treatment modalities listed in this section were taken from Maryland's Office of Problem-Solving Courts, 2007)

Drug treatment programs frequently provide ancillary services in an attempt to provide effective rehabilitation for the participants. The ancillary services commonly include

- AIDS counseling
- Community support programs
- Anger management
- Educational training
- Childcare
- Family counseling
- Cognitive behavior therapy
- Housing assistance
- Legal assistance
- Self-help groups
- Life skills training
- Sexual, emotional, domestic abuse Counseling
- Money management
- Vocational training and placement
- Parenting skills training

## SUBSTANCE ABUSE TESTING

Drug court treatment programs generally conduct frequent and random substance abuse tests of participants. The testing is designed to deter future usage, to identify participants who are both maintaining abstinence or who have relapsed, and to guide treatment and sanction decisions. Research indicates that with greater frequency of tests, drug use declines substantially and the potential for both short- and long-term successful outcomes is increased.

Frequently, the tests are conducted in probation offices, treatment agencies, and court offices. However, these tests can be conducted in any public location that will not conflict with public safety and participant's personal development, such as their home, school, or place of employment.

## GRADUATION

Many treatment programs hold graduation ceremonies for the participants when they successfully complete the program. Often, completion of the treatment court program represents the first significant achievement of their lives. A graduation ceremony is used to provide the opportunity to highlight the success of the participants and of the program. In some programs, the graduation ceremony is incorporated into the court docket. In others, it is held separately. Often relatives, friends, and support groups of the participant are invited to the ceremony. And a guest speaker is used. In many, the graduates are afforded an opportunity to speak. A certificate of graduation or other form of recognition is generally awarded.

## TERMINATION

Due process is a concern not only in the entry of participants in drug court programs, but also in the termination of drug court-mandated treatment programs. Conditions for unsuccessful termination of the treatment program include noncompliance with treatment recommendations, failure to attend scheduled court hearings, noncompliance with supervision guidelines, arrest on a new charge, and demonstrating violent behaviors towards self or others. Probably the most frequent grounds stated for treatment termination are based on the results of the substance abuse tests.

Terminating a drug court-mandated treatment program is similar in effect to revoking parole or probation; in all three contexts an offender has a conditional liberty interest that will be impacted by the decision of the proceeding. Due to the close analogy between probation and parole revocation and drug court program termination, courts addressing the matter of procedural due process protections necessary in the termination of a drug court-mandated treatment program have referred to and adopted the due process requirements applicable in probation and parole revocation proceedings (Orem and Gleckker 2006). The rights include:

- right to a written noted of claimed violations
- disclosure of the evidence used to make that determination
- opportunity to be heard
- statement of reasons for the termination

As noted in *People v. Anderson*, discussed in this chapter, the individual has a right to a due process hearing in open court before he or she is terminated from a treatment program and the case is referred to trial. There appears to be a dispute as what types of evidence should be used by a trial judge in making the termination decision and what are the appropriate reasons for terminating a program. The cases seem to reveal a pattern of most courts to follow similar rules used in the revocation of parole and probation cases. One issue that has not been addressed by most courts is the requirement for the presence of an attorney at the termination hearings.

## DRUG COURT ALUMNI GROUPS

Drug courts in some states solicit participants who have successfully completed the drug court program and establish alumni volunteer groups. Alumni volunteers can assist a drug court as follows:

- Serve as mentors to new participants
- Serve as peer counselors on DUI/DWI court hearing days
- Attend monthly meetings
- Plan social activities
- Facilitate relapse panels for current participants
- Develop and distribute newsletters
- Speak at graduations and host receptions
- Develop resource networks and support for alumni who may have relapsed or have other needs.

## ETHICAL ISSUES

As noted by Oram and Gleckker (2006), drug courts constitute a treatment-oriented judicial process, which is distinct from the traditional adversarial system that exists in the criminal court systems. In the traditional adversarial system, the state and the defendant take antagonistic positions, and the judge is considered as a detached and neutral figure with the responsibility of providing a fair hearing. In contrast, in the drug court systems, the parties including the judge part of a collaborative team along with an array of corrections personnel, treatment providers, and others, all with the common goal of treating defendants.

In criminal courts, under most circumstances, the trial judge cannot discuss the case with the defendant with the defendant's counsel being present. In drug court programs, frequently, the trial judge or his or her assistants discusses the case and the treatment program with participants without the presence of counsel. The direct interaction between the judge and defendant would constitute an ethical violation on the part of the judge.

As noted by Oram and Gleckker (2006), often defense attorneys may have a conflict of interest because they work as a team with the judge, treatment providers, prosecutor, and drug court coordinator. Public defenders often represent many drug court participants, and they may be convinced that drug court is for virtually all drug users. According to one critic, public defenders are inadequate counsels in drug court programs, because their objectives do not coincide with the defendant's objectives. Oram and Gleckker note that defense attorneys in general have had a wide range of responses to drug courts—from open hostility to

**LAW IN ACTION**

**Florida Rule of Criminal Procedure 3.170**

(m) Motion to Withdraw the Plea after Drug Court Transfer. A defendant who pleads guilty or nolo contendere to a charge for the purpose of transferring the case, pursuant to section 910.035, Florida Statutes,[ refers to referral to a drug court] may file a motion to withdraw the plea upon successful completion of the drug court treatment program.

Note: After successful completion of the drug program, the defendant's plea of guilty or nolo contendere is withdrawn and then the judge dismisses the case.

## LAW IN ACTION

### *People v. Anderson*, 358 Ill. App. 3d 1108 (Ill. App. Ct. 4th Dist. 2005)

Defendant, Charles J. Anderson, was charges with one count of burglary and a public defender was appointed to defend him. Despite having an attorney, Anderson filed a pro se motion for placement in a drug court program (pro se motion refers to a motion filed by a person without the assistance of an attorney). The trial court denied his request. Anderson waived his right to a jury trial and pled guilty in exchange for a maximum five year sentence plea bargain. Anderson's counsel requested the judge to allow Anderson to with draw his plea and to reconsider assignment to a drug court program. In April 2002, the court vacated his guilty plea and referred him to a drug court.

On May 17, 2002, Anderson signed a drug-court participation agreement, which agreed that the burglary charge would be held in abeyance for 24 months and if he successfully completed the program the burglary charge would be dismissed. Another paragraph in the agreement provided that if he failed to successfully complete the program, his case would proceed to trial on the burglary charge without delay.

On January 24, 2003, the trial court ordered his case to trial. There was no explanation in the court records as to why the trial court had summarily dismissed him from the program. He was convicted of burglary and sentenced to 14 years' imprisonment.

On appeal, defendant argued that his rights to due process were violated when he was not afforded a hearing prior to being dismissed from the drug-court program. The appellate court held that both the interests of defendant and the State were better protected if the minimum requirements of due process were met, in the form of a hearing, prior to the revocation of, or dismissal from, participation in the program. The Illinois Court of Appeals concluded that even though defendant did not have the right to participate in the program, as it was a matter of legislative and judicial grace, he should have (1) been informed of the nature of the alleged violation, (2) been informed of the nature of the evidence against him, and (3) had the right to appear and be heard before he was dismissed from the program. The case was remanded (returned to the trial court).

## Subsequent proceedings

### *People v. Anderson*, 369 Ill. App. 3d 972, 975 (Ill. App. Ct. 4th Dist. 2007)

After the case was returned to the trial court, the State then filed a motion to terminate defendant from the drug-treatment program. In December 2005, after conducting several evidentiary hearings, the trial court found that defendant had violated the program's conditions by committing a theft in January 2003. The court ordered that defendant be "revoked" from the drug-treatment program. He was re-tried on the burglary charge, convicted, and sentenced to 14 years in prison. At the punishment hearing, the trial court considered evidence that Anderson had been convicted of ten additional burglaries since the first trial and had two convictions for escaping from a penal institution. In addition, it was established that he had been convicted of numerous thefts.

On appeal, the appellate court found that the trial court had jurisdiction to order defendant removed from the drug-treatment program after the due process hearing because no provision of the Act nor any other provision of the law barred the State from resurrecting defendant's dormant burglary charge after the initial 24 months of his participation in that program. The appellate court emphasized the fact that Anderson had never satisfactorily completed the drug program.

grudging acceptance to growing endorsement. Generally, defender agencies like the Legal Aid Society have expressed support for these programs. They also note although public defenders may sometimes be pressured into advocating for and suggesting drug court, even paid defense attorneys agree that drug court is often a choice opportunity for defendants.

Prosecutors also have conflicts of interest. As noted earlier, a prosecutor's duty is not to prosecute but to promote justice. The duty to promote justice includes the duty to protect the public. The prosecutor is an essential person in the drug court team. Often, he or she is encouraged to send clients to drug court and to make plea bargains through the drug court system. The prosecutor should evaluate each defendant and decide whether to arrange a drug court entry. During this process the prosecutor's choice may be influenced by external factors such as pending case loads, members of the drug court treatment program and victim issues.

## JUVENILE DRUG COURTS

> While adults often use drugs in response to stress and increased responsibilities, juveniles may use alcohol and drugs to have fun with their peers, to experiment, or simply to cure boredom or anger. More than half of all students have tried at least one illegal drug by their senior year of high school
>
> —Kozdron, 2009, p. 373.

There is a conflict as to when the first juvenile drug court program was established. Some researchers claim that the first drug court program was established on October 1, 1993 in Monroe County, Florida. Other research data indicate that the first juvenile drug court program did not appear until 1995. At least they agree that the first one was in the State of Florida. By March 2009, there were 442 juvenile drug courts operating in all 50 states, the District of Columbia, Puerto Rico, Guam, and the Northern Mariana Islands (Kozdron 2009).

While our juvenile justice system developed with a distinctly different philosophy from the adult criminal justice system, the juvenile drug courts evolved directly from the adult drug court model. So you do not see the discrepancy in the two drug court systems as you do when you compare the adult criminal court system with the juvenile justice system.

In adapting the adult model to juvenile drug courts, the process has not been smooth, and several significant issues are apparent. For example, generally juveniles prove less receptive to rehabilitation techniques that have had some degree of success in adult drug courts. This problem could be because when adults are referred to a drug court program, they have "hit the bottom" and are addicted to a substance. However, most juveniles referred to juvenile drug courts are alcohol and marijuana users, and most are not considered as addicted to the substance (Kozdron 2009).

With many juvenile program participants, familial and negative peer influences represent a significant impediment to success, whereas often the adult has no family support network and most often few friends. Negative family and peer influences are especially significant to the juveniles because they generally must depend upon their families until they reach the age of majority. If there is substance abuse in the family or if key members of the family are abusive to the juvenile, the chances of a successful completion of a drug program are limited.

Another difficulty faced by the juvenile drug courts is that in many cases the juveniles are not represented by an attorney, and, therefore, the judge takes on the responsibility of protecting the juvenile's rights. Adult criminal courts are fairly uniform within a state. Juvenile courts, even within the same state, often share little similarity.

As noted by Kozdron (2009), while adult drug courts explicitly target offenders who demonstrate evidence of substance abuse or dependence, the population targeted by juvenile drug courts is less precise and the eligibility requirements vary even within the same state. Unlike most adult drug court programs, juveniles need not face drug-related charges to be eligible if there is reason to believe that they have a substance abuse issue. In one Indiana county, the eligibility requirements for juvenile drug court provides that juveniles may participate if they are an adjudicated delinquent. They do not need to have a history of violent convictions or have a history of dealing drug convictions.

Juvenile drug courts rely on sanctions, penalties, and rewards to reinforce their expectations. Sanctions hold juveniles accountable for their behavior while concurrently reinforcing core aspects of the program. Sanctions may range from warnings to community service to electronic monitoring to physical detention. Some juvenile drug courts use financial sanctions, which in addition to punishing misbehaving youths also help alleviate the courts' funding burdens (Rossman et al. 2004).

## PARTICIPANTS IN A DRUG COURT PROGRAM

The following describes typical drug court participants in State of Wyoming. The profile covers those active in a drug court program from January 1, 2005 to June 30, 2005 (Rubio et al. 2007).

| Participants | Adults | Juveniles |
|---|---|---|
| Percentage males | 76% | 53 |
| Average age at time of admission | 29 years old | 15½; years old |
| Average days in program | 439 | 389 |
| Race | Caucasian 90% | Caucasian 62% Native-American 35% |
| Education level | High school or GED 58% | 76% in grades 9–11 |
| Prior record of substance abuse | 65% | 63% |
| Stated as primary drugs of choice | Alcohol 88% Marijuana 65% Methamphetamines 52% | Alcohol 96% Marijuana 94% Methamphetamines 23% |

## DWI COURTS

> DWI courts are increasing in number exponentially across the country. Modeled after the effective approach of drug courts, DWI court evaluations appear to show impressive results on reducing recidivism—but is the research right?
> —Wallace 2008, 1

DWI courts focus on the high-risk drinking driver, generally defined as the repeat offenders or those drivers who had a blood alcohol content (BAC) of 0.15 or greater. According to Wallace (2008), these people are unable to live a productive life without alcohol, and more important, they are a significant threat to others on the road. Wallace notes that repeat DWI offenders are involved in disproportionately more crashes when compared to all drivers on the road. They are overrepresented in fatal crashes, and have a greater risk of involvement in other vehicle accidents. Wallace sees these defendants as individuals who are consumed by the need to drink and, unfortunately, then they drive, often with tragic results. He notes that traditional sentencing efforts do not appear to change their behavior or stop them from driving under the influence.

Organizations that have indicated support for DWI courts include Mothers Against Drunk Driving (MADD), the Governor's Highway Safety Association (GHSA), and the Highway Safety Committee of the International Association of Chiefs of Police (IACP).

According to Wallace, those organizations see DWI courts as a useful tool against impaired driving. He also concludes that DWI courts are becoming a staple in the criminal justice system.

In 2004 there were 176 DWI courts—86 designated DWI and 90 "hybrid" drug/DWI courts. (Hybrid drug/DWI courts started as drug courts, then added a separate track or docket for DWI offenders.) As of December 31, 2007, the number had increased to 396, a 233 percent increase (Wallace 2008).

### Are DWI Courts Effective?

An analysis of a large number of DWI court evaluations by Wallace (2008) found that the vast majority of the studies did not follow proper scientific protocols. He examined 41 published and unpublished evaluations, looking not so much at the results, but at whether the studies were scientifically defensible. Of the 41, he found only one study that

**COURTS IN ACTION**

**Should DWI Courts be Allowed to Use Ankle Bracelets to Ensure That Offenders do not Drink?**

According to Ames Alexander the State of North Carolina's guidelines prevent the state's drug and DWI treatment courts from using technology that has helped thousands of alcoholics stay sober. The guidelines approved in 2007 prohibit those courts from using the ankle bracelets commonly employed to ensure that offenders don't drink. Alexander contends that the decision has puzzled and frustrated some officials, who question whether opposition to the technology was sparked in part by turf battles and personality conflicts. According to Alexander, David Wallace, director of the National Center for DWI Courts, was not aware of any other state that has imposed such restrictions.

Wallace, whose organization helps train officials in setting up DWI courts, is reported to have stated that this guideline takes away one more tool that could be used to monitor people so they're not out there risking the community's safety.

North Carolina has more than 40 drug and DWI treatment courts which are designed to help rehabilitate repeat offenders who suffer from addictions. Participants are typically required to follow their jail sentences with months of intensive alcohol or drug treatment.

Judges in other N.C. courts can still order use of the bracelets, which test an offender's sweat every half-hour for signs of alcohol use. When those on probation are caught drinking, judges can order more treatment or punishment. Offenders pay a private company $12 a day for the device. A number of groups—including the National Association of Drug Court Professionals and the N.C. Conference of District Attorneys—have endorsed the technology. And a preliminary study by the National Center for State Courts found that repeat DWI offenders who wore the bracelets for 90 days or more were less likely to drive drunk again.

About 20 percent of the more than 1,000 adult offenders who participate in an N.C. drug treatment court each year report alcohol as their "drug of choice." The device can't immediately stop anyone from driving drunk, and court officials aren't alerted as soon as an offender begins drinking because the test data are typically transmitted to a central computer just once each day.

In 2005 and 2006, before the technology was banned from treatment courts, Mecklenburg County used grant money to buy 10 of its own bracelets. The county courts regularly required participants in the DWI court to use them. After the 2007 ruling, the DWI court was forced to revert to its old approach: testing offenders two to four times a week with a breathalyzer. [Ames Alexander (2010, August 13) "DWI court cannot key tools" Charlotte Observer, p. A–1.]

could be rated "good" and four others rated "marginally acceptable" in their methodological rigor. Wallace's noted that:

> The conclusion reached by the meta-analysis was that there are promising indications that DWI courts make a difference—they reduce recidivism, and they save money. However, not enough rigorous evaluations have been conducted to validate the preliminary conclusions. To use a legal analogy, the case has not been proven beyond a reasonable doubt
>
> —David Wallace 2008, 5

## Questions in Review

1. Should more due process rights be afforded individual in drug court programs?
2. What are the goals of an adult drug court program?
3. What are the issues faced by a juvenile drug court program?
4. What should be the requirements before a person facing a driving under the influence charge be offered a DWI court program?
5. In your home jurisdiction, are there drug court programs? DWI court programs? Juvenile drug courts?

## Practicum

Review the following Whitehead case and answer the below questions:

1. Is a 25 year prison term too harsh for driving under the influence?
2. Will the prison deter Whitehead from driving under the influence after he is released from prison?
3. What were the issues involved in his case?
4. Why can a lay witness (untrained ordinary witness) provide an opinion that a person was driving under the influence?
5. If an individual has a presumption of innocence, why did the magistrate indicate that there was a presumption that the lower courts which found him guilty were presumed to be correct?

### Charles David Whitehead v. Pat Book

641 F. Supp. 2d 549 (2008)

**Report and Recommendations by U.S. Magistrate Christine Noland**

This matter is before the Court on the Petition for Writ of Habeas Corpus filed by petitioner, Charles David Whitehead ("Whitehead"). The State has filed an answer and a memorandum in opposition to that petition.

**Procedural Background**

Whitehead was charged by an amended bill of information with one count of fourth offense operating a vehicle while intoxicated. He pled not guilty to the charge and proceeded to a jury trial on April 13, 2005.

Following the trial, Whitehead was found guilty as charged. He was subsequently adjudicated a third felony offender and sentenced to twenty-four (24) years imprisonment at hard labor without the benefit of probation, parole, or suspension of sentence and a $ 5,000.00 fine. The trial court ordered the sentence to run consecutively to any other sentence petitioner was serving. In addition to the sentence and fine imposed upon Whitehead, the state trial judge also ordered that Whitehead's vehicle be sold and that the proceeds be delivered to the Office of the District Attorney to be disposed of in accordance with Louisiana law.

On May 23, 2006, Whitehead appealed his conviction and sentence to the Louisiana First Circuit Court of Appeals. In that appeal, he raised several issues including whether defining the crime of Driving While Intoxicated as "operating a vehicle while under the influence of alcoholic beverages," set forth in Louisiana Revised Statutes section 14:98, is unconstitutionally vague; whether the testimony of DPS Officer Miller and Sergeant Rhodes regarding their opinion of whether Whitehead was "intoxicated" was improperly admitted as lay opinion; and whether the testimony of Officer Miller regarding the results of the field sobriety tests should have been disallowed as a result of the officer being unqualified and inexperienced to administer the tests and properly analyze the results. The Louisiana Supreme Court denied his writ application on June 22, 2007.

Whitehead then filed his present habeas petition in the United States District Court for the Eastern District of Louisiana on November 26, 2007. His case was subsequently transferred to this Court on January 24, 2008. His claims appear to be timely and exhausted, and the merits of such claims will therefore be addressed herein.

### Factual Background

On March 5, 2004, at approximately 4:39 A.M., DPS Police Officer Stephen Miller ("Officer Miller") came upon Whitehead's pickup truck blocking the intersection of Greenwell Springs and Joor Roads in Baton Rouge, Louisiana. The engine of the pickup truck was running, but Whitehead appeared to be asleep at the wheel with a beer bottle in his lap. Officer Miller attempted to awaken Whitehead by tapping on the window. He then opened the door of the pickup truck, which awoke Miller, and the truck began moving. Officer Miller put the vehicle into park and asked that petitioner exit the vehicle. [Officer Miller was in route to his employment as a security guard for the State Capital grounds.]

When Whitehead got out of the truck, he was very unsteady on his feet, and the beer that had been in his lap spilled onto the floorboard of the truck. Officer Miller escorted him to the back seat of the police unit and moved Whitehead's truck into a nearby parking lot. Based upon the alcohol that Officer Miller smelled on Whitehead's person, the fact that Whitehead had been asleep at the wheel of his vehicle with a beer in his lap, and the fact that he was so uneasy on his feet, Officer Miller decided to investigate further as to a possible DWI stop and arrest. Officer Miller advised Whitehead of his Miranda rights, which Whitehead indicated he understood. DPS Sergeant Mike Rhodes ("Sergeant Rhodes") then arrived at the scene to assist Officer Miller. Officer Miller administered field sobriety tests to Whitehead, which he failed, and Whitehead was then arrested for operating a vehicle while intoxicated ("DWI"). Officer Miller advised Whitehead of his rights relating to the chemical breath test for intoxication, and Whitehead refused to take the test.

According to Officer Miller's testimony at trial, prior to the administration of the field sobriety tests, he asked Whitehead if he had experienced any head injuries in the past and whether he wore glasses or contacts, and Whitehead responded negatively. Whitehead also indicated that he was comfortable taking the field sobriety tests in his cowboy boots.

At his trial, Whitehead testified that he had five prior DWI convictions; however, he claimed that, at the time of the offense in question, he was only drinking a sixteen-ounce Dr. Pepper. He also denied that his truck was in the intersection when Officer Miller discovered him sleeping in his truck. He testified that he dozed off while waiting for the traffic light to change. He also denied needing assistance to exit his

truck and claimed that his performance on the field sobriety tests was impacted by the fact that he was tired and because he was wearing cowboy boots when the tests were administered to him. Whitehead also testified that his performance on the tests was impacted by prior head injuries, including a fractured skull he sustained in a car accident in 1987 and a head injury that occurred during a prison fight in 1992. He indicated that the reason he did not take the chemical breath test was because he had been told by "everybody and their brother" to refuse the test and because he was upset and aggravated with Officer Miller.

According to Officer Miller's testimony, Whitehead told him at the scene of his arrest that he had consumed a few beers; however, when they reached Officer Miller's office, Whitehead changed his story and said he had only been drinking Dr. Pepper.

### Law & Analysis

Each of the claims contained in Whitehead's habeas petition was previously submitted to and ruled upon by the state courts on direct appeal. In order for this Court to grant an application for a writ of habeas corpus as to any claim which has been previously adjudicated on the merits in state court, the Court must find that adjudication of such claim: (1) resulted in a decision that is contrary to, or involves an unreasonable application of, clearly established federal law, as determined by the Supreme Court of the United States; or (2) resulted in a decision that is based on an unreasonable determination of the facts in light of the evidence presented in the state court proceeding.

In addition, determinations of factual issues made by state courts shall be presumed correct, unless particular statutory exceptions are implicated, and the applicant has the burden of rebutting that "presumption of correctness" by clear and convincing evidence. Thus, the presumption of correctness is properly invoked if the Court finds that there were no defects in the state court's procedures.

In this claim, Whitehead contends that Louisiana Revised Statutes section 40:1379D, which grants safety enforcement officers in the DPS, like Officer Miller, the same authority and protection afforded to the police employees in the Division of the State Police, is an unconstitutional extension of the state's inherent police powers and violates the Louisiana Constitution through unwarranted interference and intrusion by the state government. As a result, he contends that Officer Miller lacked constitutional authority to stop and arrest him for DWI, and any evidence seized as a result of such arrest should have been suppressed. In addressing this claim on appeal, the First Circuit Court of

Appeals did not reach the constitutional issue since courts are to refrain from reaching the constitutionality of legislation unless the issue is essential to resolution of the case or controversy. The First Circuit found that it could resolve the issue presented without addressing the constitutional question because, separate and apart from Officer Miller's challenged authority as a police officer, Officer Miller was authorized, as a private person, to arrest Whitehead for aggravated obstruction of a highway of commerce.

Specifically, the First Circuit explained that a private person may make an arrest when the person arrested has committed a felony, whether in or out of the presence of the person making the arrest. The court of appeal noted that aggravated obstruction of a highway of commerce is a felony. Considering Officer Miller's testimony at trial that he came upon Whitehead's truck blocking the intersection of Greenwell Springs Road and Joor Road, with the engine running and Whitehead asleep at the wheel therein, the First Circuit found that the requisite elements were met when Officer Miller arrested Whitehead. In other words, the First Circuit found that Officer Miller had the authority to make a citizen's arrest of Whitehead, regardless of whether he had the constitutional authority as a safety enforcement officer with the DPS, and therefore dismissed Whitehead's constitutional claim.

Louisiana Revised Statute section (La. R.S) 14:96 defines "aggravated obstruction of a highway of commerce" as the "intentional or criminally negligent placing of anything, or performance of any act, on any road or highway, wherein it is foreseeable that human life might be endangered."

Whitehead has failed to come forward with any convincing arguments or evidence demonstrating that the First Circuit incorrectly applied the law or unreasonably determined the facts in light of the evidence. Both the Fifth Circuit Court of Appeals and the United States Supreme Court have recognized that federal courts also have a duty to avoid constitutional issues that need not be resolved in order to determine the rights of the parties to the case under consideration. Thus, the Louisiana First Circuit's decision not to address the constitutional question presented by Whitehead is not contrary to, or an unreasonable application of, clearly established federal law. Because Officer Miller had authority as a citizen to arrest Whitehead for aggravated obstruction of a highway of commerce, this Court also need not reach the issue of the constitutionality of the statute in order to determine the validity of Whitehead's arrest and the related seizure of evidence. Finally, it is a settled rule of constitutional law that felony warrantless arrests made in public places, such as citizen's arrests, do not violate the Fourth Amendment of the U.S. Constitution. Accordingly, Whitehead's first claim should be dismissed.

Furthermore, the fact that Officer Miller ultimately used the power of his office to gather evidence in support of Whitehead's DWI arrest (through field sobriety tests), which power is unavailable to private citizens, does not invalidate the citizen's arrest for DWI. Courts have held that a citizen's arrest for DWI is valid where an officer develops the necessary reasonable belief that an offense has been committed (i.e., probable cause for an arrest) through means available to an ordinary citizen, such as observing erratic driving behavior, etc., and then subsequently uses his/her police power, including the use of their authority to request a defendant to step out of the car and consent to a search, the administration of field sobriety tests, and the subsequent physical arrest of the defendant. Thus, because, in the present case, Officer Miller had already developed the necessary reasonable belief that an offense had been committed to warrant a traffic stop through means available to an ordinary citizen (in that he had observed Whitehead's truck blocking the intersection of Greenwell Springs Road and Joor Road and had observed Whitehead sleeping at the wheel with a beer bottle in his lap), Officer Miller's citizen's arrest of Whitehead was valid (and the admission of evidence obtained pursuant to that arrest was proper) where he subsequently administered field sobriety tests to Whitehead and arrested him. Whitehead's arguments to the contrary lack merit.

Whitehead's argument, that Officer Miller's arrest of him without a warrant and the use of evidence obtained as a result of the stop and arrest violate the Fourth Amendment, lacks merit.

Whitehead contends that defining the crime of "driving while intoxicated" as "operating a vehicle under the influence of alcoholic beverages" is unconstitutionally. In considering this claim, the First Circuit explained that statutes are presumed to be valid and must be upheld as constitutional whenever possible. It further explained that a statute is considered unconstitutionally vague if a person of ordinary intelligence is not capable of discerning the statute's meaning and conforming his conduct thereto. A penal statute must give adequate notice that certain contemplated conduct is proscribed and punishable by law and must provide adequate standards for those charged with determining the guilt or innocence of the accused. The First Circuit referred to La. R.S. 14:3, relating to interpretation of criminal statutes, which provides that criminal provisions are to "be given a genuine construction, according to the fair import of their words, taken in their usual sense, in connection with the context, and with reference to the purpose of the provision." Id. In light of such interpretive standards, the First Circuit found that the phrase "under the influence" in La. R.S. 14:98 does not render the statute unconstitutionally vague because the terms "intoxicated" and "under the influence of alcoholic beverages" have a "certain and well-understood meaning, i.e., a person is intoxicated within the provisions of the statute when he does not have the normal use of his physical and mental faculties by reason of the use of alcoholic beverages (or narcotics), thus rendering such person incapable of operating an automobile in a manner in which an ordinary prudent and cautious man in full possession of his faculties, using reasonable care, would operate a motor vehicle under like conditions."

La. R.S. 14:98 provides, in pertinent part, that:

A. (1) The crime of operating a vehicle while intoxicated is the operating of any motor vehicle, aircraft, watercraft, vessel, or other means of conveyance when:
   (a) The operator is under the influence of alcoholic beverages.

The Louisiana Supreme Court explained that statutes which make it a criminal offense to operate or drive a motor vehicle "while intoxicated," "while in an intoxicated condition," or "under the influence of intoxicating liquor" have been adopted in practically all jurisdictions and have been generally recognized as a valid exercise of the state's police power to regulate the use and operation of motor vehicles and to safeguard the people from injury or death caused by drivers who operate their vehicles while under the influence of intoxicating liquor or narcotic drugs. The Supreme Court further noted that, in all jurisdictions where the constitutionality of such statutes has been challenged on grounds of vagueness, the courts have upheld the statutes, reasoning that the terms "while under the influence of intoxicating liquor" or "while in an intoxicated condition" are commonly used terms with a well-recognized meaning.

Like the Louisiana Supreme Court and the Louisiana First Circuit, the Fifth Circuit Court of Appeals has held that a criminal statute is not unconstitutionally vague if it defines the criminal offense with sufficient definiteness that ordinary people can understand what conduct is prohibited and in a manner that does not encourage arbitrary and discriminatory enforcement. Furthermore, when a vagueness challenge to a statute does not involve First Amendment freedoms, the court is to examine the statute only in light of the facts of the case at hand. The Louisiana First

Circuit's decision that La. R.S. 14:98 is constitutional comports with the standards under federal law for determining whether a statute is unconstitutionally vague, in that the First Circuit determined whether an ordinary person using the common meaning of the terms contained therein would understand that his/her actions were unlawful. Moreover, when that statute is considered in light of the specific facts of Whitehead's case, it is clear that La. R.S. 14:98 put him on notice of the conduct that was unlawful. Having been previously convicted under that statute five times, he certainly understood what conduct was proscribed by the statute and the punishment he could receive. Finally, Whitehead has failed to come forward with clear and convincing evidence rebutting the presumably correct findings of the state courts on this issue. Accordingly, his second claim should also be dismissed.

Although Whitehead had been previously convicted for DWI five times, he could only be charged with fourth offense DWI because that is the highest grade for that offense. As long as the State proved beyond a reasonable doubt that Whitehead had three prior DWI convictions within a ten (10) year period while he was out of prison, he could be convicted of fourth offense DWI.

Did the trial court err in admitting the testimony of Officer Miller and Sergeant Rhodes as to their opinions of whether Whitehead was under the influence? In this assignment of error, Whitehead contends that the testimony of Officer Miller and Sergeant Rhodes concerning their impressions of whether he was under the influence of alcohol at the time of the arrest should not have been admitted and that the admission of such testimony was so prejudicial that it is unlikely he received a fair trial. Specifically, the testimony of Officer Miller and Sergeant Rhodes which is in question is as follows:

Officer Miller: [Whitehead] was impaired. There's no way he could have safely operated a vehicle. I mean, he was - simply by him being passed out in the intersection in the vehicle, that speaks for itself. He should not have been behind a wheel.

Officer Miller: The basis I used for making my decision was, of course, the smell of alcoholic beverage, the beer in his lap, the fact that he was asleep and the way he performed on all the field sobriety tests. Everything was consistent with the fact that he had been consuming alcoholic beverages.

Sergeant Rhodes: In my opinion, based on what I observed from [Whitehead's] facial expression, his eyes, and the smell of alcohol from his breath as he was talking to me, I felt he was impaired.

Sergeant Rhodes: I felt [Whitehead] had been drinking, sir, at the time that he talked to me, based on my experience and my years in law enforcement and dealing with people who have been intoxicated.

State: Did you believe he was intoxicated? Sergeant Rhodes: Yes, Sir, I did.

In considering this claim, the First Circuit explained that a fact witnesses, such as Officer Miller and Sergeant Rhodes, may provide testimony in the form of opinions or inferences if such opinions and inferences are: (1) rationally based on the perception of the witness; and (2) helpful to a clear understanding of the witness's testimony or the determination of a fact in issue. The court of appeal also cited to several Louisiana cases, where it has been held that intoxication, with its attendant behavioral manifestations, is an observable condition about which a witness may testify. The First Circuit concluded that the testimony of Officer Miller and Sergeant Rhodes was proper because they were testifying as to their conclusions and opinions based upon their observations of Whitehead, and their comments were rational in light of the circumstances to which they testified.

The Louisiana Supreme Court has also specifically held that a lay opinion as to whether a person is under influence is admissible. Federal Rule of Evidence 701 similarly provides that lay opinion testimony may be elicited if it is based upon the witness's first-hand knowledge or observations. Furthermore, in prosecutions relating to charges of driving while intoxicated, opinion evidence is often admitted on the issue of the intoxication or sobriety of the defendant. The state trial court's decision to admit the opinion testimony of Officer Miller and Sergeant Rhodes (and the state appellate court's affirmation of that decision) was based upon the fact that those witnesses were merely testifying to their personal opinion based upon their rational, first-hand perceptions of Whitehead's actions. Both witnesses thoroughly explained the basis for their opinions. The Court does not find that the state courts' decisions were contrary to, or an unreasonable application of federal law; moreover, Whitehead has again failed to present clear and convincing evidence rebutting the presumed correctness of the state courts' decisions that Officer Miller's and Sergeant Rhodes' opinions were rational in light of the circumstances to which they testified. Thus, this claim should also be dismissed.

Whitehead contends that Sergeant Rhodes should not have been permitted to testify concerning his opinion of whether or not Whitehead was intoxicated because Sergeant Rhodes was not trained in making DWI arrests and had no training in the area of determining impairment for purposes of such an arrest. However, Sergeant Rhodes was not expressing an opinion as to whether Whitehead should be arrested for a DWI (in fact, the trial judge sustained objections to the State's questioning of Sergeant Rhodes as to his opinion of whether Whitehead was a danger to operate a motor vehicle); he was merely testifying, as a lay person based upon his observations, as to whether or not Whitehead appeared to be intoxicated/impaired. No formal training is required for a lay witness to express such an opinion.

Did the trial court err in allowing Officer Miller to testify regarding the field sobriety tests he administered and the results of those tests? In this claim, Whitehead contends that Officer Miller should not have been permitted to testify as to the results of the field sobriety tests he conducted because he was unqualified and inexperienced to administer those tests and properly analyze the results. Under Louisiana law, in order to lay a proper foundation for the admission of evidence of intoxication based upon a field sobriety test, there must be a showing that the officer administering the test was trained and certified in administering the procedure and that the description of the manner in which the test was administered demonstrates that it was properly conducted.

In considering this claim on appeal, the First Circuit discussed Officer Miller's trial testimony concerning his training in the administration of field sobriety tests. Specifically, Officer Miller testified that he received training concerning the horizontal gaze nystagmus (HGN) test, the walk-and-turn test, and the one-leg stand test during a forty-hour course at the Louisiana State Police Academy. He explained that such course concentrated on detecting impaired behavior and the administration of field sobriety tests in the DWI context. When he completed that course, he received a certificate indicating that he had passed standardized field sobriety and Intoxilyzer 5000 training. Officer Miller also testified that, during his training, he performed the three field sobriety tests upon numerous volunteers successfully. Subsequent to his course with the Louisiana State Police Academy, Officer Miller received post-certification training at Louisiana State University

Based upon the above testimony elicited by the State, the First Circuit concluded that the State laid a proper foundation for Officer Miller's testimony concerning the administration and results of Whitehead's field sobriety tests.

Federal courts have also held that an officer trained and qualified to perform standard field sobriety tests may testify with respect to his or her observations of a defendant's performance of those tests if such tests were properly administered, and such observations are admissible as circumstantial evidence that a defendant was driving while intoxicated (DWI) or driving under the influence of alcohol (DUI). The Court finds that the state courts correctly ruled that a proper foundation had been laid for Officer Miller's testimony concerning Whitehead's performance on the field sobriety tests. It was not only established that Officer Miller was adequately trained and certified to perform such tests but also that he administered such tests in accordance with his training. Accordingly, his observations and the test results were admissible as circumstantial evidence that Whitehead had been driving under the influence of alcohol, and this claim should also be dismissed.

### Recommendation

For the above reasons, it is recommended that the Petition for Writ of Habeas Corpus filed by petitioner, Charles David Whitehead, be DISMISSED WITH PREJUDICE.

Signed in chambers in Baton Rouge, Louisiana, September 23, 2008.

/s/ Christine Noland

# References

## COURT CASES

*Boykin v. Alabama*, 395 U.S. 238 (1969).
*Newton v. Rumery*, 480 U.S. 386 (1987)
*Robinson v. California*, 370 U.S. 660, 664-65 (1962).
*State v. Little*, 66 P. 3d. 1099 (Wash. Ct. App., 2003).

## REFERENCES

American University, "BJA Drug Court Clearinghouse Project: Summary of Juvenile and Family Drug Court Activity by State and County" (2006), www1.spa.american.edu/justice/documents/2044.pdf (accessed on July 8, 2009).

Bales, William D. et al. "Substance Abuse Treatment in Prison and Community Reentry: Breaking the Cycle of Drugs, Crime, Incarceration, and Recidivism?" *Georgetown Journal on Poverty Law & Policy* 13 (2006): 383–401.

Bamberger, Phylis Skloot. "Specialized Courts: Not a Cure-All." *Fordham Urban Law Journal* 30 (2003): 1091–1095.

Cissner, A., and M. Rempel. "The State of Drug Court Research: Moving Beyond 'Do They work?'" New York: Center for Court Innovation. 2005.

Chappel, John, Address before the National Judicial College, Reno, NV, Sept. 25, 2007. Unpublished

Cooper, Caroline. "Drug Courts" in Future Trends in State Courts." Williamsburg, VA: National Center for State Courts, 2007.

Drug Program Office, Office of Justice Programs, "Looking at a Decade of Drug Courts," Washington, D.C.: U.S. Department of Justice (1999), www.nsconline.org/wc/courtopics (accessed on July 8, 2008).

Hora, Peggy. "Drug Treatment Courts in the Twenty-first Century: The Evolution of the Revolution in Problem-solving Courts." *Georgia Law Review* 42 (Spring 2008): 417–512.

Kozdron, Nicole. "Midwestern Juvenile Drug Courts: Analysis & Recommendations." *Indiana Law Journal* 84 (Winter 2009): 393–363.

Maryland's Office of Problem-Solving Courts. "Maryland Drug Courts—DUI/DWI Treatment Court Programs." Annapolis, MD: State of Maryland, 2007.

McColl, William D. "Theory and Practice in the Baltimore City Drug Treatment Court." in James L. Nolan Jr. ed. *Drug Courts in Theory and in Practice.* 3–8. Hawthorne, NY: Aldyne de Gruyter, (2002).

National Association of Drug Court Professionals Drug Court Standards Committee.. Defining Drug Courts: The Key Components [NCJ 205621]. Washington, DC Department of Justice, 1997.

National Center for State Courts. "Final Report: Florida Statewide Technical Assistance Project: 'Development of A Plan For The Statewide Evaluation Of Florida's Drug Courts.'" www.ncsconline.org/wc/courtopics (accessed on July 8, 2009).

National Center for State Courts. "Drug Courts-FAQs" (2009). www.ncsconline.org/wc/courtopics (accessed on July 8, 2009).

Oram, Trent and Kara Gleckker. "An Analysis of the Constitutional Issues Implicated in Drug Courts." *Idaho Law Review* 42 (2006): 471–550.

Rossman, Shelli Balter, Jeffrey A. Butts, John Roman, Christine DeStefano, and Ruth White. "What Juvenile Drug Courts Do and How They Do It." In *Juvenile Drug Courts And Teen Substance Abuse*, eds. Jeffery A. Butts and John Roman. 90–109. Washington, D.C.: Urban Institute, 2004.

Rubio, D., F. Cheesman, S. Maggard, M. Durkin, and N. Kauder. *Wyoming Drug Court Performance Measures Project: Final Report*. Denver, CO: National Center for State Courts, 2007.

Wallace, David. "Do DWI Courts Work." In *Future Trends in State Courts*. Williamsburg, VA: National Center for State Courts, 2008.

# 11

# Trends and Directions in the Courts

**What you need to know about Trends and Directions in the Courts**

After you have completed this chapter, you should know:

- The courts are instruments of social change.
- In recent years, the Supreme Court has shown an increased tendency to decide issues involving state constitutional matters.
- While politics have always played a role in the operation of courts, it appears that the courts are receiving more political pressure than in the past.
- Language barriers are increasing with the diverse population making it more difficult to deliver equal justice.
- Security is an increasing issue for local courtrooms.
- More jurisdictions are establishing special courts to hand certain classes of defendants.
- An increasing area of concern in the court systems is the financing of court systems and the need to coordinate between the various branches of the governments.

**Chapter Outline**

- Introduction
- Courts as Instruments of Social Change
- Federal Courts Involvement in State Constitutional Matters
- Political Pressure
- Language Barriers
- Security in the Courtroom
- Press Coverage
- Special Courts
- Financing Court Systems
- Future Trends in Criminal Courts

## INTRODUCTION

In this chapter, the trends and predicted directions that our criminal courts will take are examined. It is always dangerous to predict the directions that any public agency or system will change. Taking a conservative approach, it appears that the court systems in the United States will:

- Either continue or increase as instruments of social change
- Be subject to more public scrutiny and media coverage
- Face language problems associated with the increasing diversity of the population
- See political pressures on local judges increase
- Be impacted by technological changes
- See Federal courts continue their trends toward more involvement in local criminal justice issues.

## COURTS AS INSTRUMENTS OF SOCIAL CHANGE

As established by the *Brown v. Board of Education* decision, the courts are instruments of social change.

## FEDERAL COURTS INVOLVEMENT IN STATE CONSTITUTIONAL MATTERS

Starting with the "Earl Warren" Court of the 1960s, the courts have become more involved with regulating state prosecutions. The general rule is that state constitutions may offer a defendant more or broader protections than those afforded by the U.S. Constitution, but a state constitution may not restrict a federal constitutional right. In other words, the state

### LAW IN ACTION

### *Brown v. Board of Education*, 347 U.S. 483 (U.S. 1954)

In the *Brown v. Board of Education* Case, the U.S. Supreme Court reviewed four state cases in which African-American minors sought admission to the public schools of their community on a non-segregated basis. In each instance, the children had been denied admission to schools attended by other children under laws requiring or permitting segregation according to race. This segregation was alleged to deprive the minors of the equal protection of the laws under the Fourteenth Amendment. The minors contended that the public schools were not equal and could not be made equal; thereby denying them equal protection of the law. The common legal question among the cases was whether segregation of children in public schools solely on the basis of race, even though the physical facilities and other tangible factors were equal, deprived the children of the minority group of equal educational opportunities. The Supreme Court held that separate educational facilities were inherently unequal.

The Supreme Court noted that in determining whether segregation in public schools deprives certain students of the equal protection of laws guaranteed by the Fourteenth Amendment, the court must consider public education in the light of its full development and its present place in American life throughout the nation; "the clock cannot be turned back to the time when the Amendment was adopted in1868 nor to the time when the Supreme Court announced the "separate but equal" doctrine in 1896, under which equality of treatment is accorded by providing substantially equal, though separate, facilities." (p. 487) constitution may offer more protection but not less than the individual rights protected by the federal constitution.

In *Mich. v. Long*, 463 U.S. 1032 (U.S. 1983), the police officers found marijuana in the passenger compartment and in the trunk of the vehicle that defendant was driving. The officers searched his vehicle because they believed that the vehicle contained weapons potentially dangerous to the officers. The Supreme Court of Michigan, which suppressed the evidence that was obtained from a search of the passenger compartment of respondent's vehicle on the ground that the sole justification of the search, the protection of the police officers and others nearby, did not warrant the search in this case. The Michigan court based their decision on both the state and the federal constitutions.

The U.S. Supreme Court reversed and held that the search was permissible for the protection of the officers. The minority in that decision accused the U.S. Supreme Court of getting involved in state issues and regulating state prosecutions. For example, Justice Stevens in a very vocal dissent stated:

> Until recently we had virtually no interest in cases of this type. Thirty years ago, this Court reviewed only one. *Nevada v. Stacher*, 346 U.S. 906 (1953). Indeed, that appears to have been the only case during the entire 1953 Term in which a State even sought review of a decision by its own judiciary. Fifteen years ago, we did not review any such cases, although the total number of requests had mounted to three. Sometime during the past decade, perhaps about the time of the 5-to-4 decision in Zacchini v. Scripps-Howard Broadcasting Co., 433 U.S. 562 (1977), our priorities shifted. The result is a docket swollen with requests by States to reverse judgments that their courts have rendered in favor of their citizens. I am confident that a future Court will recognize the error of this allocation of resources. When that day comes, I think it likely that the Court will also reconsider the propriety of today's expansion of our jurisdiction (pp. 1070–1071).

As noted by Justice Stevens, it is apparent that the Supreme Court will continue to be more involved in state issues than in the past.

## POLITICAL PRESSURE

Politics has always played a role in the operation of courts. This can be directly as the result of judges to need to run for reelection or indirectly in the form of political candidates using the courts and court reform as a political platform.

The trend in recent years is to place more and more political pressure on the judges when they make decisions in cases that have drawn media attention. It also appears that this is an issue that the courts or the legislatures will need to address. The following case of *United States v. Bayless* indicates the problems that the courts will continue to face regarding political pressures.

In the case of *United States v. Bayless*, 201 F.3d 116 (2d Cir. N.Y. 2000), on April 21, 1995, Carol Bayless was arrested for cocaine and heroin possession. The defense and prosecution agreed that the arresting police officers were patrolling the Washington Heights area of Manhattan in an unmarked police car when they observed Bayless, in a car with Michigan license plates, double-parked on 176th Street, near St. Nicholas Avenue. While Bayless was stopped, the officers saw four men load two heavy duffel bags into the trunk of her car. Almost immediately, the men stepped away from the car, and Bayless drove off alone. The officers followed Bayless for about two blocks, during which time she did not drive erratically or commit any traffic violations. They nevertheless pulled her over. After discovering that the car was a rental car and that Bayless was not an authorized driver, the officers asked her about the bags that had been placed in her trunk. When Bayless denied knowledge of the bags, they asked her for the keys, opened the trunk, and discovered that the bags contained a large quantity of cocaine, along with some heroin. (The exact amount of each was later determined to be thirty-four kilograms of cocaine and two kilograms of heroin.)

At a pretrial hearing, Bayless's counsel moved to suppress the drugs seized from her car and her post-arrest statements on the ground that the police did not have reasonable suspicion to stop her car. In early January, 1996, Judge Baer held a suppression hearing, at which the government introduced the testimony of one of the arresting officers, Officer Carroll, and the court viewed the videotaped statement Bayless gave after her arrest. Judge Baer ruled that the evidence was illegally seized and granted defendant's motion to suppress the evidence.

Judge Baer's ruling immediately drew heavy criticism in the press and from local political figures, including New York's Mayor and Police Commissioner as well as Governor George Pataki. An editorial in the *New York Times* called Judge Baer's decision "judicial malpractice," and accused him of "undermining respect for the legal system, encouraging citizens to flee the police and deterring honest cops in drug-infested neighborhoods from doing their job."

In February, the government filed a motion for reconsideration of the order granting the suppression motion. The decision, however, continued to attract attention and quickly became the focus of a nationwide controversy and a flashpoint for the 1996 presidential campaign, as Democrats and Republicans competed to enhance their reputations as proponents of law and order by denouncing Judge Baer. In early March, more than two hundred members of Congress, led by Republican Representatives Bill McCollum, Fred Upton, and Michael Forbes, sent a letter to President Clinton calling Judge Baer's ruling "a shocking and egregious example of judicial activism." The letter claimed Judge Baer had "sided with drug traffickers and against hard-working police officers and the frightened residents of violence-ridden communities," and that he had "demonstrated a level of ideological blindness that rendered him unfit for the proper discharge of his judicial duties." The writers asked President Clinton to join them in calling for Judge Baer's resignation. In March, the judge after hearing additional evidence reversed his pre-trial decision and ruled that the drugs were admissible.

Bayless was convicted, and in her appeal she argued that the district judge who presided over her pretrial suppression hearing was obliged to recuse himself [remove himself from the case]. She contended that the only reason that the judge reversed his earlier decision excluding the evidence was because of the political pressure that he had endured. The appellate court affirmed the conviction.

## LANGUAGE BARRIERS TO JUSTICE

A Report by the California Commission on Access to Justice (2010):

California is home to one of the most ethnically and racially diverse populations in the world. Of the state's 34 million people, about 26 percent (roughly 8.8 million people) are foreign born. Californians speak more than 220 languages, and 40 percent of the state's population speaks a language other than English in the home. This extraordinary diversity is among the state's greatest assets—a cross-pollination of ideas, traditions, backgrounds and cultures that has helped make California an international leader in business, the arts, entertainment, engineering, medicine, and a host of other fields.

While other states may not be as diverse in population as the State of California, there are continuing pressures on the courts to ensure that citizens are provided with assistance in understanding the language being spoken in the courtroom. As noted by one California trial judge, during each court day there are interpreters for 78 different languages in the Los Angeles county court house and every day there are defendants with languages that are not covered and for whom no interpreters are available who can provide language assistance to certain defendants.

## SECURITY IN THE COURTROOM

One big difference between the courts of the 1960s and 1970s and present day courts in the United States is the increasing need to protect the courts and participants in the everyday operation of the courts. For example, in *People v. Quiroga-Puma*, 2008 NY Slip Op 50242U, 2 (N.Y. J. Ct. 2008), a New York justice court judge noted that the Court had received a letter request from defense counsel for increased security for himself and his client.

At an earlier hearing in the Quiroga-Puma case, the State had charged defendant with the unlicensed operation of a motor vehicle and failure to provide proof of valid insurance. The trial court presumed that defendant was in the United States illegally. It then found that that Vehicle and Traffic Law § 502(1) provided that an applicant had to furnish such proof of identity as the state motor vehicles department commissioner required. However, it also noted that the department's point system made it mathematically impossible for an illegal immigrant to prove identity. The trial court then found Vehicle and Traffic Law § 502 and Vehicle and Traffic Law § 509(1) violated the state and federal Constitutions' Equal Protection Clauses, and the state and federal constitutions' Privileges and Immunities Clauses, because national security interests were not furthered by them and not being able to get driver's licenses would keep some residents from earning a living.

The trial court dismissed the charge against defendant of unlicensed operation of a motor vehicle. It found that the charge—of failure to provide proof of insurance—against defendant remained intact and the court adjourned a hearing on that charge to give

## COURTS IN ACTION

### Threats Against Judge an Increasing Trend

According to web site "Main Justice" there is an increasing trend in number of threats against judges. Main Justice noted that U.S. District Court Judge Susan Bolton, who sided with the U.S. Justice Department in a ruling against Arizona's immigration bill in August 2010, was inundated threats. Improper communications and threats to federal prosecutors and federal judges have more than doubled during the mid-2000's, according to an Office of the Inspector General report in 2010.

U.S. Marshals Service Director John Clark noted that the increased number of threats against judges was related to the wide availability of information about judges and the publication of their decisions on the Internet. According to the web site, Clark stated:

> "In today's world, there are more individuals who are more prone to threatening judges. I think a lot of it has to do with the availability of information with the use of technology and the Internet. Individuals can find out more about particular cases and judges decisions. They can use Internet sources to find out more about the judge. So if someone is prone to want to threaten someone, there are a number of ways they can find material about a judge."

Main Justice web site at http://www.mainjustice.com/ accessed on August 7, 2010 defendant and the State time to consider the trial court's decision and any plea arrangements that could arise from that decision.

The decision of the judge was not very popular with the local community and that threats had been made against defendant, his attorney, and court personnel. At the subsequent hearing, the judge stated that he was concerned about the safety of the defendant, defense counsel, others in the court, court personnel, and himself. The court ordered that a metal detector and Court Officers be placed in the courtroom or just outside of it. In making this decision, the court referred to an article in *The New Yorker* (Toobin 2008), which detailed the 2005 escape of Brian Nichols, a defendant being retried on rape charges, involving the shooting of the judge trying the case, the court reporter, and deputy sheriff, before Nichols hijacked five cars, killed a federal agent and took a hostage. The Judge also discussed the case of Hon. Allard Lowenstein, former Congressman and ambassador, who was murdered in his New York law office by a deranged former campaign worker.

The trial judge noted the increasing hostility in the public when courts made unpopular decisions and stated:

> Unfortunately, this Court has had some experience in dealing with individuals who have allegedly threatened or caused harm to lawyers, elected officials, or court personnel. Their comments and actions obviously go beyond the pale of fair comment and appropriate First Amendment protection. There are others though whose conduct is borderline; where they are obsessed with an issue or a person; whose obsession consumes them to the point where they are pushed over the edge 6 beyond pandering to their electorate (if they are elected officials), and in some cases, into a delusional, episodic psychosis. In this case, the racist rhetoric by or cowardly expression of persons, anonymous or not, will be reported to the police. When it comes to irrational behavior, the fact that this Court is just a lower Village Court with relatively minor matters before it is of no moment. This Court will not be intimidated into a renunciation of its opinions and will never back down from them (p. 4).

## PRESS COVERAGE

### Does an Accused have a Right to a Criminal Trial that is not Televised?

With reality TV and other popular media programs, the media will probably be more aggressive in televising criminal trials than in the past. The Supreme Court in *Chandler v. Florida*, 449 U.S. 560, 101 S. Ct. 802, 66 L. Ed. 2d 740 (1981) held that there is no constitutional rule barring photographs and radio or television coverage of a trial. Rather, a defendant must demonstrate that the television coverage prejudiced him.

The Court in Chandler held, that a defendant has the right on appeal to show that the media's coverage of his case-printed or broadcast-compromised the ability of the jury to judge him fairly. Alternatively, a defendant might show that broadcast coverage of his particular case had an adverse impact on the trial participants sufficient to constitute a denial of due process. Moreover, the Chandler court reasoned that, to demonstrate prejudice in a specific case a defendant must show something more than juror awareness that the trial is such as to attract the attention of broadcasters.

In his memorandum of law, defendant had cited *Estes v. State of Texas*, 381 U.S. 532, 85 S. Ct. 1628, 14 L. Ed. 2d 543 (1965) in which the Supreme Court held that a defendant was deprived of his right to due process where his "heavily publicized" and "highly sensational" criminal trial was televised. The Court noted that that was not the case in Chandler. Neither did the defendant show, nor had he even alleged, that the presence of the television cameras at his trial turned the trial into a "carnival" atmosphere, or that the jury or witnesses were influenced by the television coverage.

**COURTS IN ACTION**

**Justice by the Numbers**

Attorney Amy Bach while researching for her book, Ordinary Injustice, visited courts from Mississippi to Chicago to New York in an effort to determine how everyday justice works or according to her conclusion, doesn't work. Bach noted that in communities across the country, people use statistics on hospitals, schools and other public services to decide where to live or how to vote. But while millions of Americans deal with their local criminal courts as defendants and victims each year, there is no comparable way to assess a judicial system and determine how well it provides basic legal services.

According to Attorney Bach, this lack of data has a corrosive effect: without public awareness of a court system's strengths and weaknesses, inefficiencies and civil liberties violations are never remedied. She contends that America needs a "justice index" to show how the essential aspects of our local courts are working. The index, compiled according to national standards, would function roughly like college rankings, evaluating county courts on factors like cost, recidivism, crime reduction and collateral consequences, including whether people lose their jobs or homes after contact with the criminal justice system.

According to Bach, our hospitals and schools serve everyone, while most Americans will never directly interact with a criminal court. But she notes that an estimated 47 million Americans have criminal records, and though exact statistics don't exist, it's a good bet that similar numbers have passed through the courts as victims.

Bach contends that all citizens from better courts, which deter crime and remove public threats from the streets. She sees a justice index that would be relatively straightforward to create. It would start by amassing data from the country's 25 biggest counties, where the courts are most likely to collect large amounts of information. Then, a panel of lawyers, community representatives, statisticians and law professors would establish standards for the measurements—for example, the percentage of people who plead guilty without an attorney or average bail amounts, because a high bail figure often compels defendants to plead guilty.

Another critical measurement, according to Bach, would be the percentage of certain types of cases that get thrown out after a defined period of time, a possible indicator of inefficiency as well as disregard for traditionally under-prosecuted crimes. The index would also assess whether a county court has certain legal protections in place, like requiring that interrogations and confessions be taped.

Bach opines that this information would be analyzed by a nonprofit organization, then posted to a Web site in a ranked order and in terms clear enough for the public to understand. Users would be able to shuffle the rankings by focusing on data related to specific areas like civil liberties or crime reduction, in the same way college applicants can look at which schools are best for student life or athletics. She notes that once the data for those 25 counties has been assembled, smaller counties could gather their numbers using a detailed do-it-yourself kit from the coordinating organization. [Amy Bach (2009) Ordinary Injustice: How America Holds Court. New York: Holt]

## SPECIAL COURTS

One recent trend is establishing special courts for certain classes of defendants. Presently in some states there are courts designed specially to decide criminal cases involving:

- Veterans
- Individuals with mental health problems
- Family violence courts

In previous chapters of the text, DWI courts, juvenile courts, and drug courts have been discussed. These courts are part of the specialized court movement.

The specialized courts are also referred to as problem-solving courts. They tend to operate in a collaborative environment in which prosecutors, defense attorneys, judges, probation officers, and social service providers work together to resolve individual cases and treat the defendants. Critics of these courts contend that individual rights of the defendants are diluted, that courts should not be addressing social issues, and the courts are not economically feasible since they can handle only a limited number of cases.

Travis County, Texas, in which the state capital Austin is located, has 10 specialized criminal courts, including adult and juvenile drug courts, DWI court, felony and misdemeanor mental health courts, a family violence court, Project Recovery (a program for "chronic inebriants,") and a veterans' court. The goal of these courts is to create a framework that addresses and corrects underlying behavioral issues so that as many people as possible can be diverted from jail and prison—and can be kept from becoming repeat customers of the criminal justice system.

According to the Travis County district attorney, the problem-solving courts in the county operate in a collaborative environment in which prosecutors, defense attorneys, judges, probation officers, and social service providers work together to resolve individual cases. The National Association of Criminal Defense Lawyers has questioned, however, whether the dilution of the adversarial process weakens legal protections afforded to defendants. There are also questions about whether the courts should be addressing social issues at all and whether carving out special courts, each of which can handle only a limited number of cases, is discriminatory or inequitable.

David Grassbaugh, a criminal defense attorney, states:

> The criminal justice system is designed to operate on a strictly rational basis. That's certainly necessary to deal with crime and criminals in an orderly and predictable way, but it isn't so good at changing behavior—yet changing behavior is the only way to deal effectively with crime. We need a rational structure, but also we have to realize that the object of this system is not to deal with rational behavior; it is to deal with human behavior. That is at the heart of the specialty courts movement, which has taken a firm hold in Travis County. The county joined the movement with the creation of its drug court, the second oldest in the state, after the Jefferson County court established just four months earlier, in April 1993, and since then has steadily increased the number and type of specialty courts.
> —As quoted by Smith, 2010, p. E-1

## FINANCING COURT SYSTEMS

The court systems, like other state or federal institutions, depend on public financing. Since the fiscal power of a political system generally resides with the legislative branch, often the judicial branch appears to have no control over its funding.

As noted on the Illinois Court System home page www.state.il.us/court/General/Funding.asp, financing the state court system is a shared responsibility of the state and the 102 counties of the state. Revenue to provide court services to the people of the state comes from a variety of sources: the state income tax, county property taxes, case filing fees, court-imposed fines and assessments, and other fees.

In Illinois, like most other states, the state government pays for the salaries, benefits, and office expenses of supreme and appellate court judges, and salaries and benefits of circuit court judges. The state also pays for support staff of supreme and appellate court judges, staff in other units of the supreme and appellate courts, a small number of other personnel in the circuit courts, and mandatory arbitration staff in several counties. Part of the cost of operating the mandatory arbitration program is offset by fees paid by participants in the program. During Calendar Year 2008, the arbitration filing and rejection fees collected amounted to $6,494,801. State funding for probation departments currently covers

**COURTS IN ACTION**

**What Price for Justice?**

The court systems have struggle for years under an ever increasing case load. During the current recession, Americans are dealing with double-digit unemployment, foreclosures and businesses that are struggling to stay afloat. It has also affected the U.S. court systems. According to Stephen Zach, in 2010 eight states have resorted to closing courts on certain days every month and 19 states have instituted furloughs. Zach noted that in Vermont, for example, judges and all staff are furloughed one day per month with no pay. The Georgia state constitution prohibits lawmakers from lowering the state's Supreme Court justices' pay, however all seven justices voluntarily participated in all-staff furloughs in 2010. During 2010, California had a statewide court-closure program that shut the courthouse doors on the third Wednesday of each month. It was also reported that there were hiring freezes in 26 states, salary freezes in 12 states, layoffs in 11 states, pay cuts in nine states, and early retirement in six states. In addition, six states increased filing fees for filing civil cases. [Stephen Zach, (2010, August 2) "What Price Justice? The National Law Journal, pp. 34–35.]

approximately 3,000 probation personnel, for which the counties receive partial salary reimbursement on a monthly basis. At the present time, state funding provides for about 25 percent of the total cost of probation services in the state. The total state appropriations for the Illinois court system is approximately $308 million per year and the local appropriations for the court systems was an additional $220 million.

County governments pay part of the cost of financing circuit court operations. Counties provide office and courtroom space, maintenance, and support staff to assist the circuit court judges. Circuit clerks collect money to help pay for their operations and some court operations. They also collect and disburse revenues to help fund local and state government programs, as summarized below.

Our system of government is generally organized around the concept of three separate and independent branches: legislative, executive, and judiciary. But how can the judiciary be independent if it depends upon the other two branches for its funding? This issue was central in the *Maron v. Silver* case. The Matter of *Maron v Silver*, 2010 NY Slip Op 1528, 1 (N.Y. Feb. 23, 2010) case involved a dispute over judges' pay. In 2006, New York State ranked nearly last of the 50 states in its level of judicial compensation, adjusting for the cost of living.

In 2006, the state judiciary submitted to Governor Pataki, as part of its proposed annual budget, a request for $ 69.5 million to fund salary adjustments for the approximately 1300 judges. The intention was to restore pay parity with federal judicial salaries. Although made part of the state budget, the legislature failed to authorize disbursement of the appropriation, because the legislature and the governor could not agree on a pay increase for the legislators themselves.

The following year, Governor Spitzer included in his Executive Budget more than $ 111 million for judicial pay raises, which, if implemented, would have placed salaries of state supreme court justices at an amount roughly on a par with federal judicial compensation. The legislature removed that provision from the budget two months later.

In April 2007, the senate passed a bill (2007 NY Senate Bill S5313) increasing judicial compensation and calling for the creation of a commission to review future salary increases for both judges and legislators. Governor Spitzer refused to support this legislation, however, unless the legislature enacted campaign finance and ethics reform measures. Two months later, the governor expressed support for a "judges only" pay bill.

Shortly thereafter, the Senate passed another bill (2007 NY Senate Bill S6550) providing for an increase in judicial salaries, this time without any corresponding increase for legislators.

It also called for the establishment of a commission to examine future increases in judicial salaries taking into account the needs of the judiciary and the state's ability to pay.

Beginning in 2006, the judiciary and the state senate unsuccessfully sought salary adjustments for the state's judges. Although the parties were in accord regarding the need to adjust judicial compensation, the legislature and the executive failed to come to an agreement on legislation affecting a judicial pay increase. The New York Court of Appeals found held that because of the constitutional requirement in N.Y. Constitutional article VI, § 25(a) that judicial compensation be "established by law," the courts could not order the legislature and the governor to pass a budget that included the necessary funds.

The appellate court held that Legislature's failure to address the effects of inflation did not equate to a per se violation of the Compensation Clause, § 25(a). However, the state defendants' failure to consider judicial compensation on the merits violated the Separation of Powers Doctrine in N.Y. Constitutional articles III, IV, VI. Judicial compensation, when addressed by the legislature in present and future budget deliberations, could not depend on unrelated policy initiatives or legislative compensation adjustments.

The New York Court of Appeals noted that since the inception of the state constitution, this state has grappled with the issue of how best to establish the parameters of judicial compensation. In 1846, the constitutional convention adopted the phrase "shall not be increased or diminished;" an 1869 amendment, however, deleted the words, "increased or," allowing for the increase of compensation, but not a decrease. The 1894 Constitution restored the 1846 "shall not be increased or diminished" language, which was thereafter deleted in its entirety in 1909 and adopted a specific constitutional provision fixing salaries for certain judges at $ 10,000 per year.

In 1921, a judiciary constitutional convention was held to consider, among other things, amendments to the state constitution concerning judicial compensation. The convention criticized the 1909 compensation clause amendment's inclusion of a salary schedule in the constitution, stating that judicial compensation should, in the judgment of the present convention, be left entirely to the legislature, which, after all, is the body always directly in touch with and responsible to the people.

The New York Court of Appeals concluded with the statement:

> It is unfortunate that this Court has been called upon to adjudicate constitutional issues relative to an underlying matter upon which all have agreed; namely, that the Judiciary is entitled to a compensation adjustment. By ensuring that any judicial salary increases will be premised on their merits, this holding aims to strike the appropriate balance between preserving the independence of the Judiciary and avoiding encroachment on the budget-making authority of the Legislature. Therefore, judicial compensation, when addressed by the Legislature in present and future budget deliberations cannot depend on unrelated policy initiatives or legislative compensation adjustments. Of course, whether judicial compensation should be adjusted, and by how much, is within the province of the Legislature. It should keep in mind, however, that whether the Legislature has met its constitutional obligations in that regard is within the province of this Court. We therefore expect appropriate and expeditious legislative consideration (p. 1578).

## FUTURE TRENDS IN CRIMINAL COURTS

Writers and futuristic thinkers make bold predictions of where the court system will be 30 years from this date. The authors, who are totally without the power to foresee the future, have gathered in this section some of the predictions by others that may occur. The predictions make outstanding classroom discussion topics and serve as a reminder that the American court system is not a static organization.

**COURTS IN ACTION**

## Pennsylvania's High Court Justices Among Highest Paid in Nation

According to Debra Erdley, there is a reason why lawyers often refer to Pennsylvania's Supreme Court justices as "The Supremes." According to her report, the justices of the Pennsylvania Supreme Court were among the best compensated jurists in the nation in 2010. Erdley noted that only two states pay their top judges more than the $186,450 that Pennsylvania annually pays its justices, according to a recent survey by the National Center for State Courts. Pennsylvania's chief justice was paid $191,876 per year 2010.

In addition, Pennsylvania's seven justices have more law clerks—five to seven each—than the nine justices of the Supreme Court. And justice has a taxpayer-funded car lease topping out at $600 a month. Pennsylvania's taxpayers pay in excess of $1 million a year per justice.

Court officials say the logistics of operating the court, the nation's oldest state supreme court, are complicated. The court is a circuit court that sits in three locations—Pittsburgh, Harrisburg and Philadelphia—and there is a scarcity of public space to house justices. Top courts in Florida, Texas and Ohio meet in one location and house their justices in the state capital. In Michigan, where the Supreme Court meets in Lansing, justices are provided with offices near their homes, but all moved into state-owned facilities years ago. The court also hears cases in Pittsburgh, Philadelphia and Harrisburg, so taxpayers underwrite the costs of hotels, meals and transportation for jurists, totaling about $380,000 last year. [Debra Erdley, (2010, August 8) Pittsburgh Tribune Review, A-1.]

According to National Institute of Justice writer/editor Nancy Ritter (2006), terrorism, the growth of multicultural populations, massive migration, upheavals in age-composition demographics, technological developments, and globalization will change the world's criminal justice systems in the next three decades. According to Ritter (p. 8) three leading criminal justice experts point out issues that we need to consider:

- Bryan J. Vila, former chief of the Office of Justice Programs' National Institute of Justice's Crime Control and Prevention Research Division and now a professor at Washington State University, emphasizes the need to understand the coevolution of crime and crime fighting. Vila contends that criminals, like viruses, will evolve over time and change as their potential victims take preventive measures. For example, as more people install steering wheel locks or alarm systems to combat auto theft, thieves respond by using devices to neutralize such security systems.
- Professor Christopher E. Stone of Harvard University's John F. Kennedy School of Government, believes that a new global, professional culture will influence the world's criminal justice systems in the decades to come. Chris Stone predicts that global trends will play a significant role in how criminal justice is delivered throughout the world in 2040. Stone points to the dramatic growth in the number of foreign-born Americans and suggests that increasing diversity in populations will have a significant impact not only in the United States but worldwide. The lack of homogeneity extends beyond language to societal norms and expectations. What will foreign-born Americans expect of the U.S. justice system, given their experiences in their native countries? How will they regard the roles of the defense lawyer, prosecutor, and judge? According to Stone, answers to these questions will shape the face of criminal justice in the decades to come.
- Professor David Weisburd of the University of Maryland and Jerusalem's Hebrew University Law School opines that how criminal justice looks in 2040 will depend largely on the research path we take. In the evidence-based model, a new program

undergoes systematic research and evaluation before it is widely adopted. Now dominant in medicine—and becoming more popular in other areas such as education—the evidence-based model has been used successfully in criminal justice. For example, hot-spot policing (a policy adopted in the early 1990s, which focused police resources in high-crime areas) was preceded by studies that demonstrated its effectiveness. But Weisburd contends that the evidence-based model also has shortcomings. Research requires a large investment of time and money, and many practitioners understandably would rather spend resources implementing an innovation than wait for confirming research. Time—always a precious commodity for policymakers and practitioners—can be a particularly frustrating component of the evidence-based model. Credible research requires time to adequately test an approach, often in more than one jurisdiction, before communities can adopt it on a large scale.

As noted by Ritter, most experts emphasize the need to find new ways to work with professionals around the globe. She notes that the Vera Institute has formed alliances with academic and nonprofit organizations in other countries to conduct evaluations of the court systems and other aspects of the criminal justice system.

## LAW IN ACTION

### Should a Judge's Denial of Appointed Counsel in Federal Cases be Immediately Appealable or Must Defendant Wait Until the End of a Trial and the Customary End of Trial Appeal?

Advocates of the rights of pro se litigants [defendants without counsel] are hoping the U.S. Supreme Court soon resolve a long-simmering dispute over the right to counsel that has divided all 13 federal circuit courts of appeals.

Under several federal laws, including major civil rights statutes, trial judges are authorized to appoint counsel in certain circumstances for litigants who cannot afford them. Ordinarily, a judge's decision can only be appealed when the trial is over. But when a judge denies a litigant's request for counsel, the question is whether that action belongs to a small category of decisions that are too important and urgent to wait until the trial is over to appeal. If the decision could be appealed right away, probably more judges would avoid triggering appeals and appoint counsel in the first place.

Individuals who support the right of immediate appeal contend that the entire adversary process can be distorted by the failure to appoint counsel in the proper case. The decision whether to appoint counsel can thus be viewed as virtually outcome determinative in many cases.

The case arises as federal courts are grappling with the surge of pro se litigation and calls for a "civil Gideon" to guarantee a right to counsel in the same way that Gideon v. Wainwright established it in criminal cases. Last year, according to the Administrative Office of the U.S. Courts, 71,453 civil suits were initiated pro se in federal courts, roughly a fourth of all cases filed.

For more than 20 years, the 5th, 8th, and Federal circuits have allowed immediate appeal of denial of counsel, with the 5th asserting that there is a "great risk" that a civil rights plaintiff without a lawyer could abandon a claim or accept an unreasonable settlement, thereby making the decision on appointment of counsel unreviewable. In the 9th Circuit, immediate appeal depends on the type of claim. But the other nine circuits have rejected the argument that denial of counsel should be appealed right away. The circuit split has festered so long in part because pro se litigants are usually either unaware or too busy to realize that they could challenge the decision denying immediate appeal before the Supreme Court. [Tony Mauro, (2010, August 18) Will court wade into right-to-counsel case? National Law Journal. pp. 1–2]

## Questions in Review

1. How should the court systems be financed?
2. When does a defendant have a right to object to the use of cameras in the courtroom?
3. What steps should a trial judge take to protect the safety of the court personnel during the trial of a high profile case?

4. Under what circumstances do a newspaper's first amendment rights conflict with the defendant's right to a fair trial?

## References

*Brown v. Board of Education*, 347 U.S. 483 (U.S. 1954)

California Commission on Access to Justice, (2010) I. Executive Summary: Language Barriers to Justice in California. Sacramento: State Bar of California. http://calbar.ca.gov/LinkClick.aspx?fileticket=GQz0dj7TeEg%3D&tabid=216 (accessed August 10, 2010).

Ritter, Nancy. "Preparing for the Future: Criminal Justice in 2040." *National Institute of Justice Journal* no. 255 (2006): 8–12.

Smith, Jordan. "Travis County Specialty Courts Try to Break the Cycle of Crime." *Austin Chroncile*, March 23, 2010, Home Section, p. E-1.

Toobin, Jeffery. "Death in Georgia." *The New Yorker*, February 4, 2008, p. 32.

# GLOSSARY

**Abandonment:** The concept that once property has been abandoned, its former owner has no reasonable right of privacy in it.

**Abstract goals:** The underlying principles upon which our justice system is based.

**Adversary system:** Our concept of justice, in which one side represents the plaintiff or state and the other side represents the defendant, while the judge acts as the independent referee.

**Aggravation or circumstances in aggravation:** Facts which tend to justify the imposition of a more severe punishment.

**Allen charge:** An instruction given a deadlocked jury in attempt to get the jury to reach a verdict.

**Alternate juror:** A person who sits with the jury during the trial and is prepared to serve as a jury member if one of the regular jurors is excused or disqualified.

**Appointed counsel:** A counsel that has been appointed by the judge to represent the defendant.

**Arraignment:** A hearing before a court having jurisdiction in which the identity of the defendant is established, the defendant is informed of the charges and of his or her rights, and in some states the defendant is required to enter a plea.

**Arrest:** The seizure of a person to answer for a criminal charge.

**Atonement:** A designated price to be paid or duty to be performed by an offender to the victim or victim's family when a certain crime was committed.

**Bail:** A form of pretrial release in which the defendant is required to post money or property to ensure his or her presence at trial.

**Bailiff:** An individual assigned to assist the judge and jury and to perform other duties assigned by the judge.

**Bench trial:** A trial by a judge without a jury.

**Bench warrant:** A warrant issued by the judge during a trial. It is issued from the judge's bench.

**Booking:** The process that officially records an entry into detention after an arrest.

**Bounty hunters:** Individuals who hunt persons who have violated the terms of their bail and did not appear in court.

**Boykin advisement:** The required advice that a judge must give a defendant in open court before the judge can accept a guilty plea. Based on the Supreme Court case of *Boykin* v. *Alabama*.

**Brady material:** Material that tends to be beneficial to the defendant's case must be provided to defense prior to trial. Based on the Supreme Court decision in *Brady* v. *Maryland*.

**Certiorari:** A petition to an appeals court to invoke its jurisdiction.

**Challenges for cause:** A challenge to a potential juror based on the juror's qualifications or lack of impartiality.

**Change of venue:** Moving of the trial to a different geographical location.

**Character evidence:** Evidence of a person's character that tends to prove that the individual did or did not commit a certain act.

**Charging the jury:** The act of a judge in instructing the jury.

**Civil contempt:** The willful continuing failure or refusal of any person to comply with a court's lawful writ, subpoena, process, order, rule, or command that by its nature is still capable of being complied with.

**Code of Hammurabi:** One of the first-known attempts to establish a written code of conduct.

**Competency:** Refers to the mental state of the defendant at the time of trial. A defendant must be able to assist his or her counsel in defending of the case.

**Complaint:** A written statement made upon oath before a judge, magistrate, or official authorized by law to issue warrants of arrest, setting forth essential facts constituting an offense and alleging that the defendant committed the offense.

**Consciousness of guilt:** The concept that reflects on the defendant's knowledge of his or her level of guilt.

**Constitutional right to speedy trial:** The defendant's right to a speedy trial guaranteed by the Sixth Amendment. Speedy trial time starts when prosecution is commenced.

**Constructive contempt:** Any criminal or civil contempt other than a direct contempt. [See Direct contempt.]

**Consular immunity:** The limited immunity granted to consuls and their deputies as representatives of a foreign government.

**Contempt:** The violation of court order or disruption of court proceedings.

**Continuance:** The delay of a trial at the request of one of the parties.

**Conviction in absentia:** Conviction of a defendant in which the defendant is not present in court.

**Court rules:** Rules issued by the courts to regulate the process in the courts in the areas not regulated by statutes, regulations, and other rules.

**Court trial:** A trial by a judge without a jury.

**Criminal contempt:** Either misconduct of any person that obstructs the administration of justice and that is committed either in the court's presence or so near thereto as to interrupt, disturb, or hinder its proceedings; or willful disobedience or resistance of any person to a court's lawful writ, subpoena, process, order, rule, or command, where the dominant purpose of the contempt proceeding is to punish the contemptor.

**Cross-examination:** The examination of a witness by the party that did not call the witness; used to weaken the witness's testimony.

**Cross-section of community standard:** The requirement that the jury panel or list be representative of a cross section of the community.

**Cruel and unusual punishment:** The constitutional protection contained in the Eighth Amendment that prohibits the imposition of punishment that is considered cruel or unusual.

**Curative instructions:** Instructions given to a jury to cure any errors caused by the jury receiving inadmissible evidence or other information.

**Curtilage of a dwelling house:** A space, necessary and convenient and habitually used for family purposes and the carrying on of domestic employments. It includes the garden, if there is one, and it need not be separated from other lands by a fence.

**Daubert test:** A test used by the courts to determine if certain scientific evidence should be admitted into evidence.

**Death-qualified jury:** A jury in which the members have indicated that under appropriate circumstances they would vote for the death penalty.

**Declarant:** An individual making a formal statement.

**Definite sentence:** A sentence that has a specified period of confinement or definite terms.

**Deliberations:** The closed sessions of a jury in which the jury attempts to reach a verdict.

**Demurrer:** The formal mode of disputing the sufficiency in law of the pleadings contained in the complaint.

**Deposition:** A form of pretrial discovery in which a witness is questioned under oath and the other parties are given an opportunity to be present and ask questions. Used more in civil than in criminal cases.

**Determination of guilt:** A verdict of guilty by a jury, a finding of guilty by a court following a nonjury trial, or acceptance by the court of a plea of guilty.

**Deterrence:** Punishment based on the goal of deterring future criminal activity.

**Diplomatic immunity:** The immunity granted to diplomatic officers, their staffs, and their families by which they are free from local jurisdiction and as such cannot be arrested or detained for any offense unless they are permanent residents or citizens of the United States.

**Direct contempt:** The disorderly or insolent behavior or other misconduct committed in open court, in the presence of the judge, that disturbs the court's business, where all the essential elements of the misconduct occur in the presence of the court and are observed by the court, and where immediate action is essential to prevent diminution of the court's dignity and authority before the public.

**Direct examination:** The initial questioning of a witness by the party that originally called the witness.

**Directed verdict:** A verdict by the judge when the judge concludes that the evidence is such that a jury could not legally find the defendant guilty.

**Due process:** Those procedures that effectively guarantee individual rights in the face of criminal prosecution and those procedures that are fundamental rules for fair and orderly legal proceedings.

**Duplicate:** A counterpart produced by the same impression as the original, or from the same matrix, or by means of photography, including enlargements and miniatures, or by mechanical or electronic re-recording, or by chemical reproduction, or by other equivalent techniques which accurately reproduce the original.

**Effective counsel:** An attorney who exercises the normal standards of effectiveness in representing his or her client.

**Evidence relating to past sexual behavior:** Such a term includes, but is not limited to, evidence of the complaining witness's marital history, mode of dress, and general reputation for promiscuity, nonchastity, or sexual mores contrary to the community standards and opinion of character for those traits.

**Evidentiary hearing:** A hearing held by the trial court to resolve contested factual issues.

**Exclusionary Rule:** The rule used to exclude evidence that was obtained by the violation of a constitutional right such as an illegal search.

**Exoneration of bail:** The court's act in dissolving bail after the defendant has appeared in court as required.

**Expectation of privacy zone:** The living area immediately surrounding a home where the residents have an expectation of privacy.

**Extradition:** The surrender by one state or nation to another state or nation of a person who is charged with a crime in the requesting state.

**Farce or sham test:** A test formerly used to determine if the defense counsel adequately represented the defendant. The defense must be more than a sham or farce.

**Foreperson:** The individual jury member who has been selected by the other jurors as their spokesperson.

**Former acquittal:** A defense based on double jeopardy in which defendant claims that he or she has been acquitted of the charged offense.

**Fruit of the Poisonous Tree:** Additional evidence discovered from information obtained as the result of a constitutional violation such as an illegal search.

**Gag order:** An order by the judge to the parties to a lawsuit to refrain from discussing the case with the press.

**Grand jury:** An investigative body that meets to determine whether there is sufficient evidence to support an indictment against a defendant. The grand jury may also investigate the conduct of public officials and agencies.

**Habeas corpus:** A writ that orders the custodian of a prisoner to appear in court and explain why the individual is being held in confinement.

**Harmless error:** Any error, defect, irregularity, or variance which does not affect substantial rights and shall be disregarded.

**Hearsay:** A statement, other than one made by the declarant while testifying at the trial or hearing, offered in evidence to prove the truth of the matter asserted.

**Hung jury:** A jury that cannot agree on a verdict.

**Spousal privilege:** A communication is confidential if it is made privately by any person to his or her spouse and is not intended for disclosure to any other person. An accused in a criminal proceeding has a privilege to prevent his or her spouse from testifying as to any confidential communication between the accused and the spouse. The privilege may be claimed by the accused or by the spouse on behalf of the accused. The authority of the spouse to do so is presumed. There is no privilege under this rule in a proceeding in which one spouse is charged with a crime against the other person or property of (1) the other, (2) a child of either, (3) a person residing in the household of either, or (4) a third person committed in the course of committing a crime against any of them.

**Impaneled jury:** A jury that has been selected and sworn in by the judge.

**Impartial trial by jury:** A jury that starts the case without any preconceived opinions regarding the guilty or innocence of the defendant.

**Impeachment:** The attempt to limit or discredit evidence that has been admitted.

**Indefinite sentence:** A sentence that has no fixed term and may be adjusted to fit the offender.

**Independent state grounds:** A decision based on a state constitution or statute that does not involve an interpretation of federal law.

**Indeterminate sentence:** A sentence in which the period of confinement or other punishment is to be determined based on the need of the offender.

**Indictment:** A written statement charging the defendant or defendants named therein with the commission of an indictable offense, presented to the court by a grand jury, endorsed "A True Bill," and signed by the foreperson. The term indictment includes presentment.

**Indigent defendant:** A defendant who lacks the resources to afford to hire his or her attorney.

**Information:** A written statement charging the defendant or defendants named therein with the commission of an indictable offense, made on oath, signed, and presented to the court by the district attorney without action by a grand jury.

**Initial appearance:** The first appearance by the defendant in a criminal case before a judge. Generally, at the initial appearance, the defendant is informed of the charges against him or her and advised of his or her rights. In some states it is the same as an arraignment.

**Insanity:** The abnormal mental state of the defendant at the time that the crime was committed.

**International extradition:** Extradition of a fugitive from another country subject to the extradition treaties between the two countries.

**Joiner:** The consolidated trial of a case by joining charges or defendants.

**Judgment:** The adjudication of the court based upon a plea of guilty by the defendant, upon the verdict of the jury, or upon the court's own finding following a nonjury trial that the defendant is guilty or not guilty.

**Judicial notice:** The act of a court in accepting certain facts without the necessity to present evidence to prove them, such as the fact that New York is a state, a fact that a court can take judicial notice of.

**Jurisdiction:** The power of a court to act in regard to the individual or subject matter.

**Jury list:** A jury panel. The list of potential jurors that have been summoned from which a jury may be selected.

**Jury of one's peers:** A jury composed of a cross section of the community that was selected in a fair and impartial manner.

**Jury panel:** The list of potential jurors that have been summoned from which a jury may be selected.

**Law enforcement officer:** Any person vested by law with a duty to maintain public order or to make arrests for offenses.

**Lay witness:** A nonexpert witness.

**Legislative immunity:** Statutory provisions that grant limited immunity to legislative members while attending or going to legislative sessions.

**Limited admissibility:** Evidence that is admitted for a limited purpose only.

**Locked-down jury:** A jury that has been sent to the deliberations room to start deliberations on the findings.

**Magistrate:** A judicial officer with the power to issue a warrant, including magistrates, district judges, superior court judges, and any other judicial officer authorized by law to conduct a preliminary examination of a person accused of a crime or issue a warrant.

**Manifest necessity:** In reference to a mistrial, a condition in which the judge concludes that it is necessary to declare a mistrial.

**Material witness:** A witness whose presence is deemed necessary for the trial of the case. A person designated as a material witness may be required to post security to ensure his or her presence at trial.

**Mentally incompetent:** Refers to an accused who lacks sufficient present ability to assist in his or her defense by consulting with counsel with a reasonable degree of rational understanding of the facts and the legal proceedings against the defendant.

**Miranda warning:** Warnings required before officers can interrogate a suspect who is in detention.

**Mistrial:** The act of a judge in terminating a trial before it is concluded because of errors or issues that call into question the fairness of the trial.

**Mitigation or "circumstances in mitigation":** Facts that tend to justify the imposition of a lesser punishment.

**Motion to suppress evidence:** A motion presented prior to trial to determine the admissibility of certain items of evidence.

**Negotiated plea:** A plea that has been agreed upon by the defendant and the state; a plea bargain.

**New trial:** A retrial of a defendant with a new jury.

**Nolo contendere:** A plea of no contest that supports a conviction if accepted by the judge.

**Notice of alibi defense:** A requirement that the defendant provide the prosecution with advance notice that an alibi defense will be used.

**Open fields:** The concept that the Fourth Amendment's restrictions on unreasonable searches and seizures do not apply to items in open fields.

**Opening statements:** Statements made by counsel prior to the presentation of evidence. The statements are not considered evidence and should not contain arguments on behalf of a party.

**Order to show cause:** An order in response to a habeas corpus petition directing the respondent (warden) to file a return. The order to show cause is issued if the petitioner (prisoner) has made a prima facie showing that he or she is entitled to relief; it does not grant the relief requested. An order to show cause may also be referred to as granting the writ.

**Orientation goals:** Those goals of the justice system that are oriented in one of two opposite directions—law and order or individual rights.

**Original:** Concerning a writing or recording, the writing or recording itself or any counterpart intended to produce the same effect by a person executing or issuing it. An original of a photograph includes the negative or any print therefrom. If data are stored in a computer or similar device, any printout or other output readable by sight, shown to reflect the data accurately, is an original.

**Peremptory challenge:** A challenge that a party has to eliminate a potential juror. Each side has a limited number of peremptory challenges. While the party peremptorily challenging a potential juror normally is not required to provide a reason for the challenge, the challenge may not be used to exclude one gender or race from the jury.

**Petty offenses:** Offenses which have a maximum jail time of six months and a fine of not more than $500.

**Plain errors:** Errors or defects affecting substantial rights that may be noticed, although they were not brought to the attention of the court.

**Plain view doctrine:** The concept that looking at items in plain view is not a search because there is no reasonable expectation of privacy concerning items in plain view.

**Pragmatic goals:** Criminal justice goals related to preventing crime and developing better environmental conditions in the neighborhoods that foster law-abiding behavior.

**Precept:** A warrant or legal document issued by a court directing a person to comply with the terms of the precept.

**Preliminary hearing:** A proceeding before a judicial officer to determine if a crime has been committed, whether the crime occurred within the jurisdiction of the court, and whether there are reasonable grounds to believe that the defendant committed the crime.

**Preliminary questions:** Basic questions like name and address asked of a witness when the witness is first called to testify.

**Preponderance of evidence:** The normal burden of proof required in civil cases where the moving party is required to establish that it was more likely than not that a certain event occurred or a fact exists.

**Pretrial discovery:** The right of parties to obtain evidence from the other parties prior to the commencement of the trial.

**Pretrial diversion:** An agreement between the parties to a criminal case that the charges will be dropped if the defendant successfully meets the conditions for diversion.

**Private person arrest:** An arrest by a person who does not have a peace officer status.

**Privileged communications:** Communications between individuals that are protected from discovery or use in a trial. Generally, communications between a party and his or her attorney are privileged.

**Probable cause:** Exists when the facts and circumstances within the officer's knowledge, and of which he or she has reasonably trustworthy information, are sufficient to cause a reasonably cautious person to believe that an offense has been or is being committed.

**Probation:** Placing a defendant on conditioned release subject to revocation if the defendant violates the terms of the release.

**Public defender:** An attorney who works for the state and has the duty of defending indigent defendants.

**Public trial:** A trial that the public has a right to attend.

**Rape shield laws:** Laws designed to protect a rape victim and limit the admission of the victim's prior sexual history.

**Reasonable cause to believe:** A basis for belief in the existence of facts which, in view of the circumstances under and purposes for which the standard is applied, is substantial, objective, and sufficient to satisfy applicable constitutional requirements.

**Reasonable doubt:** The burden of proof that is required before a defendant may be convicted of a crime. The burden is on the prosecution to prove a fact with a high degree of certainty.

**Reasonable suspicion:** A suspicion based on facts or circumstances which by themselves do not give rise to the probable cause requisite to justify a lawful arrest, but which give rise to more than a bare suspicion, that is, a suspicion that is reasonable as opposed to imaginary or purely conjectural. A suspicion based on facts that would cause a reasonable person to conclude that criminal activity is ongoing or has occurred.

**Rebuttal evidence:** Evidence to rebut or negate evidence present by the other party.

**Redirect examination:** The examination by the party who called the witness to cover matters that were covered in the cross-examination.

**Rehabilitated:** The conclusion that a defendant has reformed.

**Release on own recognizance:** Release of a defendant without bail upon his or her promise to appear at all appropriate times, sometimes referred to as "personal recognizance."

**Relevant evidence:** Evidence having any tendency to make the existence of any fact that is of consequence to the determination of the action more probable or less probable than it would be without the evidence.

**Rendition:** Another term for interstate extradition.

**Resisting arrest:** The act of resisting a lawful arrest; a crime.

**Restitution:** Court-ordered sanction that involves payment of compensation by the defendant to the victim for injuries suffered as a result of the defendant's criminal activity.

**Retained counsel:** Counsel that has been selected and employed by the defendant.

**Return:** The law enforcement officer executing an arrest warrant shall endorse thereon the manner and date of execution, shall subscribe his or her name, and shall return the arrest warrant to the clerk of the court specified in the arrest warrant.

**Right of confrontation:** The constitutional right of a defendant to confront the witnesses against him or her. It includes the right to cross-examine the witness.

**Right of discovery:** The right of either a prosecutor or a defendant to discover certain evidence in possession of the other party.

**Right to trial by jury:** Right of a defendant to have his or her case decided by a fair and impartial jury.

**Search:** A governmental intrusion into an area where a person has a reasonable expectation of privacy.

**Search warrant:** A written order, in the name of the state or municipality, signed by a judge or magistrate authorized by law to issue search warrants, directed to any law enforcement officer, commanding him or her to search for personal property and, if found, to bring it before the issuing judge or magistrate.

**Seizure:** Taking any person or thing or obtaining information by an officer pursuant to a search or under other color of authority.

**Self-representation:** A defendant's acting as his or her own attorney.

**Sequestered jury:** A jury that has been secluded from the public and the press. Generally, a jury is sequestered during the deliberation phase of the trial.

**Severance:** The act of dividing multiple charges or defendants into separate trials.

**Standards:** Detail goals to improve the justice system.

**Standby counsel:** An attorney appointed by a judge to be available to consult with the defendant in cases where the defendant represents himself or herself.

**Statute of limitations:** The time within which criminal proceedings must commence after the commission of the crime. Some crimes, such as murder, have no statute of limitations.

**Statutory right to a speedy trial:** Defendant's right to a speedy trial, which is guaranteed by a statute.

**Stop and frisk:** The act of stopping a person for investigative purposes and frisking him or her for the presence of a weapon.

**Subpoena duces tecum:** A subpoena of a witness that also orders the witness to bring certain documents to court.

**Subpoenas:** Orders issued by the clerk of the court in which a criminal proceeding is pending at any time for witnesses required by any party for attendance at trial and at hearings, for taking depositions, or for any other lawful purpose.

**Summons:** An order issued by a judicial officer or, pursuant to the authorization of a judicial officer, by the clerk of a court, requiring a person against whom a criminal charge has been filed to appear in a designated court at a specified date and time.

**Suspended sentence:** An adjudged sentence whose imposition is suspended under certain conditions, and upon compliance with the conditions the sentence is vacated. If the conditions are not complied with, the suspension is vacated and the sentence is imposed.

**Symbolic restitution:** A beneficial service to the community that the defendant is ordered to perform because of his or her criminal misconduct.

**Syndromes:** Mental conditions that are often presented to excuse or justify the conduct of the defendant.

**Temporary detention:** A brief investigative detention.

**Terry stop:** An investigative stop by an officer to determine if criminal activity is ongoing.

**Torts:** A private or civil wrong or injury that is addressed in civil court.

**Transactional immunity:** Immunity granted to force a witness to testify in which the witness cannot be prosecuted for the criminal act covered by his or her testimony.

**Trial by ordeal:** An ordeal in which the accused was required to perform some physical task to prove his or her innocence.

**Unlawful flight:** Fleeing the jurisdiction of a court to avoid criminal proceedings.

**Use and derivative immunity:** Immunity granted to force a witness to testify whereby his or her testimony or any other information obtained as the result of the testimony cannot be used against him or her.

**Venue:** The geographic location of the court.

**Verdict:** A judgment by the court. In a criminal court, it refers to the finding of guilty or not guilty.

**Victim:** A person against whom a criminal offense has allegedly been committed, or the spouse, parent, lawful representative, or child of someone killed or incapacitated by the alleged criminal offense, except where the spouse, parent, lawful representative, or child is also the accused.

**Victim impact statements:** Statements which victims or victim representatives are permitted to submit for court consideration at sentencing time.

**Victim service providers:** Organizations that provide services to victims of crime.

**Victim's bill of rights:** Statutory legislation that provides certain basic rights to a victim during the trial of a criminal case.

**Victim's compensation:** Payments made to victims in an attempt to lessen the impact of the crime upon them.

**Waiver of error:** No party may assign as error on appeal the court's giving or failing to give any instruction or portion thereof, or to the submission or the failure to submit a form of verdict, unless the party objects thereto before the jury retires to consider its verdict, stating distinctly the matter in which the party objects and the grounds of his or her objection.

**Work product:** Discovery cannot be required of legal research or of records, correspondence, reports, or memoranda to the extent that they contain the opinions, theories, or conclusions of the prosecutor, members of the prosecutor's legal or investigative staff or law enforcement officers, or of defense counsel or defense counsel's legal or investigative staff.

**Writ:** A mandatory precept (warrant), under seal, issued by a court and commanding a person to whom it is addressed to do or not to do some act.

# INDEX